The Magic of Interactive Entertainment

The Magic of Interactive Entertainment

Mike Morrison

To my best friend, who provides love and happiness on a daily basis, my wife Sandie.

FIRST EDITION

International Standard Book Number: 0-672-30456-2

Library of Congress Catalog Card Number: 93-86961

97 96 95 94 4 3 2 1

Interpretation of the printing code: the rightmost double-digit number is the year of the book's printing; the rightmost single-digit, the number of the book's printing. For example, a printing code of 94-1 shows that the first printing of the book occurred in 1994.

Composed in Goudy and MCPdigital by Prentice Hall Computer Publishing

Printed in the United States of America

Trademarks

Publisher
Richard K. Swadley

Associate Publisher
Jordan Gold

Acquisitions Manager
Stacey Hiquet

Managing Editor
Cindy Morrow

Acquisitions Editor
Dean Miller

Production Editor
Sandy Doell

Copy Editors
Deborah Frisby
James Grass
Matthew Usher
Kitty Wilson

Editorial and Graphics Coordinator
Bill Whitmer

Editorial Assistants
Sharon Cox
Lynette Quinn
Carol Ackerman

Technical Reviewer
Johnny Wilson

Marketing Manager
Gregg Bushyeager

Cover Designer
Karen Ruggles

Director of Production and Manufacturing
Jeff Valler

Imprint Manager
Juli Cook

Manufacturing Coordinator
Paul Gilchrist

Book Designer
Michele Laseau

Production Analyst
Mary Beth Wakefield

Proofreading Coordinator
Joelynn Gifford

Indexing Coordinator
Johnna VanHoose

Graphics Image Specialists
Tim Montgomery
Dennis Sheehan
Sue VandeWalle

Production
Nick Anderson
Ayrika Bryant
Terri Edwards
Rich Evers
Jamie Milazzo
S A Springer
Tonya R. Simpson
Dennis Wesner

Indexer
Craig Small

Overview

Contents

3 Interactive Entertainment on Personal Computers 57

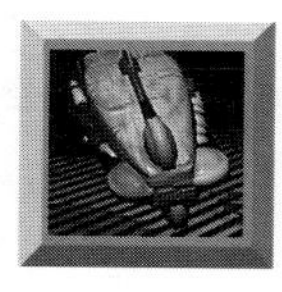

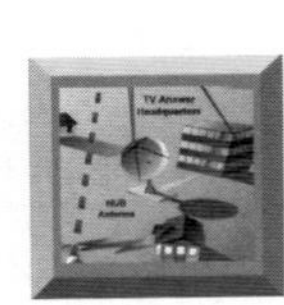

Acknowledgments

I would like to thank Richard Swadley, Jordan Gold, and Stacy Hiquet for believing in this project and getting it started. Thanks to Dean Miller, whose life gets much harder when he's working with my books. Credit also goes to Sandy Doell for her tireless efforts in editing and dealing with figure permissions. I would also like to thank the other editors, Jim Grass, Deborah Frisby, Kitty Wilson, Matthew Usher, and Johnny Wilson. Special thanks also goes to all the other people at Sams involved in the production and design of this book, especially Wayne Blackenbeckler for putting the CD-ROM together. I very much appreciate all the companies that allowed us to interview them and discuss how they develop Interactive Entertainment titles, especially those who let us include their demos on our CD-ROM. I also thank the many talented video game artists whose work graces these pages. Finally, I would like to thank my wife Sandie for providing that extra encouragement and support, without which this book may never have been finished.

About the Author

Mike Morrison has been active in computer graphics and multimedia for the past ten years. He writes for trade publications such as *Computer Graphics World* and *Computer Pictures Magazine* and is coauthor of *Using AutoCAD Release 12* from Que, and *On The Cutting Edge of Technology* from Sams.

His last Sams book, *The Magic of Image Processing* covers the basics of computer graphics. His latest book, *Becoming A Computer Animator* discusses the various fields of computer animation and gives suggestions on getting started as a computer animator.

As a resident of San Diego, California, Mike and his wife Sandie can be found during most of the summer enjoying the waves of the Pacific Ocean. You can reach him on CompuServe at `70413,3450` or Internet at `70413.3450@compuserve.com`.

Introduction

Interactive Entertainment encompasses many things: computers, video games, interactive television, and more. Today, in the United States alone, more than one out of three individuals has some type of interactive entertainment in their home. Billions of dollars are being made in this new industry, which is one of the fastest changing new technologies.

The Magic of Interactive Entertainment is designed to help you, the consumer. This is the first book to fully document the history of interactive entertainment and show where it is today. In this book you will learn not only what's available, but also how the technology works. From CD-ROMs to active matrix liquid crystal displays to fiber optics to video-on-demand, each technology is explained in easy-to-understand language.

Chapter One provides an overview of the technology and products available today. Chapter Two documents the history of interactive entertainment. From there, each chapter covers a different platform, such as personal computers, multimedia, home gaming systems, portable gaming systems, and interactive television. Chapter Eight discusses education and interactive entertainment, explaining how the human brain learns, the history of learning science, and how it is used today in edutainment products. Also included is a resource appendix for locating companies and organizations mentioned throughout the book as well as suggestions for further research. Finally, a glossary is provided to help you learn the new language of interactive entertainment.

For the icing on the cake, a CD-ROM is included that offers more than 80 playable game demos for both IBM-compatible personal computers and Apple Macintosh computers. Included on the CD-ROM are full versions of VistaPro and Distant Suns, software that brings virtual reality to your own personal computer. Before your telephone company tries to sell you video services, before your cable TV company tries to sell you local telephone service, before you purchase that new multiplayer system, read this book. Prepare yourself today for the future of entertainment.

1

Interactive Entertainment Today

Interactive Entertainment is a multi-billion dollar business. It is bigger than the motion picture industry and the broadcast television industry.

And while more than one-third of all homes in the U.S. already have some form of Interactive Entertainment, companies are investing billions to increase that figure and bring even more interactivity into the home. Government officials talk about the National Information Infrastructure—otherwise called the Electronic Highway. So what does it mean for you? Will you get a speeding ticket on the Electronic Highway or will you become road kill? How much will it cost? What's available now and in the near future?

Interactive Entertainment, even today, has gone far beyond the mindless video games of days gone by.

Another Difficult Approach...

Visibility is down to one-half mile, and the wind is gusting strongly from the southwest. You've been in the traffic pattern for 15 minutes, but conditions aren't getting any better. You finally get clearance for an instrument approach on runway 18.

As your Cessna drops below 2,600 feet and your omni-bearing indicators blink to life, you take some comfort in knowing you're in the correct glideslope and won't be plowing into the ground. Still, the snowstorm is very heavy and the ground is not visible. Fighting the controls, you stay in the glideslope as your plane drops below 1,000 feet and you see a flicker of the runway lights ahead, shining through the snow. You compensate slightly for the wind, which is trying to blow your Cessna out of its glideslope. But this does not present a problem.

Suddenly, the engine RPM starts to drop, and you feel a sickening lurch as the plane starts to fall. Quickly you scan the instruments, searching for clues to the trouble. At first everything seems normal, but then you notice that the oil pressure has dropped to near zero! The engine must have developed an oil leak. Glancing at the airspeed indicator, you realize your plane is dangerously close to a stall. With only 800 feet between you and the unforgiving Earth, you push the nose of the plane down, into a dive.

Your airspeed increases and the ground gets closer. The engines have stopped completely. About 30 feet above the ground you yank back on the yoke, and the plane's nose pulls up. Your stomach feels queasy, and you barely get the nose up before the landing gear screeches on the runway and the plane bounces back up in the air. Again the plane comes down hard and the tires squeal, but this time it stays down. As you pull your hands from the keyboard, you notice for the first time that your heart is racing.

You turn off the flight recorder and save the settings in Microsoft Flight Simulator before switching off your personal computer.

The preceding scenario is something anyone can experience with a $60 computer program and a personal computer. Is this more interesting than watching television? How about listening to Mozart's Dissonant Quartet while your computer screen updates itself every five seconds with a continuous commentary on the music playing? Perhaps you would rather direct the actions of Sherlock Holmes and Dr. Watson as they try to solve *The Case of the Thames Murders*. Instead of being led by the characters, as in a movie, you direct the action. You decide whom Holmes interviews, piece together the clues, solve the crime, and present the case before the judge. In the mood for more action? Perhaps you would like to try the interactive version of Steven Spielberg's *Jurassic Park*.

All of these technologies are here today.

In a very short time, however, even more fantastic methods of entertainment will appear. Giant entertainment companies, such as Paramount, MCA and Time Warner, are scrambling to join cable television companies, such as US West, Tele-Communications Inc., Bell Atlantic, Cablevision, and QVC. In turn, telephone companies such as GTE, AT&T, Hauser Communications, and Southwestern Bell are jumping into the fray with consumer electronics giants like Sony, Philips, Eastman Kodak, Magnavox, and Panasonic. Semiconductor firms, such as Intel, Texas Instruments, and Motorola, are joining with computer industry giants like IBM, Apple, and Microsoft.

Everyone even slightly connected to the entertainment field is involved one way or the other with the new technology of interactive entertainment (IE).

Surprisingly, one of the fastest growing segments of the entertainment industry is seldom given much thought. This segment grosses more annually than the entire American film industry and more than the three major U.S. television networks combined. This segment has found its way into one of every three homes in America. This segment is the video game industry.

Though previously limited to shoot-em-up style arcade games, the video game industry today is growing rapidly, being fueled by tremendous advances in technology. Games today are geared more for adults than ever before in history. Even educational games are finding their way into the mainstream. Further, the advancing technology is moving video games into areas where they can no longer be considered video games; instead they should be viewed as interactive entertainment.

You can hardly consider an interactive tour of the San Diego Zoo a video game, and yet it can be very entertaining. Watching a motion picture on a video compact disc and directing the characters to follow a different plot is far from the typical image of a video game. Taking an electronic piano course that analyzes your playing to determine what your next lesson should be is more sophisticated than playing Space Invaders was just a few years ago.

Yet, today's home video game (or interactive entertainment) units can do all this and more.

WHAT IS INTERACTIVE ENTERTAINMENT?

Interactive entertainment can be defined as a type of electronic game in which the user is a participant in the action rather than an observer. The classic example of IE is, of course, the video game.

In a video game you see images on a video display (a television screen, computer monitor, or arcade game) and you interact with those images by manipulating knobs, buttons, and joysticks. Usually, the game offers an incentive to reward the user for the interaction. This incentive is either a high score or a more challenging level. Along with the rewards come the punishments, usually the end of the experience or game.

Regardless of the reward, the result is the same. Just as Pavlov's dog responded to certain stimuli, so too video game players respond to the rewards and punishments of the game. Just as a good movie can get a person to care for a fictional character, so too video games can get a person involved enough to increase adrenaline and heart rate. Though this can be an exciting and distracting form of entertainment, today's interactive entertainment has moved far beyond the stimulus and response stage.

Personal-Computer–Based IE

Today IE involves much more than such simple video games. IE started on computers, and the greatest advances in IE technology continue to occur on computers despite the plethora of video game systems and arcade games. Today, personal computers lead the field of computer-based IE, and they have become the forerunners of IE technology. PCs are a good platform for IE in that there are more than 60 million of them in the U.S. alone and you can program a computer to interact with the player in practically limitless ways. Programmers have exploited this capability since the very early days of personal computers.

Today there is a huge industry devoted to creating entertainment-oriented programs for PCs. These games are not created by the typical computer nerd, working nights and weekends in his garage. Instead, they are created by talented teams of artists, musicians, designers, and testers.

Though some early PC games were created by a single individual, today's games are produced on a much grander scale. The creation of new games more nearly resembles a movie production than an accounting program created by programmers in a data processing department. The cost of creating a top-selling computer game today can easily top $1 million. Consider one company, Electronic Arts (EA). EA has produced more than 85 games which have sold more than 1 million copies. Some of EA's games sell up to 5 million copies. Keep in mind that these games can cost $25 to $75 each.

▲ Chuck Yeager's Advanced Flight Trainer from Electronic Arts sold over 1 million copies. *Used with permission of Electronic Arts.*

The flexibility of the computer made it easy to adapt new developments in graphics, sound quality, mass storage, and processing power. These four capabilities combined to produce a new breed of entertainment called multimedia.

Multimedia is the combination of sound, animation, text, and sometimes video, in an interactive program. The initial multimedia products were geared toward research and information, such as electronic encyclopedias. Soon, however, the entertainment industry began moving into the multimedia industry, using the capabilities of multimedia to entertain and educate.

The personal computer has also been exploited as an educational tool. As programmers wrote educational software, it was easy for them to make it more interesting for the user by adding game-like qualities to the lessons. For example, in a child's shooting-style arcade game, the child might be required to answer a math problem before being allowed to shoot. Or perhaps the child must type the correct letters on the keyboard to keep his car on a racetrack. This type of educational entertainment software is often referred to as *edutainment*.

▲ The components of a multimedia computer. *Photo courtesy of Apple Computer, Inc.*

Home Video Game Systems

Another area of IE is that of the home video game system. Video game systems were perhaps the first IE products to invade American homes on a mass scale. Video game systems have seen their ups and downs, but currently they are in an "up" period. With total industry sales of $5.3 billion in 1992, video games, without a doubt, are the major player in the IE industry.

Home video systems usually use cartridge-based or CD-ROM–based games. For cartridges, the game is built directly into a computer chip. The chip is then manufactured into a cartridge that plugs into the game unit. These game cartridges provide the consumers with an endless variety of games, while providing the manufacturers with an endless supply of customers.

▲ The Super Nintendo System, one of the most successful home video game systems in history. *Photo courtesy of Nintendo of America.*

The early video games produced for these systems were rather simplistic because of the limited capabilities of the video game system. Even the earliest PC-based games outmatched them in complexity. Today however, the technology inside the average cartridge-based game system is getting close to, if not surpassing, that of the average personal computer.

Custom video graphics and sound chips are being designed and produced to give game systems capabilities that far surpass personal computers. Even now, most game systems include stereo sound systems and graphics with tens of thousands of colors. Information about CD-ROM is presented in the section of this chapter titled "Memory."

Portable Video Game Systems

In 1989, the Nintendo corporation released the first true portable video game system, called *Game Boy*. This hand-held portable unit was more than a miniature video game system. It was small, sleek, and even sexy. It immediately opened up the world of video gaming to the adult community. Half of Game Boy players were adults. Amazingly, Game Boy also appealed to that untapped market of adult females.

▲ The Nintendo Game Boy. The first cartridge-based portable video game system. *Photo courtesy of Nintendo of America.*

The success of the Game Boy was so outstanding that other companies soon released their own versions. Atari had the Lynx, NEC released Turbo Express, and Sega had Game Gear.

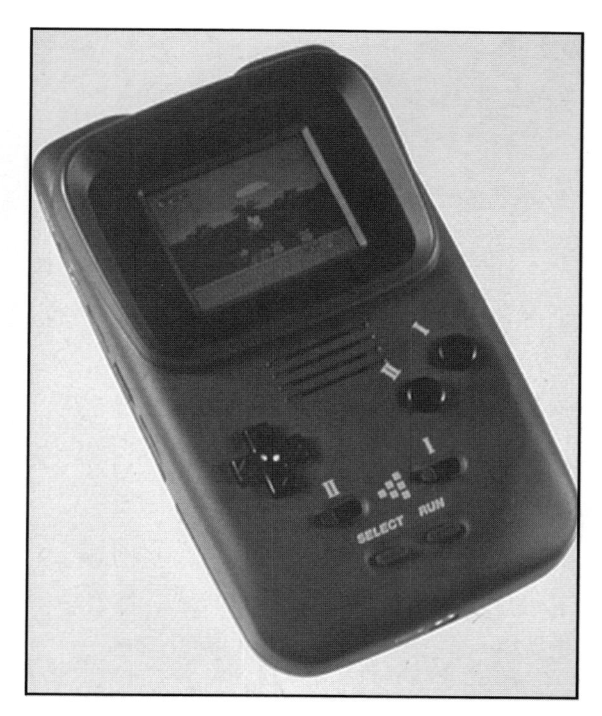

▲ The NEC Turbo Express. This portable system is compatible with the same game cartridges that run in the home system. *Photo courtesy of Aldrich and Associates.*

▲ The Sega Game Gear. This system has a television tuner cartridge available. *Photo courtesy of Sega of America, Inc.*

▲ The Philips CD-I system. This platform has more adult-oriented edutainment titles than any other system. *Photo courtesy of Philips.*

Today the portable market continues to increase in both sales and technology. Faster, smaller, and better have always been the benchmarks of the electronics industry and these benchmarks apply to portable units as well. Screens now support full color (some portables even offer television tuner adapters that enable you to watch television on them), and some support digital stereo sound.

Edutainment

Edutainment has popped up now and then in PC-based IE and video game systems, but never has it been so fervently pursued as in a new home entertainment device called the *Philips CD-Interactive* (CD-I). CD-I looks like a typical stereo compact disc player with a joystick added.

Philips appears to be targeting an adult audience that wants to use an interactive experience to learn, as opposed to the passive learning experience of reading a book or watching an education program. An older audience is clearly targeted with such titles as *Luciano Pavarotti* and *Great Impressionists of the 20th Century.*

Philips has even introduced a portable version of the CD-I player. The portable unit can run the same CDs as the home system.

▲ The Philips CD-I portable system. *Photo courtesy of Philips.*

Virtual Reality Entertainment

Some of the multimedia technologies have been combined to create low-cost *virtual reality* systems. These systems include a new product from Sega that offers immersion virtual reality, where players wear gloves and video helmets to interact with the virtual world. Virtual reality is a process in which players are hooked directly into the computer game through gloves or VR helmets. By using these features, players can, in effect, enter a game and manipulate it directly.

Other developers are working hard to fit existing PC-based games into the virtual reality arena. Hoods are available to fit over existing video monitors. These hoods enable each eye to see a separate part of the computer monitor. Then with some programming sleight of hand, images appear to the user to be three-dimensional. Other developers are using very fast computer monitors to flip quickly between two views. When combined with special eyeglasses worn by the user, the images on the computer monitor appear in 3-D.

THE DRIVING HARDWARE TECHNOLOGIES

Hardware advances made by researchers in the past decade have spurred immense growth in the interactive entertainment industry. Hardware is the physical electronic components in any interactive entertainment system, including the cables, joysticks, keyboard, monitors, and so forth.

The progress of the past decade has produced such advanced hardware as CD-ROMs, high-speed computer chips, low-cost memory chips, and colorful graphics displays.

Computing Power

The most significant factor in the increased capabilities of today's IE products is the increased speed and capacity of computer chips or integrated circuits (IC). In a typical video game or computer system, a single chip performs most of the calculations. This chief component or "system brain" is called the *central processing unit* (CPU). As IC technology has advanced over the years, CPUs have become increasingly powerful. This is a result of faster processing speed and more powerful computational powers. The CPUs commonly used in personal computers today are very advanced compared to the CPUs of just a few years ago.

Even with super-powerful CPUs, the old adage of strength in numbers still applies. In the past, one CPU typically performed all the tasks of a computer or video game. This has slowly changed over the years.

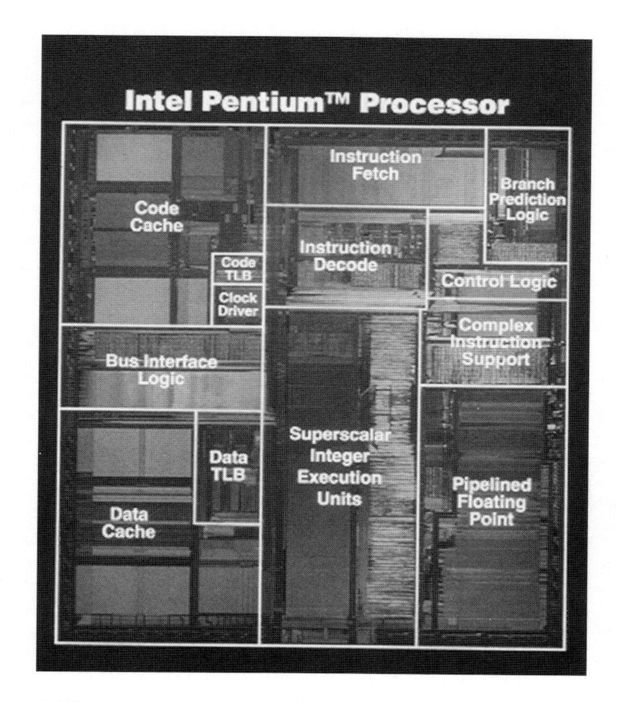

▲ This is the most advanced CPU available for personal computers, the Intel Pentium. *Photo courtesy of Intel Corporation.*

▲ The multimedia computer card from ATI Technologies sports a number of custom chips for digital sound and digital video. *Photo courtesy of ATI Technologies, Inc.*

Today, most systems include specialized custom chips. Some chips deal with only the graphics, and others handle the digital stereo sound. This in turn leaves the CPU to coordinate the activity of all the specialized chips in the machine. With this lighter CPU workload, game developers have been able to make games faster, more detailed, and more interesting.

Memory

The cost and quality of electronic memory also has played an important role in the advancement of video games. Memory is one of the few things in the world that gets better and cheaper every year. If the price of automobiles had dropped as quickly and as much, proportionally, as the price of memory has over the years, today you could buy a Rolls Royce for $1!

Though electronic memory may be similar to human memory in its ability to store information, electronic memory differs greatly, of course, from human memory in the method that information is stored and retrieved. Whereas the human brain stores information by complex biological and chemical reactions, electronic memory stores information with simple gates. These gates can be either open or closed, on or off. Mathematically, the gate is represented as a 1 or a 0.

You can touch a light switch and know by feeling it, even with your eyes closed, whether the light is on or off. That is because you know that a switch in the up position means that the light is on and a switch in the down position means the light is off. Likewise, the CPU can "read" the contents of electronic memory, the patterns of ones and zeros, and determine what they represent.

These individual units of "off" and "on" are called *bits*. A collection of eight bits makes up one *byte*. With the eight bits in a byte, you have a total of 256 possible combinations. If you were to assign every letter (upper- and lowercase) to a specific number (A=65, B=67, and so forth), a single byte could easily store any letter of the alphabet, given the 256 possible combinations. Of course, in storing a large amount of information, terms like *kilobyte*—which means one thousand bytes—are used. To describe 1 million bytes, you use the term *megabyte*. Today's games require storage in the megabyte range, from 1M up to 600M! Six hundred megabytes is enough space to store over 1,000 books, such as the complete works of Shakespeare, or multiple translations of the Bible, dictionaries, or encyclopedias.

There are three basic types of memory: electronic, magnetic, and optical. Electronic memory works when electric current travels into a capacitor and deposits a charge. The CPU can then poll that

capacitor to determine if it is charged or not. Thus a capacitor can have two states: charged (on) or not charged (off). A capacitor, however, will drain and lose its charge if it is not constantly refreshed with a fresh supply of electricity. As long as your computer (or video game) is on, there is no shortage to this electricity. When you turn off your computer, no electricity is available to keep the capacitor charged, so it quickly drains. Everything that was stored in memory simply disappears.

▲ This is a photograph of the circuitry on a memory chip (magnified 400 times). *Courtesy of International Business Machines Corporation.*

To solve this problem, magnetic memory was developed. By magnetizing iron particles in a circular disk or piece of magnetic tape, a computer can store patterns of "off" and "on." Naturally, magnetized iron particles do not need a constant flow of electricity to stay magnetized. When computer memory is stored on magnetic media such as disks and tape, you can turn off the computer without any loss of data. A downside to magnetic media is that there are physical limits to how small you can make a magnetic read/write head.

▲ This is the read/write head of a hard disk drive. *Courtesy of Maxtor Corporation.*

To overcome this limitation, lasers and optics are used. Optical memory is similar to magnetic memory in that it does not require a constant flow of electricity. It is better than magnetic memory because a laser beam can be focused into a much smaller area than a magnetic read/write head. Compact discs (CDs) are the most common type of optical memory. Though most of us know CDs as a method of playing back high-quality music, they are really data storage devices. The music you hear from a CD is broken down into a long series of ones and zeros. As with a music CD, you can not write to a computer CD. That's where the name CD-ROM comes from; ROM stands for read-only memory.

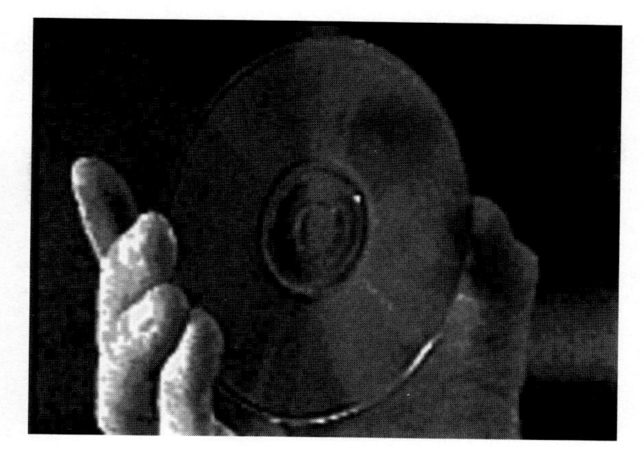

▲ A common CD-ROM, used for the storage of data.

To store sequences of "off" and "on" using a CD, small patterns of pits and bumps (called *lands*) are manufactured into the CD's surface. A laser beam is projected onto the CD, and where there are lands, the beam is reflected back. Where there are pits, the beam is dispersed. The reflected beam is then detected by an optical sensor and compared to the speed the disc is spinning. The CPU can convert these patterns into useful information. The tremendous benefit to CD-ROMs is their optical properties. Because a laser beam can focus on a much smaller area than a magnetic read/write head, much more information can be packed in the same amount of space. One CD-ROM, for instance, can hold about 600 megabytes of data.

▲ In this highly magnified view of a CD-ROM, you can see the pits and lands.

▲ Microsoft's Multimedia Mozart: The Dissonant Quartet.

▲ Microsoft's Multimedia Stravinsky: The Rite of Spring.

The development of the CD-ROM has heralded a new generation in interactive entertainment. Some CD-ROMs, known as *mixed mode*, allow computer data to be interleaved with standard CD audio data. This means that computer programs can load data off the CD-ROM and play CD-quality music or sound effects at the same time. Good examples of this are the music exploration titles from Microsoft, including *Multimedia Beethoven: The Ninth Symphony*; *Multimedia Mozart: The Dissonant Quartet*; and *Multimedia Stravinsky: The Rite of Spring*.

Each music exploration title features four main areas. These include a "Pocket Audio Guide" that enables the user to see a quick overview of the entire musical score and an "Artist's World" function that takes you through a tour of the artist's life and times and enables you to explore the social and artistic environment in which the work was created.

The "Listening" section explains details about each composer's musical style. Music samples help explain complicated concepts. Finally, "A Close Reading" function plays the entire score directly from the CD-ROM while at the same time giving you a real-time commentary on the screen. In the case of Beethoven's Ninth Symphony, the user can toggle between German and English text for the singer's performance of Ode to Joy while the music and commentary are simultaneously running.

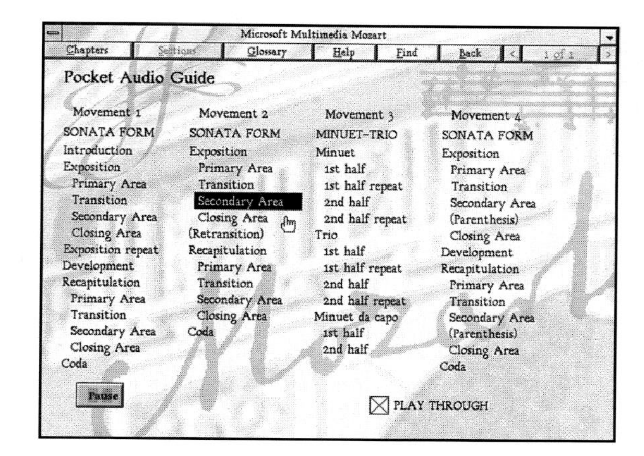

▲ The "Pocket Audio Guide" of Multimedia Mozart: The Dissonant Quartet.

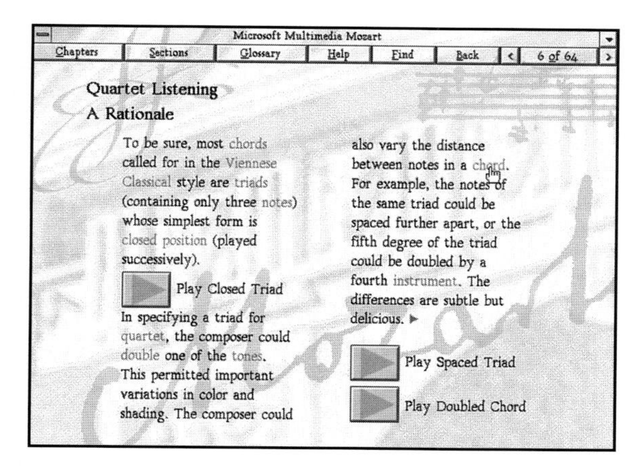

▲ "Quartet Listening" explains the inner workings of Mozart's Dissonant Quartet.

▲ "Mozart's World" provides a biographical background of Mozart.

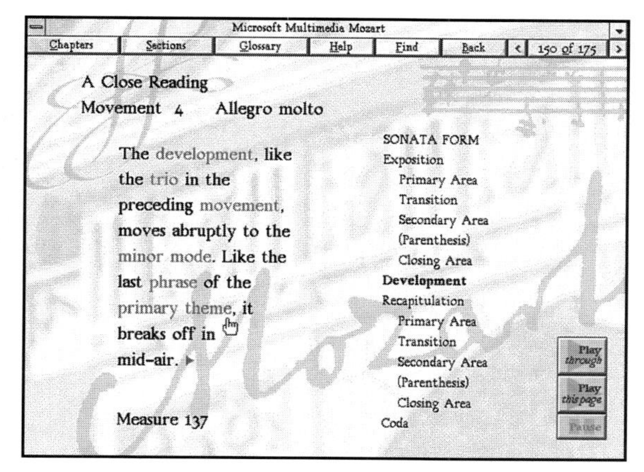

▲ "A Close Reading" offers a real-time commentary as the musical piece plays from the CD-ROM.

You may be wondering, "Why so much emphasis on memory? Why is it so important to interactive entertainment?" Memory involves much more than just keeping score in a video game. All the beautiful digital stereo sound that comes from the game system's speakers must likewise be stored in memory. The internal software that runs an IE system also must be stored in memory. The more memory a PC or game cartridge has, the larger and more complex the program can be. Additional memory makes IE much more interesting by providing for lengthy digital sound-tracks and complex programming. However, these are not the only areas that benefit from added memory.

High-Color Graphics

The quality of the color the resolution of graphics is directly proportional to the amount of memory available. Generating graphics is a fairly straightforward task. First, consider that the screen is divided into rows and columns just like a chessboard. On a chessboard, the rows and columns are fairly wide, so it is easy to see the individual squares of the board. If you put twice as many rows and columns into the same space, then the board squares are only half as big. Also, you would have twice as many squares on the same board. This is called the *resolution* of the graphics.

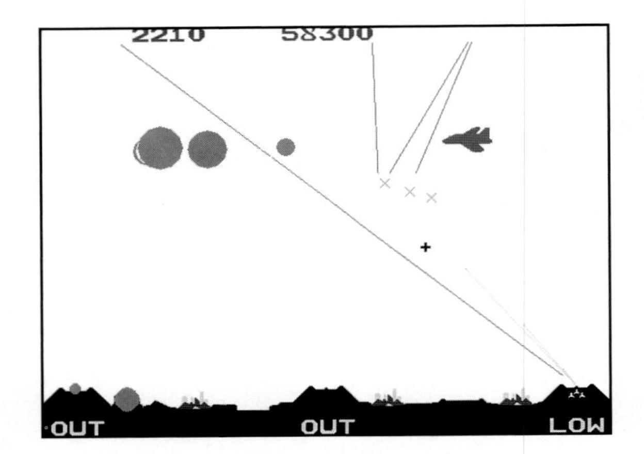

▲ An older video game using low-resolution graphics.

▲ A new high-resolution video game.

Early video games had very low resolution, so much so that you could see the individual squares of color that comprised the image. Imagine that each square on a chessboard is represented by one bit in the computer. Naturally, the more bits you have, the more squares you represent. So with memory, the more you have, the finer the resolution of the resulting image.

The analogy goes even further. The individual squares of a chessboard alternate between white and black. With only two separate colors, it would be straightforward to use one bit per square, too. If the bit was set to 0, it could be a black square. If the bit was set to 1, it could be a white square. Suppose, however, you had a special chessboard with a third color square—gray. Now with three possible colors for each square, could you still represent each square with only one bit? Remember, a single bit can have only one state: it is either on or off (1 or 0).

In this new situation, you would have to use at least two bits for each square. You could set up a fairly simple code, such as:

Bit #1	*Bit #2*	*Color*
0	0	Black
0	1	White
1	0	Gray

In theory this works fine, but consider the fact that the amount of memory required to store the chessboard has now doubled. Now two bits per square are needed to store the chessboard as opposed to one bit. Think now of the complexity involved in representing detailed pictures and you can see why the cost of memory has limited (and driven) the graphics market for years. The limitation in graphics wasn't so much a matter of the technology as of cost.

Going back to the two-bit chessboard, is three the limit of colors you can have with two bits per square? No, there is a fourth combination, 11, that could be used to represent a fourth color. At this point, we should start calling the graphics squares by their real name—*pixels*. Pixel is short for "picture element."

As you add more memory per pixel, you get more color possibilities out of that pixel. In the example, if we double the memory again to eight bits per pixel, it could have up to 256 different colors for each pixel. This is called 8-bit graphics. As the cost of memory dropped, however, color increased even more. Today there commonly are 16-bit (65,000 colors) and 24-bit (16,700,000 colors) graphics. Again, remember that all those impressive graphics that video games display must be stored in memory.

One of the most recent developments in video games is that of full-motion video. The speed of graphics and the number of colors are now high enough that today's IE systems can simulate a television picture in the ability to play live video sequences. The need for memory increases dramatically in full-motion video. Instead of moving a little ball or player around a fairly static screen, you now have the entire screen (every pixel on the screen) changing 15 to 30 times a second.

The high speed must also be combined with at least 8-bit graphics, if not 16-bit or 24-bit. The result however is stunning. You actually have a movie you can not only watch but interact with.

Some existing systems are simply unable to handle the high-speed, high-color graphics needed for video playback. To solve this problem, many manufacturers are creating high-speed custom circuitry

▲ An interactive game that uses live video sequences.

High-Speed Custom Circuitry

Performing a challenge like displaying live video along with digital sound is beyond even many of today's advanced CPUs. To solve this problem, custom chips have been developed to handle specific tasks. The chips are commonly called coprocessors, because they assist the central processing unit. Some coprocessors handle the creation of digital stereo sound, while others handle the problems associated with syncing that digital sound to video sequences. Still other coprocessors deal with the problem of getting graphics information to the screen fast enough to simulate video.

A custom coprocessor can be created to perform virtually any task. The only problem is that of cost. It is expensive to develop and manufacture coprocessors. Often special software must be developed to take advantage of the capabilities of coprocessors. This often leads to a chicken-and-egg scenario, in which hardware developers don't want to invest in creating special-purpose coprocessors when there is no software available. Likewise, software developers are hesitant to write programs for special-purpose coprocessors when it appears that the market may be very small.

As a result, even though the technology to produce high-performance interactive entertainment systems has existed for a number of years, it has not been done until recently. As development has become less expensive, and the demand has grown strong enough, hardware manufacturers and software developers have taken the leap and jumped into production.

Digital sound chips that convert sequences of numbers to analog wave forms that simulate music are a good example of the custom circuitry that graces practically every IE system on the market today. The special chips, often called DACs (digital-to-analog converters) or ADCs (analog-to-digital converters), convert analog sound waves to digital patterns and then back to analog sound waves again.

Computer gamers know the outcome of this process as digital voice and stereo digital sound. The difference between games that use them and games that don't is like the difference between an old silent movie and a modern movie with digital surround sound.

In 1992 a company called 3DO announced a home game system technology that was subsequently released in the fall of 1993. Instead of simply making another game machine, 3DO designed a technology based on high-speed custom circuitry. This reduced the price for a high-speed graphics computer down to the level of a video game. The following chart compares personal computers, game systems, television, and the 3DO system.

As you can see, the graphics display speed of the 3DO is many times faster than current technologies. Added to the high-powered technology of the 3DO are the high-powered backers of the product. Time Warner, Electronic Arts, AT&T, and Matsushita (the parent company of Quasar, Technics, Panasonic, MCA-Universal, and many others) are partners in 3DO. Thus the makers of 3DO plan to offer not just shoot-em-up style video games, but full-length motion pictures that can be viewed directly from a CD-ROM. One of the first titles will be an interactive version of the MCA movie *Jurassic Park*.

▲ The 3DO system offers custom circuitry for generating high-speed graphics. *Courtesy of The Bohle Company*.

	Personal Computer	*Game System*	*Television*	*3DO*
Max Colors	16.7 million	256	2 million	16.7 million
Pixels per second	1 million	1 million	6 million	36-64 million

Other companies, such as Sega, have released products, such as the Sega-CD Virtual-VCR, that offer more than one hour of video on a single CD-ROM. They currently have titles such as "Prince" that features music and footage of the popular rock star and his band. Also available is "March of Time" from *Time* Magazine, which features old newsreels narrated by Orson Welles.

IE system manufacturers and developers are also creating coprocessors for computing detailed 3-D computer graphics on-the-fly. These custom 3-D chips used to be the domain of very expensive graphics workstations costing tens of thousands of dollars each. They enable the computer to simulate a three-dimensional scene in its memory and then project that scene onto the screen.

▲ Microsoft Flight Simulator 5.0 uses state-of-the-art 3-D graphics.

The number of mathematical calculations required to simulate a 3-D scene in the CPU is astounding. However, CPUs can do it with the right software, and many IE programs over the years have been developed, including Microsoft Flight Simulator. Still, the cost of weighing down the CPU with the complex mathematics of 3-D graphics really slows down the games. Now with low-cost 3-D graphics coprocessors, 3-D computer graphics are becoming increasingly popular in IE.

THE DRIVING SOFTWARE TECHNOLOGIES

If the technological advances in hardware seem to be happening quickly, the advances in software appear mind-boggling. It may seem like science fiction to think of games that use artificial intelligence to watch your actions, then re-program themselves to closely fit your interest and your style of playing, but it's becoming science fact. Just as hardware has made great advances over the years, software has also. Software often has advanced even faster than hardware. Software is fairly easy to create and requires little overhead to produce, when compared to prototyping and manufacturing electronic components. There are five key areas where software advances really shine:

1. Player Analysis
2. Artificial Intelligence
3. Digital Sound
4. 3-D Graphics
5. Digital Video

Player Analysis

From the very beginning, video games have monitored and responded to the actions of the player. Perhaps the game monitored the movement of a joystick and shifted the patterns on the screen accordingly. The game might record the score of the player and display it on the screen, or as a result of a high score, the game might enable a player to progress to some new level. Regardless of what form it took, even the most early video games had some form of player analysis.

The basic problem, however, was that all games tended to be based on a win or lose attitude. If you won, you progressed. If you lost, the game ended. As video games advanced, alternate possibilities developed. Maybe the player didn't find all the secret doors, but managed not to get himself killed. Perhaps the player went on a mission but failed to achieve the major goals before returning to base. Early games tended to view this type of scenario as a loss. Thus the game demanded that the player repeat the level or mission and complete it perfectly before continuing.

Game playing reached a higher level of sophistication during the winter of 1989 with a new space-combat simulator called Wing Commander from a company called Origin Systems. The game simulated a world in the far future in which, in the role of a rookie space dogfighter, you were assigned combat missions. Some missions were defensive and others offensive in nature. Another interesting feature of the game was a plot. Instead of going on one mission after another, games), (as was standard for other flight simulator/combat Wing Commander included animated sequences that carried the story line along between missions.

Also surprising was the fact that even if you failed to fulfill the primary objectives of a mission, the game let you progress to the next mission. Though this was not so astounding in itself, a real shock came when players of Wing Commander started talking among themselves.

Players of Wing Commander realized that they were assigned missions that other players had never seen. Some players even received a new story line. The game actually changed itself based on the individual's performance. If you did well and completed all the mission goals, the next mission would be more aggressive and exciting. If you failed, you were severely reprimanded by your commanding officers and sent on more defensive missions (which were sometimes equally exciting). This type of flexibility is known as using *pathway trees*. The game essentially was constructed like a "tree" with various branches. As players played the game and made certain decisions or performed in certain ways, the computer branched to different parts of the game.

Not only did the missions change, based on your performance, but so did the story. If you failed to escort a freighter full of supplies and it was

▲ Completing the mission objective in Wing Commander.

▲ The next mission.

▲ A successful mission briefing.

▲ Failing to complete the mission objective.

destroyed by enemy fighters, then the planet it was attempting to supply would eventually get overrun by the same enemy. As a result, you would be forced to fly more defensive missions. On the other hand, if you succeeded in escorting the freighter to its destination, the enemies would be driven out of that sector, and your ship could progress deeper into enemy territory on more aggressive—and glory-filled—missions.

The Wing Commander series was an instant hit, selling over 500,000 copies. Because of its new software technology, it was an instant hit with adults. More recently video games have taken this technology a step further by modifying the way the

▲ The Wing Commander mission briefing after failing to meet the objectives.

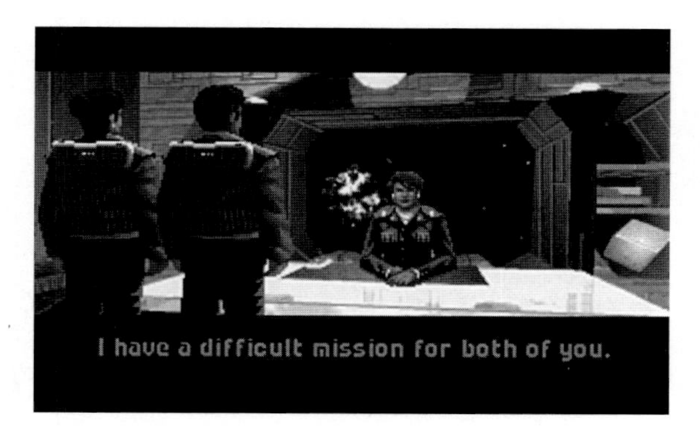

▲ The next Wing Commander mission.

game works based on the player's actions. A graphics adventure game released in 1991 by LucasArts Entertainment Company called Indiana Jones and the Fate of Atlantis monitors the choices you make early in the game and then modifies the rest of the game to suit your style of playing.

▲ Indiana Jones and the Fate of Atlantis from LucasArts Entertainment Company.

For younger players—who like more action than puzzles—the game modifies itself more toward an action-oriented melodrama. For older players who enjoy a good puzzle, there is the classical puzzle-solving mode. Finally there is the social interaction (or team) mode, where you need to interact with other computer-controlled characters to solve problems.

▲ Indiana Jones and the Fate of Atlantis in action mode where Indy hits first and asks questions later.

▲ Indiana Jones and the Fate of Atlantis in puzzle mode. Here Indy, with your help, tries to repair ancient Atlantean machinery.

▲ Indiana Jones and the Fate of Atlantis in team mode. Now Indy has to rely on cooperation with other teammates.

After completing the game by following a certain style of playing, the player can play the game again using another style. Again this type of "self-tuning" makes modern games very appealing and interesting to practically any audience.

Artificial Intelligence

Of course, almost all games require the computer to calculate a response to your input. Even mindless shoot-em-up style video games require that the object shooting at you must aim at you. If you move your character to the left, the enemy needs to aim to the left. If you move your character to the right, the enemy needs to aim to the right. Of course, the computer-controlled enemy could nail you every time he shoots at you. So the software must limit his abilities somewhat so you have a fighting chance.

This can quickly become very complicated. For instance, what if you move your character behind an obstacle? Does the computer-controlled enemy have enough intelligence to move to a new position where it can shoot you, or does it remain static, shooting straight at you as its bullets are blocked by the obstacle? Not only shouldn't the computer opponent shoot through obstacles, but it shouldn't walk through them either. The software needs to monitor the movement of the opponent as well. To make matters worse, there's the issue of strategy.

Everyone is familiar with the common chess-playing games and how successful they can be at developing winning strategies. Most chess programs try as many combinations as possible before choosing and making the best move. Some action games may require that the computer opponent use some sort of strategy. But in action games, deciding a strategy must be done quickly; otherwise the pace of the game will be too slow.

Modern game developers use the term *artificial intelligence* (AI) when referring to the software that controls computer opponents. The section of the program that controls AI is known as the *AI engine*. AI has become extremely complex in simulation-based games. These are games that simulate real-life events; such games include racing simulations, historical military simulators, sports simulations, and flight simulators.

Consider a game that simulates a road race. Cars in the race need to take corners as quickly as possible to pass other cars. What, however, does a computer-controlled opponent car do when it needs to pass you when a sharp corner is coming up? Does it swing wide, and risk losing speed as it passes? Does it try to pass on the inside, and risk getting run off the track? Should it simply hang close behind you until after you've both rounded the corner?

Consider a navy military game, in which you are in command of a fleet of ships. The computer opponent must have a large amount of AI, so that it can analyze the strengths and weaknesses of its fleet. It also needs to quickly develop a strategy, then constantly check that strategy in case you make some move to block it. There may be also simulated weather and sea conditions to deal with.

Sports games often need very complicated AI engines. In a single-player sport, such as javelin throwing, the computer needs to monitor the moves of the player and verify that the computer equivalent would be physically capable of performing the moves. Is the athlete too tired to continue running? How heavy is the javelin? How far will it travel, based on the strength and angle of the athlete's throw as compared to wind conditions?

Perhaps the ultimate challenges in AI are the combat-oriented flight simulators. Imagine the complex AI engine needed to replicate a typical jet fighter dogfight. The computer-controlled enemies need to know where you and they are in three-dimensional space. They also need to be aware of the aircraft maneuvers their plane is capable of performing, such as Immelmanns, high and low yo-yos, and lag rolls. In the process of fighting, the computer enemies also have to be aware of the flight characteristics and tolerances of their planes, so they do not stall while attempting some impossible maneuver. Once computer enemies get you in their sights, they need to choose which weapon would be most effective against your plane. If you are being chased by an aircraft using guns, the enemy needs to anticipate your turns so it can fire at a point in space ahead of your plane, hoping you fly into the stream of bullets.

▲ An enemy (computer-controlled) pilot lines you up in his sights using artificial intelligence in Origins' Strike Commander.

Artificial intelligence makes interactive entertainment very challenging and realistic. However, another advancement in software technology has made IE even more realistic: digital sound.

Digital Sound

The advent of realistic digital sound is due as much to software advances as to the development of the digital-to-analog converters mentioned earlier. Even before the arrival of DAC and ADC chips, imaginative PC programmers had created games that included software-based digital-to-analog conversions. These software-based DACs ran in the cycles of the CPU along with the rest of the game. This, of course, slowed down the game, and the quality of the digital sound left a lot to be desired. It sounded more like a cheap AM radio receiving a bad signal than realistic sound. Still, it was digital.

Today's game systems and personal computers feature state-of-the-art digital sound chips, and IE software takes these chips to their limit. Multimedia-based personal computers now are coming equipped with sound cards that offer high-quality digital sound synthesis. You can hook the output of your sound card directly to your home stereo and play your favorite game while blasting out 100 watts of stereo digital sound.

The music and sound effects you receive also are not the typical beeps and blips of video games gone by. Instead, IE titles come with beautiful soundtracks composed by some of Hollywood's best composers. Strike Commander, a jet combat simulator from Origin Systems, features a gripping sound track from the composer of such Hollywood hits as *Lethal Weapon III*.

▲ In this scene from Strike Commander, a computer-controlled character talks to you using digital voice.

There's also a lot to be said for having non-playing characters (NPCs) actually speak to you, so you don't have to read subtitles.

Actors are even getting roles, as in LucasArts' *Day of the Tentacle*. The game designers were brainstorming when they thought that the voice of Richard Sanders, who played a news reporter in *WKRP in Cincinnati*, would make a great voice for one of the game's characters. Sanders had done extensive voice-over work in the past and was excited to get involved with the project. In the game, Sanders played the part of a nerdy scientist named Bernard.

Day of the Tentacle is like an interactive cartoon. Colorful, entertaining sequences keep the action lively, and puzzles and digital sound keep the player involved.

High-quality stereo digital sound is a necessity for interactive entertainment today. Sound conveys a wealth of feelings and emotions in our everyday experiences, so it's only natural that we exploit it to enhance entertainment with sound.

▲ Actor Richard Sanders, known for his role as Les Nessman in WKRP in Cincinnati, did the voice-over for a new LucasArts CD-ROM–based game, Day of the Tentacle. *Photo courtesy of LucasArts.*

▲ Sanders was cast in the role of Bernard, the nerdy scientist.

▲ Here the player needs to find a solution to the puzzle in Day of the Tentacle.

▲ A frame from an animated sequence in Day of the Tentacle.

3-D Graphics

In the same way that digital sound first appeared in software, so 3-D computer animation first appeared in software. Bruce Artwick started developing 3-D graphics software in 1977 for the then-current Tandy TRS-80 and the Apple II. Artwick decided to make the first PC-based 3-D flight simulator, and he released it two years later under the company name of subLOGIC. Although the device was very crude and used only simple lines, it was nonetheless a full 3-D simulator. Of course, it pales in comparison to more recent 3-D simulators such as Comanche from Nova Logic.

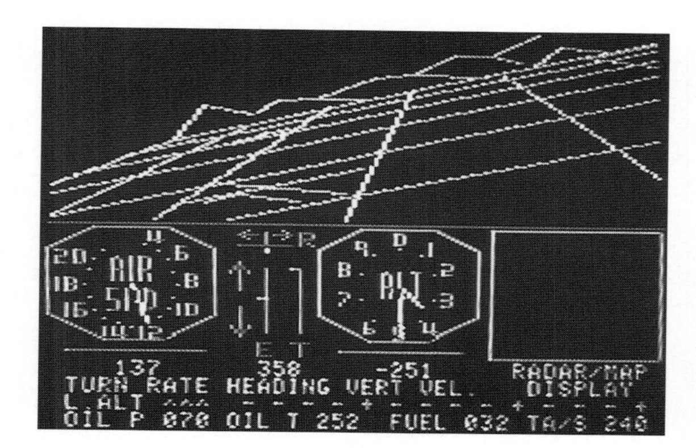

▲ subLOGIC's Flight Simulator Version 1.0 for the Apple II. *Courtesy of subLOGIC. Flight Simulator is a registered trademark of Bruce A. Artwick.*

▲ Comanche from Nova Logic uses the latest software-based 3-D graphics technology.

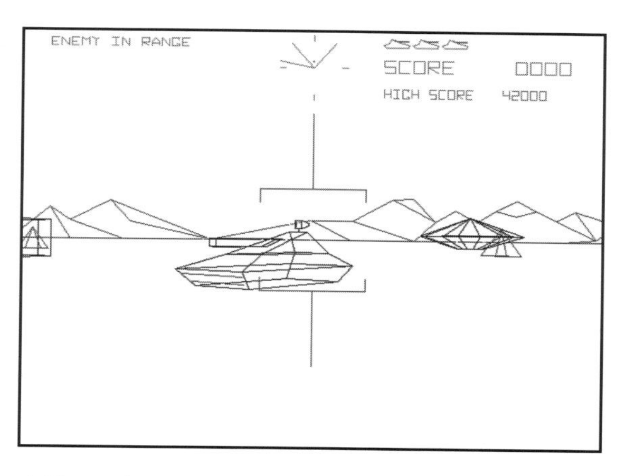

▲ This early arcade game, Battlezone from Atari, featured 3-D wireframe graphics. Notice how you can see through everything (including other tanks).

For 3-D graphics, there are three basic techniques used: real-time 3-D, bit-map scaling, and pre-rendering. These techniques can be used individually or in combination with each other. Following is a discussion of how each type works and the pros and cons of each.

Real-Time 3-D

Making real-time 3-D graphics means the computer has to generate 3-D scenes on-the-fly. Without special hardware to do this (and sometimes even with special hardware), this is a computationally expensive process. That means it takes most of the CPU's capabilities just to compute the mathematics involved, let alone carry out the rest of the game. There are three basic types of real-time 3-D graphics being used today: wireframe, polygon, and voxel.

3-D wireframe graphics are the simplest method of getting quick 3-D imagery. The only problem is its lack of realism. An advantage to 3-D wireframe is the speed at which the computer can create 3-D imagery.

Polygon graphics are a great improvement over wireframe in that polygon graphics provide solid-looking objects and allow some shading and detail. The computer accomplishes this by calculating small triangles in 3-D space and filling them with a color. Each triangle is called a "face" or "polygon." Flight simulators such as Microsoft's Flight Simulator v5, Dynamix's Aces of the Pacific, and Spectrum Holobyte's Falcon 3.0 have taken this technique to its current limits.

Because performing many 3-D calculations on-the-fly can tax even the fastest PC, older polygon-based graphics were usually solid blocky objects with little detail. As processor speeds have increased, we see more detail in polygon-based graphics. This translates to more and smaller polygons in each scene. In some cases, bit maps (small pictures stored in the computer's memory) are mapped onto the polygons like wallpaper, as in Aces of the Pacific.

The final method of real-time 3-D graphics is called *voxels*, which stands for "volume pixels." This technique was borrowed from professional flight simulators and scientific visualization systems costing millions of dollars. A few years ago, developers at a game company called Nova Logic realized that today's high-performance personal computers have enough computational power to perform voxel graphics for a flight simulator. The result of this work stunned audiences at the January 1993 Consumer Electronics Show. Nova Logic's stunner was *Comanche Maximum Overkill*, a helicopter simulator with graphics that are, without a doubt, the best ever seen on a PC-based flight simulator.

▲ In this screen shot from Nova Logic's Comanche, you can clearly see the beauty of 3-D voxel graphics.

3-D Rendering and Bit-Map Scaling

Another method of creating 3-D graphics is by taking flat two-dimensional pictures and scaling them on-the-fly. For instance, if you are flying to the right of a ship in space, you need only see the right side of that ship. The game can display an image of the right side of the ship you are viewing. As you fly around the ship the image changes from a side view to a three-quarter view and then to a front view. In this way, a very complex ship can be drawn and a fly-by can be simulated without very much processing by the CPU.

The pictures or different views of a 3-D object | can be hand painted, for example those in Wing Commander I. They also can be rendered from 3-D models, as in Wing Commander II.

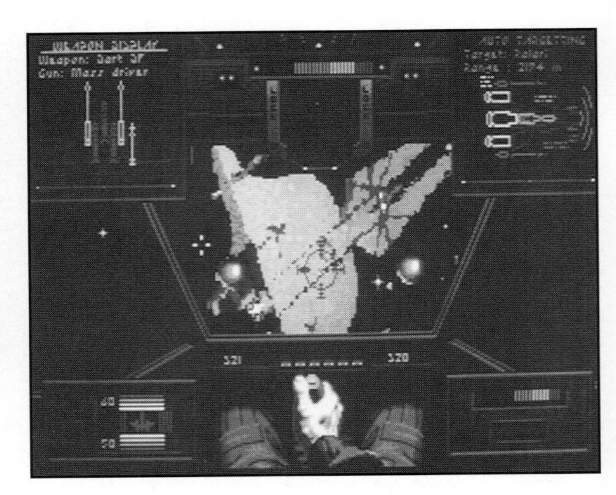

▲ In Wing Commander I, hand-painted views were used for bit-map scaling. *Courtesy of Origin Systems*.

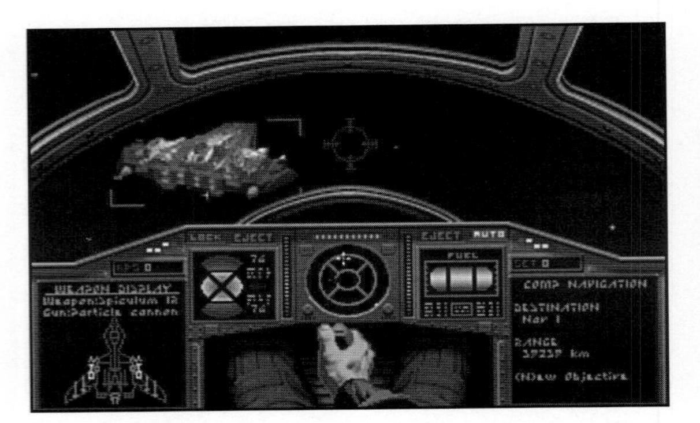

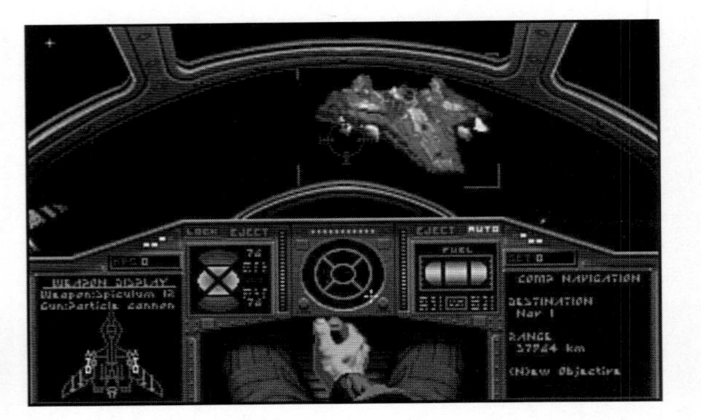

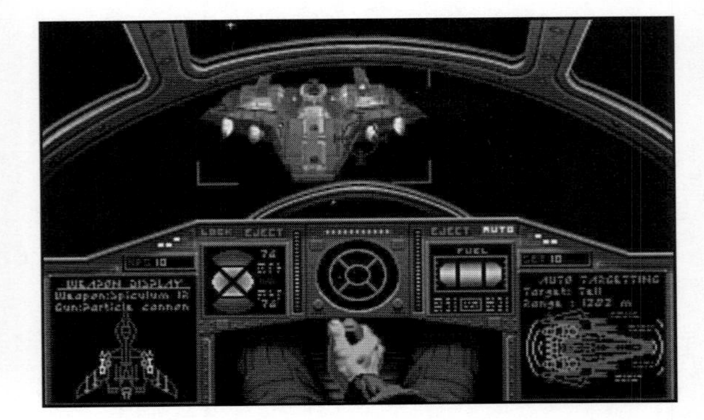

▲ Wing Commander II used computer-rendered views for bit-map scaling.

▲ Ultima Underworld by Origin Systems.

3-D Rendering is the process of creating a 3-D wireframe model of an object or scene. Realistic bit maps are then applied to the surface of the object to make it look real. Next, the computer spends hours creating a highly realistic image of that 3-D model, complete with reflections, shadows, and transparent surfaces.

These 3-D renderings can be still images, or a number of still images can be rendered and then viewed in quick succession. As long as the individual images are viewed at 12 frames per second or higher, the human mind thinks it is seeing real motion; 3-D computer animation is thus possible. These images and animations are very realistic and beautiful, but require hours to render. Therefore, most 3-D rendering is used for creating still shots or for quick cinematic sequences, such as those the Wing Commander games use to carry the story line.

▲ Notice the realism that can be achieved with bit-map scaling, as seen in this scene of Secret Weapons of the Luftwaffe, from LucasArts. *Courtesy of LucasArts*.

When two-dimensional views are created with 3-D rendering, the realism is enhanced, and development time is reduced. A spaceship, for instance, needs to be created in 3-D only once. Afterward, the computer can render as many views from different angles as needed. When Origin Systems started using 3-D rendering technology to produce these bit maps, the company cut production time by up to 70 percent!

Ultima Underworld, another Origin Systems product, likewise uses this bit-map scaling technique to simulate walking around inside a dungeon. "The effect is very convincing, and easily lends itself to future virtual reality titles," according to Chris Douglas, graphic artist for Origin. Bit-map scaling can even be used in traditional flight simulators, as Secret Weapons of the Luftwaffe, from LucasArts, demonstrates.

▲ In this scene from Ultima Underworld, the player is too close to a character, which causes the character to appear pixelated.

▲ Interplay's Star Trek: The 25th Anniversary uses a dithering technique to smooth the jaggies when you get too close to an object. *Courtesy of Interplay*.

A current limitation to bit-map scaling is that you can only move so close to an object before the bit-map resolution becomes lower than the screen's resolution. When this happens, bit maps tend to pixelate. *Pixelation* occurs when the pixels in a picture become very large and blocky. A company called Interplay has developed a method of smoothing out the blocky edges; the method is called *dithering*. If you fly too close to an object in Interplay's Star Trek: The 25th Anniversary, dithering blends the edges with each other.

With the large amount of storage on CD-ROMs, some companies are rendering entire games. Such games, including The Seventh Guest by Trilobyte, enable a player to choose different exits from a room. The player then sees a pre-rendered scene of walking out of the selected exit. The result is a very realistic game, with 3-D graphics rivaling those on television and in motion pictures.

Here is a sequence of images taken from The Seventh Guest from Trilobyte/Virgin Games. Notice the beautifully rendered 3-D graphics.

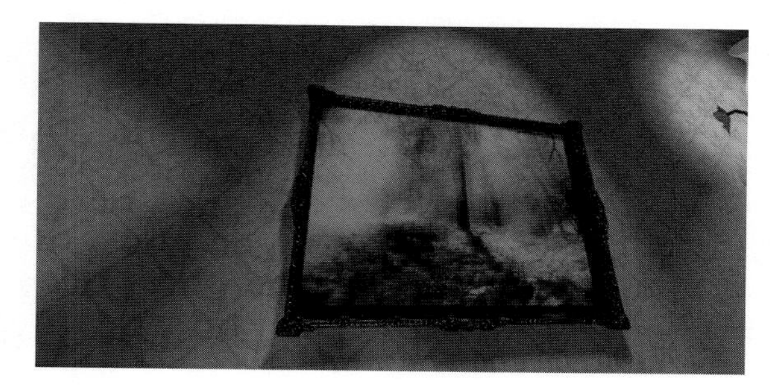

Building the Virtual World

Regardless of the method used to represent a three-dimensional scene to the user, a true 3-D environment or "virtual world" must exist mathematically in the computer. How are virtual worlds built? There are many ways to build them, ranging from using fractal formulas to hand sculpting the world. Perhaps the most interesting is the new technique of using satellite-scanned data.

Fly the Grand Canyon by Hyacinth offers the state-of-the-art in this regard. It contains satellite-scanned 3-D elevation data of more than 1,800 square miles of terrain in the Grand Canyon. The game includes more than 3 million points of actual topographical data which portrays the canyon accurately. As a simplified flight simulator, it lets you fly through a 3-D wireframe representation of the canyon. Though the 3-D graphics themselves may not be cutting-edge technology, they are effective because they appear in stereo. By viewing the image through red- and blue-lensed glasses, you can see the canyon in true stereo 3-D. The technology makes your monitor look as if it's about five feet deep. The fascinating thing is that games based on satellite scanned data could, theoretically, allow you to explore areas of the earth that no human has ever seen before (if such an area exists)!

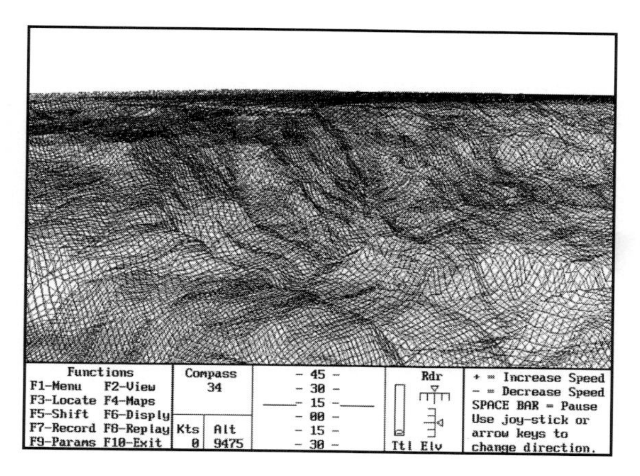

▲ This stereoscopic view is from Hyacinth's Fly the Grand Canyon.

Note: Use the 3-D glasses in the back of the book to view these two images as they appear in Color Inserrt 4.

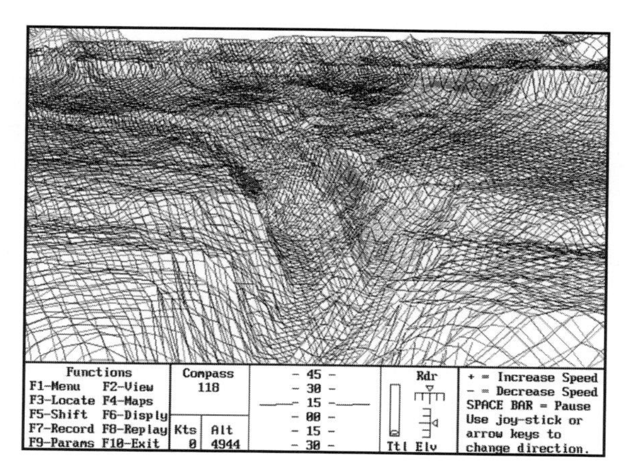

▲ In this stereoscopic view, the player is flying just above the Colorado River.

Digital Video

A final topic concerning developments in software technologies is digital video. You already know about the problem of playing digital video back on electronic gaming equipment or personal computers. The major problem has been that most game systems and personal computers don't come close to the speed required to move full-color images from a disk or CD-ROM to the screen.

Consider the math needed to make the transition from a disk or CD-ROM to the screen. A typical television tube picture has an approximate video resolution of 512 (height) × 486 (width). That brings the single image to 248,832 total pixels, and each pixel stores up to 16,700,000 colors (24-bit graphics). A 24-bit pixel requires three bytes (one byte = eight bits), so the total amount of memory for this one frame is 746,496 bytes. Now consider that normal television video runs at about 30 frames-per-second. That means that every second the CPU has to move 22,394,880 bytes (22 megabytes) of data from disk to memory to video. Twenty-two megabytes would be equivalent to all the information in two 500-page phone books every second.

The speed of the average CD-ROM drive is about 300,000 bytes-per-second, a far cry from the required 22,394,880 bytes-per-second. If sound accompanies the video, that adds to the storage requirements. Even the tagline "Hasta la vista, baby" in Terminator II requires about 210,000 bytes to store in stereo CD-quality sound.

Not only is the speed of the modern game system and PC a problem, but even modern storage techniques are severely limited when it comes to the enormous space requirements of digital video. A single two hour movie would require 2,687,385,600 bytes (2.6 gigabytes) of storage. That would be equivalent to a stack of phone books 32 feet tall (about 256 500-page books).

These seemingly insurmountable problems have been overcome by software engineering. Imagine a video sequence of a typical street as a car drives by. In this case, the camera does not move, so the background stays relatively the same throughout the entire sequence. If software could be developed that would compare every frame with its previous frame and analyze exactly which pixels need to change, it would only need to adjust (and store) those pixels that change. In the example, the software need only update the pixels that comprise the car as it moves across the static background .

This form of video compression is added to other standard image compression techniques. For example, if the camera is pointing at a blue sky, the computer does not need to store all those blue pixels with identical color values. It can simply store the color blue, along with the number of pixels to make blue on the screen. This is a common form of image compression.

Note

For more information on image compression, see *The Magic of Image Processing*, by Mike Morrison. Published by Sams, ISBN 0-672-30315-9.

An unexpected aid to compressing video is that the human mind tends to fill in missing data when images move quickly. That means that the quality of each frame need not be very high for acceptable results. Even modern television transmissions take advantage of this human trait. When color television first appeared on the scene, the standards agencies wanted to make color TV transmission compatible with black-and-white TV transmissions. So they kept the high-resolution black-and-white transmission and tacked a low-resolution color image onto it. When the two are overlaid by your TV set, your eye is fooled by the movement and high quality of the black-and-white images; it does not see that the color is really in a lower resolution.

▲ This scene from Return to Zork by Activision shows some slight degradation in the digital video.

The human eye tends to focus on areas of the video screen that contain movement. Because the human eye may not see every pixel of every frame in a video sequence, the computer doesn't need to update all of them. Some pixels can simply be left over from previous frames without any noticeable degradation. In this case, some of the data is considered "lost" or "missing" from the original video sequence. This is where the term *lossy compression* comes from.

Today special hardware can compress and decompress video at much higher speeds than compression software on a typical CPU. This method of compressing digital video data—which first appeared in software—not only solves the problem of bandwidth (how fast the computer can move the data through the system) but it also solves the data storage problems.

Compression ratios of up to 200:1 are possible with digital video compression techniques. A ratio of 200:1 would mean that the 22,394,880 bytes-per-second of digital video can be compressed to 111,974 bytes-per-second. Even the slow speed of CD-ROM drives can handle that bandwidth. Using a compression ratio of 200:1 on a 500-page phone book would bring it down to only 2 1/2 pages.

All these software advances have pushed the level of interactive entertainment to new heights. Just as television is a socially acceptable method of entertainment for both adults and children, so too the video game is now being accepted as a legitimate method of entertainment. All that remains is to look to the future and imagine how far IE will progress.

A VIEW OF INTERACTIVE ENTERTAINMENT'S FUTURE

Each of the following chapters in this book will present the current IE platforms on the market. Each chapter also will discuss the future of that platform. The following is a brief, general discussion of the future of IE.

If you could sum up all the goals of IE developers in two words, those words would be "mass market." That's where the money is, and money is definitely a driving force behind IE. As indicated in the discussion of the driving software and hardware technologies, the trends of IE are toward the mass market. One example is that of digital video and interactive television.

Interactive Television

Soon, you may be able to bypass the programming plans of broadcast networks and cable systems. Viewers will have instant access to pay-per-view "libraries" of movies or shows. Say, for example, that you decide to watch Quantum Leap on interactive television. After selecting Quantum Leap for viewing, you may be presented with a list of all episode titles. After choosing one, the system may prompt you for the type of view service you want. You may be able to choose to watch the episode with "maximum advertising" (for a viewing discount, of course), "minimum advertising" (for the standard viewing fee), or "no advertising" (for an extra viewing fee).

Next you can choose an "expanded research" option. This option, for an additional cost, will enable you to pause the episode and view extra information relating to the time period the episode occurs in, the historical figures depicted, or hyperlinks to previous episodes for more information on a character you don't recognize.

Finally, the episode begins. In this episode Sam goes back in time to the wild west. Before long, an advertising break starts. Because the local station knows the basic theme of this episode is western, it automatically runs an advertisement for "Bob's Big Cowboy Hats." You find that you have a sudden interest in cowboy hats, so you interrupt the commercial and request a catalog. Back at your local station, an automatic fax system faxes your name and address to Bob's Big Cowboy Hats, along with your catalog request.

Because you've ordered a catalog, the commercial ends (as a reward for your voluntary submission to their mailing list), and you are returned to Quantum Leap. As the episode continues, you notice a nice pair of western boots. You pause the episode and click on the actor's boots. A menu appears with the options to research the period dress of that time, or you can enter a mall program and go shopping. After choosing the mall, you see a list of stores that offer Western clothing.

Once you choose a store, you are placed into an online catalog. You select the footwear section, and after browsing through a number of boots, you find a pair similar to those in the episode. You verify that they have your size in stock, then click the purchase option. After choosing your method of payment and delivery, you return to Quantum Leap episode. Now, however, you may be awarded a free "no advertising" view for the rest of the show because you made an online purchase.

Some people may consider this scenario "couch potato hell," where any television show can turn into an infomercial in the blink of an eye. Still, there are many other possibilities for this technology. For instance, if you became curious about the name of a western character mentioned, you could pull up the on-line encyclopedia and look up "Doc Holiday." While in the encyclopedia, you could browse through the articles, graphics, and digital video clips about Arizona and the city of Tombstone. At your convenience, you could exit the encyclopedia and return to the program.

As you can see, this new technology has benefits for viewers, the providing service, and the advertisers. It's a win, win, win situation. Though technologies such as virtual reality may seem more exciting and provocative, the more practical mass market aspects of IE will be developed first.

WHAT'S NEXT

Interactive entertainment takes many forms, from hand-held game systems to personal computers. Modern technology has advanced game system technology far past other entertainment products like television. There is big money in interactive entertainment. Billions of dollars are made and spent every year with the technology. Still, there seems to be a stigma about adults playing a video game.

What caused IE to get this reputation? Does this stigma come from the average person's aversion to threatening technology, or is it simply a matter of entire product lines geared only to children? Also, how closely has IE paralleled other entertainment related industries?

In the next chapter you'll look at the history and origins of interactive entertainment. This should help answer these questions and more.

2

The History of Interactive Entertainment

Pong—"As the ball bounced off a paddle or one of the top or bottom walls, it made a little "pong" sound like a sonar. The only line of instructions read, 'Avoid missing ball for high score.'"

The designers of the first computers would be surprised to find their creations entertaining people. The designers of Colossus and ENIAC (the world's first electronic computers) certainly never imagined that computers would become so commonplace that they would be used in the entertainment field.

Originally, computers were treated almost like gods. Humble worshipers submitted requests (programs) to a priesthood (the computer operators) who, in turn, offered the request to the almighty machines. After the gods considered the request, they responded to the priesthood, who then presented the response to the humble worshipers. Computer users seldom touched the computers themselves. They were completely isolated from the machines by the priesthood of operators. You could hardly call these early systems interactive.

▲ The DEC PDP-1. *Courtesy of Digital Equipment Corporation, Corporate Photo Library.*

1950—1960

In the 1950s, CRTs (cathode ray tubes) started appearing on computers. The CRT made interactive computing possible. These new computers offered instant feedback because programs could direct and manipulate patterns of light on the screen. When computers became interactive, one of the first programs written was a game.

In 1959, a small startup company called Digital Equipment Corporation (DEC) released a computer called the PDP-1 (programmed data processor) that had a CRT. DEC sent one of the first PDP-1 units to the Massachusetts Institute of Technology (MIT).

1960—1970

One of the first and most outstanding programs for this interactive computer was a video game. The students at MIT had previously conducted some experiments with interactive entertainment. One involved a computer called the TX-0 from Lincoln Lab, a military development laboratory affiliated with MIT. The students created a program called Mouse Maze that enabled the player to draw a

maze on the screen with a light pen. Then the computer would draw a little dot on the screen representing the mouse. The mouse would work its way through the maze in search of a group of dots representing the cheese.

However, with the arrival of the PDP-1, the students decided that a sci-fi game program would make interesting use of the capabilities of the PDP-1. Thus was born the idea for a simple game called Spacewar. Originally written in 1962 by a student named Steve Russell and modified extensively by other students thereafter, the game soon began burning more hours on the PDP-1 than any other program.

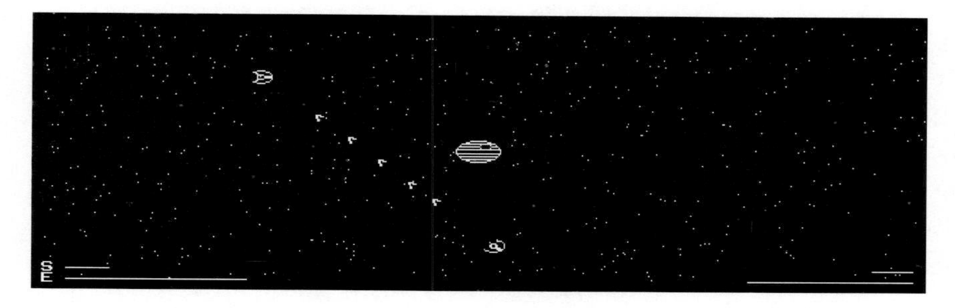

▲ This modern personal computer-based version of Spacewar follows the same basic structure of the original game.

The controls for the game were four switches on the side of the PDP-1. Two ships were on the screen (one for each player). The ships could rotate in any direction and accelerate in the direction they pointed. Players could turn the ships clockwise or counterclockwise by flicking two switches. The ships could also fire torpedoes by means of a third switch. The game simulated a gravity-free environment, so as a ship moved forward it continued to glide along that path until the player rotated the ship and applied more acceleration to change its direction. The object of the game was simple: shoot the other player's ship.

Of course, flicking the switches on the side of the PDP-1 was very uncomfortable. Students Alan Kotok and Bob Saunders found extra parts lying around the MIT Model Railroad Clubroom and constructed the first joystick. It was actually more like a wooden box with four switches mounted on the top than one of today's modern joysticks.

Compared to today's standards, this game would seem hopelessly simplistic. However, imagine its effect when students showed the game to the public for the first time at the 1962 MIT open house. Until then, the popular view of computers involved data punch cards and stern-faced scientists. It seemed almost impossible to believe that these young students were playing a science fiction game controlled by the computer!

Spacewar was an instant success. Copies started flowing to other PDP-1 owners and eventually even DEC got a copy. The engineers at DEC used it as a diagnostic program on new PDP-1s before shipping them. The sales force picked up on this, and when installing new units, they would run the world's first video game for new customers.

John McCarthy, a professor in the computer department at MIT, left his teaching position in 1962 to start up the Stanford Artificial Intelligence Lab (SAIL) in California. Spacewar, of course, went with him. New students later refined and enhanced the game with extra features, including a five-player mode. By the late 1960s, DEC had released a number of newer PDP systems, including the PDP-10. It was also at SAIL that another programmer by the name of Donald Woods used a PDP-10 to create an entirely new form of video game, one destined to live on throughout all advances in technology, down to the present day.

Woods' game, called Adventure, was totally unlike Spacewar. Adventure used no computer graphics whatsoever. Instead, it used text to tell a J.R.R. Tolkien-like story that players could interact with. The computer would tell you where you were and what you would see, then you could enter simple commands like "Go west" or "Get box."

Following is a sample from a personal computer game called Zork. Zork, released in 1981 by Infocom, was roughly based on the original PDP-10 Adventure game.

```
ZORK: The Great Underground Empire
Copyright (c) 1981, 1982, 1983 Infocom,
Inc. All rights reserved.
ZORK is a registered trademark of Infocom,
Inc.

West of House
You are standing in an open field west of
a white house, with a boarded front door.
There is a small mailbox here.

>LOOK IN MAILBOX
The small mailbox is closed.

>OPEN MAILBOX
Opening the small mailbox reveals a
leaflet.

>PICK UP LEAFLET
Taken.

>READ LEAFLET
"WELCOME TO ZORK!
ZORK is a game of adventure, danger and
low cunning. In it you will explore some
of the most amazing territory ever seen by
mortals. No computer should be without
one!"

>GO NORTH
North of House
You are facing the north side of a white
house. There is no door here, and all the
windows are boarded up. To the north a
narrow path winds through the trees.

>GO NORTH
Forest Path
This is a path winding through a dimly lit
forest. The path heads north-south here.
One particularly large tree with some low
branches stands at the edge of the path.
You hear in the distance the chirping of a
song bird.

>CLIMB UP TREE
Up a Tree
You are about 10 feet above the ground
nestled among some large branches. The
nearest branch above you is above your
reach.
Beside you on the branch is a small bird's
nest.
In the bird's nest is a large egg
encrusted with precious jewels, apparently
scavenged by a childless songbird. The egg
is covered with fine gold inlay, and
ornamented in lapis lazuli and mother-of-
pearl. Unlike most eggs, this one is
hinged and closed with a delicate looking
clasp. The egg appears extremely fragile.

>PICK UP EGG
Taken.

>EXAMINE EGG
The jewel-encrusted egg is closed.

>OPEN EGG
You have neither the tools nor the
expertise.
You hear in the distance the chirping of a
song bird.

>CLIMB DOWN
(down the tree)
Forest Path

>GO SOUTH
North of House

>GO EAST
Behind House
You are behind the white house. A path
leads into the forest to the east. In one
corner of the house there is a small
window which is slightly ajar.

>OPEN WINDOW
With great effort, you open the window far
enough to allow entry.

>ENTER WINDOW
Kitchen
You are in the kitchen of the white house.
A table seems to have been used recently
for the preparation of food. A passage
leads to the west and a dark staircase can
be seen leading upward. A dark chimney
leads down and to the east is a small
window which is open.
On the table is an elongated brown sack,
smelling of hot peppers.
A bottle is sitting on the table.
The glass bottle contains:
 A quantity of water
```

```
>OPEN SACK
Opening the brown sack reveals a lunch,
and a clove of garlic.

>EAT LUNCH
(Taken)
Thank you very much. It really hit the
spot.

>DRINK WATER
You have to be holding the glass bottle
first.

>GET WATER
You can't reach something that's inside a
closed container.

>GET BOTTLE
Taken.

>OPEN BOTTLE
Opened.

>DRINK WATER
Thank you very much. I was rather thirsty
(from all this talking, probably).
```

The original Adventure game proved to be very addictive. Students and staff members at SAIL stayed weekends and nights trying to discover solutions to the puzzles. However, as quickly as players solved the puzzles, Woods and his friends expanded the game to create new ones. The new type of video game combined the best of literature and puzzles to create an entirely new form of entertainment.

Other companies, such as Magnavox, slowly started making consumer-oriented video games. In 1966, Ralph Baer created a home video game that was later licensed to Magnavox and called the Odyssey. Though it was very simplistic and required fairly inexpensive electronic parts, it enabled the player to move points of light around on a screen. With the help of color overlays and a little imagination, it passed for a video game.

Also in 1966, Ivan Sutherland at the MIT Lincoln Laboratory invented the first computer controlled head-mounted display (HMD). Called the *Sword of Damocles* because of the hardware required for support, it displayed two separate wireframe images—one for each eye. This enabled the viewer to see the computer scene in stereoscopic 3-D. Sutherland later joined the University of Utah and perfected his HMD. Twenty years later, NASA would rediscover his techniques while doing virtual reality research. In 1968, Intel Corporation was founded by Gordon Moore and Robert Noyce. Intel went on to develop dynamic RAM and the first microprocessor.

1970—1980

As Spacewar found its way into colleges and universities around the country, it likewise found its way into the imagination of many young students. One such student was Nolan Kay Bushnell, a student at Utah State College, who in the mid-1960s started spending a large amount of time hanging around the school's computer lab playing Spacewar.

Bushnell always had a propensity for fun and adventure. This carried on into his adult life, and after graduating from the University of Utah in 1968, he took a job as an engineer in the computer graphics division at Ampex Corporation. Still, the draw of Spacewar pulled at him.

At home, Bushnell moved his daughter out of her room and into the living room to create a laboratory. It was here that he created his own version of Spacewar called Computer Space. Computer Space was vastly different from Spacewar in that it did not require a $120,000 computer to run. Instead, the game required several fairly inexpensive electronic parts. Bushnell imagined his electronic game standing beside pinball machines in pool halls and arcades throughout the country.

Bushnell left Ampex in 1971 to accept a position as a product engineer at Nutting Associates, a small pinball machine company. Nutting manufactured 1,500 computer space games, but the games didn't catch on and were never sold. Bushnell still believed in the game, but he knew it needed to be simplified. The Computer Space game was too complex, requiring players to read a full page of instructions before they could play. Putting the failure of Computer Space behind him, Bushnell left Nutting Associates in 1972, determined to create a successful, and simpler, video game.

The microprocessor also appeared on the scene in 1971, thanks to the development of the integrated circuit (IC) in 1959. The IC permitted the miniaturization of computer-memory circuits and reduced the electronics of a computer processor down to a single chip, the microprocessor or CPU. One of the first desktop microcomputers designed for personal use was the Altair 8800 from Micro Instrumentation Telemetry Systems (MITS). Coming through mail order in kit form, the Altair (named after a planet in the popular "Star Trek" television series) retailed for around $400.

Bushnell, along with a friend, formed a company called Syzygy. After both invested $250 in Syzygy, they found that the name had already been taken by another company. So they came up with the name Atari, which is the Japanese equivalent of *Check* in the game Go. It's a polite warning to your opponent that he is in peril. It seems almost comical today to think of an American electronic game company using a Japanese name. With a firm determination that its first video game would be easy to use without instructions and would allow a player to hold a beer while playing, Atari started developing Pong.

Without the finances for an assembly line manufacturing process, Bushnell created Pong himself and completed it in the fall of 1972. The game simply showed a black screen with a solid line across the top and bottom. On the left and right sides, the screen was blank except for two small vertical lines (the paddles), one on each side. The two lines were controlled by two knobs mounted into the case of the game. As you rotated your knob, the small vertical line on your side moved up and down.

When the game started, a small white dot would dart across the screen, and your job was to move your paddle into position so it reflected the ball back across the screen to the other player's side. If you missed a ball, it went off your side and a new ball was served. As the ball bounced off a paddle or one of the top or bottom walls, it made a little "pong" sound like a sonar. The only line of instructions read, "Avoid missing ball for high score."

Without realizing it, Bushnell hit on two key features for successful video games. First, make it a multiplayer game. Second, model the game after a real-life activity (in this case, ping pong). Even today with high-technology video games, it's the games that incorporate these two features that always tend to be most successful.

▲ The Atari Pong video game. *Courtesy of Atari Games Corporation.*

Compared to the pinball machines sitting beside it, Pong did very well. While pinball machines took in $30 or $40 a week, the Pong game earned about $300. Bushnell tried to get financial backing from some large amusement-game companies like Bally's Midway, but was refused. He was forced to make a go of it by himself. He secured a modest loan from a local bank and set up an assembly line in an abandoned roller skating rink. He also hired low-cost electronics technicians to do the assembling. The industry was so new that they couldn't even buy monitors. Instead they bought Magnavox televisions, threw away the plastic cases and tuners and cannibalized the electronic parts.

Also in 1972, Magnavox released the Odyssey home video game. The simplified video game system was designed back in 1966 by Ralph Baer, a supervising engineer at a company called Sanders and Associates. Magnavox licensed the technology and sold more than 100,000 units the first year. A toy and playing-card manufacturer in Japan by the name of Nintendo Company, Ltd., negotiated a license with Magnavox to manufacture and sell the Odyssey home video game. Nintendo, however, lacked the technical capabilities to produce the system, so it teamed up with the electronics firm Mitsubishi and began work on a Japanese version.

History was also being made in the early 1970s at an obscure laboratory called the Xerox Palo Alto Research Center (PARC), in Palo Alto, California. About 100 scientists there were given free rein and told to "discover the future of computing." In 1973, they unveiled the results of their work with the release of the Xerox Alto personal computer. It offered 128KB of RAM, a 2.5MB removable hard drive, and a high-resolution (608 pixels by 808 pixels) graphics screen. Most importantly, it used a completely new type of human interface. PARC had developed a graphical user interface (GUI), in which a mouse controlled graphical representations of everyday objects. Surprisingly, the Alto never took off, and during the next six years only 1,000 units sold. Graphical user interfaces affectionately became known as WIMP interfaces (Windows, Icons, Menus, and a Pointing device) by hard-core programmers.

It wasn't long until Pong was a great success, and Bushnell had to expand his workforce. One of his earliest new workers was a lanky youth by the name of Steve Jobs. Jobs, who had dropped out of Reed College after one semester, answered Atari's help-wanted ad. Bushnell hired him, and in 1974, Jobs became Atari's fortieth employee.

▲ The Apple computer created by Steve Jobs and Steve Wozniak. *Courtesy of Apple Computer, Inc.*

Meanwhile, Atari continued to develop new games, such as Gran Trak, which used a real steering wheel and simulated racing around a curvy road at night. Atari also developed other new games such as Goth, Tank, and Breakout. In 1974, Bushnell started to plan a new home version of his Pong game that might compete with the existing Magnavox Odyssey.

Jobs was joined at Atari by a schoolmate—Steve Wozniak. While Wozniak was still an engineer for Hewlett Packard (HP), he started helping with the video games. It wasn't long until Jobs and Wozniak started work on their own project (sometimes using parts lifted from Atari). This project, the Apple personal computer, would have a profound effect on the future of video games.

Wozniak certainly had the experience for designing and building electronic devices. In 1971, an article about a person known as Captain Crunch, who built electronic "blue boxes" to make (illegal) free long-distance phone calls, inspired Wozniak. A "blue box" enabled anyone to explore freely the vast worldwide telephone network. Jobs and Wozniak built their own blue boxes, and even sold them door-to-door at the Berkeley campus dormitories.

Zilog, a semi-conductor company, was formed in 1974 by Dr. Fredrico Faggin, Ralph Ungermann, and four other employees from Intel. They went on to create the Z80 microprocessor.

In 1975, Alan Baum, a workmate of Wozniak's at HP, invited him to a meeting of the local Homebrew Computer Club. Homebrew, started by Fred Moore and Gordon French, was founded to help amateur computer enthusiasts. It soon became a hotbed of ideas about building your own personal computers. From the Altair 8800 to TV typewriters, the Club discussed and built virtually anything that resembled a computer. A friend at the Homebrew Club eventually gave Wozniak a box full of parts that would work with a Motorola 6800 microprocessor. Later Wozniak switched to the 6502 microprocessor from a company called MOS Technology because it was inexpensive, readily available, and very similar to the Motorola chip. It wasn't long before Wozniak was showing off his own personal toy/personal computer at the Homebrew meetings.

In the same year, Bill Gates dropped out of Harvard. He joined his boyhood friend, Paul Allen, and together they founded a company called Microsoft. They wrote a version of the BASIC programming language for the Altair 8800. Microsoft BASIC was copied and pirated before it even shipped. When it did ship, few copies sold because most Altair owners already had a pirated version. Gates, who was a little impetuous, wrote a passionate letter that basically called computer hobbyists thieves. This didn't sit well with hobbyists, and earned Gates a reputation that took quite a while to overcome.

In 1976, Gary Kildall founded a company called Intergalactic Digital Research (later called Digital Research) in Monterey, California. Digital Research led the microcomputer industry by developing an operating system for 8-bit microprocessors based on Intel's 8080 design and Zilog's Z80 design. The operating system called CP/M (Control Program for Microprocessors) enabled the microprocessor to communicate with the other components, including memory, video, and disk storage.

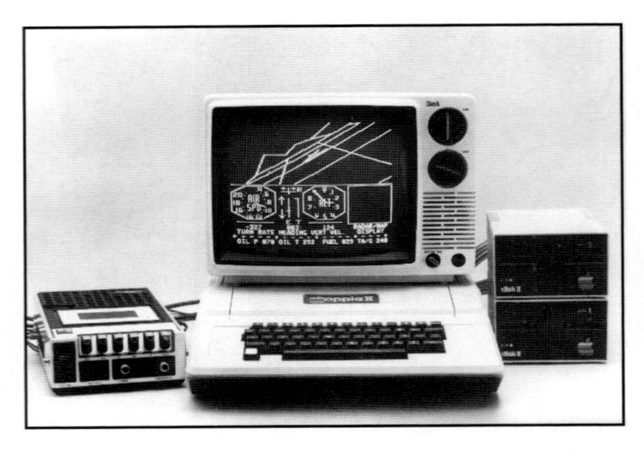

▲ The Apple II computer with its advanced graphics. *Courtesy of Apple Computer, Inc.*

Jobs, on the other hand, saw more potential in Wozniak's personal computer. He named it the Apple and encouraged Wozniak to start producing and selling it. They built the units in a garage and sold them for $666.66. While Wozniak continued to improve his design, Jobs secured financial backing. In early 1976, he showed the prototype Apple II computer to the Homebrew Club. Apple Computer was formed on April Fool's Day in 1976 and was incorporated in March 1977. The company's six employees then moved into office space in Cupertino, California.

Apple's new computer offered some very advanced features for personal computers of that time. With expanded memory (4KB RAM), disk drives for storing programs and data, and sound and color graphics, it led the technology of personal computers. It came fully assembled with a list price of $1,298. The Apple II+ with 48KB RAM was introduced in 1979. Apple Computers became the fastest growing company in U.S. business history.

After the success of Apple, other companies began entering the burgeoning computer field. Commodore Business Machines in West Chester, Pennsylvania, released a personal computer called the Commodore PET (personal electronic transaction). The Commodore PET was a low cost CP/M-based machine that became very popular. Tandy Corporation (Radio Shack) introduced its own personal computer in 1977, the TRS-80. It came with a CRT display, a keyboard, and the capability to store programs or data by means of standard audio-cassette players.

Tandy next released the TRS-80 (Tandy Radio Shack) Model II, to be followed later by the Model III. In 1978, Radio Shack led the field with only Apple and Commodore offering any real competition. However, Tandy's market share would fall to 10 percent by 1982 due to increased competition and the IBM personal computer. The TRS-80s were good machines, overall, although those who used them affectionately called them "trash-80s."

In 1977, Nintendo entered the Japanese home video game market with Color TV Game 6, which played six variations of the Pong game. The game was developed jointly by Nintendo and Mitsubishi, with a license from Magnavox for the Odyssey home video game.

In 1978, Apple hired Trip Hawkins, the company's first marketing manager. Hawkins stayed with Apple only four years. In 1982, he left to form his own computer game company—Electronic Arts. Hawkins later lured people from Apple, Atari, and Xerox PARC to his company. He even persuaded Wozniak to sit on the board of directors.

In 1978, Taito, a Japanese corporation, released the hit arcade game, Space Invaders, which became the only game to produce a physical malady, called Space Invaders' Wrist by the *New England Journal of Medicine*. Also in that year, Bushnell made plans to introduce a slimmed-down, home version of Pong, called the Atari 2600. Because Bushnell had passed on the chance to be a founding partner in Apple, Atari also started work on a personal computer. This computer was called the Atari 800. Texas Instruments also released a personal computer in 1978 called the TI-99. It retailed for $1,100, and was a dismal failure for four years, until Texas Instruments cut the price.

▲ The TRS-80 computer from Tandy Corporation. *Courtesy of Tandy Corporation.*

Atari was not alone in the home video game arena. By 1976, about 20 different companies were making home video game systems. Companies such as Fairchild Camera, Coleco, RCA, National

Semiconductor, and Magnavox were all competing for the market. Bushnell, who had Sears as a retailer since 1975, was doing $40 million in business annually. Still, he needed more cash and so sold Atari to Warner Communications for $28 million. Bushnell remained as chairman, but company profits continued to decline. In 1979, Bushnell left Atari.

Intel released its first 16-bit microprocessor, the 8088, in 1979. It featured 29,000 transistors and a clock speed of 4.77 MHz, and it would become the most successful microprocessor in the history of computers. Activision, the first independent game developer, also was founded in 1979. Activision has survived through the years and still remains a major force in interactive entertainment. Gregory Fishbach, a lawyer in entertainment law, became president of Activision International. Fishbach would later found Acclaim Entertainment in 1987.

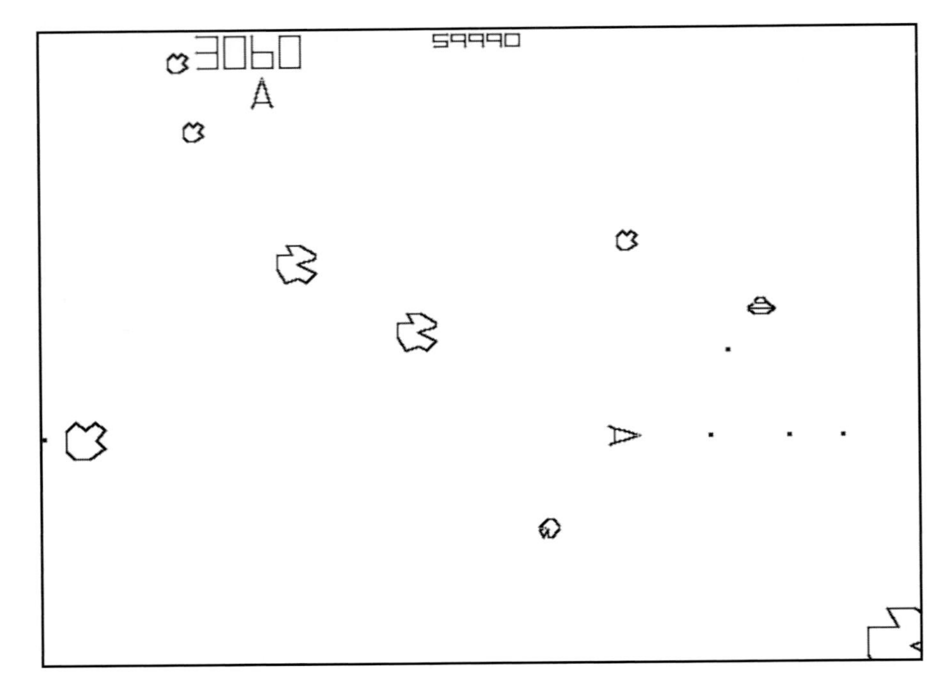

▲ The Atari Asteroids coin-operated video game. *Courtesy of Atari.*

1980—1990

For home video games, the 1980s were a roller coaster ride. Atari started to turn around and went from $200 million in sales in 1978 to $2 billion in 1982. Enjoying great success, the Atari 2600 game unit dominated in 1980 with 44 percent of the market. In the following two years, Mattel and Coleco both entered the market.

In the personal computer arena, Apple released the Apple III computer. However, it never caught on in the business community and was not quite 100 percent compatible with the Apple II line. Leading Edge Products, founded in 1980, shipped the first overseas IBM-compatible personal computer.

In 1980, Atari released Asteroids, the all-time arcade video game hit. In the game, players battled flying rocks and flying saucers (that shot back) in free-floating space. Asteroids is viewed by many to be perfection in the art of video game design.

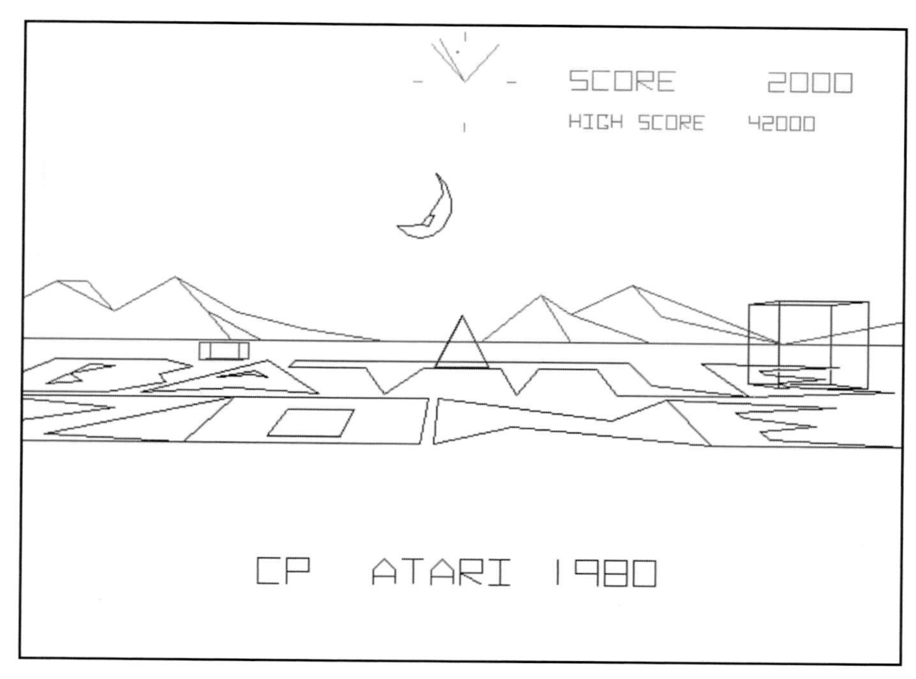

▲ Atari's Battlezone coin-operated video game. *Courtesy of Atari.*

During 1980, Atari produced another smash hit video arcade game, Battlezone. It was the first arcade game to use 3-D computer graphics. The game was a three-dimensional tank battle, where you played it from a first-person view inside your tank. It was such a sensation that the U.S. Army ordered modified versions to use in training.

In 1980, IBM approached Kildall of Digital Research and asked him to provide an operating system for an upcoming personal computer they were about to release. Kildall, in probably the biggest mistake of his life, wouldn't agree to certain IBM demands, so they dropped him. Next, IBM approached Microsoft's Gates with the offer.

Gates remembered an operating system for Intel 8080 microprocessors (the one used in the IBM PC) written by Seattle Computer Products (SCP) called 86-DOS. Taking a gamble, Gates bought 86-DOS from SCP for $50,000. He rewrote it, renamed it DOS, and licensed it (smartly retaining ownership) to IBM as the operating system for their first personal computer. Ironically, DOS was modeled after Digital Research's CP/M.

A young couple, Ken and Roberta Williams, living in Simi Valley, California, decided to try out the new Apple II computer. Ken was a programmer and computer consultant during the day, but Roberta had a strong aversion to computers. One day, Ken brought home a terminal and dialed into the IBM mainframe at his office to show her a game called Adventure. This was the same adventure game written nearly twenty years earlier by Don Woods. Roberta was immediately enthralled and began to formulate an adventure game of her own called Mystery House.

Mystery House was the first adventure game to use computer graphics to illustrate the story line. Roberta made the graphics, and Ken wrote the program to control the adventure and display the graphics. Within a month, they had finished. Ken scrapped his pet project of making a FORTRAN compiler for the Apple II, and used his business name of On-Line Systems to sell Mystery House.

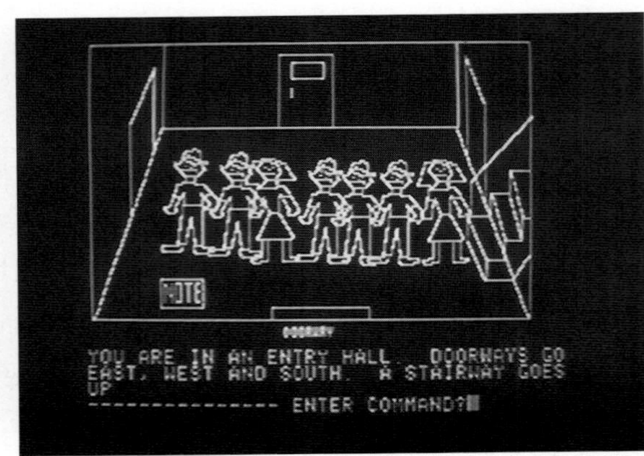

▲ The first graphic adventure game, Mystery House from Sierra On-Line. *Courtesy of Sierra On-Line, Inc.*

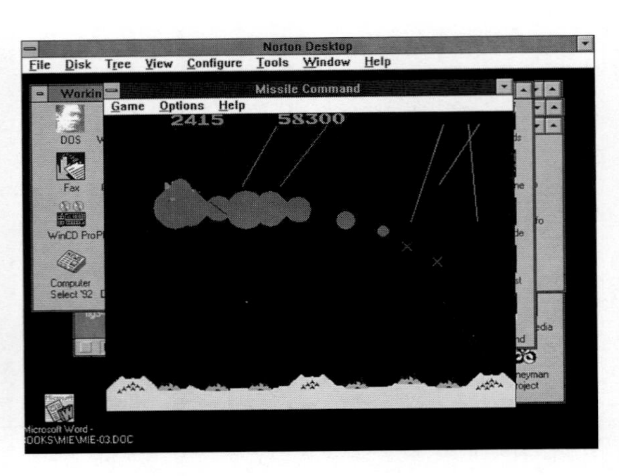

▲ Atari's Missile Command.

They advertised it for $24.95 in the May 1980 issue of MICRO magazine. In May, they made $11,000 on Mystery House. They made $20,000 in June and $30,000 in July. They followed up Mystery House with Wizard and the Princess, another graphic adventure game for the Apple II. Wizard and the Princess sold more than 60,000 copies at $32.95. Ken and Roberta jumped into their dream, moved into the Sierra Nevada mountains, and created Sierra On-Line, a computer game company still going strong today.

Toward the end of 1980, Atari completed Missile Command, an immensely popular arcade game that combined great game play with a rather chilling message about the dangers of war. It involved protecting a group of cities from incoming nuclear missiles with your own anti-ballistic missiles.

In 1980, Douglas Carlston, a lawyer with a small firm in Maine, purchased a Tandy TRS-80 personal computer and wrote a sci-fi strategy game called Galactic Empire. Your mission was to protect the good guys, the Brøderbund. Joined by his brother Gary, Douglas founded Brøderbund Software. Creators of the hit edutainment series Carmen Sandiego, which has sold more than 3 million units, Brøderbund still is going strong today.

▲ The Edutainment title Carmen Sandiego from Brøderbund Software.

▲ The original IBM Personal Computer. *Courtesy of International Business Machines Corporation.*

By now, arcade video games were doing better than ever, taking in 20 billion quarters, earning $5 billion, and consuming 75,000 player man-years in 1981 alone. The $5 billion in earnings represented twice the amount made in all the casinos of Nevada, almost twice as much as the entire U.S. movie industry, and three times more than the combined television revenues of major league basketball, football, and baseball.

IBM introduced its first personal computer, the IBM PC, in August 1981. The IBM PC, while not the most technologically advanced personal computer, seemed to break PCs into the business community in a serious way. It used the Intel 16-bit 8088 microprocessor and offered 10 times the memory of other personal computer systems. From then on, personal computers became serious tools that business needed. This new attitude sparked tremendous sales as PCs spread across the country into practically every business. Still, with all those business machines, spread the spirit of the first computer game—Spacewar.

Also in that year Atari released a new arcade game, Tempest. It was a fast-paced game in which you fought odd geometric shapes at breakneck speeds. Your screen character crawled around the top of 3-D tunnels of varying shapes and sizes. Meanwhile, enemies slowly worked their way up the tunnel toward you. If you successfully cleared the tunnel of all enemies, you would zoom through to the next level.

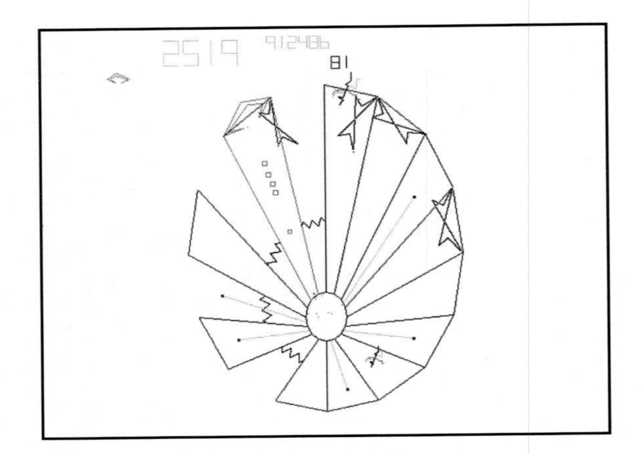

▲ Atari's Tempest coin-operated video game. *Courtesy of Atari.*

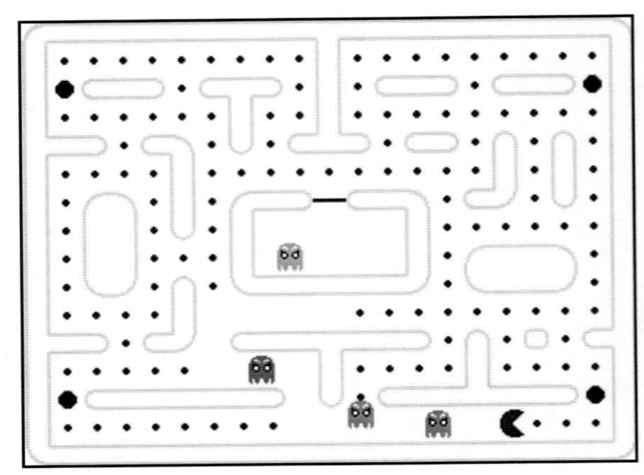

▲ Namco's Pac-Man.

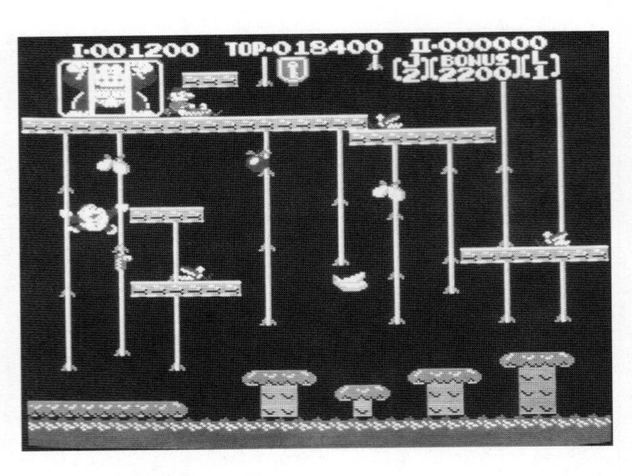

▲ Nintendo's Donkey Kong. *Courtesy of Nintendo of America.*

Xerox released another PARC wonder in 1981: the Star personal computer. It was, however, as unsuccessful as the Alto and sales were low. However, it provided inspiration for the future Apple personal computers: the Lisa and the Macintosh series.

Namco (Nakamura Manufacturing Company) produced Pac-Man in 1981, one of the greatest coin-operated arcade games. Pac-Man was a run-away hit, making the cover of *Time* and *Mad* magazines. According to David Sheff's book, *Game Over*, Masaya Nakamura made hundreds of millions of dollars on Pac-Man, and rewarded the engineer who designed the game with just $3,500. Disgusted, the designer left the video game business.

Nintendo moved into the American coin-operated game market in 1981 with a horrible game called Radarscope. The Nintendo employees in Seattle were very dismayed when Nintendo's next game arrived with the name Donkey Kong. The designer, Sigeru Miyamoto, had named the game that because at the top of the screen was a menacing giant ape, who had captured the player's girlfriend. The player, at the bottom of the screen, had to work his way up to the ape in order to free his girl. When Miyamoto was naming the game, he discovered that donkey was the English translation for the Japanese words stupid or goofy (according to his Japanese-to-English dictionary); he used the word Kong to denote the rival ape, thus the name Donkey Kong.

The rest of the characters, however, arrived without names, so the employees in Seattle came up with suitable names for the game's characters. The owner of their rented warehouse happened to be named Mario Segali, so Minoru Arakawa (president of Nintendo of America) named the star of Donkey Kong "Mario." The following year, Mario appeared again in the arcade game Donkey Kong Jr., and his first starring role appeared in the 1983 arcade game Mario Bros. Since then, Mario has been the star of 12 Nintendo home and arcade video games and is recognized by more American children than Mickey Mouse. He became Nintendo's mascot in 1985, and has been the subject of two feature films along with many TV

Colo
Gallery
ON

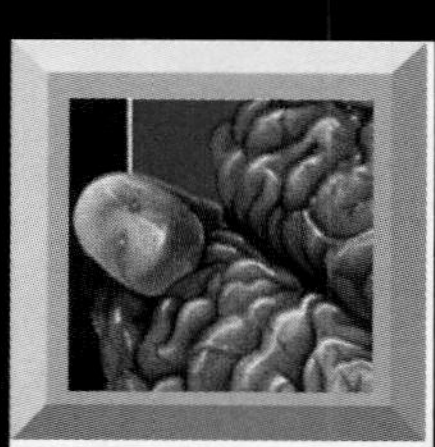

PUSH

When the original Life & Death game from Software Toolworks hit the market in the late 1980s, it caused quite a stir. Here was a PC-based game that broke through the popular perceptions of what entertainment software should be. At a time when most games were based on some form of shoot-em-up situation, Life & Death was a surgery simulator! Life & Death II is the latest version and offers 256-color graphics for that added touch of realism. As with the first Life & Death, Version 2 requires that you obtain a basic knowledge of surgical techniques. You also must examine your patients with CAT scans, MRIs, X-rays, and ultrasound methods to make a proper diagnosis before you operate. Once in the operating room, you must master a dizzying array of procedures. You must learn which drugs to administer, how to read EKGs, and how to clamp and cauterize "bleeders" so the patient does not lose too much blood. Your performance determines whether the patient goes to recovery or to the morgue.

Courtesy of Software Toolworks.

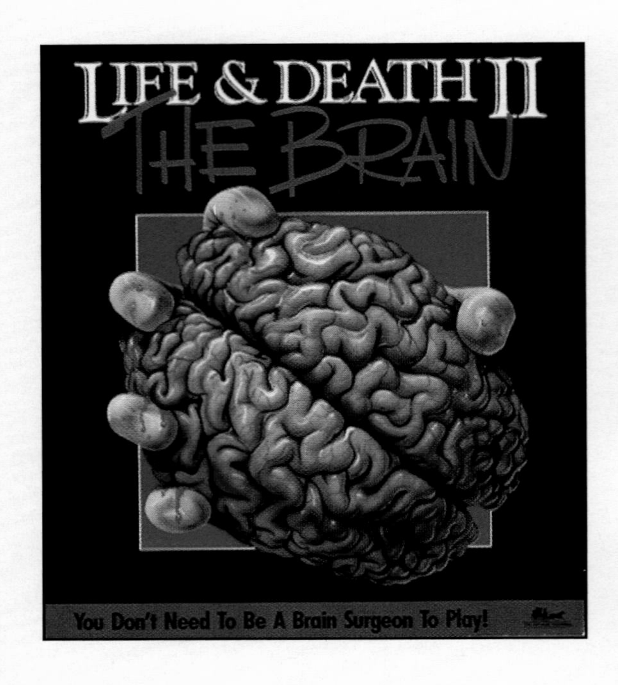

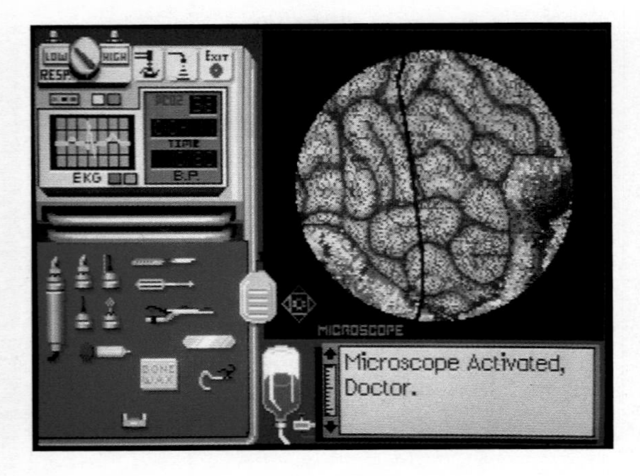

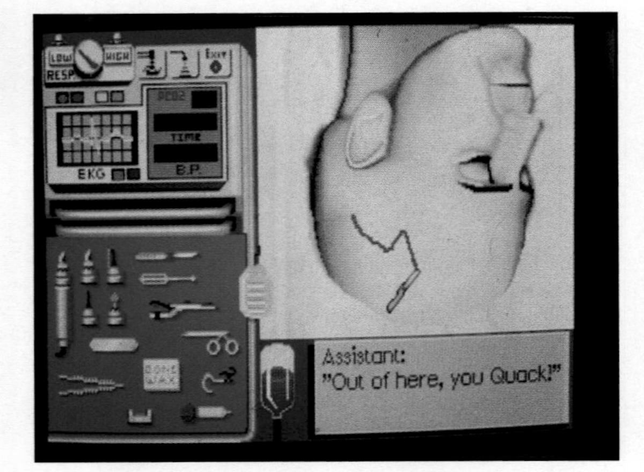

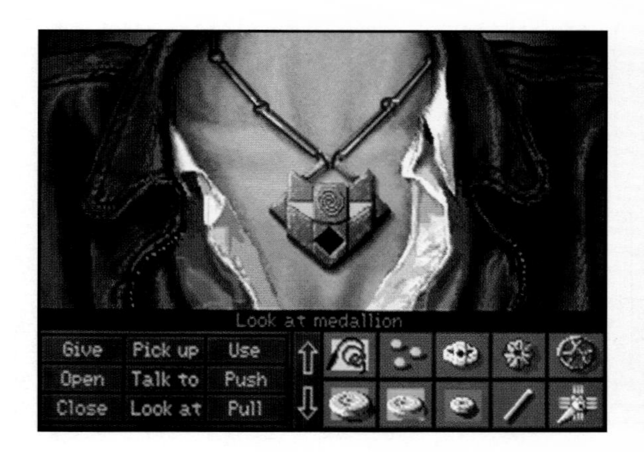

Indiana Jones and the Fate of Atlantis, a graphic adventure game from LucasArts, is the first computer game to be produced by Hollywood film writer and producer Hal Barwood. Barwood worked in the film industry for 20 years and co-wrote and produced such movies as *Corvette Summer* and *Dragonslayer* before joining LucasArts. Fate of Atlantis is the first Indiana Jones game to branch out with an original storyline separate from the motion pictures. Available on CD-ROM as a "talkie," Fate of Atlantis features the digitized voices of actors to add emotion and a dimension of reality. As gaming technology increases, we should see more creative endeavors between Hollywood and Silicon Valley.

Courtesy of LucasArts.

Based on the comic-strip characters created by Steve Purcell, Sam & Max Hit the Road is a new cartoon graphic adventure from LucasArts. Hit the Road stars the sarcastic characters Sam and Max—"Freelance Police"—as they track down a runaway Sasquatch from a freak show. Along the way you have to avoid various pitfalls, play game sequences such as "wak-a-rat," and interact with other characters in the game. Sam & Max Hit the Road is a good example of taking content from a successful product and applying it to interactive entertainment.

Courtesy of LucasArts.

The "Where … is Carmen Sandiego" series from Brøderbund includes some of the most successful educational games ever created. Following the likes of Mario and Sonic the Hedgehog, Carmen has even spawned her own television series, broadcast daily on PBS. While chasing Carmen through time, and space, players learn about the places they visit through questions and puzzles which they solve with the help of the almanacs and reference material provided with the game.

The National Geographic "Wonders of Learning CD-ROM Library" is a content-based reading series for young children. Each CD-ROM in the series comes with its own full-color book. The book, accompanied by background music and sound effects, is read to the child. A World of Plants teaches children about the life of plants from seed to full growth. Children learn many aspects of plant life, such as how trees change with the seasons and why plants are important.

Courtesy of National Geographic.

Armed with the most advanced hardware technology, the Atari Jaguar is leading the way to high-performance/low-cost home gaming systems. The Jaguar features a 64-bit RISC-based microprocessor along with a 64-bit data path and real-time 3-D graphics. These specifications appear to be the goal that other video game manufacturers are shooting for. This includes Nintendo with its scheduled 1995 roll-out of Project Reality (a joint venture between Nintendo and Silicon Graphics) and Sega with its upcoming Saturn game system. These new 64-bit game systems will offer computing power equivalent to today's fastest personal computers, but at a price tag 80 percent cheaper.

Courtesy of Atari Games Corporation.

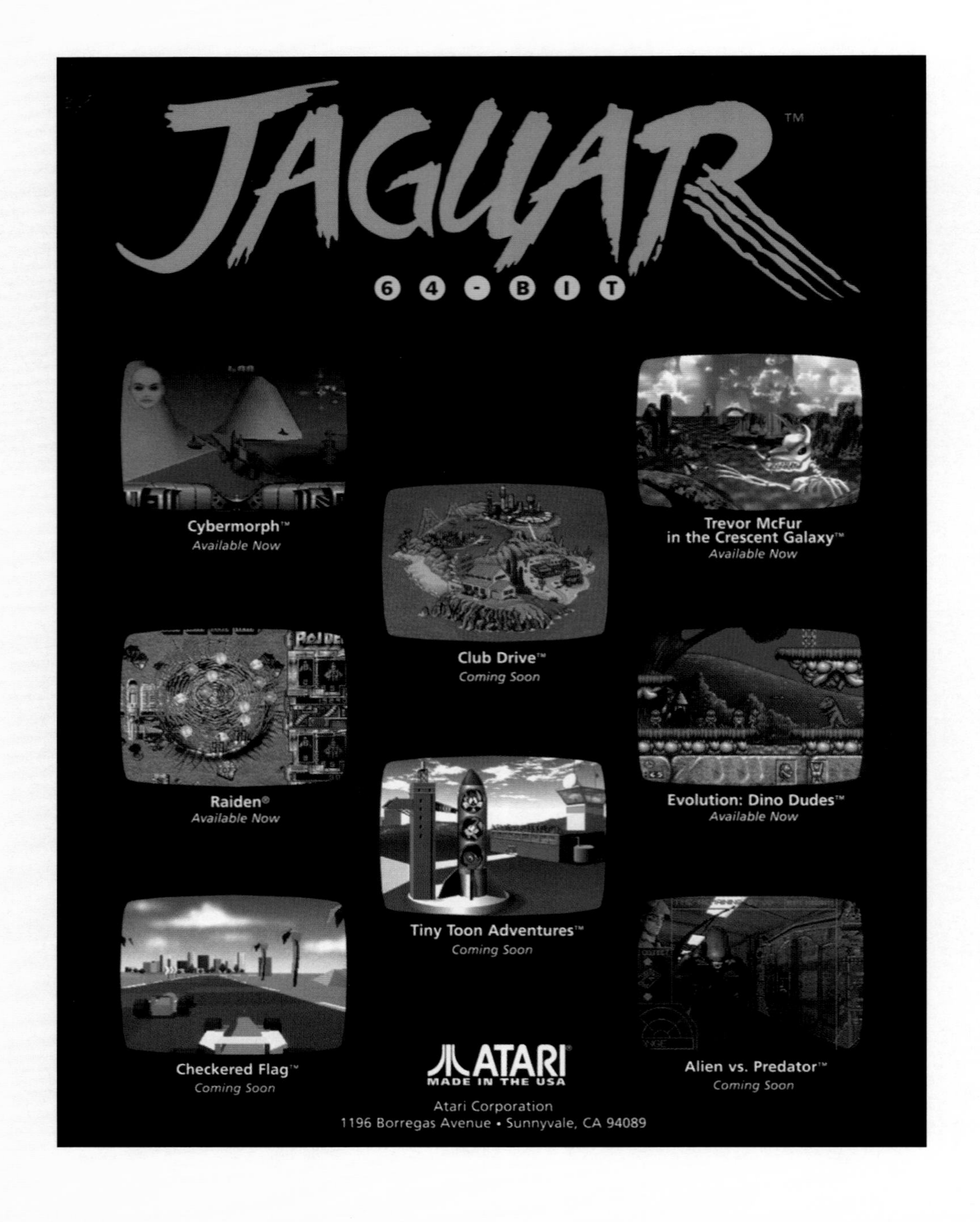

Day of the Tentacle is another "talkie" CD-ROM-based graphic adventure game from LucasArts. It features voice-overs from professional actors including Richard Sanders who played Les Nessman in the television series "WKRP in Cincinnati." The scenario is that a purple tentacle from outer space is trying to conquer Earth. You must guide three characters to travel through time, find a solution, and save the Earth. The gameplay and soundtrack are exciting enough to make you forget that you're playing a game—it's as if you are taking part in a cartoon.

Star Trek: The Next Generation for the 3DO multiplayer takes a quantum leap forward in computer graphics technology for video games. Characters from the hit TV series have been digitized and placed over 3-D computer models of their faces. These models are then animated to simulate the actor talking. The effect is very realistic, but this technique won't be putting actors out of work for a long time. Three-dimensional computer graphics also grace the rest of the game, giving it a clean, hi-tech look. Artwork created by 3-D computer imagery is clearly the direction in which video games are moving.

Courtesy of Absolute Entertainment.

Mad Dog McCree is a good example of a successful arcade coin-op ported to personal computer and video game platforms. By far the best-looking port is the Philips CD-I version with Full Motion Video (FMV). Following that comes the 3DO version, then the PC version and finally the Sega CD version (which really suffers from the limited colors of the Sega Genesis and the slow access speed of the CD). Still, this trend of porting successful arcade coin-op games to other platforms is destined to become more common as video game systems and personal computers become more powerful. Nintendo's Project Reality gaming system is going to be released first as a coin-op arcade game in the fall of 1995. It will later be "downsized" into a home unit costing less than $200.

Courtesy of American Laser Games.

Rise of the Robots is a new hand-to-hand combat game from Absolute Entertainment. Available for the Amiga, PC, SNES, and 3DO platforms, it uses advanced 3-D computer-generated imagery. The switch to nonhuman characters is considered one way of lessening the violence commonly associated with hand-to-hand combat games.

Courtesy of Absolute Entertainment.

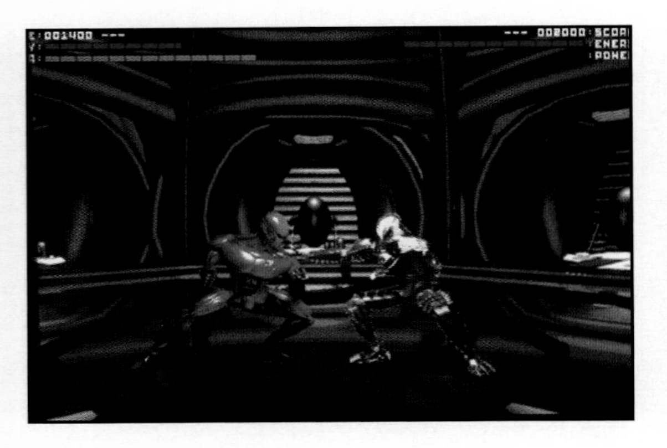

Pop Rocket touts Total Distortion as the first "music video adventure game." A hybrid cross between a rock & roll CD and a multimedia CD-ROM, Total Distortion offers the best of both worlds. On one hand, you can play a 3-D adventure game with beautifully rendered animation sequences, and on the other hand you can listen to music clips, watch video clips, and even compose your own rock video.

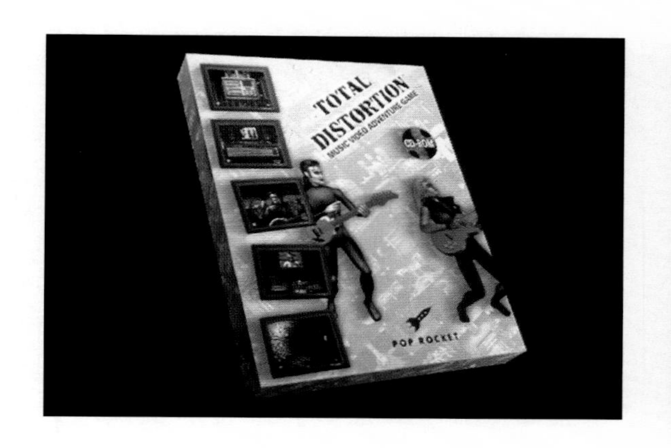

A blue hedgehog named Sonic has been the mascot of Sega video games and game systems since his introduction in 1991. Sonic-related software has grown to a multi-billion dollar business. Just as the Macy's Thanksgiving Day parade saw Sonic flying high in the sky, game system sales for Sega have been flying high allowing it to capture about 60 percent of the 16-bit video gaming market, surpassing the mighty Nintendo. Today, Sonic appears on everything from McDonald's Happy Meals and Saturday morning cartoons to candy.

Courtesy of Sega of America, Inc.

Alphabet Blocks from Bright Star Technology (a subsidiary of Sierra On-Line, Inc.) teaches young children the basics of reading. It comes with four games: identifying letters by name, matching letters, identifying letters by sound, and identifying words that begin with a letter sound. To guide your child through the lessons, there's a monkey named "Bananas" and a Jack-in-the-Box called "Jack." These characters provide instructions on playing the game and offer verbal encouragement for correct answers.

Courtesy of Sierra On-Line, Inc.

Designed for ages 3 to 6, Early Math from Bright Star Technology follows a similar teaching method as Alphabet Blocks. However, in this game a funny pink alien named "Loid" guides your child through the math lessons. The games teach math applications such as counting, geometric shapes, adding, and subtracting.

Basic Spelling from Bright Star Technologies follows the same structure as the company's other two games. Again, digital voice is used to carry a child through the lessons.

Courtesy of Sierra On-Line, Inc.

Licenses such as Donald Duck, Aladdin, Tom & Jerry, and Spider-Man continue to make up a large percentage of video games. However, the license itself does not guarantee a bestseller. Take for instance Aladdin, which won "Sega Genesis Game of the Year" in *Electronic Gaming Monthly*. It wasn't the huge success of the motion picture that made the video game a success, it was the beautiful artwork, animation, and captivating gameplay of the video game itself. As proof, games such as Home Alone 2 and the Rocketeer have not reached the bestseller lists despite the popular licensee and content.

Sports games continue to dominate popularity polls with video game systems. It's believed that sports games are going to be the main method of attracting adults to the world of video games and interactive television. Licenses continue to be a major concern with software developers. Sega Sports has signed on Joe Montana, and "NFL Football '94 Starring Joe Montana" was named "the best football game ever" by *DIEHARD GAME FAN* magazine.

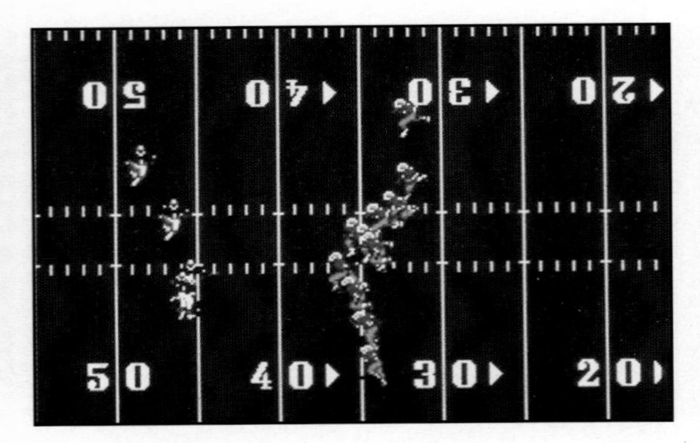

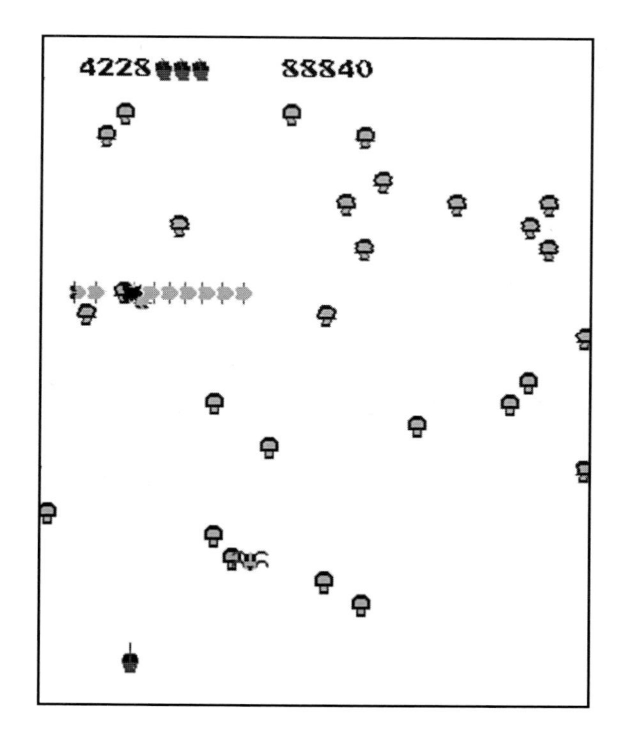

▲ Atari's Centipede Game.

programs and comic books. One of the games, Super Mario Bros. 3, has grossed more than $500 million since its release in 1990. If the game had been a music album, it would have won 11 platinum records.

In 1981, Atari created Centipede, a game of action, bright colors, and smooth play. It quickly won a wide following in arcades. Set in a mushroom world, your job was to shoot centipedes as they snaked down from the top of the screen.

The entire home video game industry roared up to $3 billion in the final quarter of 1982. Personal computer sales were strong as well. Timex released by far the cheapest personal computer yet, the Timex/Sinclair for $99. It came with built-in BASIC, and sold 600,000 units in 1982 alone. Commodore rolled out the VIC-20 for $299 and sold close to a million units. The VIC-20 was soon followed in late 1982 by the Commodore 64 (64KB) for only $595. The Commodore 64 was an extremely popular PC, and has sold more than 10 million units to date. Next, Commodore rolled out the Commodore 64C, which used an icon-based user interface. Amazingly, the 64C is still on the market today, some 12 years later.

In 1982, Atari unveiled the Atari 400 ($299) and Atari 800 ($899) personal computers. The Atari PCs were ideal game machines with 256 colors (8-bit), four separate sound generators, and built-in sprite graphics to assist with high speed video games. Atari shipped almost 200,000 Atari 800 models and about 400,000 Atari 400 models in 1982. Texas Instruments finally dropped the price on its TI-99 computer from $1,100 to $450. Bolstered with a snappy marketing campaign using actor Bill Cosby, and an upgraded keyboard, sales took off. Texas Instruments shipped a total of 530,000 units in 1982. Still, personal computer sales for TI were never as great as its semiconductor business, and they eventually pulled out of the PC business altogether.

In 1982, one of the most important developments in the history of interactive entertainment was released: the Compact Disc (CD). Developed jointly by Sony and Philips, the CD could store an amazing amount of digital data, enough to store an entire digitized music album. The 4.5-inch CD can hold about 600 megabytes or 250,000 printed pages of text. The huge data storage capabilities of CDs opened the way for a new industry, multimedia.

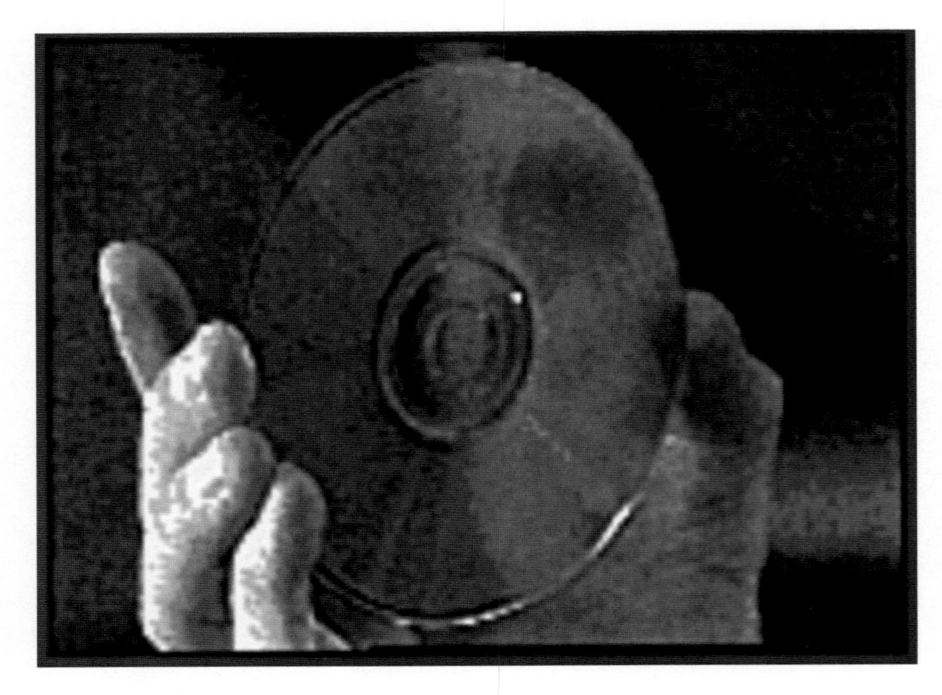

▲ A compact disc.

The Apple II still led the personal computer market in 1982, with more than 700,000 units sold since its release, including 270,000 in 1982 alone. The outstanding success of the Apple II computer was largely due to its huge software base. By 1982 some 16,000 programs were available.

The time was now ripe for Trip Hawkins, who left Apple Computer in May 1982 to found Amazing Software. Company creators were inspired by how the movie studio United Artists was organized, with independent artists coming together to work on a single project. Later, Amazing Software changed its name to Electronic Arts. In 1982, there were 135 competitors in the field of video game software. Today, only four of these companies are still in business. Electronic Arts is the largest of those four.

In 1982, conditions couldn't have been better for the home video game industry. Atari had just signed up with Lucasfilm (the company founded by Hollywood producer-director George Lucas) for the first of its kind venture between a film studio and video game company. Atari planned to create a home video game based on the hit movie *Raiders of the Lost Ark*. They also made plans to develop arcade games and computer software together. Some of LucasArts games include PHM Pegasus, Koronis Rift, Labyrinth, Ballblazer, Rescue on Fractalus, and Strike Fleet. They also developed Habitat, a networked game that is still very popular in Japan.

The increase in sales was outstanding. An October 1982 New York Times survey predicted that revenues from home video games would soon exceed those of the U.S. motion picture industry. The survey found that total revenues for both the arcade and home video game industry reached $7 billion in annual sales. Home video games alone had revenues of $1.7 billion in 1982 and were expected to reach more than $3 billion in 1983, while the domestic motion picture industry sold about $3 billion in tickets a year.

By the end of 1982, almost 15 million U.S. households had home video games. The Consumer Electronics Group, an industry trade organization, states that 8 million game modules and 60 million game cartridges sold in 1982, double the amount sold in 1981. At the time there were 16 companies selling modules, cartridges, or both. The top three were Atari, with its Atari 2600, Mattel with the

Mattel Intellivision, and Coleco Industries with Colecovision. According to *Billboard* magazine, the top five arcade games for the month of October were: Coleco's Donkey Kong, Atari's Berzerk, Atari's Defender, Parker Brothers' Frogger, and Atari's Pac-Man. Even a motion picture about video games appeared in 1982; *Tron* from Walt Disney Studios was a science fiction fantasy about a game programmer who is sucked into the computer to play his own games. Though the computer animated sequences were beautiful, the lack of story line eventually caused the *Tron* arcade game to do better than the movie itself.

The home video game industry appeared to be on a winning streak and no one suspected it was about to face its worst crash. But on Dec. 8, 1982, Warner Communications—Atari's parent company—announced that fourth quarter earnings would be lower than expected due to slow sales of video game cartridges. The value of Warner stock immediately plunged—a dramatic blow considering Atari was the industry leader. The stocks of competitors Coleco Industries and Mattel also started sliding. During the next three days, Warner Communications stock fell an incredible 19 3/4 points from 51 7/8 to 34 3/4. At the same time, concerns were raised about possible bad effects computer games might have on children. Around the world—in the Philippines, Singapore, and Malaysia—bans started appearing on video game arcades, and they were closed.

Atari quickly tried to respond. The company laid off 600 California workers on February 22 and announced plans to move its home computer and home video game production to Asia, and eliminate 1,700 of its 7,000 employees in U.S. plants. Despite these moves, the downward spiral continued. In the first quarter of 1983 alone, Atari lost $45.6 million, causing parent company Warner to lose $18.9 million, its first loss in more than seven years. Warner reported that Atari lost another $310.5 million in the second quarter. By the end of 1983, video game industry sales had dropped to $2 billion. Cartridge games that once sold for $35 were selling for $5 by the end of the year. It was this year that Commodore bravely released a new home video game system called the Max Machine.

The *New York Times* blamed the industry losses on declining interest in the games. This included boredom with the fad among children and teenagers, the games' principle market; the growing disapproval of parents; restrictions on video game arcades by municipalities across the nation; and the emphasis by home computer manufacturers on other uses for their machines. The *Times* also noted that, while the number of arcades nationwide had grown to 10,000 in 1982, they suffered a 75 percent decrease in profits in 1983. More than 1,500 arcades closed in 1983 alone.

Warner also continued to suffer from Atari's fall. The company laid off 250 people, one-third of its corporate staff, on October 13. The following day Warner announced a $122.3 million loss for the third quarter. The Atari subsidiary itself posted a third quarter loss of $180.2 million compared to a profit of $109.6 million during the same period of the previous year.

Some of the first IBM PC compatibles appeared in 1983 as Compaq Computer company successfully cloned the IBM PC. In 1983, the company shipped 53,000 PC-compatible Compaq Portables creating $111 million in revenues and setting an American business record. Steve Jobs, inspired by a trip to the Xerox PARC, released the Apple Lisa (named after his first daughter). It used a PARC-like user interface but was very slow and cost a whopping $10,000.

Scott Fischer, Brenda Laurel, Jaron Lanier, and Thomas Zimmerman worked at the Atari Research Center (ARC) during the early 1980s. In 1983, Jaron Lanier developed the DataGlove, a glove wired with switches to detect and transmit to the computer any movements you make. The computer interprets the data and enables you to manipulate objects in 3-D space within a computer simulation. Lanier left Atari later that year to team up with Jean-Jacques Grimaud. Two years later, they founded a company called VPL Research, which developed and marketed some of the first commercial virtual reality products. Zimmerman, an MIT graduate who had developed "air guitar" software and a DataGlove that enabled you to play a virtual guitar, also joined VPL Research. Zimmerman left in 1989, while Lanier stayed with VPL Research until November of 1992.

Despite the gloomy U.S. video game market, Nintendo Corporation announced and released a new home video game in Japan called the Family Computer System (Famicom). Sega also released a home video game called the SG-1000. The Sega game failed while Famicom sales soared. Selling at half the price of most game systems (about $100), the Famicom boasted better graphics and higher speed. Also in 1983, Robert and Richard Garriot found Origin Systems, most known for its Ultima series of games. Origin Systems would sell more than 1.5 million units worldwide by 1992.

To help cut losses, game makers in the States turned to the home-computer industry. Meanwhile home video game sales continued to plummet—dropping to $800 million by the end of 1984. Mattel closed its electronics division. Coleco ceased manufacturing. Atari had a horrible year. Though Atari had posted a $300 million profit in 1982, in 1983 it lost $536.8 million. For the leader of the video game industry, this painted a bleak picture.

▲ The Nintendo Famicom (NES). *Courtesy of Nintendo of America.*

In July, Warner broke Atari in half and sold the hardware division to Jack Tramiel, former president of Commodore, for $332 million. Tramiel promptly laid off 1,000 Atari workers, reducing the staff to 5,000 employees. Warner sold Atari's arcade coin-operated divisions to Namco under the new name of Atari Games. Atari Games would later spawn a new company called Tengen, and would compete against its older brother (Atari Corporation) in the home video game and personal computer video game market.

In January 1984, Apple released the first Macintosh computer. The Macintosh used the same graphical interface as Apple's Lisa. Continuing the 'Woz' tradition, the 'Mac' was based on a Motorola microprocessor. It also used a single floppy drive; 128KB of memory; a 9-inch, high-resolution screen; and a mouse. It would become the largest non–IBM-compatible personal computer series ever introduced. IBM forged ahead by releasing the IBM AT personal computer, using the Intel 80286 microprocessor, a true 16-bit CPU.

At the 1984 Consumer Electronics Show, Atari Corporation released a new personal computer, the Atari ST line. At the same show, Commodore introduced the Commodore 128 personal computer, and Tandy released its first IBM-compatible PC, the Tandy Model 1000. Alan Miller and Robert Whithead, two of the original founders of Activision, formed a new video game company called Accolade in December.

Despite the bleak picture in the home video game industry, Nintendo's Famicom system sold more than 6.5 million units in Japan in 1985. That fall, Nintendo began test marketing a new home video game in New York called the Nintendo Entertainment System (NES). Nevertheless, the total U.S. market of home video game sales fell to a record low of $100 million.

Multimedia began making an entrance into the home computer market in 1985. The International Standards Organization created the first standard for Compact Discs with Read-Only Memory (CD-ROM). This new standard was called High Sierra, after the area near Lake Tahoe, where ISO created the standard. This standard later changed into the ISO 9660 standard.

In Russia, Alexey Pajitnov was busy creating a mega-hit video game. The ancient Pentomino puzzle inspired Pajitnov. He created a video game version in which different geometric shapes slowly fell from the top of the screen while the player needed to furiously fit them together at the bottom. Because each puzzle piece comprised four squares, Pajitnov called the game Tetris, after the Greek word for four. Through a series of international licenses, Pajitnov's game was finally released in the United States. Later, Nintendo introduced Tetris in America for the Game Boy and NES systems.

Also in 1985, Commodore launched the new Amiga personal computer line. It offered many advanced features, including hardware compatible with the IBM personal computer line. The Amiga used Motorola's 68000 microprocessor and had its own proprietary operating system. The base unit's retail price was $1,295. Electronic Arts was one of the chief game developers to support the Amiga.

▲ The game Tetris was developed in Russia.

Scott Fisher left the Atari Research Center in 1985 and joined NASA's VIVED (Virtual Visual Environment Display) project. Fisher ordered DataGloves from VPL Research. Warren Robinett, another Atari programmer, joined Fisher. Robinett had previously created and programmed the game Rocky's Boots and Atari Adventure.

Another virtual reality researcher by the name of John Waldern came across Sutherland's 1968 paper describing the head-mounted display system. Waldern was working on his Ph.D. in Computer Science at the Human Computer Research Center in Loughborough, England. He quickly saw the implications of virtual reality in interactive entertainment systems. With three other partners, he formed W Industries in 1986. With extra funding from a company called Wembley PLC, W Industries developed the world's first virtual reality game system. It was called Virtuality VR.

Sales of home video games began resurging in 1986. Nintendo released the NES (Famicom) system in the United States; Sega released the Master System; Atari and INTV also released new home video games. In 1986, Nintendo sold more than a million units and captured 70 percent of the "new generation" of home video games sales. Also in that year, Spectrum HoloByte, a new video game company, was founded. Spectrum HoloByte is best known for its highly realistic flight simulator, Falcon.

The home video game market continued rising from its slump in 1987. Industry sales bounced back up to $1.1 billion. Nintendo remained the clear industry leader, and its licenses earned more than $800 million. Sega Enterprises signed on with Tonka Toys, and Atari Games reopened. Industry-wide, 4.1 million home video game units sold in 1987, including 3 million Nintendo units alone. The Legend of Zelda became the first million seller of this "new generation" of home video game software. At the same time, NEC, another giant Japanese company, entered the home video game market with the Japan release of PC Engine in October.

LucasArts started to bring serious competition in the computer game field of graphic adventures. They released Maniac Mansion, a graphic adventure that used the LucasArts proprietary development system called SCUMM (Script Creation Utility for Maniac Mansion). SCUMM continues to play the leading role in all LucasArts graphic adventures today. Gregory Fishbach became founder of Acclaim Entertainment Inc., an independent video game developer. Acclaim continued to grow and became the top independent video game publisher in the United Kingdom, with revenues of $216.6 million in 1992.

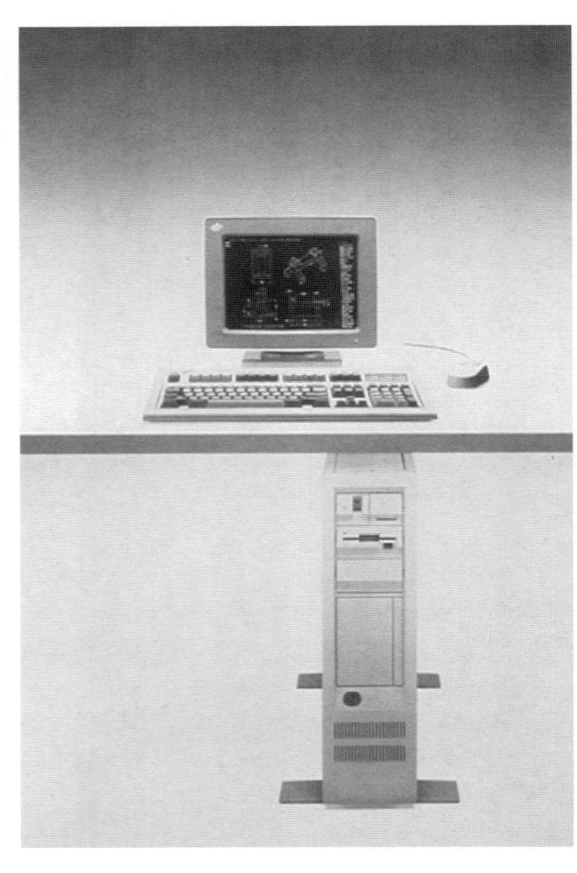

▲ The IBM PS/2 Model 80. *Courtesy of International Business Machines Corporation.*

IBM shocked the PC industry in 1987 by releasing its new personal computer, the PS/2 line. Instead of supporting the existing de facto standard, IBM moved ahead with a new bus architecture. The new machines were good, but the momentum behind the old standard remained strong, and PS/2s never really took off. The PS/2 did set a few new standards, however, including 3.5-inch, high density floppies and VGA graphics.

Home video game sales continued to skyrocket in 1988, with $2.3 billion in sales, and more than 7 million units of hardware and 33 million software units sold. Two Nintendo products, The Legend of Zelda and Mike Tyson's Punch Out! sold more than 2 million units. The year also saw a rise in the level of adult and female players playing games. Nintendo's data revealed that 20 percent of players were ages 25 to 44, and 25 percent of all players were women.

▲ Mike Tyson's Punch Out!, pictured here with other titles from Nintendo Corporation, sold more than 2 million copies in 1988. *Courtesy of Nintendo of America.*

▲ The Philips CD-I system. *Courtesy of Philips.*

In November of 1988, Philips and Sony announced a new CD-ROM standard called "Green Book." Philips planned on using it for its upcoming CD-I (Compact Disc Interactive) home multimedia device, which would offer motion video capabilities. Microsoft, Philips, and Sony also developed a new CD-ROM standard called the CD-ROM XA (eXtended Architecture). This new format would run on both PC-based CD-ROM players and CD-I players.

By May of 1989, Matsushita, Philips, and Sony entered an agreement to jointly develop the new CD-I technology. In September of 1989, Philips demonstrated the capabilities of CD-I, including full motion video (FMV). Work continued on the establishment of motion video compression standards by a committee called the Motion Picture Experts Group. Philips, committed to MPEG for CD-Is full motion capabilities, waited for the MPEG standards to finalize.

The end of the decade continued to see a sharp increase in the popularity of home video games. Total industry retail sales in 1989 reached $3.4 billion, and the home penetration of Nintendo games reached an amazing 22 percent. Sega Enterprises launched the first 16-bit home video game system, called Sega Genesis. Even though Sega Genesis was a 16-bit machine, it was compatible with Sega's previous 8-bit system (Master System). This proved to be important as Sega slowly started to increase in popularity and sales.

▲ The NEC Turbografx-16 home video game. *Courtesy of Aldrich and Associates.*

▲ The Nintendo Game Boy, the first hand-held game unit. *Courtesy of Nintendo of America.*

NEC finally entered the U.S. market by releasing Turbografx-16, another 16-bit video game. While Turbografx-16 was a technically superior machine to Nintendo's 8-bit NES, NEC had neglected to create quality video games for its machine. Video game developers also were reluctant to help NEC because they were busy developing for Nintendo's large market.

Nintendo meanwhile released the first hand-held video game system, the Game Boy. It featured stereo sound and cartridge games based on existing NES titles. The Sega Game Gear was also released in 1989. Game Gear featured a color display, with 8-bit game play. Sega sales would double every year for the next three. Fujitsu released a multimedia PC system in Japan called the FM-Towns. It is IBM PC-compatible, comes with a built-in CD-ROM drive, high-resolution graphics, and high-quality audio. List price for the FM-Towns is $2,000 to $3,000.

1990–PRESENT

In May 1990, Microsoft shipped Windows 3.0, which was immediately adopted as the environment of choice for software developers. Windows follows the graphical user interface structure similar to the Apple Macintosh, and lays the foundation for a future growth in multimedia. While in 1990, only two of the nation's 10 top-selling programs ran under Windows, this rose to 9 of 10 by 1991.

Trip Hawkins of Electronic Arts formed the 3DO Company. 3DO was designed to create a standard for interactive entertainment hardware. Taking a new approach, 3DO decided not to manufacture a retail product. Instead, they developed and licensed it to various hardware and software developers. With the backing of major companies such as AT&T, Matsushita, Time-Warner, and MCA, 3DO hopes to quickly establish a new standard in high-performance interactive entertainment.

In August 1990, Virtual World Entertainment opened the first BattleTech Center at North Pier in Chicago. The BattleTech Center enables up to 12 players to drive futuristic robots in a 3-D computer simulation. Each simulator has its own realistic cockpit and is networked to all the other cockpits, so you can play against or with your friends.

▲ The 3DO System. *Courtesy of Panasonic.*

In September 1990, Eastman Kodak Company announced the development of a new technology to enable 35mm film images to be stored on a compact disc (CD). This disk would contain high-resolution images suitable for printing and viewable on a television. The Photo CD technology promised the capability to convert the images to digital formats and store them on common CDs.

▲ The current Photo CD formats available. *Courtesy of Eastman Kodak Company.*

There were two immediate advantages to doing this. First, storing the images would be greatly simplified. Furthermore, by converting the images to digital information, you could make unlimited duplicates without any image degradation. Still, a number of obstacles faced Kodak. The cost alone of mastering equipment for CDs was very expensive, and Kodak would need to design new players for both the old music CDs and the new Photo CDs.

▲ Kodak's consumers' Photo CD players. *Courtesy of Eastman Kodak Company.*

MPC CM

Multimedia PC

▲ The Multimedia PC Marketing Council's certification mark.

Kodak turned to Philips Corporation to build custom Photo CD players. This worked well for Philips because the company already built new CD Interactive (CD-I) machines that played multimedia titles from CDs on television. In September 1991, Philips Interactive Media Systems announced that they would market dedicated Photo CD players beginning in the summer of 1992. They also announced that existing CD-I players would be Photo CD-compatible.

Kodak announced in March 1992 that the major CD-ROM drive manufacturers, Philips, Sony, Toshiba, and Pioneer, would offer fully Photo CD-compatible drives. These drives came to be known as multi-session drives, for their Photo CD compatibility. In early August of 1992, the first Photo CD players shipped to consumers. Kodak released three different consumer players in 1992. By this time, the Photo CD format already enabled sound to be included on the CD along with images.

With around 60 billion photographs taken worldwide every year, Kodak has an incentive to set standards and stay on top of them. According to president of CD Imaging at Eastman Kodak, Dr. Leo J. Thomas, photo CD will become a billion dollar business in a "very foreseeable period."

The MPC Level 1 Specifications

Minimum Requirements	
RAM:	2MB
Processor:	16MHz 386SX
Hard Drive:	30MB
CD-ROM Drive:	150KB/sec. sustained transfer rate
	1 second maximum seek time
Sound:	8-bit digital sound, 8 note synthesizer, MIDI playback
Video Display:	640×480, 16 colors (4-bit)
Ports:	MIDI I/O, joystick
Recommendations	
CD-ROM Drive:	64KB on-board buffer
Video Display:	640×480, 256 colors (8-bit)

With the backing of Microsoft and Tandy, the Multimedia PC Marketing Council was formed in October of 1991. The council's goals were to create a standard by which PC-based multimedia hardware and software could be created. In 1990, they published the MPC Level 1 specification for PC-based systems qualified to run multimedia software. The council also defined a Multimedia PC certification mark.

In 1991, Commodore entered the home multimedia market with the release of its CDTV (Commodore Dynamic Total Vision) system. CDTV was a CD-based system that connected to any TV, and played CD-ROMs and audio CDs. It was designed to compete with Philips' CD-I system. In November of 1991, the MPEG full motion video compression standard was finalized, and Philips moved ahead with its FMV implementation of MPEG for the CD-I with encoder tools and decoder chips. Also in 1991, W Industries took its first virtual reality game, Virtuality, on a tour around the United States.

In 1992, Philips publicly demonstrated FMV from a CD at the Multimedia and CD-ROM conference (now called Intermedia). Philips also signed an agreement with Motorola to develop chips for future CD-I applications. On September 10, 1992, Electronic Arts acquired Origin Systems, which had an estimated value of $35 million. Electronic Arts became the largest interactive entertainment company in the U.S., with 100 titles selling more than 1 million units and 30 titles selling more than 5 million units.

The total industry sales for home video games in 1992 reached $5.3 billion. Nintendo announced a new chip, called Super FX, that offered real-time 3-D animation and texture mapping for the Super Nintendo Entertainment System (SNES). In 1993, Nintendo released Star Fox for the SNES, the first game to use the Super FX chip. In 1992, the estimated installed base of personal computers was 20 million. Paramount Communications entered the IE market in the fall of 1992 by forming Paramount Interactive, a company designed to create, acquire, develop, and market interactive entertainment titles.

FMV cartridges for CD-I machines became market-ready in 1993, and 10 different studios began developing FMV titles. Philips provided FMV cartridges to all its CD-I developers, and by the fall of 1993, the first FMV titles were released. In May, the Multimedia PC Council released the MPC Level 2 specification for multimedia PCs.

The MPC Level 2 Specifications

Minimum Requirements	
RAM:	4MB
Processor:	25MHz 486SX
Hard Drive:	160MB
CD-ROM Drive:	300KB/sec. sustained transfer rate
	400 milliseconds maximum seek time
	CD-ROM XA & Multi-session capable
Sound:	16-bit digital sound, 8 note synthesizer, MIDI playback
Video Display:	640×480, 65,536 colors (16-bit)
Ports:	MIDI I/O, joystick

Recommendations	
RAM:	8MB
CD-ROM Drive:	64KB on-board buffer
Sound:	CD-ROM XA audio ability
	Support for IMA adopted ADPCM algorithm
Video Display:	Delivery of 1.2 megapixels/sec. given 40 percent of CPU bandwidth

While Sega reached $2.8 billion in sales in 1993, the company also announced a new cable TV channel called The Sega Channel. It was tested in markets by Tele-Communications Inc., Time-Warner Entertainment Co., and Sega of America. The service works by delivering video games through a special decoder box. The service price is $10 to $20 a month.

In 1993, Atari attempted to leapfrog ahead of the competition by announcing a 64-bit video game called the Jaguar. By signing a 30-month contract worth $500 million, IBM joined up with Atari to produce this new multimedia entertainment system. Under the terms of the contract, IBM will assemble, do component sourcing and quality testing, package, and distribute the new Jaguar.

▲ The Atari Jaguar 64-bit home video game system. *Courtesy of Atari Games Corporation.*

Not to be outdone, Nintendo announced an agreement with Silicon Graphics, Inc. (the leader in computer graphics technology) to produce a 64-bit 3-D Nintendo platform for home use. The first product from "Project Reality" will be an arcade game to be released in 1994. A home version is planned for late 1995. The home system's target price will be $250. Nintendo remains the industry leader with 80 percent of the home video game market and $4.3 billion in retail sales. The 8-bit NES system sold more than 2.7 million units in 1992—which brings the total to 35 million units, and 230 million game units sold during its eight-year history. The total number of Nintendo game units sold (to date) is 750 million.

Sega also has announced agreements with U.K.-based W Industries (creators of Virtuality) and Martin Marietta for advanced technology to appear in a new generation video game. W Industries offers virtual reality technology while Martin Marietta offers advanced 3-D texturing and training simulation capabilities. These technologies will enable Sega to create virtual reality arcade games and a VR-based home gaming system.

Commodore announced the development of an Amiga-based multimedia system called the Amiga CD32, designed to directly compete with the Philips CD-I and 3DO platforms. The system uses Motorola's 32-bit microprocessor. It supports an optional full motion video (MPEG-based) module for playing video CDs and other CD formats.

Pioneer launched its LaserActive system in October 1993. The LaserActive is a combination laser disc/CD player with optional modules to support Sega Genesis and NEC Turbo Technologies video games. It has built-in support for laser discs, audio CDs, and video CDs.

▲ The Pioneer LaserActive system. *Courtesy of Pioneer Electronics*.

▲ The official video CD logo.

JVC, Matsushita, Philips, and Sony jointly announced in 1993 the new Compact Disc Digital Video (video CD) format. Video CDs will allow up to 74 minutes of full-motion video along with CD quality audio. The video CDs will also provide two extra features: a choice of either normal or high-resolution, still-picture playback, and special effects playback codes for fast-forward, still-frame, and frame-advance viewing. The backers have also agreed on an official logo that combines the format designation with the familiar logo used for multimedia and audio compact disc.

Kodak unveiled the first battery-powered photo CD player at the summer Consumer Electronics Show. Kodak plans to ship the unit for a retail price of $449. Philips plans to release the first linear FMV movie applications in 1994. All new CD-I players after 1993 will be shipped with FMV built-in.

CHAPTER SUMMARY

The field of interactive entertainment has been very active. Advances in hardware and software, along with keen competition, keep the market constantly changing. Beginning in the 1970s, IE shifted from an adult-oriented to a youth-oriented market. Now the market is expanding again as developers target adults with more educational related products and titles, including many multimedia products.

Interactive entertainment appears to be like a vine, slowly growing over and intertwining among forms of entertainment, including motion pictures, television, music, literature, and so forth. Will some entertainment industries get choked out, or will new symbiotic relationships develop within IE? The future, most likely, will hold a combination of the two. Sega, Viacom, and GTE are now conducting research to develop interactive cable television. This would prove to be a useful symbiotic relationship. On the other hand, if interactive cable is successful and makes movies-on-demand possible, will the movie rental industry suffer? Insight into the future of interactive entertainment is needed to answer this.

The following chapters will examine the various hardware and software currently available for each IE system. Industry leaders will also give their views about the future of interactive entertainment. To begin with, the next chapter will look at the platform that started it all: the computer.

3

Interactive Entertainment on Personal Computers

"By the end of the decade there may be only two computing devices: one for the home and one for the office. Models could combine the personal computer, television, stereo, and telephone in one unit."

This book begins now to cover in detail each interactive entertainment platform: personal computers, multimedia, home gaming systems, portable gaming systems, edutainment, and interactive television. Each chapter provides a brief discussion of how the technology works, how a selected software title was developed, current titles that make the most of the platform being discussed, and, finally, a look into the future of each platform. It's only natural to first look at the platform that started it all: the computer.

The most common computer used today for interactive entertainment is the personal computer. There are a number of popular PCs, including the Apple Macintosh and IBM compatibles. Although all of these PCs support multimedia capabilities, such as CD-ROM, multimedia hardware and software is discussed in the next chapter. This chapter focuses strictly on diskette-based entertainment software, excluding any CD-ROM–based software.

HOW COMPUTERS WORK AND PLAY

Computers can be divided into two areas: hardware and software. Hardware is comprised of physical components of the computer. Software is comprised of instructions that tell the hardware what to do. You can liken this to an audio cassette player. The cassette player and the cassette itself could be considered hardware, and the music recorded on the cassette tape is equivalent to software. In fact, early microcomputers used standard audio cassette tapes and players to store software (see Chapter 2, "The History of Interactive Entertainment").

The use of software differentiates the computer from all other machines. Before computers, every machine was designed to perform a specific function. The computer completely changed that tradition.

The computer is a machine that is not predesigned to perform a specific task. The same computer that can take the place of an accountant's desk calculator can also serve as an engineer's drafting table. You can't draw with a desk calculator, and you can't add a series of numbers with a drafting table. Yet with software, the computer can easily perform both these tasks and myriad others. Thanks to software, the computer is the first all-purpose machine.

HARDWARE AND SOFTWARE

How does a computer work? By performing three simple operations: addition, subtraction, and comparison. The computer can add two numbers, subtract one number from another, and compare two numbers to see which is larger. This is all a computer can do.

▲ An enlarged view of the Pentium™ microprocessor's circuitry. *Photo courtesy of Intel.*

What makes a computer so powerful is that it can perform millions of these operations (or instructions) per second. The typical desktop computer today is rated at 10 million instructions per second (MIPS). These three operations are performed by a single chip (integrated circuit) called a *microprocessor*. The microprocessor, commonly called the

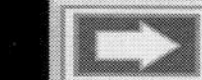

central processing unit (CPU), is the "brain" of the entire computer. Without the CPU, and software, a computer would only be slightly more useful than a push-button telephone or electric typewriter.

The CPU coordinates all the components of your computer system. It is mounted on the *motherboard* or main circuit board of your computer. The CPU loads information from magnetic disks into electronic memory. It then performs addition, subtraction, or comparison on the data until a satisfactory result is achieved. The computer then stores that result in memory and later sends the result to the monitor (display), printer, or back to magnetic disk for storage.

It's almost impossible to understand how these three operations enable the computer to run complex interactive entertainment software, so I will begin with simple examples. Consider how the computer's elementary operations can be enhanced. If you want to multiply two numbers, 3×4, for instance, you could simply instruct the computer to add 4+4+4. Likewise, if you want to divide 10 by 2, the computer can subtract 2 from 10, subtract 2 from 8, 2 from 6, 2 from 4, and 2 from 2. Then the computer adds the total number of subtractions performed, which is 5. Thus computers perform multiplication and division by repeating simple addition and subtraction.

The final operation, that of comparing, is perhaps the most important. It allows the computer to progress beyond the level of a fancy desktop calculator. You can instruct the computer to compare two numbers to find the largest, the smallest, or if the numbers are equal. This simple operation can be advanced to the point where a computer flight simulator can simulate realistically how a jet maneuvers at high speeds. This is where software comes into play.

Software is nothing more than a long to-do list for the CPU. It's a list of additions, subtractions, and comparisons that need to be made in a specific order. Also included with software is some type of information. In an air combat simulator, for example, the software contains data regarding how fast the jets fly and how quickly they turn. This could be stored in the form of data or rules.

Rules are a practical application of the comparison operation. For instance, if the rule is: Jet speed cannot be greater than 500 mph, and the player tries to increase the speed of his jet, then the software compares the jet's current speed with the rule. If the current speed is less than the maximum, then the simulator increases the speed of the player's jet. If the jet is already at the maximum, then the simulator does nothing.

This is a very simplified example, because typically there are many rules governing a step such as increasing the speed of a jet aircraft. For example, the computer will evaluate external conditions, wind speed, and altitude. It will also examine the status of the flaps, rudders, ailerons, and landing gear. It may also consider the weight of the jet, including how much fuel or armaments are onboard. Still, all these complicated rules can be handled fairly easily by a well thought out to-do list involving comparison.

SOFTWARE

Just as computer memory must break everything down into simple ones and zeros, so too the CPU can only handle sequences of 0 and 1. What this means is that the rules and to-do lists of a program must be converted into sequences of 0 and 1. As you can imagine, writing a to-do list for a computer using only 1 or 0 would be very difficult. For example, say you wanted to create a simple program to count from 1 to 100 and display each number on the screen as it counts. It would be wonderful if you could write a program by typing the following line into the computer:

```
Count from one to one hundred and display
each number on the screen.
```

The computer, however, isn't nearly smart enough to understand a command in English. To speak to a computer, you must speak a computer language. Just as a United Nations translator translates messages from one language to another, a programming language for the computer translates messages from a semi-English version of a program to a computer version made up of ones and zeros. There are many computer programming languages. Below is the above mentioned program using the Beginners All purpose Symbolic Instruction Code (BASIC) programming language:

```
10 FOR X = 1 TO 100
20 PRINT X
30 NEXT X
40 END
```

In this program, the CPU would start at the top line (line 10), and assign the variable `X` the number 1. Then it would move onto line 20 and print the current value of `X` to the screen. During the first pass, `X` would equal 1. Line 30 tells the computer that if `X` is still less than 100 then increment `X` by one and go back to line number 20. This time through `X` equals 2 so line 20 prints the number 2 on the screen. The computer comes to the `NEXT X` statement again, and since `X` is still less than 100, it increments `X` by one and returns to line 20. This process will repeat until `X` reaches 100, at that point the computer drops below line 30 to line 40 and the program ends.

You'll notice that our little program requires four lines of code or instructions to accomplish what we previously said in one English sentence. A typical video game today may require tens of thousands of lines of code.

Surprisingly enough, even though this BASIC version of our program may seem very computer-oriented, it is still too complicated for our CPU to understand. Again, all the CPU can understand is machine language, which is a series of ones and zeros. The good thing about BASIC, however, is that software exists that can compile it into assembly language. Assembly language is the last step before a program is converted to machine language. Below is our little program in assembly language.

```
0100     MOV     AH,02
0102     MOV     CX,0064
0105     MOV     DL,00
0107     RCL     BL,1
0109     ADC     DL,30
010C     INT     21
010E     LOOP    0105
0110     INT     20
```

Now the program is starting to become very cryptic. Here are specific commands that speak directly to the CPU and give it step-by-step instructions. Still, even this assembly language is too complicated for the CPU to understand. The final machine language version of the program follows.

```
1011010000000010
101110010110010000000000
1011001000000000
1101000011010011
100000001101001000110000
1100110100100001
1110001011110101
1100110100100000
```

Now it's just right for the CPU, nothing but ones and zeros. While I have separated the instructions (one per line) the CPU does not need such a distinction and would group all the instructions in one big lump. As you can imagine, it is impossible for any human to program directly in machine code. The closer you get to the natural language of computers, the harder programming becomes. The best programmers today can only go as far as assembly language.

Software requires memory to store all of those ones and zeros. As mentioned in Chapter 1, computers use two types of memory: electronic and magnetic. The electronic memory only stores information as long as it receives electricity. Magnetic memory (such as on floppy and hard disks) can retain information even when there is no electricity.

THE OPERATING SYSTEM

When you turn on your computer, its electronic random access memory (RAM) is totally blank because there is no software loaded into it. Without software the computer can't even perform the simplest tasks. All it can do is search for a magnetic disk, such as a floppy or hard disk, and try to load software from whatever disk it can find. This initial software is called the *operating system* because it tells your computer system how to operate itself, and how to load and run other programs.

While the operating system itself is a program, you can think of it as an air-traffic controller. Just as an air-traffic controller directs planes to land and take off from an airport, the operating system tells the computer how to load, execute, and unload other programs. Once the operating system is loaded, it instructs the computer to load other programs. The operating system is something unique to the personal computer platform. All other interactive entertainment platforms, including home and portable game systems and set-top boxes for interactive television, do not use operating systems; instead they have the initial software burned into special chips.

EXPANSION SLOTS

Today almost all personal computers come with expansion slots. These are electronic connectors mounted on the motherboard of your computer. They enable you to plug in different circuit boards for specific tasks. The disk drives need to communicate with the CPU. To accomplish this, a disk controller circuit board plugs into an expansion slot on the computer's motherboard, then cables connect it to the disk drives. Data passes from the disk drives through this cable into the disk drive controller. From there the data passes into the expansion slot and travels along a pathway called the *bus* until it reaches the CPU. The expansion slots are also called the *expansion bus*.

These expansion slots are critical to interactive entertainment because they enable devices such as joysticks, modems, video display cards, and sound cards to be connected to the personal computer. The rest of the computer is fairly simple. You have a keyboard, in which each key is a small switch that passes a unique value to the CPU when it is pressed. The CPU then reads this value to determine which key you pressed.

There is also some type of display monitor. Data is passed from the CPU to the expansion bus, to a video adapter card plugged into the bus. Once in the video adapter card, the digital signals are converted to analog signals by means of a *digital-to-analog converter* (DAC). Those signals are then sent through another cable to the display monitor. The data is then displayed on the video monitor.

COMPUTER DISPLAY MONITORS

Some of the best-looking interactive entertainment is on personal computers. The reason is that a computer display monitor has far better technology behind it than the average television. Standards for television were set back in the 1950s by the *National Television Standards Committee* (NTSC). While technology has greatly improved since the 1950s, the NTSC standard has remained in effect to ensure compatibility.

Personal computers, on the other hand, do not have such longstanding benchmarks. Even though many of the first personal computers, such as the Apple II and Commodore 64, used the NTSC standard for their displays—which enabled them to be hooked to televisions—the outmoded standard was quickly dropped in favor of better quality.

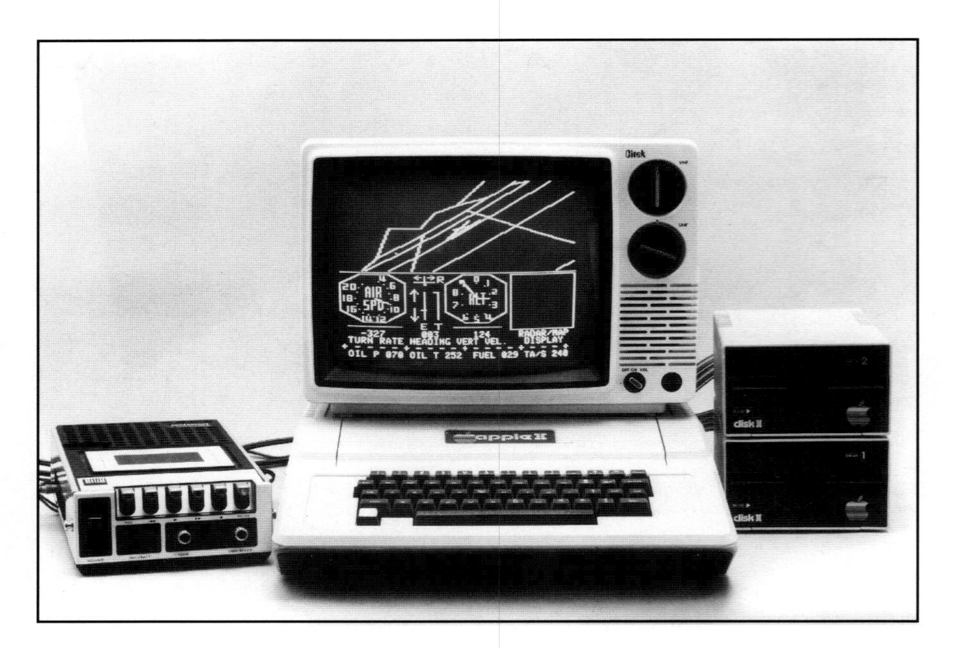

▲ Here the Apple II computer, using a television for a display monitor, is running SubLOGIC's Flight Simulator Version 1. Notice the low quality graphics. *Courtesy of Apple Computer. Flight Simulator is a registered trademark of Bruce A. Artnick.*

If you were to describe normal television in terms of graphics resolution it would have about 512 pixels width and 480 pixels in its height. In terms of computers, 512x480 is not really very high. Resolutions up to 1280x1024 are common in modern personal computers. Keep this in mind when reading about home video game systems, such as the Atari Jaguar and the 3DO, that boast more graphics processing power than many personal computers. Even if the game systems do have more power, most of it is frittered away by using low-resolution televisions for the display output.

JOYSTICKS

The expansion bus of the computer enables input/output (I/O) cards to be used to get data in and out of the computer. I/O ports are commonly used to enable the computer to communicate with external peripherals such as printers, modems, and joysticks.

Printers use parallel ports which transmit data simultaneously over a number of wires in the cable, thus the name "parallel." Modems use serial ports which only transmit one byte at a time through a single wire in the cable, thus the name "serial." Joysticks use game ports, which communicate in a manner similar to parallel ports.

A joystick is similar to a flight stick in a jet aircraft. There is a vertical grip usually with one or more buttons or triggers on it. You can tilt the grip forward, backward, left, or right. Springs keep the grip vertical, while the position of the grip is registered by small encoders and transmitted to the computer through a cable attached to the game port. Pressing any buttons on the joystick likewise sends a signal to the computer. Joysticks offer an intuitive method of controlling video games and flight simulators.

MODEMS

Modems enable your computer to communicate over standard telephone lines to other computer systems. While computers deal with digital information, telephones only deal with analog information—sound waves. When your computer sends data to the modem through the serial port, the modem in turn modulates that digital data into an analog electronic wave form. This analog wave passes through the telephone system to the receiving modem. The receiving modem then demodulates this wave back into digital data. The name modem is derived from MODulate/ DEModulate. There are two types: external and internal. The external modem sits on your desktop and connects to the computer via a cable and the serial port. The internal modem is plugged directly into your computer's expansion bus.

Modems are essential in computer games with multiple players, where players on different computers play together on the same game. These types of multiplayer games can be as simple as Chess or as complex as a three-dimensional simulation of a modern military campaign, in which one player would drive a tank while another provides air cover in a jet fighter. However, in most multiplayer games, only two people can play, because most personal computers only have one modem.

▲ Players flying Spectrum HoloByte's Tornado flight simulators attack an enemy runway together. *Photo courtesy of Spectrum HoloByte.*

▲ An ATI stereo sound card. *Courtesy of ATI.*

SOUND CARDS

Another hardware device that requires a computer expansion bus is the sound card. While some personal computers, including the Apple Macintosh and Commodore Amiga, offer built-in sound capabilities, IBM compatible personal computers require additional hardware for high-quality stereo sound. This is where sound cards come in.

Sound cards plug directly into the computer's expansion bus. They typically have numerous stereo output jacks on the back of the card. These enable you to plug in a microphone to record sound on your computer or hook your computer to your stereo, so that you can play back sound over your home stereo system. Computer games use sound cards extensively to generate sound effects, digital voices, and music.

NETWORKS

Like modems, networks also allow multiplayer games. However, they take computer-to-computer modem games one step further by enabling more than two players to compete at the same time. Networks are collections of computers tied together, usually through a central computer called the server. Each computer on the network uses a special communications port that is either built into the computer or plugged into the computer's expansion bus. This communications port enables the computer to send and receive information from the server (the central computer). Networks are naturally expansive, and are only found in business. For this reason, network-based games have been very slow to take off. Game developers are gambling that network-based game players will sacrifice their lunch hour or stay after work to play games. They are also gambling that businesses will allow the game on the network in the first place. These factors have really hindered the development of networked games.

Now that you have a understanding of the technology involved with computer-based interactive entertainment, let's take a look at the development of a specific title, Privateer by Origin Systems.

▲ A player flying Spectrum HoloByte's MIG-23 simulator prepares to gun down another player over a network.

▲ Landing at New Constantinople.

THE CREATION OF A PC-BASED IE TITLE: PRIVATEER BY ORIGIN SYSTEMS

I certainly never planned on smuggling Brilliance, especially with the frequent searches by the militia. However, the increased cash flow soon helped soothe my conscience…and fears.

It all started so quickly, I hardly had time to think about it. Hearing rumors from a bartender about a heavy fixer by the name of Sandoval on New Constantinople, capitol of the Gemini Sector, it seemed like a good idea to head there and try to pick up some work.

All I found there was a very nervous man, who offered me a smalltime merchant mission hauling ore to a refinery. Oddly enough, he wanted me to hang onto a strange ancient artifact for him during the mission. By the time I returned to New Constantinople, Sandoval was dead. I ran into a woman by the name of Tayla who informed me of Sandoval's death (I'm not so sure she didn't have something to do with it herself).

I had heard rumors of an operator by the name of Tayla for quite a while. Mostly in seedy bars where people thought I might be interested in smuggling contraband. Tayla herself seemed to be innocent enough, and better still, she knew about this strange artifact. Promising to give me information on the artifact after my return, she sent me on a typical merchant mission, transporting iron to the planet of New Detroit.

Still, she offered no information other than my life would be worth little if I hung onto the artifact long enough. This of course only served to pique my interest in discovering the truth about it. My adventure started with a small shipment of the illegal drug Brilliance to a little known section of the Humbolt quadrant. It was true, I found out, that she had bribed the militia patrols to ignore my contraband cargo. They performed their normal cargo searches only to come up empty. It made me wonder how corrupt the militia really was, and how 'safe' they kept the shipping lanes. The thought did not last long, however, when I was searched by a second militia squad who obviously were not bribed. They found the Brilliance, and opened fire while telling me I would not make it out of the quadrant alive.

▲ Sandoval was responsible for sticking me with that cursed artifact.

▲ Tayla lured me into smuggling.

▲ The artifact.

▲ The militia opened fire after detecting my contraband.

▲ First of the militia to fall under my new tacheon lasers.

▲ Lynch was one of the less scrupulous individuals I've worked for.

▲ The University Square on Oxford.

Fortunately, I had just upgraded my lasers and shields, thanks to the profits from my legal trade runs. The militia light fighters proved no match for my upgraded ship. Surprisingly enough, I found that destroying those who upheld the law was not harder than destroying the occasional pirates and retros (Church of Man fanatics who use technology to destroy technology).

This started my decline into the world in which I now live. I have been involved in countless smuggling missions from a pirate base hidden in the asteroid field of the Pander's Star system. I've worked for such notable personalities as Lynch (an organized crime boss). Lynch suckered me into my first assassin mission by sending me to deliver a message to someone (his enemy) who immediately opened fire. Lynch himself later tried to have his goons ambush me in order to get the artifact.

Now with a price on my head, I'm performing escort missions for the University on Oxford, trying to weasel my way into their library archives in order to get more info about the artifact. If I can just keep those pirates and retros off my clients long enough, I should find some answers in the university's archives.

OVERVIEW OF PRIVATEER

And so goes the storyline of Origin System's Privateer. Released last fall, it is still entrancing players with its rich plot and nefarious characters. Privateer continues on in the same universe as the highly successful Wing Commander series: the 27th century. The Wing Commander series focused on a war in the far future between humans and an alien race called the Kilrathi. Those games always put you as the soldier/space combat ace flying the missions of the Confederation. Privateer, on the other hand, places you in a much more flexible situation as master of your own destiny.

▲ The game Privateer from Origin Systems (box shot).

As a fortune seeker, you have access to over 60 different bases/planets in about 90 systems. You start out with a rickety ship and a few cash credits, and from there perform various merchant missions to make money. As you build up wealth, you can use it to purchase a better ship, or upgrade your existing ship with better shields, more cargo space, bigger engines, and so forth.

Even though it is grounded in exploration and trade, Privateer is still mostly a space combat simulator. Even if you decide to run legal cargoes through well-patrolled systems, you'll still bump into pirates and retros (or even stray Kilrathi if you wander too close to the edge of the frontier).

Most of the gameplay is based on a first-person viewpoint. When piloting your craft you see the interior of the cockpit, and you can turn your head left or right to look out the side viewports. When docked on a base or port you can see all the available exits and simply click on one to enter. To engage an individual in a conversation, you simply click on that character and a conversation ensues.

Currently Privateer is only available for IBM compatible personal computers with a 386-DX or higher capability CPU. The system needs VGA graphics capabilities along with at least 4MB of RAM and 20MB of free space on a hard disk drive.

THE DEVELOPMENT PROCESS

Game development at Origin Systems follows a fairly structured and organized approach. When a designer comes up with an idea for a game, the designer submits his idea to a review board. The review board evaluates the idea and decides whether or not it is worth investigating.

If a game design is approved, the designer gets a software engineer (programmer) to help develop the idea further. What follows is a period of research and development where the designer and programmer work closely together to build the basic framework of the game.

After a period of time, the designer and programmer take their results back to the review board. At this point, if the game still looks like a winner, more funding is provided and a development timetable is set. Artists and more programmers begin work on the project. Programmers and designers work hand-in-hand to get the artwork and data merged together into a workable game.

Toward the end of development, the music and sound effects are added. The product goes into testing six to eight weeks before shipping. Product testing includes Beta testing and play testing. Designers and programmers track down any bugs or software problems that arise during this time. The public relations department kicks into gear by sending press releases to prospective reviewers and members of the press. At last the product is bug free and it ships (hopefully on the projected ship date). Based on sales and customer response, a sequel or add-on product may be added, and the development sequence begins anew.

INITIAL CONCEPTS

For Privateer, designer Chris Roberts came up with the initial game concepts. As the designer of some of Origins greatest games, Roberts is held in much respect. Roberts designed the hit Wing Commander series, along with Times of Lore and Bad Blood. Naturally, with his successful background, Roberts did not have any trouble getting the approval of the products review board for Privateer.

When Privateer was introduced, the only similar games on the market were fairly old ones called Elite and Space Rogue. They both featured arcade style action, and communication with other characters. In-house at Origin there really were no other game ideas in competition at the time.

GAMEPLAY DESIGN

The main goals in the design of Privateer were to create a commerce trading system within the Wing Commander universe. Another goal was to provide a game with random missions that players could play over and over again. That freshness ensures the game never ends.

Some initial ideas never quite made it into the final game. One such idea involved player finances. The game initially enabled players to get loans from banks or other (less reputable) characters. In this scenario, you might run into debt, and be pursued by creditors or bounty hunters who were after the price on your head. Privateer took about a year and a half to make, and so during this period, many such ideas were dropped while others were developed and added to the game.

Tom Kassebaum, a game designer, joined Origin at the start of Privateer and jumped straight into game design. His background involved some computer programming and a lot of math and physics. "A lot of what a game designer does is data manipulation," says Kassebaum, "setting up missions, setting up the universe. We also go through and make sure the game stays within the initial constructs. Privateer had a lead designer, who had a pretty good image. As the game was fleshed out, the programmers would say whether or not certain features were doable. If it couldn't be done in a reasonable fashion, the design was modified. By staying with the entire project, the game designer gave the programmers more freedom."

The game designer sticks with the project through development, right to the end. According to Kassebaum, "I work with a lot of the artwork. And I'm in charge of overseeing the artwork. The game designers and programmers stick with the entire project. Artists, on the other hand, will go in and out of various projects."

As a game designer, one of Kassebaum's responsibilities involves directing the artwork and programming. He solves a graphics problem by telling an artist what he wants, then puts that artist's product into the game. The programmers take care of the music. The lead designer oversees the main musical pieces to make sure they sound good with the game and fit his overall design.

ARTISTIC DESIGN

Rough sketches are created and approved before work begins on any artwork. For the computer graphics, the artists at Origin Systems used 3D Studio from Autodesk for all the 3-D work. The two-dimensional painting and animation was done in Deluxe Animator by Electronic Arts, and an internal drawing program called "Eor."

A number of artists worked on Privateer, including Chris Douglas (3D Artists), Danny Garrette, Brian G. Smith, Beverly Garland (who did the scenic art), Jake Rodgers (3D Artists) and Bob Frye. All together, the artists spent about eight months working on Privateer.

PROGRAMMING

Programmers at Origin Systems are known as software engineers. This title is definitely more descriptive of the work of a programmer. In creating software, the programmers are engineering very precise relationships between the available hardware and software-based instructions.

The programmers at Origin use 386- and 486-based personal computers for development. They use C++, along with some assembly language routines, for programming. Because C++ enables programmers to create modules that can be reused from game-to-game, programmers do not have to "reinvent the wheel" every time they create a new game. The assembly language routines enable programmers to squeeze the most speed out of the personal computer for animation and other computer-intensive operations.

The programmers were Reinaldo Castro, Alex Jen, Edwin Herrell, Arthur DiBianca, and Charles Cafrelli. Like the artists, the programmers worked on Privateer eight months.

MUSIC AND SOUND EFFECTS

Music and sound effects have become just as important to video games as they are to motion pictures. You would hardly expect to see a new feature film without a soundtrack and spoken dialog. Likewise, all computer games today have either a sound track, digital sound effects, or both.

Dana Glover composed all the music for Privateer. Glover comes from a professional background in music. He created the Nightshift Network, a group of composers that has been ghostwriting for motion pictures for the past thirteen years. Glover's work was heard in movies such as *Rain Man*, *Misery*, *Robocop II*, *Apocalypse Now*, and *Beetlejuice*. For sound effects, Nenad Vugrinec is the expert at Origin. Vugrinec has created sound effects for several Origin games, including Ultima VII and Strike Commander.

TESTING

After the pieces of a new program are brought together and a workable version is created, the testing begins. Testing can be divided into three stages; Alpha testing, play testing, and Beta testing. Alpha testing is usually performed by only a few people at Origin, or sometimes only the project leader. Because there are usually a large number of glitches and problems in early software, Alpha testing requires someone who has an intimate understanding of the software programming. This knowledge enables an Alpha tester to distinguish between minor and major code problems. After Alpha testing is completed, a Beta version is released for further testing.

Dan Orzulak of Origin Systems has a fun job as a play tester. The responsibility of a play tester is to play games and uncover software bugs. A software bug is a glitch or mistake in a program. The mistake can be caused by an error or typo on the programmer's part, or by an unexpected event that occurs when a game is played. The ways bugs manifest themselves are as varied as the bugs themselves, from totally freezing up the computer (the most common result) to throwing graphics garbage on the screen.

Play testers look for any bugs in the software. When a problem is found, the tester documents it and reports it back to the programmers. The programmers correct the problem, then send the play tester a new version of the program. The play testers also keep a close eye on the artwork. If any pixels appear out of place, or some piece of art is difficult to understand, the play testers report this to the art department, and artists correct the problem.

The seven play testers at Origin Systems also do customer service. After playing a game for weeks on end, they are naturally the most qualified to handle technical support calls from customers. During the testing period play testers have some input on game design. Their goal is to make the game easier and more fun, so they may suggest new features, change the game flow, or make the game easier or harder to play.

Play tester's reactions to Privateer were very similar. According to Dan Orzulak, "Everyone really liked the game. I've played 300 to 400 games in my lifetime and I feel it's one of the best I've ever seen."

When it came to suggesting changes for Privateer, Orzulak explains: "There were a lot of things people wanted in the game, but most were too difficult to implement. So we tried to focus on simple things that would make the game easier and more fun. One change I recommended, that made its way into the final game, was to allow the user to double-click the mouse button to access the computer console. Another change made by the play testers was to add a second weapon to the Tarsus (the initial ship that a player gets when the game starts). This extra weapon on the Tarsus made the game easier for new players just starting out."

The play testers also keep notes about playing the game. These notes, along with extended details about playing the game, maps, and hints, are compiled by the Creative Services department at Origin. Creative Services then produces a "Play Testers Guide" to assist players and make the game more interesting. The guide includes detailed maps of all the game's solar systems and asteroid belts. Each mission has a full step-by-step walkthrough. Detailed charts are provided for each weapon and various trade opportunities.

The Beta version of the program also moves into a phase known as Beta testing. In the software industry, Beta testing is usually performed by a select group of users (the consumers). Origin, however, doesn't use outside testers due to the fear of software piracy. For Privateer, Origin used a bonded company, as well as their own inside testers. Both tested Privateer for a number of weeks, on many different computer configurations, and reported any bugs to Origin.

When testing does turn up a bug after the program is released to the public, the programmers fix it, and the fix is then released through diskette or online services such as CompuServe and the Origin Bulletin Board System.

PRODUCT RELEASE

About three months prior to the release of Privateer, the Marketing department kicks into gear and sets up advertising. Advertising is the key to a successful launch. As soon as the product ships, press releases are sent to major media outlets.

▲ The ad slick for Privateer that appeared in game magazines. *Photo courtesy of Origin Systems.*

CONSUMER REACTION

Initial consumer reaction was outstanding. Privateer sold out in most stores, and is now available worldwide through Electronic Arts distribution. A lot of people really liked the randomness to the game, including the mission generators. There were only a few negative reactions. Some players didn't like the fact that you can't stop at any bases during a mission. Some have complained that the guns don't have automatic fire.

The concern about landing at other bases during missions was an original concern of the designers. But as the programmers developed the code, it became a very complicated process. First, the game would have to deal with cargo that was on your ship, selling it or keeping it. Secondly, there would need to be a timer added to the game, to make sure that a mission got completed and that the cargo was still valid by the time you eventually got it to its destination. These and other problems caused the programmers to reject the ability to land at bases during a mission.

THE FUTURE OF PRIVATEER

With more than 50,000 copies of Privateer sold in the first few months of release, there will definitely be some type of follow-up game. It may be a Privateer II or a Special Missions disk. Any new game ideas, even spin-off games, must go through the complete review process. A good market response always makes it easier to design and introduce a sequel.

CURRENT PERSONAL COMPUTER-BASED IE TITLES

The following section discusses a few of the current personal computer-based IE titles and the technologies that make them popular. While there are a number of personal computers on the market, this section focuses more on the titles than the platforms they run on.

On personal computers, IE titles can be divided into three areas: action, adventure, and simulation. Action games include any video games similar to shoot-em-up coin-operated arcade games. Action games rely mostly on manual dexterity. Adventure and role-playing games tend to rely more on intellect than reflexes. While Adventure games may be text-only, the current trend is to make them more graphic-oriented. The last area is simulation games. Simulations usually require a combination of both reflexes and intellect. A good example of simulation games are flight simulators, in which you, as a pilot, need both a steady hand and an understanding of the dynamics of flight to play the game. A large part of simulation-based games are sport simulations that cover everything from Indy 500 racing to football.

ACTION AND ARCADE GAMES

In the action and arcade arena, there are many games that are very popular. Three such games are: Microsoft Arcade for Windows, Wolfenstein 3-D from Id Software, and Wing Commander Academy from Origin Systems. These games all run on IBM compatible personal computers.

Microsoft Arcade is the result of a licensing agreement between Microsoft and Atari. The agreement enables Microsoft to create personal computer versions of classic Atari games. Arcade runs under Microsoft Windows, a graphical user interface, and comes with five different arcade games: Asteroids, Battlezone, Centipede, Missile Command and Tempest.

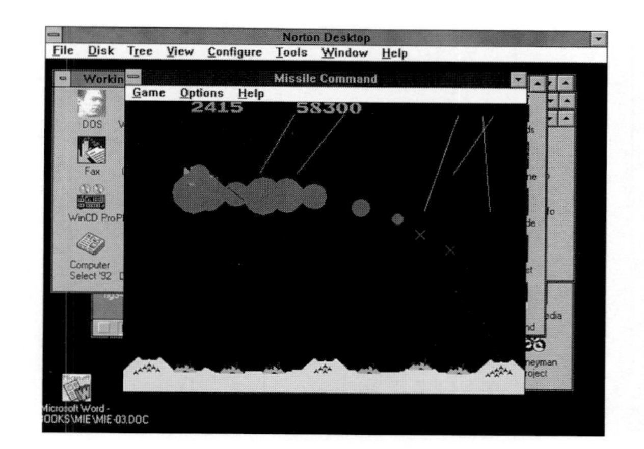

▲ The Microsoft arcade version of Missile Command running under Windows.

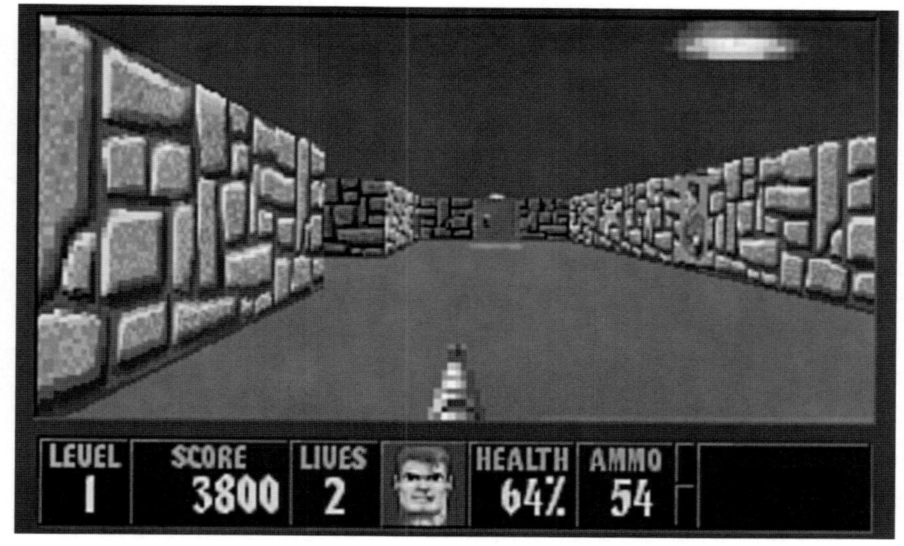

▲ The first-person view of Wolfenstein 3-D.

Microsoft went through great pains to perfectly duplicate the original coin-operated games under Windows. The Windows versions are so accurate that even the subtle strategies used in the original coin-operated games work with Microsoft's versions. Microsoft even digitally recorded the sound effects from the original games and included them in the Windows versions. Even running under Windows, the games are just as fast as the originals.

Another highly popular arcade-style game for personal computers is Wolfenstein 3-D. In September of 1992, Wolfenstein was given the Editor's Choice award by Shareware Magazine. Shareware is a term used to describe software that can be distributed freely through online computer systems. You can download Shareware from these systems and try it, but if you decide to use it, you are required to send the author a registration fee.

Wolfenstein 3-D is first person graphics action game. You play the role of a World War II commando who has been captured by the Nazis. As a prisoner, you are kept eight floors down in Wolfenstein. One day you overpower a guard, steal his gun, and escape your cell. The object of the game is to work your way through each floor until you reach ground level.

▲ The difficulty settings for Wolfenstein 3-D.

▲ Wolfenstein 3-D features plenty of graphic violence.

▲ The warning screen for Wolfenstein 3-D.

Four separate difficulty levels are available; Can I Play, Daddy? (very easy), Please Don't Hurt Me (moderate), Bring 'Em On (difficult), and I Am Death Incarnate (very difficult). Depending on the difficulty level you choose, the game will throw more obstacles at you: everything from slow-witted German guards, to machine-gun toting SS guards, to vicious German Shepherd guard dogs. One mission even includes machine-gun toting mutants and the scalpel-throwing mad scientist that created them.

Your character's health begins at 100 percent and drops every time you're attacked or shot. Finding food or first-aid packs along the way will revitalize your health. As you are wounded and your health level drops, a picture at the bottom of the screen reflects your character's physical condition—complete with bloody lips, black eyes, and worse.

This brings up another aspect of Wolfenstein 3-D that makes it unique—its violence. As you run down corridors blowing away Nazis with your machine gun, they get thrown backwards, screaming, as the blood splatters in the air. The floor quickly gets littered with dead, bleeding bodies. Even before the game starts, you are presented with a warning screen regarding the violence.

A number of other features make Wolfenstein 3-D an interesting action game. The actions of the characters change as you move and act. There is a level of randomness built in, so that other characters are never in the same place or act the same way twice. Support for sound cards provides digital music and sound effects. If a Nazi guard walks into the room behind you, you can hear the metal door shut.

Wolfenstein 3-D is included on the enclosed CD-ROM.

Following the theme of the Wing Commander series, Origin Systems has released Wing Commander Academy. Academy is an arcade style shoot-em-up space combat engine extracted from the Wing Commander II game. In Academy, you set up your own missions with a combat simulator. You then fly these missions with your own choice of ship and wingman.

The mission computer enables you to specify the type of enemy you wish to encounter and where they are placed. These missions can be immediately played, or saved to disk to trade with other Academy players. The ability to save missions to disk is a unique feature to personal computer-based games. It opens up the world of game design to the players themselves. Scenarios that players design can be traded with friends or even uploaded to online computer systems.

The actual combat takes place in 3-D space. You can dogfight with other ships, dodge asteroids and mines, and pick up lost cargo and ejected pilots with your tractor beam. If you don't feel like designing your own mission, the computer can randomly build missions for you. You can also play the Gauntlet, where ships come at you continuously throughout 15 progressively difficult levels.

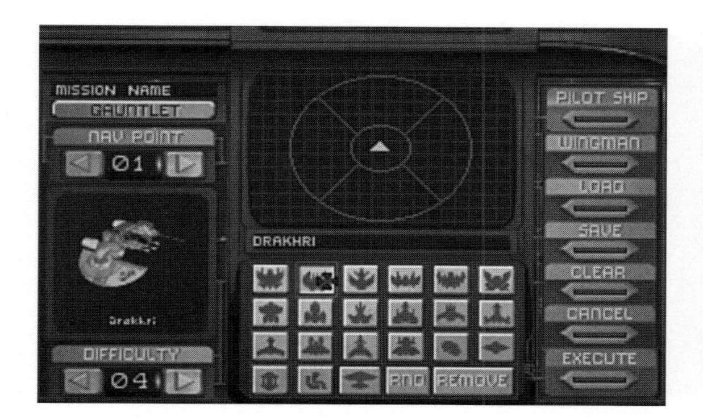

▲ Wing Commander Academy's mission builder.

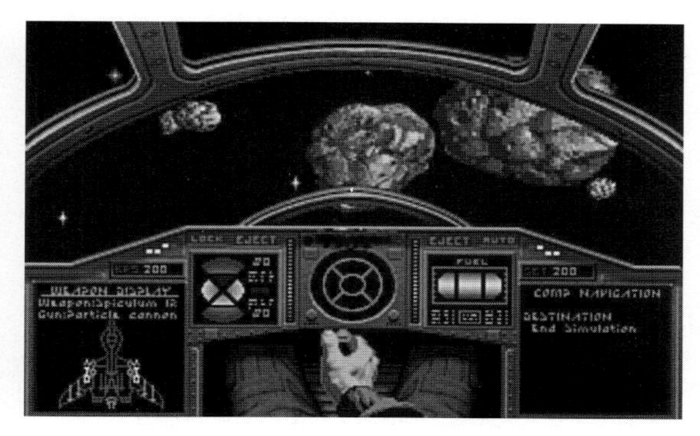

▲ Navigating an asteroid field.

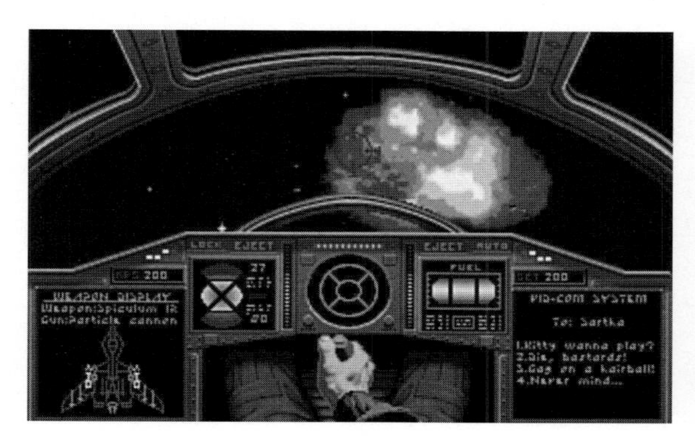

▲ Dogfighting in Wing Commander Academy.

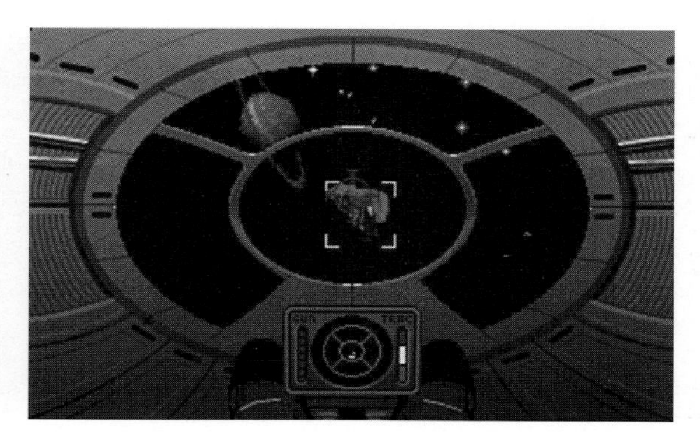

▲ Capturing an ejected pilot with the tractor beam.

ADVENTURE AND ROLE PLAYING GAMES

Adventure and role-playing games (RPGs) tend to take a larger share of the personal computer-based entertainment software. Role-playing games are similar to adventure games, except they usually involve much more complex player characteristics. RPGs keep track of information about each player's computer character, including the character's strength, charisma, endurance, wisdom, and so on. As players progress through the game storylines, and face various obstacles, all the factors regarding that character are taken into consideration.

RPGs are strong on strategy. For instance, if a character with a high wisdom quotient and a low strength quotient meets a group of thugs, the player would probably want to try talking his way out of potential conflict. If the character has more strength than wisdom, the player's character might be better off shooting first and asking questions later. Or if you command a squad of men, the men with short-range weapons are better at guarding tight doorways, while men with long-range weapons are more effective guarding long hallways.

Space Hulk from Electronic Arts is a program that combines strategy with role playing. Space Hulk started out as a 3-D board game from Games Workshop called Warhammer 40,000. The computer version combines real-time arcade style action with strategy and impressive 3-D graphics.

The storyline in Space Hulk takes place tens of thousands of years from now, when mankind has access to "warp space" enabling them to travel to distant planets faster than the speed of light. This warp space, however, is very unpredictable, and some travelers get washed off course and are doomed to float in and out of warp space for eternity. The extraterrestrials that exist in this future scenario stowaway and overrun these lost ships, called "space hulks."

The main threat to humanity is an evil alien race known as the Genestealers. Unable to breed and reproduce among themselves, they choose to infect other species. To do this, they implant 'eggs' in the victims bodies that alter their victim's genetic makeup. Thus the normal offspring of the victim becomes a hybrid combination of the Genestealer and victim's species. After four generations of this, the Genestealer is physically identical to the victim's race. Genestealers smuggle themselves into unwary systems by infesting huge space hulks, and waiting until that hulk happens to fall out of warp space near a habitable planet.

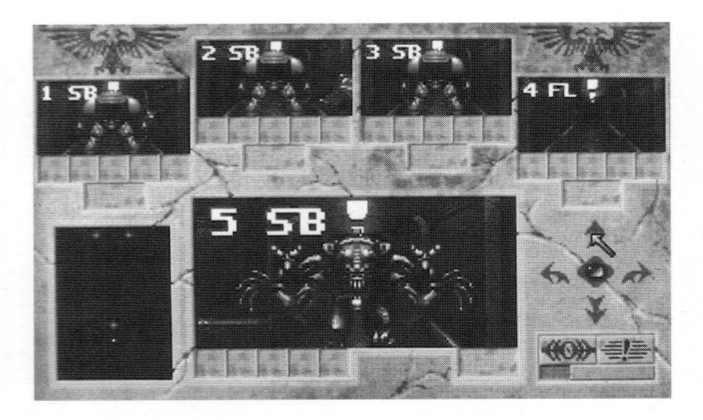

▲ The first-person views available in Space Hulk.

This is where your character—a Space Marine—enters the scene. The emperor supplies the orders, and you assemble a squad and arm them. The game offers 12 different types of weapons for close- and long-range warfare within space hulks. Scenarios range from a single Marine to two full squadrons (10 Marines). Based on the weapons and strengths of your team members, you maneuver them through the abandoned space hulks, destroying aliens, to complete your mission.

The game is played through a combination of first-person views and a planning screen. In the first-person perspective, you see the visor views of all your squad members. This enables you to monitor their progress, and even take control of a member at any time during the game.

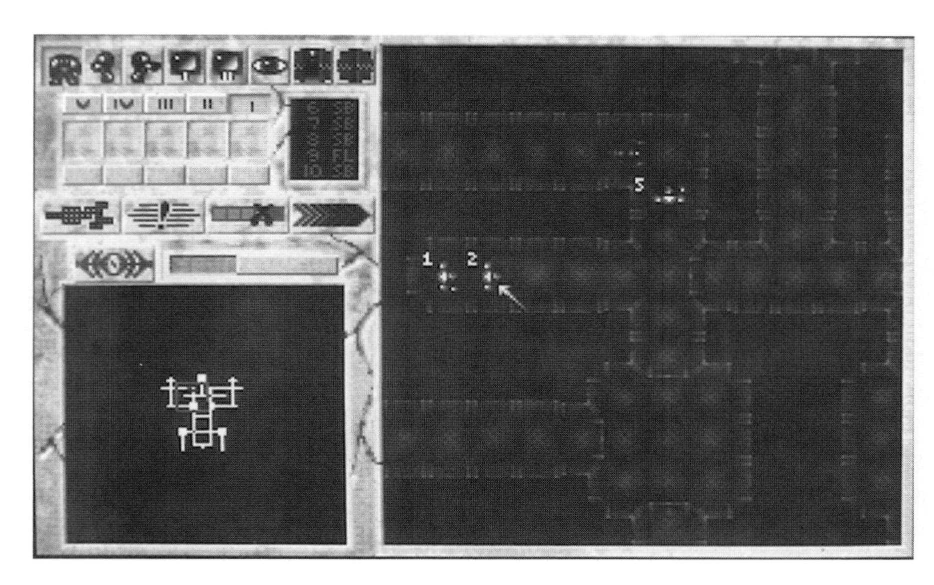

▲ The Space Hulk planning screen.

From the planning screen you can give orders to the terminator units in your squad. Icons on your screen enable you to program how a character moves and turns, and when and where a character shoots or opens or closes doors. You can program each of the marines under your command with up to five different orders at a time. You can use other features to see the firing range available to any squad member based on his particular weapon. Not all your orders may be carried out, however, because aliens may unexpectedly burst from corridor walls to disrupt your strategy. The game is definitely not a game of dexterity. The challenge is in giving orders to your squad, based on their weaponry and the layout of your current location.

Coordinating the planning phase of the game requires you suspend real time with a freeze time button. To keep the pace of the game active however, you only have a limited amount of freeze time. The freeze time allocation grows with the amount of time you spend in real time, and diminishes while you are in freeze time mode. Controlling the game in real time, when you have to coordinate the movements and actions of up to 10 Marines, however, is nearly impossible.

The game comes with a series of basic and advanced tutorial missions, along with a full campaign with many missions to complete. Upon successful completion of a set of missions, you may appear before the high court of Space Marines to receive a commendation. The game makes full use of sound board capabilities through digital music, voices, and sound effects. As you walk down the seemingly deserted corridors, you can hear the wails and shrieks of aliens somewhere on the ship. Members of your squad yell out warnings, and even scream when attacked by aliens.

While Space Hulk may qualify as a good RPG, it is not in the classical adventure style. For classical adventure, you should consider Return to Zork from Activision. Return to Zork is the latest installment in a long series of adventure games, which started in 1982 with the original Zork.

▲ The first-person perspective of Return to Zork.

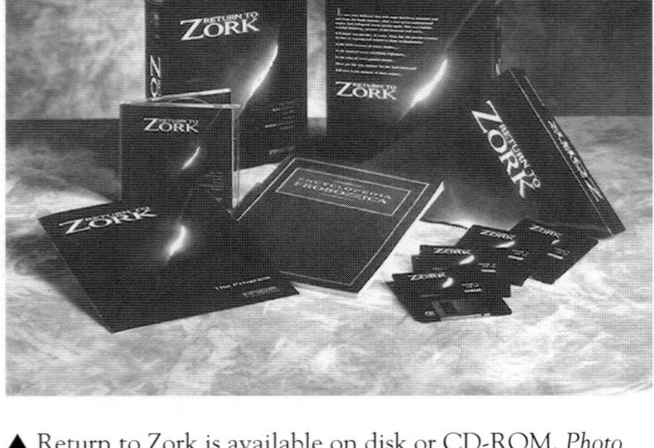

▲ Return to Zork is available on disk or CD-ROM. *Photo coutesy of Activision.*

Return to Zork takes place in the Great Underground Empire of Zork. This underworld is dominated by an evil force. Your job is to remove the force. Using only graphics, the game enables you to explore caves, rivers, lakes, and towns from a first-person perspective. As with all adventure games, you come across puzzles that are solved by manipulating objects in the environment. For example, to traverse the river you must cut some vines with a knife and use them to bind boards into a makeshift raft. Once you create the raft, you continue your journey on by shooting the rapids of the river.

The user interface was originally conceived at the Massachusetts Institute of Technology. It uses animated icons to represent actions that can be taken. Icons are simplified pictures that represent a command to the computer. RTZ takes icons one step further by animating them. For example, the icon representing the action "drop object" shows an animated hand dropping something. From talking to fighting, everything can be controlled by the animated icon interfaces. Instead of typing "Put the rat in the box." you simply click the "put" icon, click the rat, then click the box.

The game itself allows you to explore a rich 3-D world by pointing with a mouse and clicking anything you see. Most of the scenery created for RTZ was done with 3-D computer graphics technology and provides a clean, high-tech look. Some of the mazes in the game generate themselves while you play, so each player maps their own way through some areas of the game.

In addition to the 3-D computer graphics, live video is also used extensively throughout RTZ. When you communicate with people in the game, you see on the screen a video sequence of that person talking. Activision hired professional actors such as Robin Lively from the television series "Twin Peaks," and Jason Harvey from "The Wonder Years" to play roles in the adventure. Even the advertising that promotes RTZ is more like a movie and less like a computer game.

▲ The ad slick for Return to Zork. *Photo courtesy of Activision.*

SIMULATIONS

Simulation-style games are by far the largest segment of the personal computer game market. The main reason for this is that the computer is naturally suited for large computational tasks, such as calculating 3-D scenery for a flight simulator or determining the best move in a Chess game. Simulation games include vehicles such as planes, tanks, race cars, submarines, and so forth. Also included in this category are war simulations (historical and fictional) and strategy games like chess. Game developers are even starting to push the simulation envelope with products like SEAL Team (a 3-D simulator for Navy SEAL combat operations) and SimLife (a simulator that enables you to create your own ecosystems by designing plants and animals at the genetic level). Not to be left out of the simulation category would be sports simulators, such as football, basketball, golf and almost any other sport.

It would be beyond the scope of this book to try and touch on all the various types of simulators available for personal computers. Instead, we'll examine a few of the more popular simulators today that use the latest in hardware and software technology.

One of the most outstanding flight simulators for personal computers is Comanche Maximum Overkill from Nova Logic. Comanche is a 3-D military simulation of the Boeing Sikorsky RAH-66 Comanche attack helicopter. It brings personal computer-based flight simulation to a new level by using voxel graphics. Voxel graphics create beautiful, lush scenery that not only looks better than other simulators, but moves faster than traditional scenery methods.

▲ Voxel Graphics enables Comanche's scenery to outshine all other simulators.

First-time players of Comanche will probably find themselves spending more time exploring the scenery than barreling down canyons and blowing away enemy tanks. The game assigns missions for you to fly, such as taking out a landing field full of Kamov-50 Werewolf helicopters before they can get airborne. If you are too slow, each chopper that takes off becomes another enemy chasing you around the canyons.

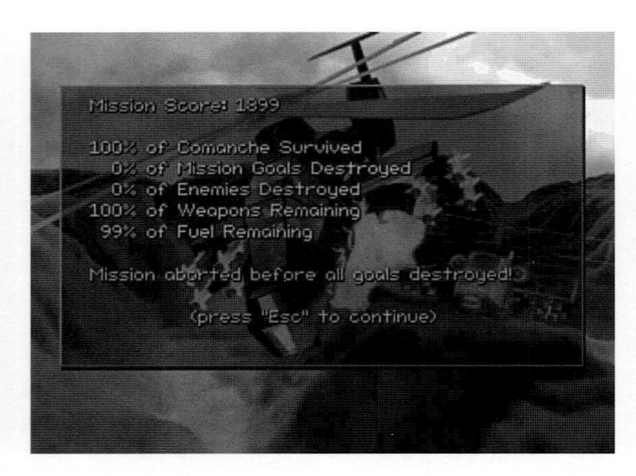

▲ The Comanche mission statistics screen.

Based on the outcome of each mission, a 3-D rendered image is displayed along with the statistics relating to your performance. The enemies you face during the missions show a level of intelligence. If you target a surface-to-air missile launcher and miss, the SAM will move to cover. Tanks and SAM launchers will rotate to face you before firing. Each mission uses different terrain, from burning desert badlands to the frozen mountains of Alaska.

To keep the plot going, Nova Logic has released Missions Disks 1 and 2. The add-on missions supply Comanche with new music, terrain, missions, and enemies. The second mission disk incorporates new river terrain, and snowstorm/limited visibility missions. After Comanche, flight simulators will never be the same.

Computer-based simulations today are not limited to flight simulators. For example…

As the PBR (Patrol Boat, River) glides in quietly to the shore, members of the SEAL Team jump out, and fall to prone positions in the cool mud. It's 0200 hours as the PBR pulls slowly away from shore and you give the four-fingered column formation signal. Your team falls into line behind you.

Inching your way through the mud and mosquitoes, you can easily hear the insects swarming around you. Near a group of bunkers, you spot a Viet Cong patrol lurking around the edge of the camp. As point man, you could open fire with your silenced rifle. If you want to take the VC alive, you give the cease fire signal to the rest of the team.

▲ Chasing down a renegade helicopter pilot in the frozen mountains of Alaska.

▲ River bend terrain from Comanche Mission Disk 2.

▲ The PBR inserting your SEAL team into Vietnam's Mekong Delta.

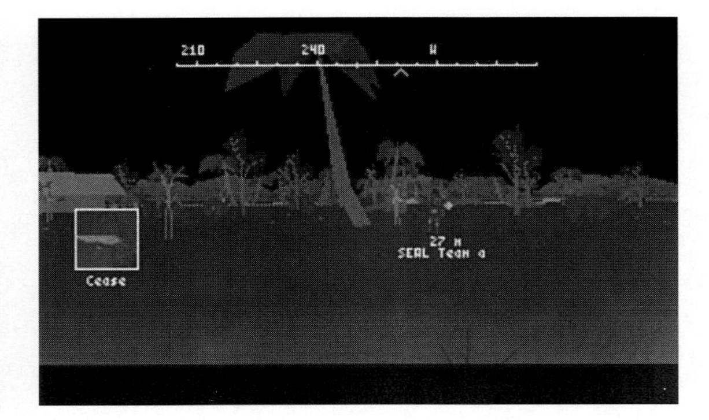

▲ You give the cease fire signal, hoping to take prisoners alive.

▲ Huey Seawolves fly in for extraction and air support.

Suddenly everything breaks loose as your team is spotted. As AK-47 rounds shriek overhead, you give the fire at will signal and your team opens fire on the VC patrol. You find yourself being surrounded and your flanker is hit. You radio for air support and a dust off and suddenly the night is ablaze with tracer bullets and shock waves as multiple Seawolves come to your aid. This is the Forest of Assassins: Vietnam's Mekong Delta, a typical scenario with Electronic Art's SEAL Team combat simulator.

SEAL Team is state-of-the-art in simulation techniques. From the moment you pick up the 150 page manual, you realize this isn't a typical shoot-em-up style arcade game. This game practically requires that you *become* a Navy SEAL just to play and understand it. When you begin SEAL Team, you choose a team point man and a starting year for your tour of duty. The years available are from 1966 to 1969, with missions getting progressively harder in the later years of the war. The missions you can choose to play are based on actual missions performed by SEAL teams in Vietnam.

As your team successfully completes missions, their abilities and skills increase. They become better shots, gain agility and strength, and other qualities that are considered during their performance on the battlefield. An intelligence briefing enables you to select a mission, then a mission briefing follows that explains mission objectives, support craft, and enemy activity in the area.

After a few further details—such as picking the marching order, inventory, and patrol order—you move to the battlefield. A 3-D zoom-in sequence shows the insertion of your team. Once on the battlefield, you have full access to a panoramic 3-D view of the action. You can see the situation from any team member's viewpoint. You can target possible threats with the aid of a targeting diamond. You can supply orders to your teammates, to help them avoid booby traps, specify a particular formation, and even split the team up.

After the mission objectives are met, (or perhaps before then if things don't turn out as planned) you radio for helicopter pickup and return to base. You undergo mission debriefing back at the base. After debriefing, you receive a post-mission report, followed by a historical report. The post-mission report provides a summary of your performance, while the historical report summarizes the performance of the men who actually performed that mission during the Vietnam War. The historical report displays the results of the men who played for keeps. While it may not necessarily be the ideal outcome, it was the *real* outcome.

▲ SEAL Team makes extensive and effective use of digitized pictures

▲ Microsoft Flight Simulator Version 5.0.

The 3-D engine makes this simulation much more interesting. Digitized images are also sprinkled throughout the game to add additional realism. The key lesson learned from SEAL Team is that even the most complicated environments can be simulated on a computer. Some environments can be simulated very close to the real thing, as in Microsoft Flight Simulator Version 5.0.

▲ Cockpits from actual planes have been digitized for realism.

▲ In this scene from Microsoft Flight Simulator Version 5.0, you can see the satellite scanned imagery overlaid onto Meigs field in Chicago.

▲ Here is the view above San Francisco, using satellite-scanned scenery from Mallard Software.

Microsoft Flight Simulator Version 5.0 (FS5) is the latest installment of the most realistic flight simulator available. FS5 is so realistic, it conforms to the Federal Aviation Administration's minimum visual flight rules and instrument flight rules. Actual cockpits of planes have been digitized and appear when you choose the type of plane you want to fly. The sounds from using various instruments have also been digitized, so when you lower the flaps or drop the landing gear you hear the appropriate sound made by the plane you are flying.

By far though, the most impressive aspect of FS5 is its out-of-the-window 3-D graphics. It's the first PC-based flight simulator to take satellite imagery and use it as a texture map on the surface of the ground. This imagery adds a new level of realism to the flying experience. Such rich scenery makes simulated flying seem more like watching a video of an actual flight than viewing computer-generated images.

FS5 even enables you to fly a Schweizer Sailplane in search of ridge lifts and thermals. Or you could choose to fly a Learjet at speeds of up to 460 mph at a ceiling of 41,000 feet. A Cessna Skylane and Sopwith Camel are also available for your flying pleasure. All of the planes can be controlled by realism and reliability factors. This means you can test your skills, when suddenly instruments start to fail during your flight.

Even environmental conditions are accurately simulated with FS5. You can program the weather simulator to simulate any type of weather condition from calm summer days, to hurricane winds and thunderstorms. Any time of day or night can be easily simulated. During long flights, time progresses naturally (although you can speed up simulated time), and day turns to dusk and eventually night.

▲ Another view of Mallard Software's satellite scanned San Francisco scenery for FS5.

FS5 takes realism to new heights with the addition of add-on products from Mallard Software. One product, called Real Weather Pilot (RWP), uses a modem to dial the national weather service. RWP then downloads the current weather conditions for the entire U.S., and programs the weather simulator in FS5 to duplicate those conditions. So when you cruise around in your Learjet with its digitized cockpit and sound effects, you can also experience the actual current weather conditions of your particular location.

The 285-page manual includes a seven-chapter flight school section that discusses everything from basic flight physics to advanced aerobatics and radio navigation. FS5 includes many online flight lessons to teach you in conjunction with the manual's discussions. Microsoft Flight Simulator is also available on the Apple Macintosh platform.

One other simulator worth mentioning is the new Kasparov's Gambit by Electronic Arts. Kasparov's Gambit is the state-of-the-art in Chess simulation. With high-resolution, 256-color graphics, and digital video of the world's greatest chess players, nothing else compares.

While you are playing, Chess Master Gary Kasparov himself coaches you through digital video sequences. Over 120 different tutorial positions were written by Chess masters, and the training lessons are based on Kasparov's own training techniques. It also offers the strongest chess engine available; it even beat a Cray Super Computer during the 1992 World Computer Chess Championship.

MULTIPLAYER INTERACTIVE ENTERTAINMENT

Matching your wits against another living, breathing person has always been more challenging than playing even the most brilliantly conceived artificial intelligence software. In this area, personal computer-based interactive entertainment is leading the field. There are four types of multiplayer games: modem-to-modem, direct connection, networked, and online services.

Modem-to-modem games involve two personal computers communicating through modems. Many new PC-based chess games enable players to play to challenge each other over the phone. Other games, such as Microsoft Flight Simulator 5.0 and F15 Strike Eagle III from MicroProse, enable more complex simulations to take place between two remote players.

In these flight simulators you can fly against other players. In F15 Strike Eagle, you dogfight with another person, or fly with that person on a computer-generated mission. You can have a head-to-head dogfight, fly a mission together as pilot/navigator, or be a protective wingman.

▲ F15 Strike Eagle III enables you to play via a modem or direct connection with another player. *Courtesy of MicroProse*.

A direct connection is similar to a modem-to-modem connection. However, instead of hooking your computer to a modem, you hook your computer directly to another computer. This means that the two players (and computers) must be physically close to each other. Practically any game that allows modem-to-modem connections allows direct connections. Both modem-to-modem and direct-connection multiplayer games are limited in that only two players can interact in a game at the same time. This limitation, however, does not exist in network and online service games.

Networks enable multiple computers to be connected and share information. While that information may be word processing files and electronic mail, it also can be flight simulator data. Some flight simulators, such as Spectrum HoloByte's Falcon 3, enable multiple players to compete against one another. In Falcon 3, up to six players can fly with each other, either in a multiplayer dogfight, or a multiplayer attack.

Another network capable multiplayer game is Spectre Supreme from Velocity Development. It is available for both Macintosh and IBM compatible personal computers and enables up to eight players to compete in a 3-D environment.

For those who want multiple player games, but do not have access to a network, there are many online services that offer online interactive games. These games enable many players to interact with each other.

The most popular online system dedicated to computer games is ImagiNation. It has been in service for about four years and is owned by Sierra Online Systems. It is not the largest online system (it has only about 25,000 subscribers), but is dedicated solely to online gaming.

When you log on to ImagiNation, you are presented with a graphical picture that looks like a fairy tale. The picture represents all the areas available within the ImagiNation software.

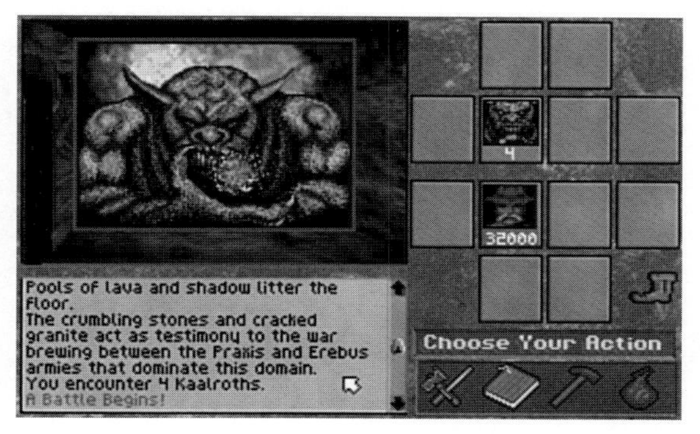

▲ The ImagiNation service.

By simply moving and clicking with the mouse you can select any location on the map, which joins you into the game in progress, starts a new game, or enables you to communicate with other online users.

One of the games available is a graphical multiplayer adventure called Shadow of Yserbius. In Shadow, users create their own graphical representation of themselves that other online players see as they enjoy the game. Shadow enables you to become a gnome, dwarf, monster, or any other alter ego. You then compete against other players in a medieval fantasy setting.

There are many other multiplayer games available from ImagiNation, including the Red Baron flight simulator and various classic board and casino games. ImagiNation costs $12.95 a month which provides you with 30 hours of connect time.

One of the most popular online services is CompuServe. With millions of users around the world, CompuServe is the giant of the online services. While CompuServe's online games may not be as graphical and lush as those offered by ImagiNation, the service offers some of the longest-running online games around. Island of Kesmai and British Legends are two such adventure games, in which multiple players compete against one another.

GEnie from General Electric is another popular online system that offers games. The pride and joy of GEnie is Air Warrior, a high resolution, 256-color multiplayer flight simulator. The software, available from Konami and Kesmai Corporation, enables you to dogfight modem-to-modem with a friend or go online and dogfight multiple players.

America Online offers a graphical role playing game called Neverwinter Nights. Written by Strategic Simulations Inc., Neverwinter Nights uses a beautiful graphical interface that enables you to see other players and objects while playing.

Multiplayer games are going to play a big part in interactive entertainment of the future. As interactive cable television becomes reality, you can bet that some of the first applications will be versions of these existing online games.

THE FUTURE OF PERSONAL COMPUTER-BASED INTERACTIVE ENTERTAINMENT

Looking ahead at the future of PC-based games is very difficult. It is highly unlikely that another new form of video game will be introduced. The basics of action, adventure, and simulations have endured through the years despite hardware and software advances.

What you can expect, however, is for PC-based entertainment to become visually richer and more engrossing. Action games will likely progress until they equal or surpass today's existing coin-operated and home game systems. Adventures will continue to grow in realism until they match and surpass the quality of television and motion pictures. Simulations will progress in the same areas. It may soon become more fun to actively play in a simulated sporting event instead of passively watching one on television.

In the area of flight simulation, it shouldn't be too long until the scenery for flight simulators is all scanned from satellites, and include both realistic colors and elevations. This may open the doors to virtual exploration, as travelers can visit places in their computers that they never explored on foot.

By the end of the decade there may be only two computing devices: one for the home and one for the office. Models could combine the personal computer, television, stereo, and telephone in one unit. This speculation, however, is controversial. For one thing, word processing and electronic mail are mainstay applications in home personal computers. Until broadcast television standards change, and higher definition televisions become available, current televisions cannot even be used for tasks as simple as word processing.

Many feel that the disk-based games will become obsolete in the near future, completely replaced by CD-ROM technology. For more information on this, see the following chapter, "Interactive Entertainment and Multimedia."

LucasArts producer Kalani Streicher looks to a future of personal computer games with more storage space, whether information comes on disk or CD-ROM. "The future holds more space for us, the developers, more space for 3-D images and animation, more music, more speech, and more sound effects," said Streicher. "Our future games such as TIE Fighter will offer advanced 3-D shading, and multiple mission paths that do not restrict the player to a single linear storyline. With newer personal computers, such as the Intel Pentium, we will be able to add much more capability to our software. Instead of rehashing older plots from movies, we are enhancing and adding to them."

One thing is certain, the costs of game development will increase. Higher production costs means that game quality will generally improve. But higher costs also means the end of the rebel garage programmer. No longer can one individual crank out a best-selling computer game at home in his spare time. Today's games cost millions of dollars to produce. They require teams of artists, composers, sound effects specialists, software engineers, game designers, and so on. Regardless of an individual developer's talent, you likely won't see any more hit single-authored games.

The future likely will bring even greater cooperation between game developers and movie studios. Game companies even now are filming software footage in conjunction with film footage. One example of this is the movie *Demolition Man*. Expect a Demolition Man game to debut soon. Even so, most developers agree that even great films do not necessarily make best-selling games. They point to the Nintendo platform, where only three of the top 100 video games are based on movies. It takes good gameplay, gorgeous graphics, and striking sound to build a bestseller.

CHAPTER SUMMARY

In conclusion, personal computers have driven the interactive entertainment market. At times, up to 60 percent of all software sold for personal computers was game software. That percentage has dropped as personal computers became more common. Nevertheless, personal computer-based games, such as Comanche and SEAL Team, continue to push the boundaries of video games.

One thing is certain, personal computers are the only IE platform that can be used to both program and play games. This fact alone should ensure that PCs will always lead the field in new advances in game design or software engineering.

While advances in personal computer-based entertainment are fascinating, the biggest step in IE during the past three years is the creation of multimedia. The next chapter will discuss what multimedia is and how it works, how a multimedia program is created, and what outstanding titles are now on the market.

4

Interactive Entertainment and Multimedia

"Multimedia, in its simplest form, can be described as the presentation of information on a computer, using sound, pictures, text, and animation."

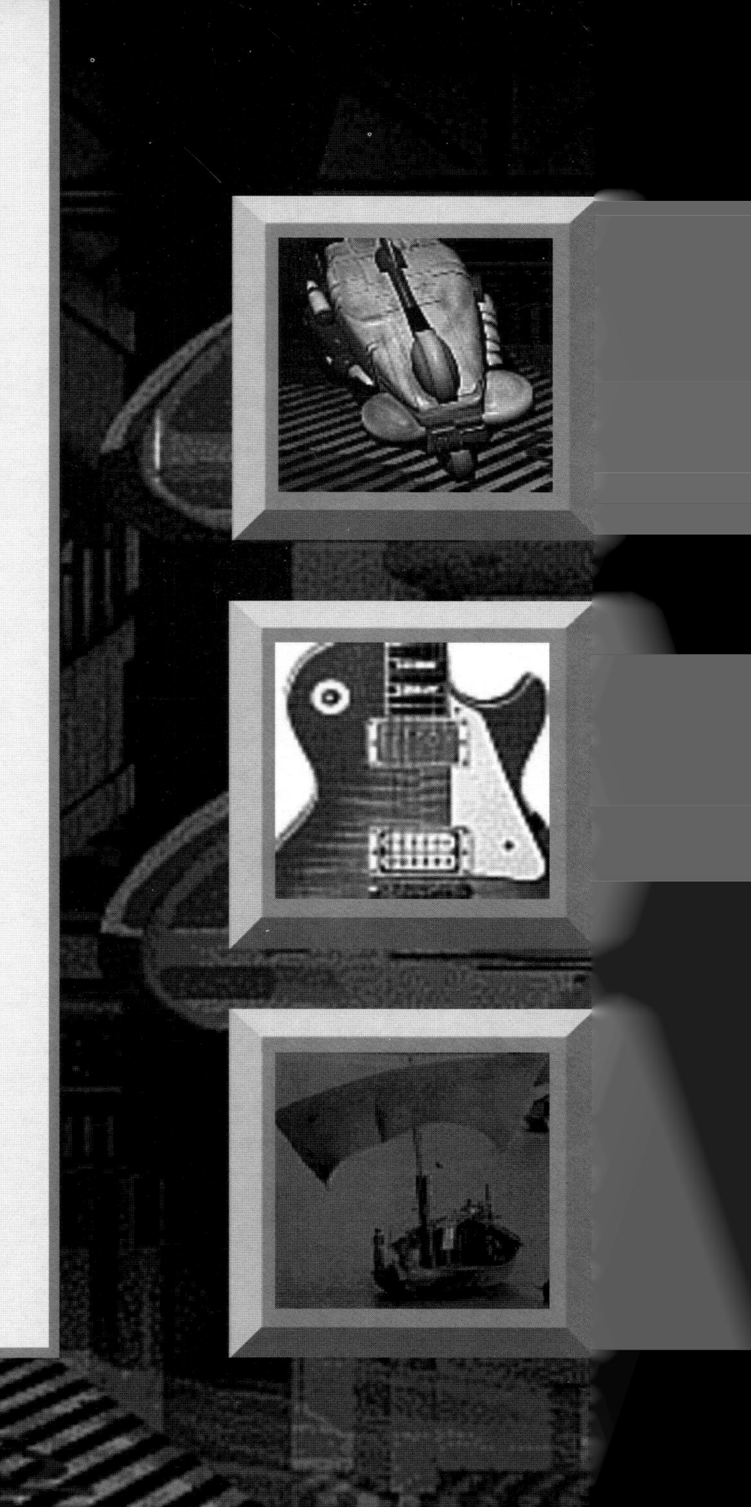

The terms *interactive entertainment* and *multimedia* are synonymous to many people; however, multimedia is simply one aspect of a wide range of interactive technologies. Furthermore, though many interactive platforms claim to be multimedia, the personal computer is the platform on which multimedia was first created. The personal computer platform is also the one that continues to carry the most multimedia titles.

When multimedia appeared on the personal computer scene a few years ago, software developers jumped at the chance to create multimedia titles. Today multimedia has become a mainstay of the personal computer industry. With its tremendous success in the personal computer market, it has expanded into other interactive platforms, such as home gaming systems and interactive cable television.

This chapter discusses what multimedia is and how the hardware of multimedia works. The chapter also presents how a multimedia title is developed, documenting step by step the production of The Journeyman Project, a new multimedia title from Presto Studios. The chapter reviews some innovative titles that are newly available, looks into the future of multimedia and where industry leaders think the technology is going.

WHAT IS MULTIMEDIA?

Multimedia, in its simplest form, can be described as the presentation of information on a computer, using sound, pictures, text, and animation. Information presented with pictures and sound is much more interesting than information in text form; however, information from pictures and sound is not always enough. For instance, though television has been around for quite some time, no video encyclopedias are on the market. That's because the video form is not practical for the depth of information presented in the text of an encyclopedia. You can't put an encyclopedia into video. What if, however, video information could be presented along with the text and pictures of the encyclopedia?

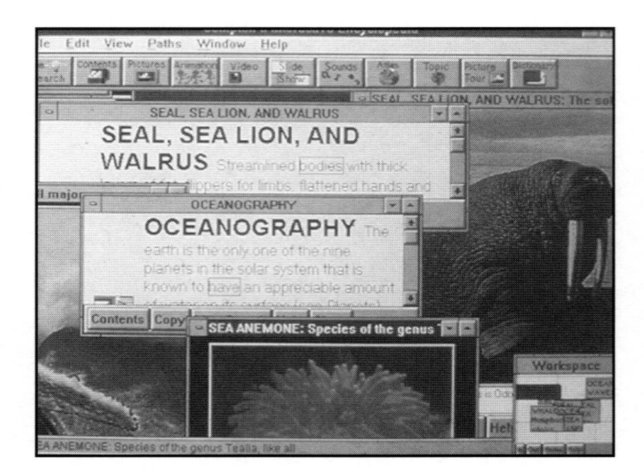

▲ A screen shot from Compton's Interactive Encyclopedia.

You know how pictures serve to enhance the information content of the traditional encyclopedia, so you can imagine how videos would enhance the information further. For example, instead of merely looking at a picture and reading a text description of how a sea anemone feeds, you could watch a video sequence of a sea anemone feeding.

While you are watching the video sequence, a helpful narrator could explain what's happening. Later, if you need to examine the facts more closely, you could read the text and review the information or watch the video sequence again. This is what multimedia is about, and, in the case of the multimedia encyclopedia, the possibilities have become reality. Multimedia has made text, graphics, and sound work together to supply you with as much information as you can absorb in the least amount of time.

The possibilities and benefits of multimedia do not, however, stop with encyclopedias. Imagine that you are trying to decide which video to rent for the evening. You could take one of the popular movie review books and flip through it, looking for a good movie. On the other hand, you could use an existing multimedia movie review program. Not only does the program contain the same information as the book, but also, when you select a movie, you can—through the multimedia program—listen to a sound clipping or even watch a short video sequence.

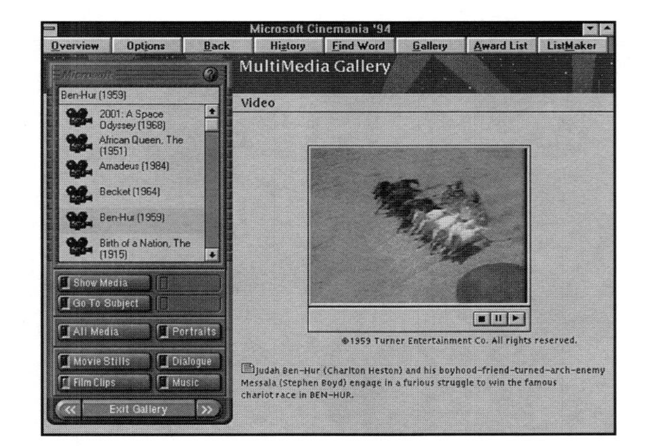

▲ This is Microsoft's Cinemania, a multimedia movie review guide that features video clips of selected movies.

Furthermore, if you love the movie but have already seen it, you can click the name of the actor or director and instantly see a list of other movies created by the same person. You can choose the producer or writer and instantly get a brief biography of that person. If you see mentioned in the biography a movie that you have never seen, you can use the mouse to click that movie and obtain its review and information screen.

These are the wonderful advantages of multimedia. Multimedia is more than a book with video sequences. It's an entirely new way to obtain information quickly and intuitively. Best of all, it's fun.

HOW MULTIMEDIA WORKS

How does multimedia work? What are the technologies behind it? Multimedia titles are available for many different platforms. The first platform, however, was the personal computer, and from the beginning, the personal computer has driven the multimedia market. Later chapters of this book discuss some of the newer multimedia platforms, such as the Philips CD-I and the 3DO. This chapter focuses on personal-computer-based multimedia.

First, not every computer has the capability to run multimedia titles. As discussed previously, moving large amounts of graphics and sound through a computer system to its display screen and speakers requires some serious computing power. Because of this, the CPU for IBM PC-compatible computers must be at least a 386-DX or higher; 386-DX-based CPUs can process 32 bits of data at once, allowing them to handle the throughput needed for multimedia. Of course, if you have a 486 or Pentium CPU, this is better. For Macintosh computers, you need to have at least a Motorola 68030 CPU or something faster, such as the 68040 or PowerPC processors. Once your personal computer has the muscle to handle multimedia, it needs the tools: graphics, sound, and storage.

Graphics

For multimedia graphics, there are three main considerations, in this order of importance: speed, color, and resolution. Nothing is worse than trying to watch a multimedia video sequence when your graphics card is so slow that the video runs in slow motion, with the screen updating only a few times per second. For this problem, high-speed graphics cards are available for both the Macintosh and IBM PC-compatible personal computers. These high-speed cards often have custom circuitry to assist the CPU in playing digital video. This helps solve the problem somewhat, but IBM PC-compatible personal computers have another handicap, the expansion bus.

The standard expansion bus for IBM PC-compatible personal computers can move only 16 bits of data at the rate of 8 megahertz (MHz). The graphics of personal computers suffer from this because the video card must plug into that slow 8 MHz expansion bus. When you consider that most CPUs for new IBM PC-compatible computers run at speeds of 33 MHz to 66 MHz, there is a tremendous data bottleneck between the CPU and the video card. It's like channeling the rush hour traffic of an eight-lane freeway through a one-lane dirt road.

To solve this problem, a consortium called the Video Electronics Standards Association (VESA) created a new PC expansion bus standard that can run at speeds up to 66 MHz with 32 bits of data. Previously, the Industry Standard Architecture (ISA) ran at only 8 MHz with 16 bits of data. This allowed for a total data throughput of only about 16 megabytes per second (16 bits × 8 MHz). Contrast that with the average local bus, which can transmit 32 bits of data at speeds up to 66 MHz; this gives you a throughput of about 264 megabytes per second (32 bits × 66 MHz), more than enough speed to handle the most demanding graphics. Apple Computer has upgraded the expansion buses of the Macintosh line over the years, and now the NuBus of the latest Macs can reach speeds of 100 megabytes per second.

With higher-speed graphics adapters, personal computers can display more colors at higher resolutions. Most multimedia titles today demand a minimum of 256 color capabilities (8 bits per pixel), and newer titles are starting to demand more color. For example, 256 colors simply are not enough to play back high-quality digitized video sequences: the colors will not appear smooth enough. This problem is eliminated by going to high color "depth," such as 16 bits per pixel (65,000 colors) or even 24 bits per pixel (16.7 million colors). Resolution likewise must be at least 640 pixels horizontal by 480 pixels vertical for most multimedia titles.

▲ An image from Mad Dog McCree. In the first color insert, notice the lack of color gradations in the 8-bit, 256-color video sequence of Mad Dog McCree. *Courtesy of American Laser Games.*

Sound

For Macintosh personal computers, sound has never been a problem. The designers have cleverly thought to include sound capabilities since the first Macs. IBM PCs, on the other hand, never had such a nicety. To compensate, hardware manufacturers such as Media Vision and Creative Labs have developed advanced stereo sound cards that can be plugged into the expansion bus of an IBM PC-compatible computer. Thus, IBM PC sound is on par with the Macintosh. Today, most sound cards available for IBM PC-compatible personal computers support multimedia titles. The only disadvantage to IBM PC sound cards is that they require external speakers. You can hook the sound card into the auxiliary input of your home stereo, or you can purchase inexpensive self-amplified speakers.

Though multimedia technology has been available for a number of years, industry standards have been lacking. Thus, for a period of time, software developers were cool on creating any multimedia titles because of the fairly small market in which to sell them. Likewise, few people wanted to invest money in some proprietary multimedia hardware for better sound or graphics without software to run on it. What helped this situation was the creation of a multimedia standard.

Standards

The Macintosh computer never had a problem with standards, because all of its multimedia hardware was created by Apple Computer and thus conformed to a set standard. On the other hand, the PC-compatibles again were left lagging. Plenty of sound boards and CD-ROM drives were available, but there were no standards, and most manufacturers created software interfaces that were proprietary.

In 1990, a number of companies involved in the PC-compatible market banded together to set a multimedia standard. They formed an organization called the Multimedia PC Marketing Council.

A multimedia personal computer (MPC) specification was developed to serve as a baseline standard for the implementation of multimedia capabilities as an extension of the PC standard. Published in 1990, this new MPC specification became accepted worldwide as the technical standard for the hardware implementation of multimedia on IBM PC-compatible computers.

The following chart compares key requirements and recommendations of the Multimedia PC Level 1 and Level 2 Specifications. Complete information about the specifications is available from the Multimedia PC Marketing Council.

	MPC Multimedia PC Level 1	MPC2 Multimedia PC Level 2
Minimum Requirements:		
RAM	2 MB	4 MB
Processor	16 Mhz 386SX	25 Mhz 486SX
Hard Drive	30 MB	160 MB
CD-ROM Drive	150 KB/sec. sustained transfer rate, maximum average seek time 1 second	300 KB/sec. sustained transfer rate, maximum average seek time 400 milliseconds, CD-ROM XA ready, multisession capable
Sound	8-bit digital sound, 8 note synthesizer, MIDI playback	16-bit digital sound, 8 note synthesizer, MI\DI playback
Video Display	640 x 480, 16 colors	640 x 480, 65,536 colors
Ports	MIDI I/O, joystick	MIDI I/O, joystick
Recommendations:		
RAM		8 MB
CD-ROM	64 KB on-board buffer	64 KB on-board buffer
Sound		CD-ROM XA audio ability, support for IMA adopted ADPCM algorithm
Video	640 x 480, 256 colors	Delivery of 1.2 megapixels/sec. given 40% of CPU bandwidth

Please note that the above requirements are *minimum* system requirements and not a recommendation by the Multimedia PC Marketing Council for a particular system configuration.

▲ The MPC standards for Level 1 and Level 2 compatibility.

To assist end-users in purchasing MPC-compatible hardware and software, an MPC trademark was created and licensed to more than 100 hardware and software developers. Currently 95 software developers are licensed, with some 230 multimedia titles available for IBM PC-compatible computers. Buyers can now look for this trade mark and be assured that the product they are buying will be compatible with any existing multimedia products.

In May 1993, the Multimedia PC Marketing Council specified yet another standard to further enhance multimedia capabilities. This new standard is known as MPC Level 2, with the previous standard now being called MPC Level 1. Notice that the Council has upped the ante for the CD-ROM data transfer rate, sound quality, CPU speed, and color depth, and the Council now specifies a pixels-per-second throughput for video adapters.

Storage

For storage, a hallmark of multimedia is its use of CD-ROM technology. As mentioned in Chapter 1, a compact disc (CD) can be used to store not only digital stereo sound, but also computer data. When used to store data, a CD can hold about 650 megabytes. This CD space gets used up rapidly when you start storing digital video and stereo sound, but it is this massive amount of storage that allows multimedia titles to have such rich content. The next sections explain how CDs are created and also their advantages and disadvantages.

CD-ROM TECHNOLOGY

The small, 4 1/2-inch piece of polycarbonate called the *compact disc* (CD) not only has revolutionized the music industry, but also is bringing the computer industry into the 21st century. When CDs hit the computer scene, people were stunned. On a CD, you had the ability to store about 500 times more data than you could store on a high-density floppy diskette. What was more amazing was that manufacturing CDs cost no more money than manufacturing floppy disks.

For distributing software, here was a new medium on which storage space was virtually unlimited. The use of CDs to store reference data started immediately. For example, entire phone books were slapped on a single CD. Ford Motor Company started publishing a CD containing an inventory of more than 300,000 parts and shipping it each month to their approximately 2,400 dealers. It wasn't long after companies like World Library started packing classical books onto a CD. At last count, the World Library CD has some 1750 books on a single CD, including the Bible and other religious works, all the works of Shakespeare, all the Sherlock Holmes books by Sir Arthur Conan Doyle, and three John Steinbeck novels, to name a few.

Despite their tremendous advantages, CDs have one drawback. CDs are manufactured with the data already on them. You can't write information to a standard CD as you can to some other type of magnetic disk. This fact is what gave data-storing CDs the name Read Only Memory or ROM. Today we call CDs that store data CD-ROMs.

The Introduction of CD-ROM Technology

The North American Philips Corporation and Sony jointly developed the original digital audio (DA) CDs in 1982. This first standard for storing digitized audio on a CD was called the Red Book standard. Audio CDs were introduced in the U.S. in 1983, and in 1986—only three years later—the sales of audio CDs and disc players exceeded the sales of LPs and turntables. Though the CD-DA was capable of storing vast amounts of computer data, there were no standards to follow.

The International Standards Organization (ISO) played a major role in setting the standard for storing data on CDs. An ISO committee met in an area near Lake Tahoe, Nevada, in 1985 to create this new standard. When the committee members finished, they decided to call it the High Sierra standard (named after the resort they stayed in). Later, ISO tidied up the High Sierra standard, creating the ISO 9660 standard that became known as the Yellow Book standard. Many hardware manufacturers started making personal-computer CD drives to read these 9660-format CDs. These drives were available in both internal and external models, and a controller card was required to attach them to the expansion bus of the personal computer. Often, the controller used for the hard drive and floppy disk drives also could be used to control the CD-ROM drives.

In 1988, Sony, Philips, and Microsoft created a new enhanced CD-ROM standard called *CD-ROM eXtended Architecture* (CD-ROM XA). This new standard—also called the Green Book standard—allowed for the narration of text by supporting audio and video to be played simultaneously from the CD, accomplished by interleaving the computer data with digital audio. The standard allowed for up to 9 1/2 hours of AM-quality stereo or up to 19 hours of monophonic audio. A standard CD-ROM player can read a CD-ROM XA, but only with an XA compatible controller card.

Recently, other standards have emerged, such as the CD-WO (ISO 9669). WO stands for "write once." With CD-WOs, you can write the data once, but after that these CDs can not be erased or rewritten because they become normal CD-ROMs. Recordable CD-ROMs—called CD-Rs or the Orange Book standard—are similar to CD-WOs except that, instead having to write an entire CD in only one session, with the new CD-R recorders you can write a recordable CD-ROM in multiple sessions. That means you can add a little data to a blank CD-R, then later go back and continue filling the CD-R. You can repeatedly stop and fill until the CD-R is completely filled. However, once it is completely filled data cannot be erased or rewritten.

Kodak's Photo CD depends heavily on this "multisession" capability. When you take your 35 mm film to the photo developer, you can ask the photo developer to scan the pictures onto a Photo CD. Then, as you take more pictures later, you can have the pictures added later to the same Photo CD.

How Compact Disc Technology Works

Compact discs store data in a way different from that of magnetic hard and floppy disks. Whereas data on a magnetic disk is stored on concentric tracks, data on a CD-ROM is stored with one long spiraling track, similar to the way songs are laid down on records.

CD drives use constant linear velocity (CLV), which means the optical sensor of the CD drive always reads information from anywhere on the CD at a constant speed. To achieve this constant speed, the CD must change rotation speeds, depending on how far the read head is from the center of the disc. If the sensor is near the outside edge of the disc, the drive spins slower. As the sensor gets closer to the center of the disc, the drive speeds up.

CLV is an archaism that recent CD standards have carried on from the original Red Book specification. The early audio CDs required that the disc play at a constant speed in order for the optical sensor to pick up correctly all the microscopic pits and lands. If the CD used constant angular velocity (CAV), data at the outside edge of the disc would be read three times as fast as data on the inside edge of the disc.

As mentioned in Chapter 1, the CD-ROM stores information by the use of microscopic *pits* and *lands*. When a laser beam is focused on the CD, either the beam hits a pit, in which case the beam is absorbed, or it hits a land, in which case the beam is reflected back to where it came from.

With a prism, the reflected laser beam is deflected to a light-sensing diode. This diode converts the flashes of light to electrical impulses. These impulses, when timed with the current rotation of the disc, are translated into binary data. This data can be used in the same way as any other computer data.

How a Compact Disc Is Created

The process of creating a compact disc is not a simple one. Typically, to start with, the data to be stored on a CD-ROM must be in the correct format, known as the "image file." The data used to create a CD-ROM is usually submitted on computer backup tapes. These tapes are read and converted to an image file. From the image file, a proof disc can be created on a CD-R machine. This proof disc can be used to test the CD-ROM before production. Next, any digital audio must be premastered—that is, digitized into standard Red Book audio digital files—and added to the image file.

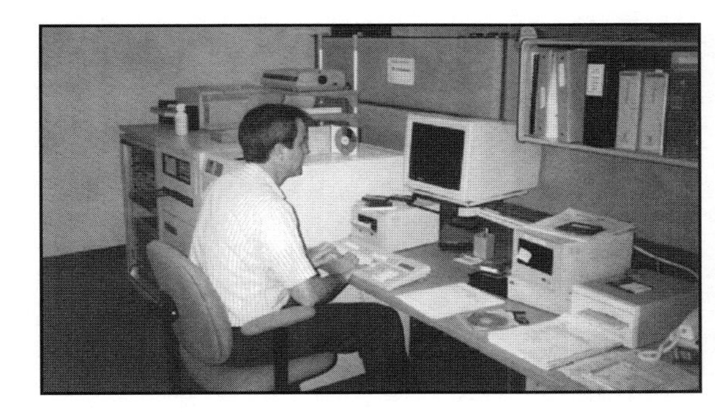

▲ Here a CD proof disc is produced.

Once the data is in the correct format, a mastering unit called a laser burn recorder (LBR) is used to expose the data to a glass master. The glass master is a disc made of glass and larger than the average CD, about 8 inches in diameter. This glass master is coated with a material called photoresist. The LBR uses a laser beam to expose the photoresist on the glass master with the correct pattern of lands and pits, based on the proof disc. From this point on, the production environment of the CD manufacturer must be absolutely clean. These "clean rooms" are hundreds of times cleaner than hospital surgical units.

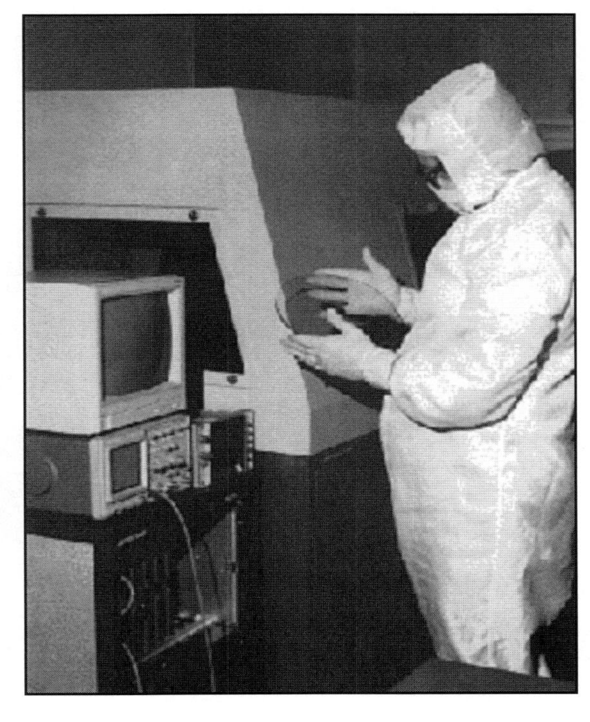

▲ The glass master produced on a laser burn recorder.

After being exposed in the LBR, the disc is placed in a liquid developer that etches the unexposed areas of photoresist on the glass master. What remains is a pattern of pits in the surface of the glass master. After the developing, you have a complete glass master, with the data in the form of lands and pits in the remaining photoresist material.

Photos on this page courtesy of Disk Manufacturing, Inc.

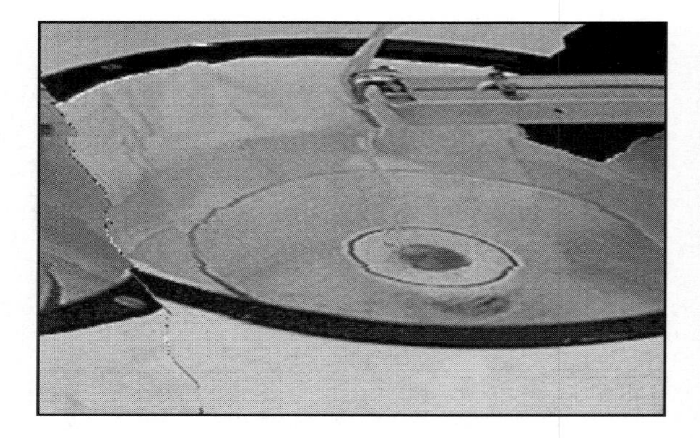

▲ Developing the photoresist on the glass master.

A thin silver coating is then applied to the glass master by sputter application. This silver coating makes the surface of the glass master conductive. Each pit is about one micron in size, so the slightest particle of dust could easily corrupt the pattern of pits and interfere with the accurate recording of the data.

The next step is electroplating. The glass master is mounted on a holder and lowered into an electroplating bath. This plates the surface with layers of nickel. The nickel build-up is known as the father part. This father part is separated from the glass master, washed, examined for defects, and crimped to size. The father part is a mirror image of the glass master; it has a bump for every pit in the glass master.

Photos on these pages courtesy of Disk Manufacturing, Inc.

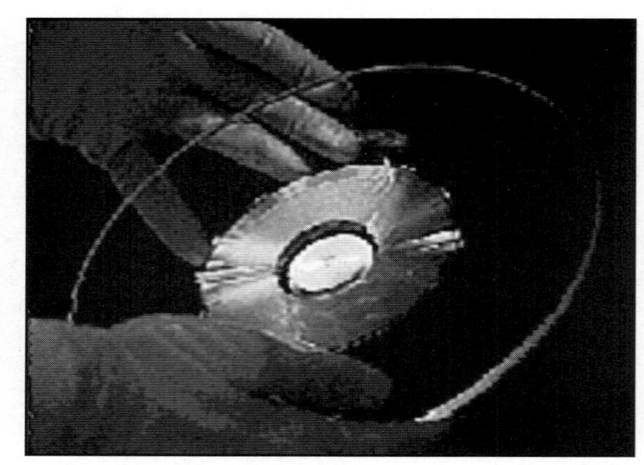

▲ A silver coating has been applied to the glass master.

▲ After electroplating, the father part (top) is separated from the glass master (bottom).

▲ The stamper is mounted onto a molding machine.

A stamper is produced from the father part. The stamper is what comes into contact with the molten polycarbonate to form the image area on a CD. The stamper is trimmed to size and mounted on a molding machine. A holding ring holds the stamper by its outer edge on the molding machine.

Clear discs of molten polycarbonate are then pressed against this stamper in the molding machine. The polycarbonate hardens, with the exact pattern of pits from the stamper hardened into one of side of the disc. These clear discs are stacked on a spindle for transport to the metalizing phase.

▲ Molded polycarbonate is stacked on a spindle after being pressed with the stamper.

Metalizing is the process of applying a thin coat of aluminum over the side of the disc containing the pits. This thin reflective coat of aluminum is what allows lasers to reflect off the surface of the disc and read the patterns of pits and lands. Next, the discs receive a lacquer treatment. This keeps the natural oils of human skin from damaging the sensitive aluminum coating on the surface of the CD.

Right after receiving the lacquer treatment, the discs are spun at high RPM. This causes the lacquer to form a smooth, even coat over the CD. The discs are allowed to dry. Labels and graphics are then added to the back side of the CD surface, using traditional graphics screening techniques. A robotic assembly line packages the finished CDs into jewel boxes (those clear plastic boxes that CDs come in). The assembly line also inserts front pamphlets and back inlays.

▲ The polycarbonate disc is metalized with a layer of thin aluminum.

As you can see, the manufacturing of CD-ROMs is not a simple process. Once the stamper has been created, however, the materials used in producing the discs are fairly inexpensive. In 1993, the costs for producing CD-ROMs were as follows. The premastering step—where a CD-R drive is used to create a "one-off" or "proof disc"—costs about $250. The entire mastering process costs around $1,300. For a quantity of 5,000 discs, the manufacturing cost is about $2.31 per disc. The total cost for a 5,000 disc run would be, therefore, about $11,550.

▲ The CDs are spun at high speeds to smooth the lacquer coating.

▲ A robotic assembly line assembles the CD jewel boxes and inserts the finished CDs.

The Advantages and Disadvantages of CD-ROMs

The single greatest advantage of the CD-ROM is its storage capacity. The more than 650 megabyte capacity is incredible, considering the low production cost of the discs. The low production cost is itself an advantage to CD-ROM technology. Another advantage is the low cost of CD-ROM drives. You can find drives in the $200 to $500 range, depending on interface and access speed. This is a great deal, considering the storage capacity.

The main problem with CD-ROM technology is the access speed. Because most CD standards have been hindered by the inherited Red Book standard, they are all slow, as much as 10 times slower than hard disk drives. Some manufacturers are beginning to overcome this limitation with new CD-ROM drives called "double speed" drives. These double speed drives increase speed for reading data and drop back down to normal speeds for playing music.

Another limitation is that once pressed, the CD-ROM data is unchangeable. Though this might be an advantage for archiving information such as medical records, it is not an advantage for personal computers. Most PC users expect read/write capabilities on storage devices.

Images on these pages are courtesy of Presto Studios.

▲ The Journeyman Project.

Despite its shortcomings, CD-ROM technology still is an incredible advance for the personal computer and consumer electronics industry. The awesome storage capabilities of compact discs have opened up completely new levels of interactive entertainment. One such example is The Journeyman Project by Presto Studios.

THE CREATION OF A MULTIMEDIA TITLE, THE JOURNEYMAN PROJECT OF PRESTO STUDIOS

The Journeyman Project is an interactive movie that takes place in the future year 2318. In this year, technology has become very advanced. Biotechnology-based implants have become as common as sunglasses. Implants can be inserted in the human brain to give a person enhanced abilities, such as spatial mapping and massive data storage; even the handicapped can be assisted thus with motion algorithms. Gravity neutralizing technology has brought about progress in space exploration and has enabled the creation of floating cities. Perhaps the most amazing technological advancement is the time machine called Pegasus.

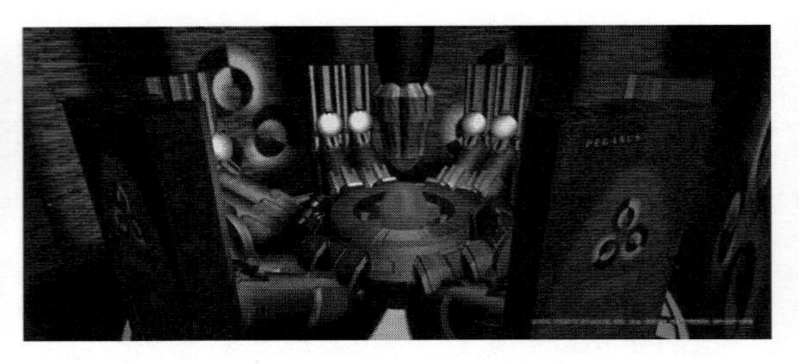

▲ The Pegasus Time Machine.

Considering the delicate nature of time, the citizens of this future world have realized how dangerous a time machine could be in the wrong hands. After all, the slightest change in history could have unimaginable repercussions in the far future. The government has acted quickly to halt any further development or research in time travel. The government has also created the Temporal Protectorate, an elite guard squad whose main assignment is to protect and safeguard history. This is where you fit into the story line; you are a guardian of time in the ranks of the Temporal Protectorate.

The background of this future world continues thus: When the time machine was being developed (about the year 2185), humans had their first contact with alien life. A cargo pilot landing a shuttle at the Morimoto Mars Colony spotted an alien spacecraft. Soon after the sighting, the alien spacecraft sped off at light speed toward the outer edge of the solar system. The scanners of the landing bay confirmed and documented the encounter, and the existence of intelligent alien life forms was thus proved.

Still, nothing of consequence occurred until the year 2308, when Earth was formally contacted by an alien race known as the Cyrollians. During a visit to Earth, the aliens invited the Earth to join an alliance called the Symbioty of Peaceful Beings. This alliance would foster the sharing of culture and knowledge. After making this proposal, the Cyrollians left, giving humans 10 years to deliberate the proposal, after which another delegation would land and present a more formal invitation.

It is now the year 2318. While the Earth has prepared for the peaceful arrival of the Cyrollian delegates, a disillusioned scientist has developed a bad case of xenophobia toward the extraterrestrials. Unfortunately, the disillusioned scientist happens to be a person who worked on time travel techniques.

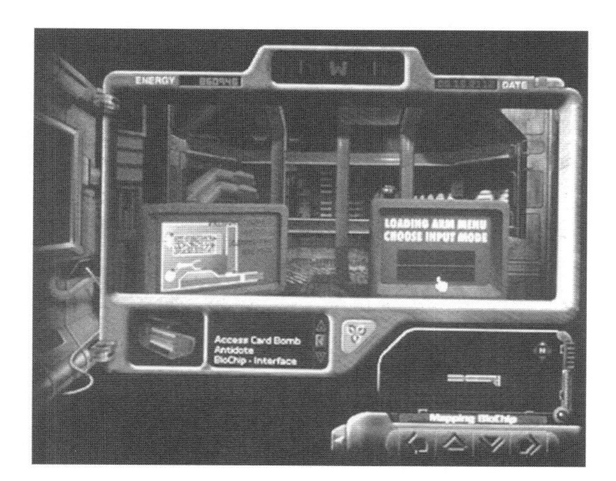

▲ With the BioTech Interface you can interact with the world.

You "awaken" in your apartment. You hear the radio report of the crowds waiting to see the alien delegation. Interacting with the world via your neuroprosthesis implant, you make your way to work at the Temporal Security Annex. While you are on duty at the Annex, a rip in the fabric of time is detected. Somewhere in the past, an event was changed. To avoid the effects of the temporal rip before it reaches the present time, you use the Pegasus time transporter to jump back in time 200 million years, thus escaping the reality-altering effects of the rip.

It's at 200 million years that a disc containing all known history is placed each day. Two such discs are created every day at the Temporal Security Annex. One is stored in the Annex, and the other is taken back in time 200 million years. By collecting the disc and bringing it back to the future to compare with the disc in the Annex, you can detect any discrepancies. This allows you, the Temporal Security Agent, to determine exactly where and when the rip in time occurred.

Traveling back and forth through time, you begin to uncover the xenophobic scientist's plan to prevent any peace between the Earth and the Cyrollians. Feeling that he must save the Earth from a wicked plot, he creates a series of artificially intelligent robots to travel back in time and alter history to deter aliens from coming to earth; to make earth a less palatable target for the aliens. Your mission is to stop these robots at all cost.

From the underground tunnels of the Mars colony to the bottom of the Atlantic ocean, your journey leads you throughout a rich and varied landscape. From dogfights in outer space to chases through the canyons of Mars, you must pursue and stop these robots.

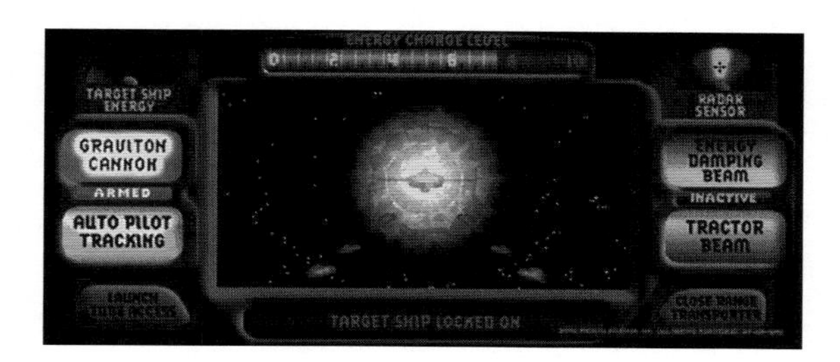

▲ A dogfight in space.

▲ A flight through the canyons of Mars.

Throughout the game, there are multiple solutions to the problems and puzzles that you will encounter. You are credited more points for finding non-violent solutions, but these are much more difficult than the easy, violent solutions you come across. The realism of the game is enhanced by the more than 30 minutes of digital video sequences shot with professional actors.

The Journeyman Project is available for both PC and Macintosh platforms. On the Macintosh side, you need a 256-color-capable Mac II, 8 megabytes of RAM, a CD-ROM drive, and System 6.0.7 or later. For the PC, you need a 33 MHz 386-DX or faster CPU, 8 megabytes of RAM, Windows 3.1 with a 640×480×256 color video driver, a sound card, and a CD-ROM drive.

THE CREATION OF JOURNEYMAN

The initial concepts for The Journeyman Project were formed by Dave Flanagan and Michel Kripalani. They envisioned a sci-fi space/time travel adventure, but nothing came of their idea until the 1991 Macworld Exposition in San Francisco. There they saw a product called Spaceship Warlock, a graphical adventure that made use of some 3-D animation and rendering. At the time, Kripalani was in the middle of another project, called Verbum Interactive, for *Verbum* magazine (Verbum Interactive is a CD-ROM–based multimedia title that uses video, graphics, audio, and text to present information to the user). Kripalani and Flanagan knew that it was time to act on their space/time adventure idea. Kripalani left Moov Design, the company he was with then, and founded Presto Studios in order to create The Journeyman Project. Kripalani was joined by computer animator and programmer Farshid Almassizadeh, 3-D artist Jose Albanil, programmer Greg Uhler, musician Geno Andrews, and art director Jack Davis. Davis really made a difference in the final look and design of the game. Together they created the compelling new multimedia title called The Journeyman Project.

The first step in producing The Journeyman Project was the script. The script began as a rough story concept that, after multiple revisions, led to a final script and game play summary. The summer of 1992 involved a lot of brainstorming for the Presto Studios group. Though they came up with many good ideas, not all the ideas were included in the final game. Much of the game design was done first hand, while the environments were being created. For instance, if a particular puzzle or problem was too hard to solve, a voice hint or sign was added to assist the player. After the script and play summary were complete, it was time for artist Phil Saunders to step in and start designing. Saunders began by drawing rough conceptual sketches.

▲ Detailed conceptual drawings, showing multiple views.

Initially, the design called for 10 or 12 different "time rips" to be repaired. That was scaled back to four and then to three as the project progressed. Some early ideas were rejected. For example, one early mini-game idea was that when you first arrived at the undersea NORAD complex, you would face a hallway with 3-D fireballs you must dodge to gain entrance. The balls would bounce off the walls in 3-D space, and they made for a very interesting challenge. It was discovered, however, that on slower personal computers the game was too slow to be any fun. Finally, the mini-game was removed.

Images on these pages are courtesy of Presto Studios.

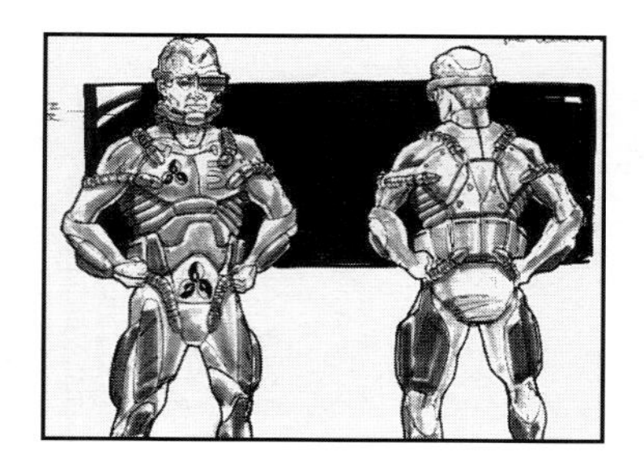

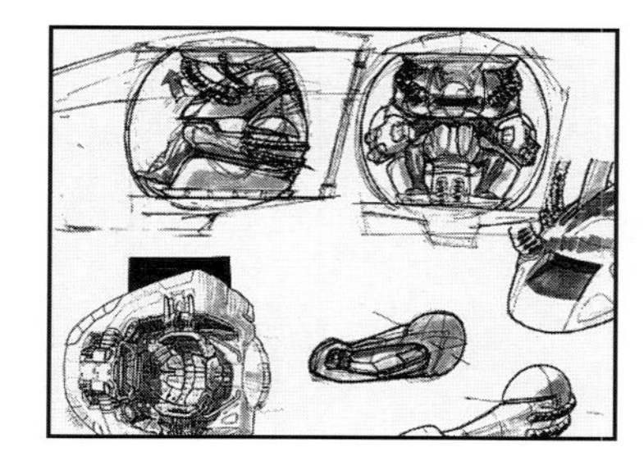

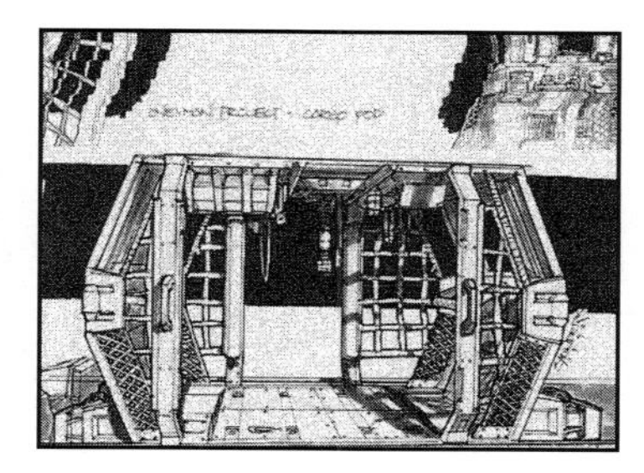

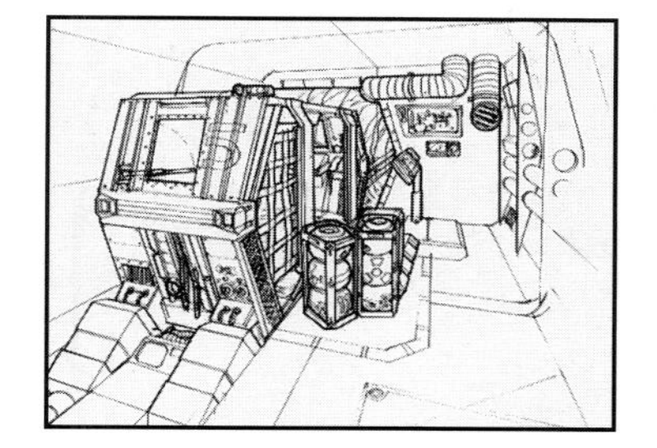

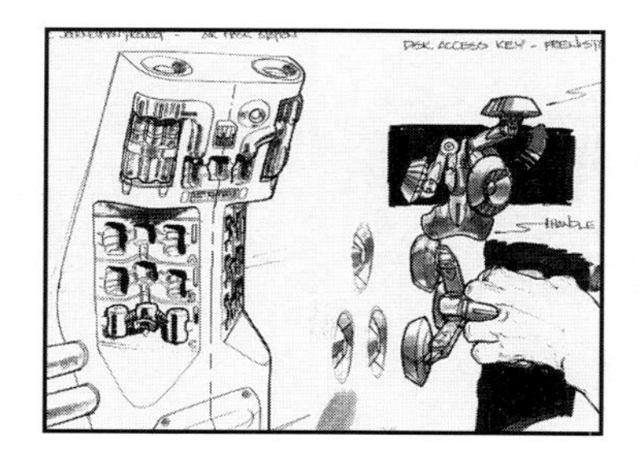

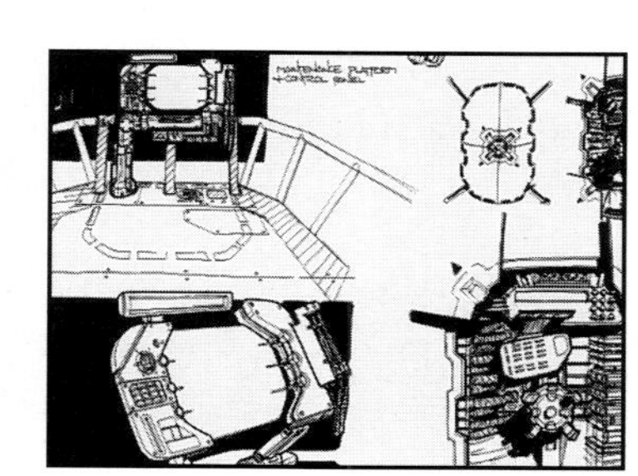

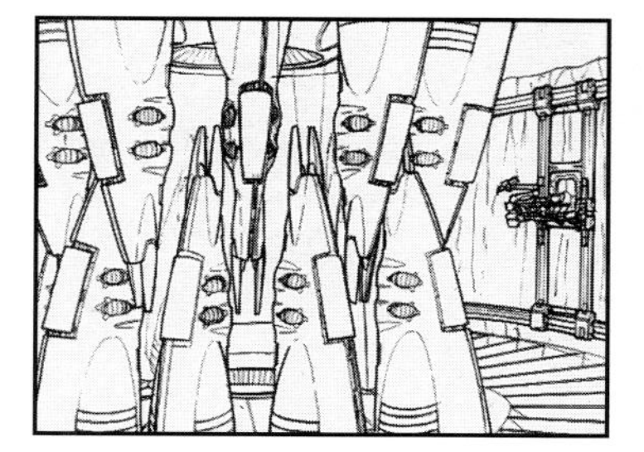

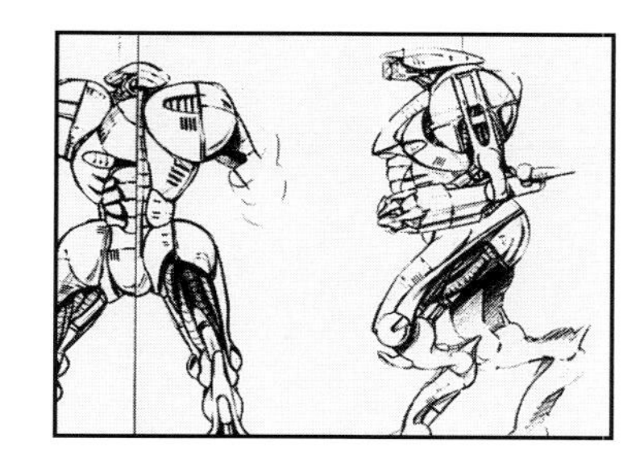

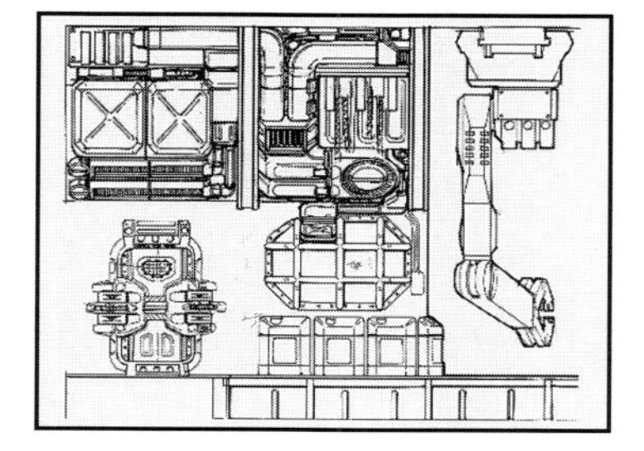

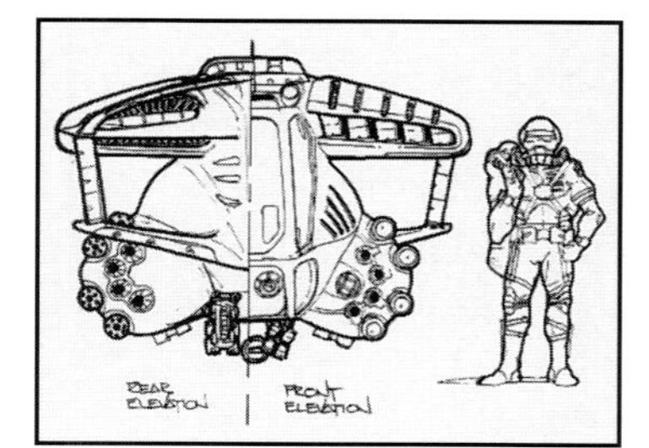

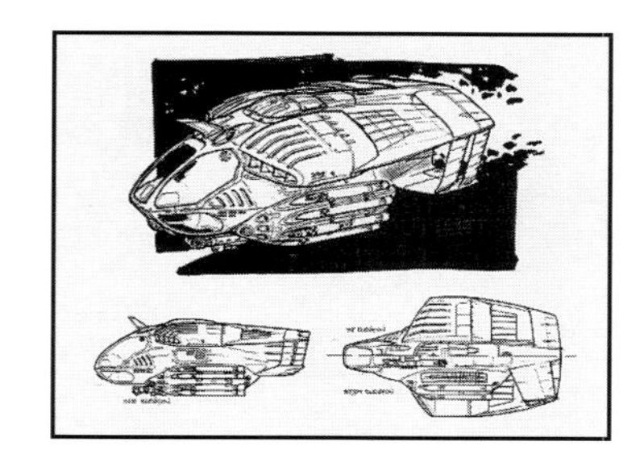

▲ Some early conceptual sketches for The Journeyman Project.

As the early drawings took shape, more detailed drawings were produced. These drawings sometimes showed multiple views of the same object. These drawings would help later, when the 3-D artist would need to create the objects in 3-D space. Starting in the summer of 1992, the artist at Presto Studios began full-scale production, using some of the most advanced graphics tools available for the Macintosh.

Artistic Design

Jose Albanil was in charge of modeling all the objects and scenery with three-dimensional computer graphics. Albanil had studied art at the University of California, Santa Cruz, but building the 3-D models for Journeyman proved to be a monstrous task. A single room in Journeyman could require 100 to 200 separate 3-D objects. 3-D modeling requires that you specify how the surfaces of an object look in three-dimensional space. This is complicated when you must use 2-D input (the mouse) to describe 3-D data to a computer and when you must view the results on a 2-D display (the computer monitor). Using various programs—such as Swivel 3D, Form Z, and Macromind Three-D—Albanil created about 95 percent of all the 3-D models used in Journeyman. Each 3-D model Albanil created contained anywhere from 50 to 100,000 individual 3-D surfaces (often called *polygons*).

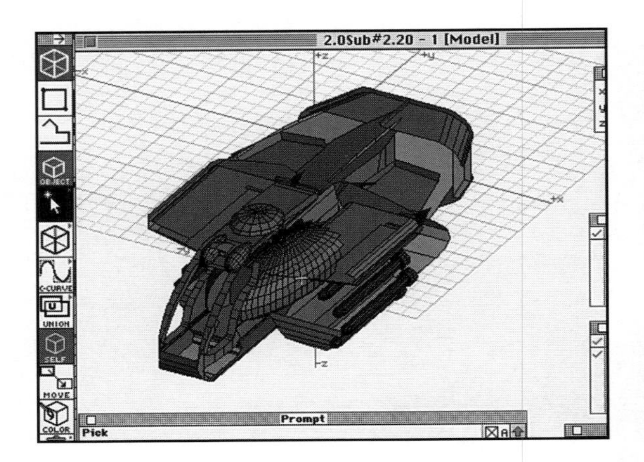

▲ The creation of a spaceship in a 3-D modeling program.

▲ A 3-D scene with flat colors assigned to the objects.

In general, after a 3-D model is created, the computer needs to know what the surfaces of the model should look like. The artist can specify a particular color for the computer to use to shade the surfaces; but that leaves the models looking fairly flat because the only color variation across the 3-D surfaces will be that caused by the light sources that are set on the object.

Images on these pages are courtesy of Presto Studios.

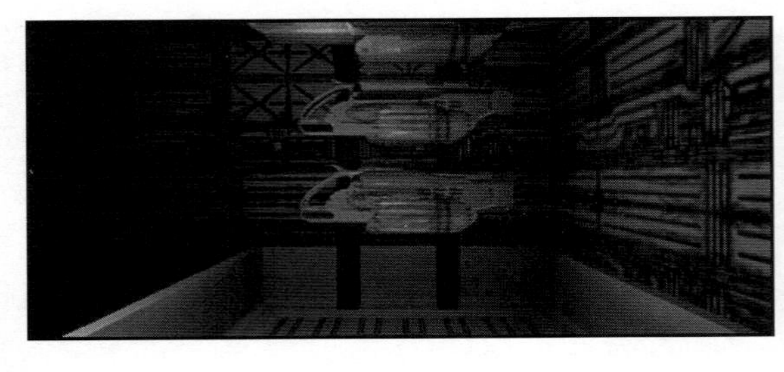

A way to make any 3-D model more realistic and appealing is to use texture maps. Texture maps are simply scanned or hand-drawn images. These images are applied to the surfaces of 3-D models in a process known as *texture mapping*. This results in more realistic images.

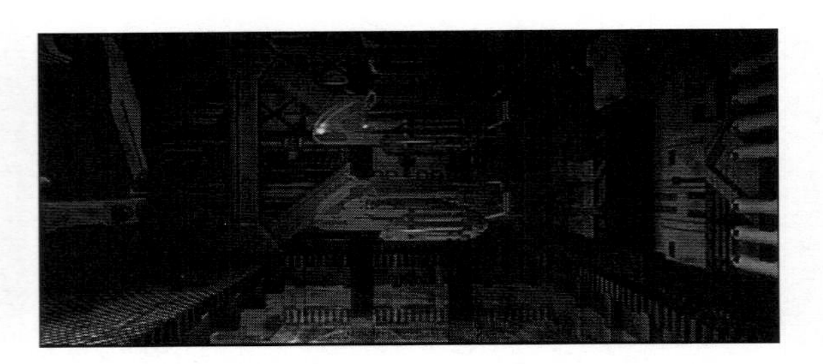

▲ The 3-D scene after textures have been applied to the surfaces.

The texture mapping for Journeyman was done mostly by Michel Kripalani, and the final images were rendered on Macintoshes with software called Electric Image. One scene or one room in Journeyman could easily contain 50 to 100 texture maps. Two other types of surface mapping were also used: bump mapping and transparency mapping.

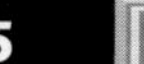

In *bump mapping*, the computer takes a 2-D image and applies the image to the surface of a 3-D model. Instead of simply mapping the colors from the image to the surfaces of the model, the colors from the image make 3-D dents or bumps in the model. The lighter areas of the image make bumps, and the darker areas of the image make dents. Using a bump map with light and dark variations, you can make the surface of a 3-D object look as if it has texture or roughness.

Similarly, a *transparency map* uses an image to specify the areas of the 3-D model that are transparent. The white areas of the image allow the object to remain opaque, and the black areas of the image make the object transparent. In this way, it becomes fairly simple to model complex 3-D objects like a chain link fence. Instead of modeling every fence link in 3-D, the modeler can simply create a solid wall. Then with a black-and-white drawing of a chain link fence applied to that solid wall as a transparency map, the black areas of the bump map make holes in the 3-D wall, creating the illusion of a fence.

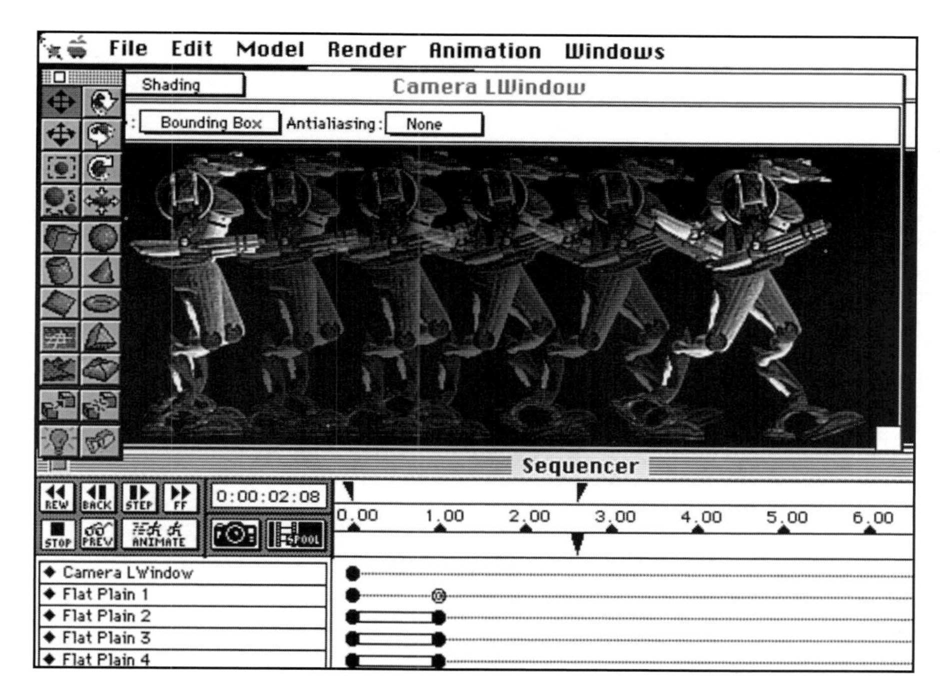

▲ The animation for a robot's walk is being created.

In Journeyman, after modeling and texture mapping were complete, it was time to bring the models to life. Farshid Almassizadeh, the lead animator at Presto Studios, took the models and scripted animations for them, using many of the same packages used in the modeling process.

Animation involves telling the computer where and when to move the objects in 3-D space. It also involves moving the camera and sometimes even lights. The animator could be compared to the director in a motion picture. He directs the action, camera angles, and pace of a scene.

After the animation is set up, the next step is rendering. In rendering, the computer takes the mathematical descriptions of the 3-D models and scenes and then, using advanced mathematics, computes an image of what that scene would look like. The more complex a scene (the more textures and objects it contains), the longer it will take to render. Bump and transparency maps, shadows, and reflections give each scene added realism, but they add to the rendering time. For Journeyman, the average time to render the most complex scenes turned out to be between 15 and 20 minutes per frame. Almassizadeh used a program called Infini-D to spread the task of rendering across a network to multiple computers. This allowed each computer to work on its own frame, so instead of one frame taking fifteen minutes, five frames could be rendered with five different machines on the network during that same fifteen minute period.

In this area, the artist had a real challenge in animating the robots in the game. Many little technical problems kept plaguing the artist. For one, the robots were created and animated in Swivel 3D, but when the robots were being rendered in Electric Image, the animation information did not translate from the Swivel 3D program. This meant that the artist had to render the robots in Infini-D. Even this presented some problems, however, in that the texture maps did not come out looking as good as the Presto group wanted. Finally the group did manage to finish the robot animation, and the results were very good, as you can see from the screen shots.

Jack Davis, the art director and lead artist at Presto Studios, used the image editing program Adobe Photoshop to touch up all the finished renderings. He added rust to make computer-rendered metal look more realistic. This turned out to be a daunting task, considering that the entire project had more than 2,100 individual frames.

Toward the end of November and the beginning of December in 1992, all the artwork was finished. During the last hectic weeks of production, the team worked between 90 and 100 hours a week. According to the 3-D artist for the production, Eric Hook, "We would wake up and start work at 9:00 a.m., work throughout the day, and into the night until about 2:00 in the morning, go to sleep for a couple of hours, and repeat the same process the next day."

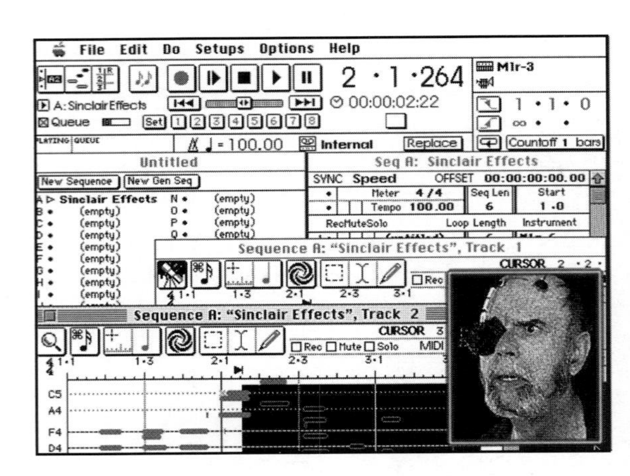

▲ Sound effects software running on a Mac II computer.

Music and Sound Effects

To accompany the photo-realistic artwork, Geno Andrews—a musician/sound effect specialist who prefers the title of audio sculptor—created a stunning sound track and sound effects. Pictures of the environment were passed to Andrews for music and sound effects, and Andrews used advanced music MIDI software on a Mac II computer. Unfortunately, the beautiful CD-quality stereo sound that Andrews composed for Journeyman did not get into the game that way. For playback speed considerations, the quality of the digitized sound was reduced from the CD-quality 44 KHz sampling down to 22 KHz sampling. The stereo was even converted to mono.

Color Gallery TWO

2

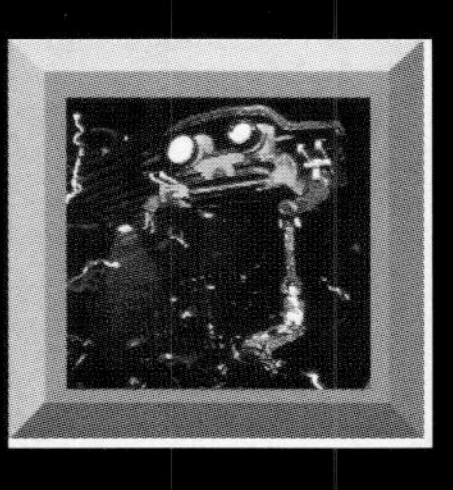

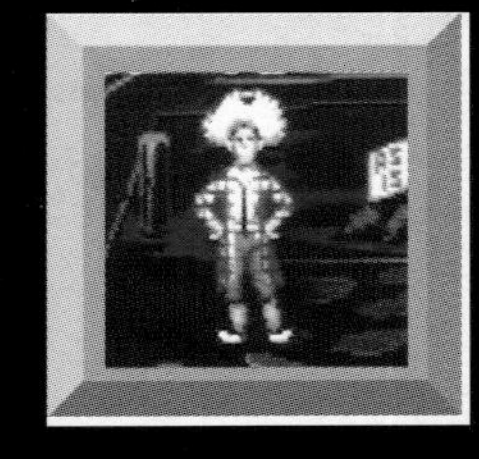

PUSH

This game, Civilization from MicroProse Software, is a good example of a successful PC-based game that was ported over to the Macintosh platform. Likewise, successful Macintosh games such as Spaceship Warlock and The Journeyman Project are quickly ported over to the PC platform to take advantage of its large market. On the whole, practically every interactive entertainment title available for the Macintosh is available for PC-based systems. Even Apple has recognized this trend and supports PC development with its Mac-based multimedia authoring software. Forever Growing Garden is a good example of this—it was originally developed on the Macs. Once development was finished, run-time versions were created for both Macs and PCs, allowing the creators to take advantage of both markets.

Courtesy of MicroProse Software.

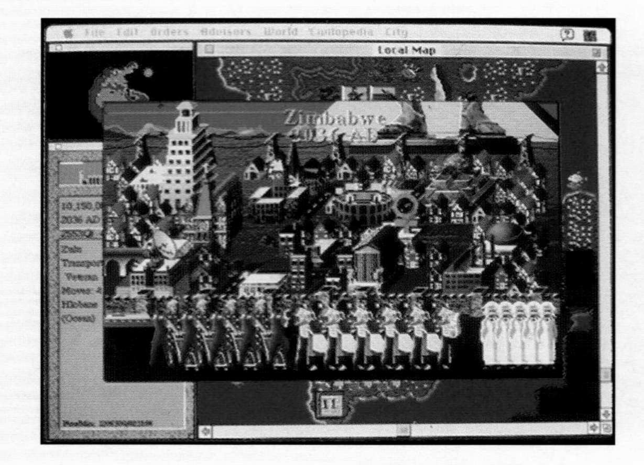

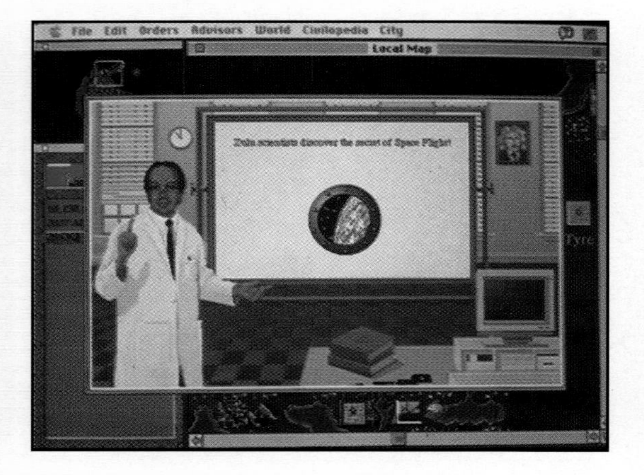

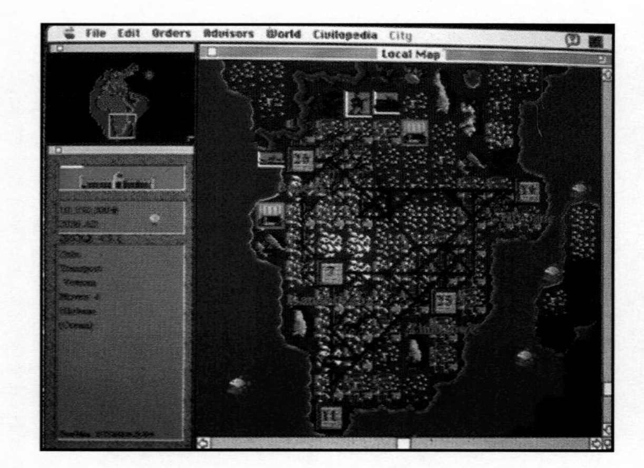

Little Mermaid and Beauty and the Beast Fairy Tale Factory from Hi-Tech Expressions allows small children to create pictures by arranging pre-drawn images on the screen. The resulting picture can then be saved to disk or even printed. The user interface is designed for very young children. It only involves pressing the space bar and moving the mouse. These pictures were created by 6-year-old Anastasia Nikoulina from Moscow.

In 1993, LucasArts introduced its first space combat simulator, X-Wing. Based on the "Star Wars" universe, X-Wing depicts the Rebel Alliance's effort to destroy the evil Empire. As a rookie pilot for the Alliance, you fly a variety of starfighters, such as the X-Wing, Y-Wing, and A-Wing, each with its own strengths and weaknesses. Using these fighters, you fly various missions against the Empire following a storyline that intertwines with the original motion pictures.

Courtesy of LucasArts Entertainment Company.

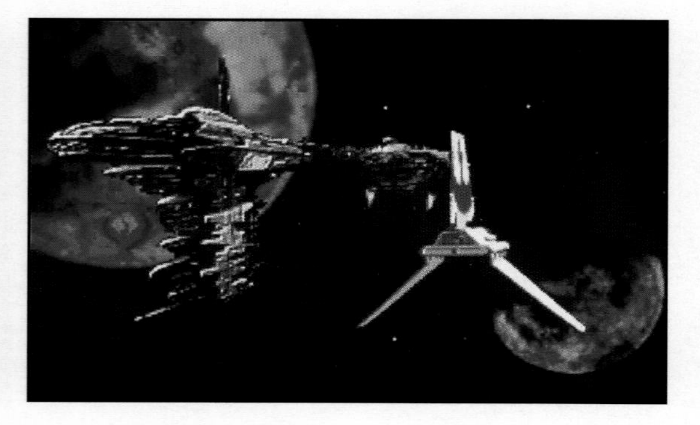

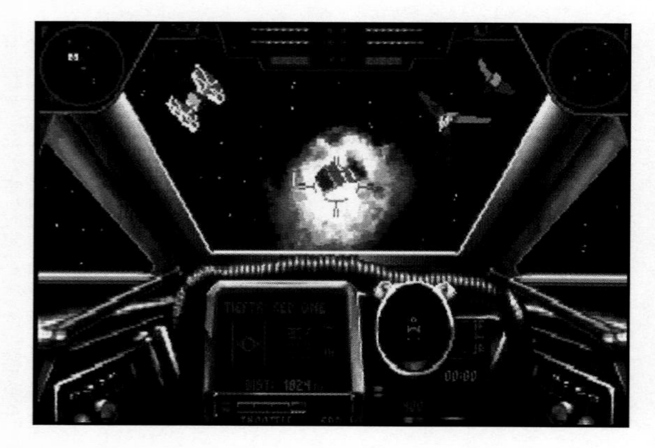

Following closely upon the success of X-Wing were two add-on expansion disks. For practically any type of simulation game, a tremendous investment is required for the initial development. The details do not require such extensive efforts on the part of the programmers. By the time players truly master the controls, they have often finished all the missions. Expansion disks solve these problems by allowing the developers to sell more products based on an existing simulation engine. All that is required is the creation of a new missions database. For the game players, expansion disks mean new and exciting missions in which to invest their hard-earned skills.

The Imperial Pursuit Tour of Duty expansion disk offers 15 new missions along with new cinematic sequences, digital sound effects, and a new sound track. Also available is the B-Wing Tour of Duty expansion disk, which offers 20 new missions and includes a new starfighter, the B-Wing, in which to fly missions.

If you are curious about what an interactive movie would be like, purchase Rebel Assault. With the original sound track performed by the London Symphony Orchestra, 3-D computer-rendered special effects, and digitized sequences straight from the motion pictures, it's the closest thing to a true interactive movie on the market today. Rebel Assault, a 3-D arcade game from LucasArts, is its first title created specifically for CD-ROM. The 3-D animation and rendering sets a new standard that is unsurpassed by any other video game across any platform. If Rebel Assault is any fore-gleam of LucasArts' future CD-ROM titles, we have a lot to look forward to.

Courtesy of LucasArts Entertainment Company.

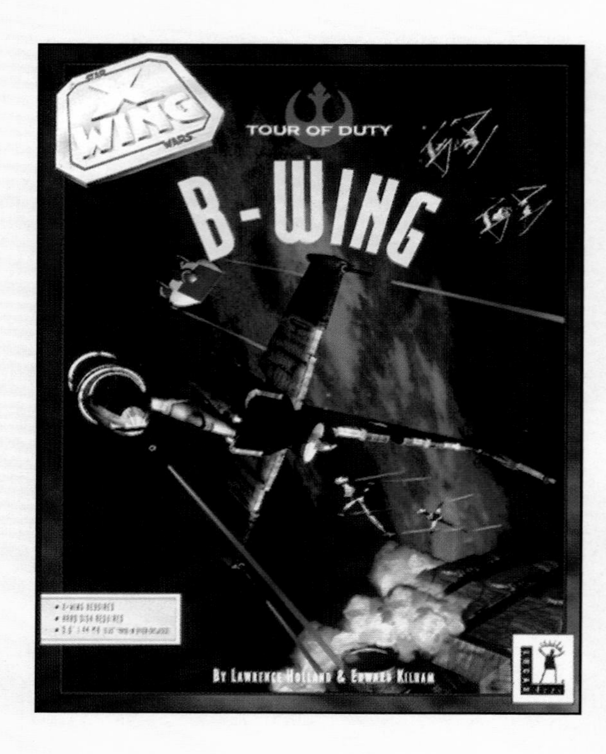

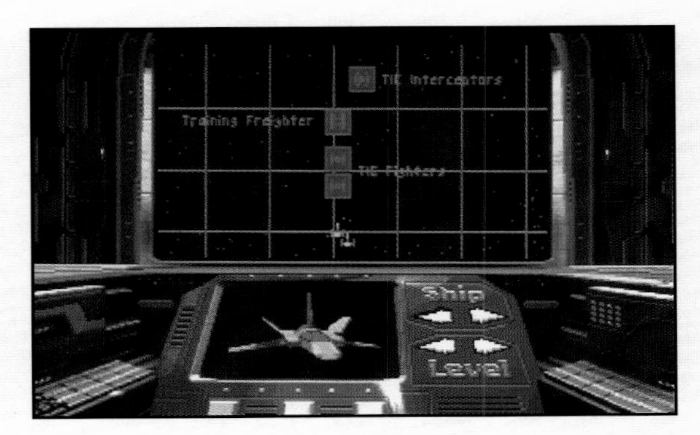

For those who are tired of blasting hapless Imperial fighters and want a change of pace, LucasArts has released TIE Fighter, a sequel to X-Wing. For the first time in any LucasArts game you get to play the role of an Imperial pilot fighting for the side of the Empire. TIE Fighter includes advanced 3-D graphics and more cut scenes than X-Wing along with an original storyline. Tying into the Star Wars universe, a character from Timothy Zahn's best-selling Star Wars novels, Admiral Thrawn, is included in the storyline. TIE Fighter will be available in the Spring of 1994.

Media Vision has released a unique educational title for multimedia personal computers called Forever Growing Garden. Garden allows children to experience the fun of planting flower or vegetable gardens, even if they live in a city. It simulates all aspects of growing gardens, from choosing the seeds, trapping gophers, planting, watering, harvesting, and even selling the vegetables or flowers that they grow.

The plant's growth is simulated by the computer at any speed you choose, from real-time growth to one real second equals one simulated day. As time passes, Garden features animations of each individual plant's growth. It also monitors the actual time you are cultivating your garden, so you can turn off your computer, come back a week later and find that your plants have grown during that week.

The Secret of Monkey Island was created by Ron Gilbert to have the flavor of a sarcastic rendering of the Disneyland ride Pirates of the Caribbean. Gilbert tried to make Secret as nonlinear as possible for a graphic adventure game. It took two and a half years to design the game. From the Piranha Poodles guarding the governor's mansion, to the advertising pirate in the saloon trying to sell you another LucasArts game, there are plenty of gags, and Gilbert has created his own following with his unique sense of humor.

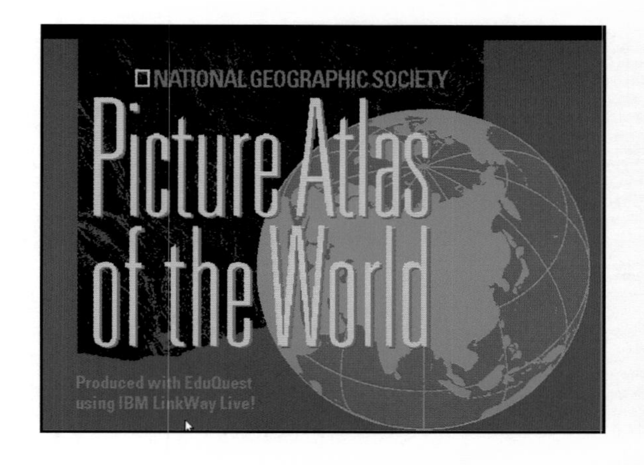

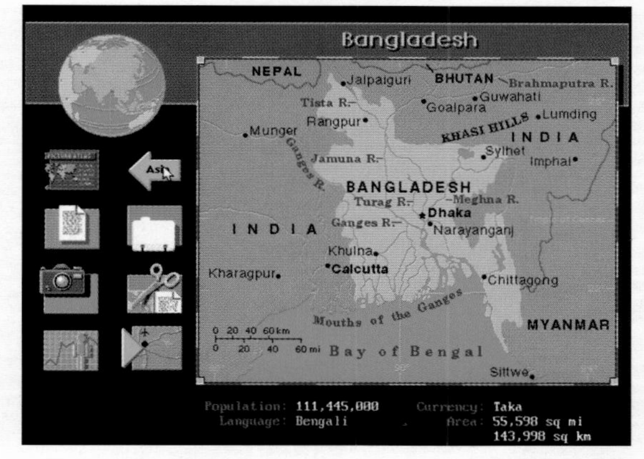

National Geographic Society's Picture Atlas of the World is a good example of putting existing content to practical use. It features more than 800 interactive maps indexed to take you directly to any part of the world you wish to view. Each area has political, physical, and topographic maps. As you examine each continent, you will run across some of the 50 video clips, 1,200 full-screen photographs, audio segments with music, and over 100 different spoken languages from around the world. Vital statistics are included with each country, such as population, industries, religions, income, climate, and so forth. Narrations explain map projections, time zones, and other aspects of the Atlas. Even the glossary is interactive, allowing you to jump directly to a particular item. As more owners of information start to take advantage of multimedia, we should see more outstanding titles like this one.

Courtesy of National Geographic Society.

Iron Helix, created by Drew Pictures and published by Spectrum Holobyte, uses the latest 3-D computer animation techniques to bring to life a 3-D Sci-Fi universe. Iron Helix is one of the few new programs that has a complete 3-D world pre-rendered by 3-D computer artists. 3-D animation gives the illusion that you are really traveling through an environment. These types of 3-D rendered games require extremely large amounts of storage, so they are based on CD-ROMs but CD-ROM players have slow access speed. You can't play back full-screen computer animation smoothly from a CD-ROM, so most of these types of games (The Journeyman Project, The Seventh Guest, Spaceship Warlock, Critical Path, and Quantum Gate) simply restrict the viewing area to a small window on the screen. This reduces the amount of data that comes off the CD-ROM and allows it to play back faster. As CD-ROM access speeds increase, we can expect full-screen 3-D rendered games.

Released in 1993, Pirates! Gold from MicroProse Software is perhaps the longest-awaited sequel in video game history. The original version (Pirates!) was released in the mid-1980s when 16-color EGA displays were the latest and greatest technology. The latest version lives up to the legend of the original version, with historically accurate adventures in high seas of the 17th century. Not only is the game entertaining, but it is very educational. You learn volumes of information about the 17th century from first-hand experience in dealing with fellow pirates, sailing your galleon though storms and rough seas, sword fighting, crew management, and navigating the reefs of the Caribbean. This is an excellent example of how video games can be educational and entertaining at the same time.

A popular subject in multimedia educational software is that of language instruction. The Berlitz Think & Talk series from Hyperglot Software teaches you foreign languages by pronouncing the words correctly for you and then recording your efforts through your multimedia systems microphone. The software plays your voice back for comparison with the correct pronunciation. These types of interactive drills in comprehension and grammar help sharpen your skills and provide an interactive way to learn a new language.

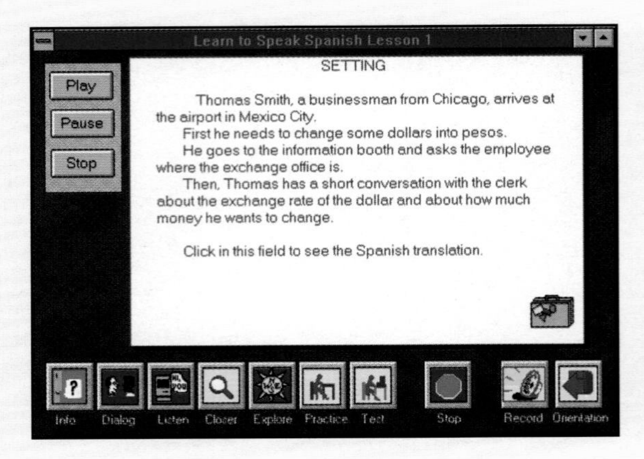

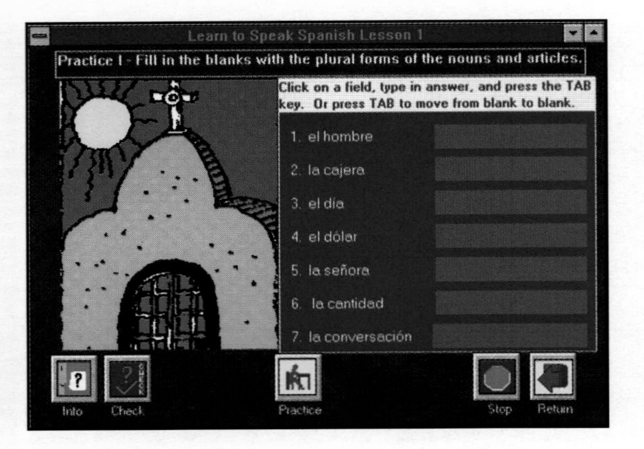

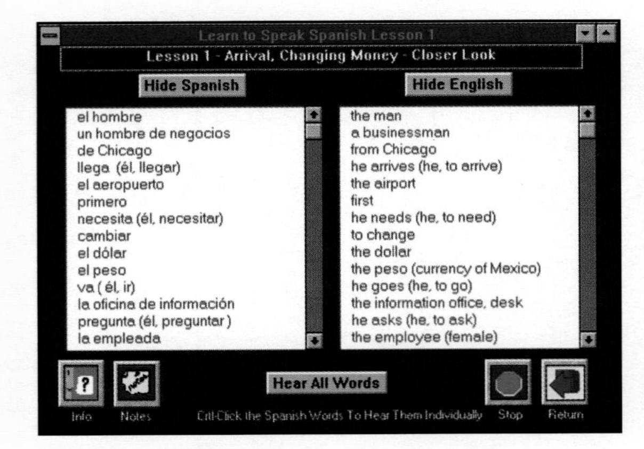

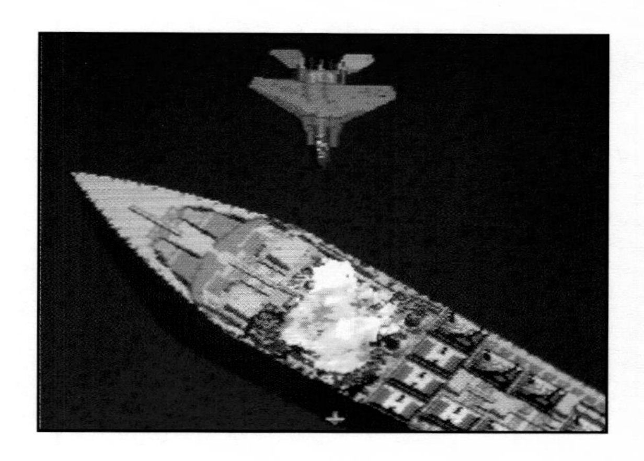

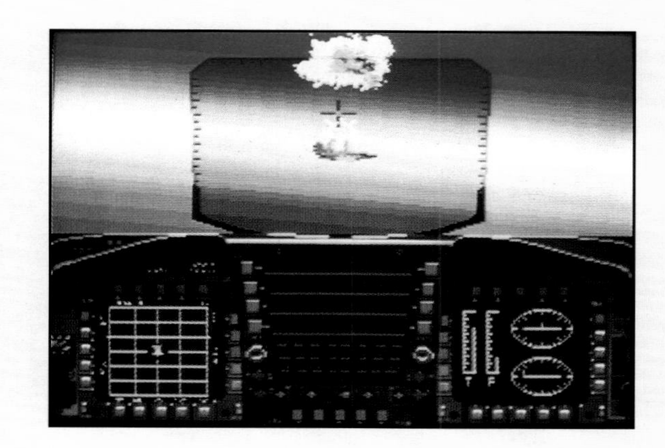

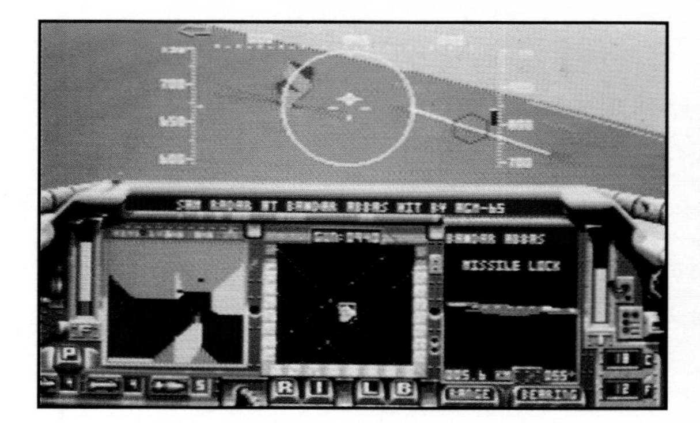

MicroProse has long held the reputation of having some of the best air combat flight simulators on the personal computer market. Today it has branched out into the home gaming system market as have many other PC game developers. Here are two examples of PC games that MicroProse ported over to the Nintendo SNES and Sega Genesis home gaming systems. Super Strike Eagle for the SNES offers true 3-D flight with 256 colors and digitized stereo sound. F-15 Strike Eagle for the Genesis likewise offers true 3-D flight and realistic enemy dogfights.

Courtesy of MicroProse.

LHX Attack Chopper is another example of a successful game that has been ported from the personal computer to other platforms such as the Sega Genesis. You can fly the LHX or AH-64 Apache helicopter on over 30 missions in Europe, the Middle East and Southeast Asia.

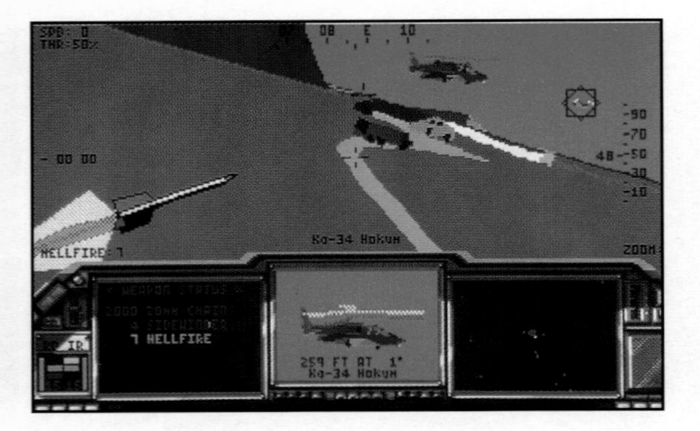

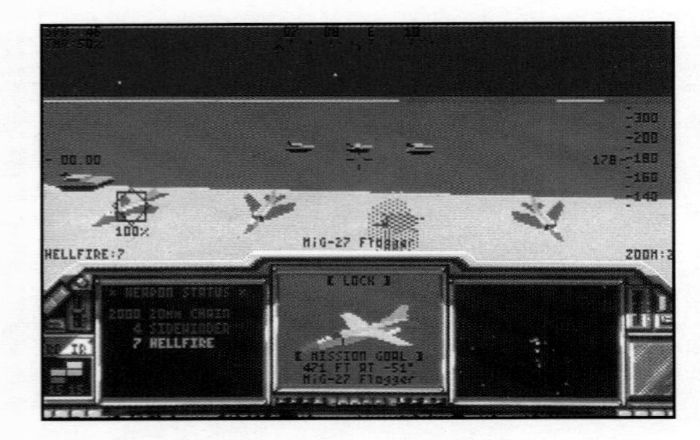

Andrews was useful in another unexpected way: when Presto was looking for an actor to play the role of the evil scientist, Sinclar, Andrews recommended Graham Jarvis. Jarvis had been a professional actor for a long time and had even co-starred in *Star Trek: The Next Generation* (the "Unification" episode). Presto was able to obtain Jarvis for the role, and the video sequences of him were very good. Another role was that of the Computer Generated Personality; this was played by Kristi Pado.

▲ The user interface of Journeyman helps limit the viewing area to a small portion of the screen. *Courtesy of Presto Studios.*

Programming

As artwork was completed, it was passed to the lead programmer, Greg Uhler. Using an off-the-shelf multimedia authoring tool called Macromind Director, Uhler started integrating the computer animation sequences into an interactive interface. Kripalani and Almassizadeh assisted in the programming. Flanagan did the programming for all the mini-games throughout Journeyman, such as the space dogfight sequence.

Because there are serious limitations to the data throughput of most CD-ROM drives, Kripalani decided to create a user interface that offered a small viewing window through which all animations would play. Though Spaceship Warlock used half of the screen, Journeyman therefore used a third (even so, because of the large, beautiful user interface, most people think Journeyman has a larger viewing area than Warlock). The creation of the interface alone took many months, according to Kripalani.

Uhler had to program all the interaction in Director, using the Lingo language. The only problem with Director is that when a program of instructions is created for the computer to follow, the program stays in the English-based Lingo language. Director does not compile (or convert) the Lingo language into the machine language of ones and zeros. For Journeyman, this means that every time you run Journeyman, the computer must convert the instructions into machine language while you are playing. This means you get a slower response than you would get from a compiled game.

Another problem the programmers had was the difficulty of Journeyman. It truly pushed the Macromind Director system to its full potential by using detailed interactive interfaces, on-screen mapping, scoring throughout the game, and even a countdown timer for each time zone. Some features had to be left out because of the capabilities of personal computers. For instance, the compass originally spun smoothly as the player turned around; but this slowed the game down too much, and the spinning compass was eventually replaced by a compass that simply snapped to each new direction. This problem of creating exciting programming that would run smoothly on most systems was a constant issue.

On the positive side, Director makes it very easy to combine and sequence various still images, animations, sound effects, and music. All together, with programming, artwork and composition, Journeyman took more than 15,000 man-hours to produce.

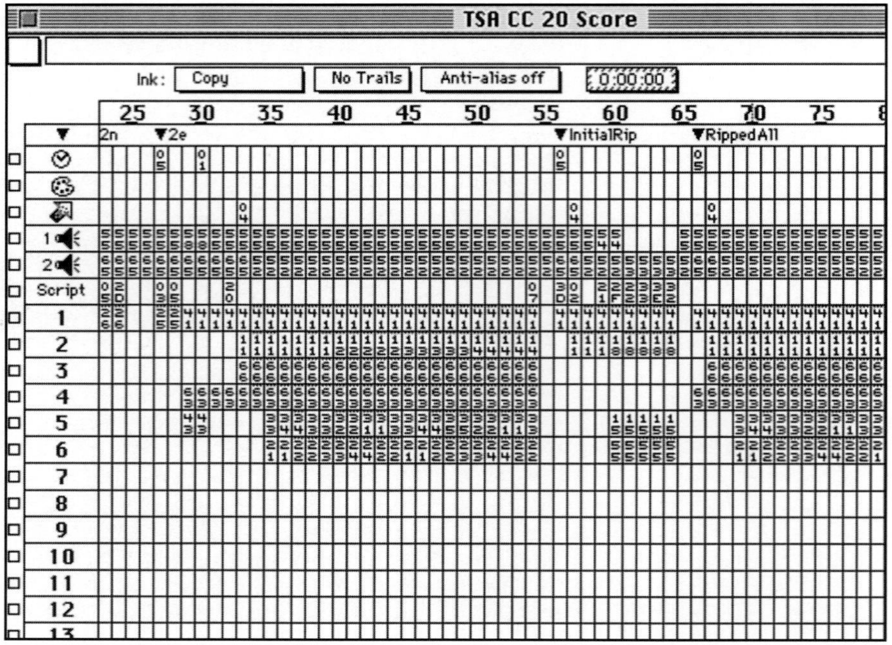

▲ The sequencing sheet of Director allows images, animation, and audio to be sequenced together.

When Journeyman was finished, most of the testing took place in-house at Presto Studios. Presto did try to release early copies to outside testers, but as Eric Hook of the marketing department states, "The outside testers did not work out as well as we had planned. Many of the bugs they reported didn't exist, while others slipped through and were never reported. Our best results came from bringing family and friends in-house and watching over their shoulder as they played the game. This not only helped us track down any bugs, but it also assisted us in learning where the game was too hard. In those areas, we were able to add sound hints to guide the player along."

Product Release

Initially, Presto Studios wanted to publish the game through a large, well-known publisher. Oddly enough, however, Presto could not find any publisher interested enough to take on this CD-ROM 3-D adventure. Finally, the Presto group decided to publish it themselves. For the first disc pressing, they ran only about 5,000 discs. As soon as The Journeyman Project hit the market, it was a success.

This created a lot of footwork and phone work for Eric Hook. Hook had initially worked on the project as a 3-D artist, and later became the marketing department. Hook contacted members of the press, as many as he could, who might be able to review or promote Journeyman. The Presto Group worked all the Macintosh trade shows and made connections with distributors, for example, EduCorp and MacConnection. Since then, Presto has turned over the publication of Journeyman to Quadra Interactive. Quadra now publishes both the PC and the Mac versions of Journeyman, and has dropped the retail price from $99.95 to $79.95.

Bandai, a large Japanese toy manufacturer, made a deal with Presto to create a Japanese version of Journeyman. Bandai flew Uhler and Andrews to Japan to help with the conversion, and the finished Japanese version was released at a Japanese Macintosh Exposition.

▲ The ad slick used to promote The Journeyman Project. *Courtesy of Presto Studios.*

Consumer Reaction

Consumer reaction to Journeyman has been extremely positive. Not only are players sending in their registration cards, but they are also sending full-page letters proclaiming their undying devotion to Presto Studios and promising to purchase Presto's next product, sight unseen. The few negative responses have been mainly about the speed issue. This is the current limitation of CD-ROM technology. Speed was expected to be a problem from the earliest design meetings.

The Future of The Journeyman Project

Production and enhancements are still being made to The Journeyman Project. Currently, Presto Studios is on version 1.2. In the latest version, you can "walk around" without waiting for the current sound bite to finish. Work has already started on Journeyman II. According to Hook, "It's not just going to be another day at work for you, the Temporal Protectorate. It is still based on characters from Journeyman I, but under a completely new story line. The interface will change, and we are attempting to increase the motion and size of our video window."

CURRENT MULTIMEDIA TITLES

Multimedia titles currently on the market can be divided into five categories: action, adventure, simulation, personal enrichment, and research. The action, adventure, and simulation categories are similar to those in personal-computer-based interactive entertainment, as discussed in the previous chapter. Multimedia titles in these categories, however, are much more rich in artwork, animation, and sound because of the increased storage of the CD-ROM.

The personal enrichment category is one of the main focuses of multimedia. Geared more toward adults, personal enrichment software provides users an entertaining education and offers users a chance to explore at their own pace. The research category, however, takes in the bulk of CD-ROM titles. Most research titles are text based, but this is changing with the creation of products such as Microsoft Encarta and Compton's Multimedia Encyclopedia, both of which are multimedia encyclopedias with graphics, text, audio, animation, and even digital video. This category appeals to all ages, from the youngest to the oldest computer user.

The following sections present each of the multimedia categories and examine some of the more popular titles and their enhanced features.

Action

In the action category, there are several popular titles, including Mad Dog McCree from American Laser Games and Rebel Assault from LucasArts. Both titles are true action games that were specifically created for the CD-ROM platform.

Mad Dog McCree began in 1990 as a coin-operated arcade game based on a laser disc. It became so popular that in 1991 it was one of the top-rated video arcade games in the world. In the fall of 1991, the Amusement Machine Operators Association (AMOA) nominated Mad Dog for the Most Innovative New Technology Award. Since then, Mad Dog has been translated into five languages and is distributed worldwide. Its new technology involved an entire western movie in which the player takes the role of hero. While you watch, the live action takes place in front of you, played on a television monitor from a laser disc. You hold a "gun" and, by pointing it at the screen, you can pick-off the bad guys when they jump out to shoot you or any of your friends.

▲ Here you weren't able to save your friend from being shot. *Courtesy of American Laser Games*.

▲ You have to draw fast to take out this gunslinger in the saloon. *Courtesy of American Laser Games*.

The arcade coin-operated version works with a branching laser disc player. The multimedia version, however, was created by digitizing all the video sequences and compressing them onto a CD-ROM. Naturally, this cuts down the quality of the live video, but the excitement stays with the game as you interact with live video footage. Using the mouse as your gun, you pick off sharp shooters and engage in saloon shoot-outs. You can even engage in showdown draws in which you have to keep your gun down until the other person draws.

▲ Keep your eye on his trigger finger before drawing. *Courtesy of American Laser Games*.

Rebel Assault by LucasArts is another action title on the cutting edge of multimedia entertainment. Rebel Assault is the first "CD-ROM only" title for LucasArts; that is, Rebel Assault was created specifically for the CD-ROM platform. In Rebel Assault, you take on the role of a fledgling Rebel pilot in the continuing sci-fi *Star Wars* saga of rebellion against the Empire.

During game play, you go through about 15 levels of arcade action. From dog fighting with TIE Fighters in space, to taking on Imperial Walkers in a Snowspeeder, to taking on Storm Troopers with only your blaster in defense, each mission becomes more difficult as you progress through the game.

You will also encounter TIE fighters while cruising the valleys of the planet Tatoonie. As a grand climax to the missions, you fly an X-Wing fighter through the Death Star trench to re-live the heroic destruction of the Death Star from the original movie.

All of the graphics in Rebel Assault were created with 3D Studio, a 3-D rendering and animation program from AutoDesk. Game levels are tied together by skillful use of film clips taken directly from the Star Wars movies. A CD-quality sound track features the original music score of John Williams performed by the London Symphony Orchestra. Before the creation of Rebel Assault, the personal computer multimedia market was not considered a strong one for arcade/action style games. Rebel Assault has changed that.

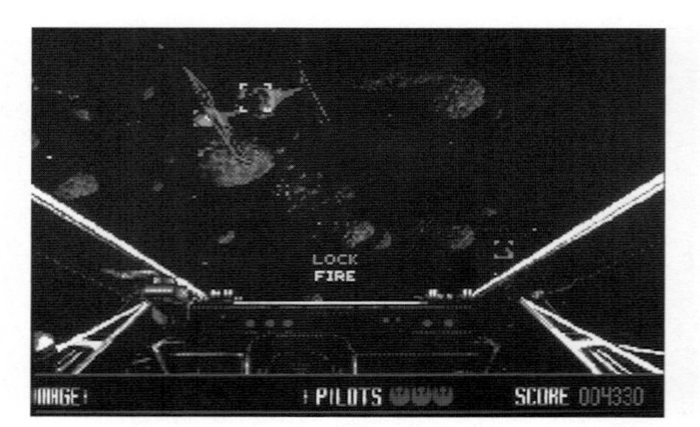

▲ Dog fighting TIE fighters in Rebel Assault by LucasArts.

▲ Quick reflexes are required to take out the Imperial storm troopers.

▲ Attacking an Imperial Walker in a Snowspeeder.

▲ Chasing a TIE fighter through the canyons of Tatoonie. *Screen shots courtesy of LucasArts.*

▲ A 3-D rendered scene from The Labyrinth of Time.

▲ The action icons can be seen at the bottom of the screen.

Adventure

One of the more popular categories for multimedia and CD-ROM is graphic adventures. Graphic adventures lend themselves well to CD-ROM technology, because most require large storage requirements to store pictures of every possible location you can go to in the game. With this added space, some developers are trying to push the edge of the envelope by incorporating smooth, 3-D rendered animation as you move from room to room or location to location. Other developers are relying totally on digitized video sequences. One multimedia graphic adventure that makes good use of 3-D rendered graphics is The Labyrinth of Time, from Electronic Arts.

The Labyrinth of Time features some 250 megabytes of high-resolution (640×480), 3-D rendered graphics. In the game, you interact with the environment, picking up items and using items by moving the mouse cursor on special action icons. Periodically, animated sequences appear, bringing the environment of game to life.

True to its name, The Labyrinth of Time takes the player on a voyage through various historical times, competing with characters from ancient Greek mythology in order to solve the mysteries of the Labyrinth. In this adventure, you play a role opposite that of The Journeyman Project. In Labyrinth, you must travel through history and try to set of a chain of events that alters the future and destroys the Labyrinth of Time once and for all.

Leading the pack in the use of digital video in graphic adventure games is Viacom New Media (VNM), formerly known as ICOM Simulations. VNM prefers digital video as opposed to 3-D rendering. VNM's successful series called Sherlock Holmes: Consulting Detective is a good example of this. In Sherlock Holmes, the player gets to guide and direct Sherlock on a variety of interviews with possible suspects to solve a given case. The interviews are live video clips that play directly from the CD-ROM in some of the best-looking digital video to come off of a CD-ROM, thanks to VNM's custom in-house video compression techniques. Once you have determined who committed the crime and how, you appear before the judge to plead your case. If you are correct, the computer grades you on how quickly you solved the mystery, based on the number of interviews you took.

Some graphic adventure games have both 3-D rendering and digital video techniques. Return to Zork, from Activision, is one example of combining both technologies; another example is The Seventh Guest, from Virgin Games. The Seventh Guest comes on two CD-ROMs, which contain a total of 1.2 gigabytes of data (the equivalent of about 390,000 pages of text). The reason the game requires so much storage is that it offers high-resolution 3-D computer-animated sequences that enable you to explore an entire house. Instead of cutting from one location to another, the 3-D animation takes you smoothly from place to place.

For instance, you may find yourself in the foyer with a beautiful view of a large marble staircase. Clicking the staircase will smoothly walk you over to the staircase and glide you up to the top. From there, you can walk through the hallway and explore various rooms in the house. The Seventh Guest represents the state-of-the-art in multimedia graphic adventures.

Simulations

The added storage space of CD-ROMs has also been a benefit for the category of simulation software. Finally, extensive data can be stored in an interactive title to allow for detailed and complex simulations. One of the largest suppliers of multimedia CD-ROM titles is Software Toolworks, from which come the following three simulation titles.

Oceans Below is a simulation with which you can explore the world of scuba diving. You are taught about diving gear, dive sites around the world, and the varied sea life you will encounter in your

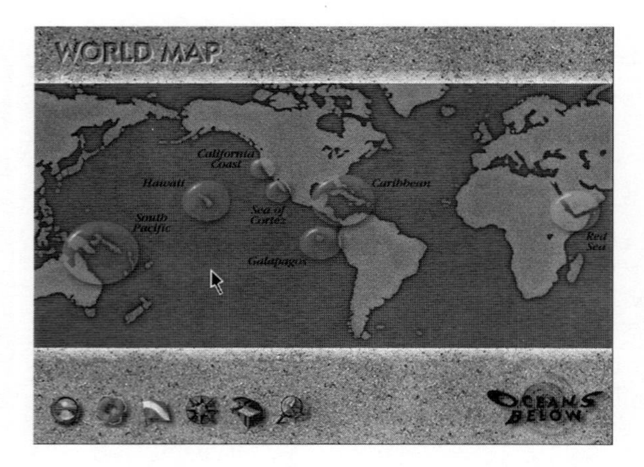

▲ You can choose the dive location from various parts of the world.

▲ Watching a video of dolphins during your dive off the coast of Maui.

simulated dives. The first-person perspective enables you to "dive" in various parts of the world. For example, you could choose the Caribbean ocean and dive down 70 feet to feed an eel. You could dive the northern coast of California to get a close-up view of the great white shark.

Each dive experience gives you access to more than 100 high-resolution underwater photographs and more than 200 digital video sequences. While diving, you can discover lost treasure, sunken planes, and shipwrecks. You can simply click to navigate through the water. Oceans Below is a product of Amazing Media and, as stated, it is available from Software Toolworks.

Have you ever wanted to explore the Capitol Building without a tour guide? You can do this with Capitol Hill, a new simulation from Amazing Media. You can take a 3-D walking tour of the Capitol Building, seeing photographs of any place you go in the building. Clicking any painting or sculpture that you come across gives a high-resolution picture and a text explaining more about the art.

Furthermore, through the multimedia audio, text, graphics, and video, you can explore the history and purpose of the United States legislative system. After learning how Congress works, you can play the role of a congressman and deal with the day-to-day tasks encountered by a freshman congressional member on the way to becoming Speaker of the House or Senate Majority Leader.

The third simulation title is Space Shuttle, also from Amazing Media. Space Shuttle is an advanced simulator for NASA's space shuttle program. You can experience NASA's training program "first hand." You can follow along with any of NASA's 53 recorded shuttle missions.

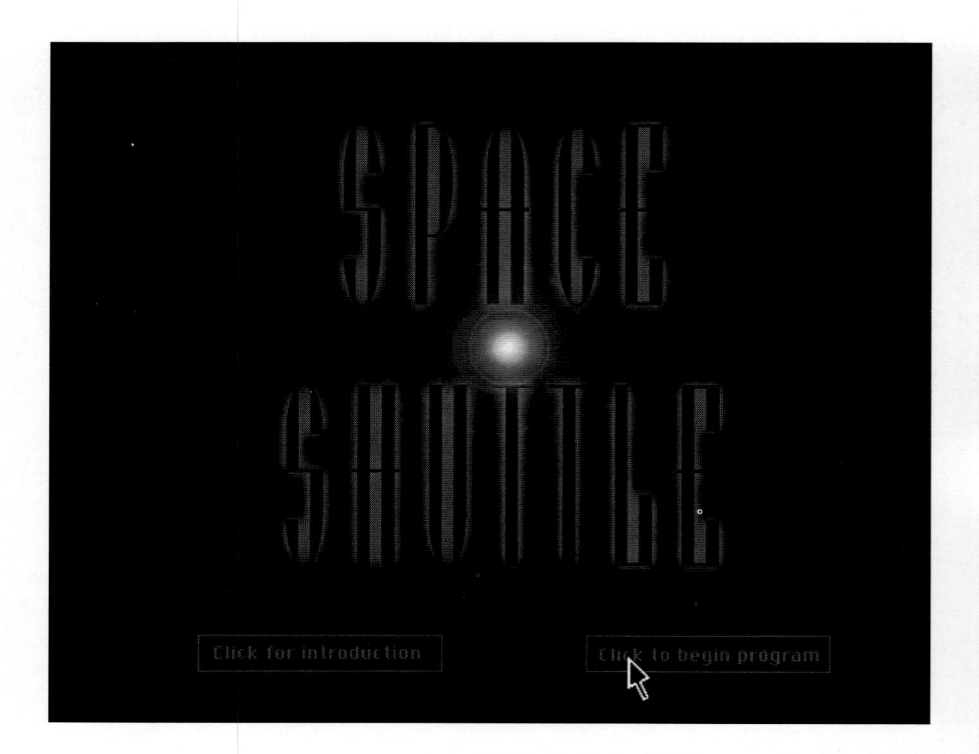

Each shuttle mission is complete with a video sequence of the launch and landing. This includes even the horrifying video sequence from the Challenger's final launch (mission 25), in which all the astronauts lost their lives. For nonclassified missions, you can view video from various aspects of the mission, such as satellite deployment, maintenance, and science experiments.

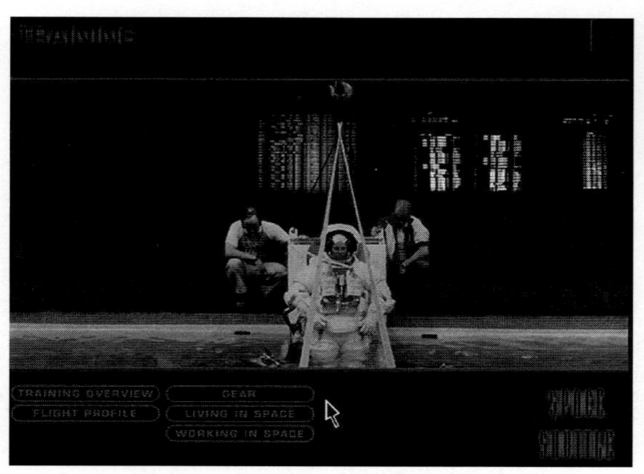

▲ The trials and tribulations you'll experience in NASA's training program.

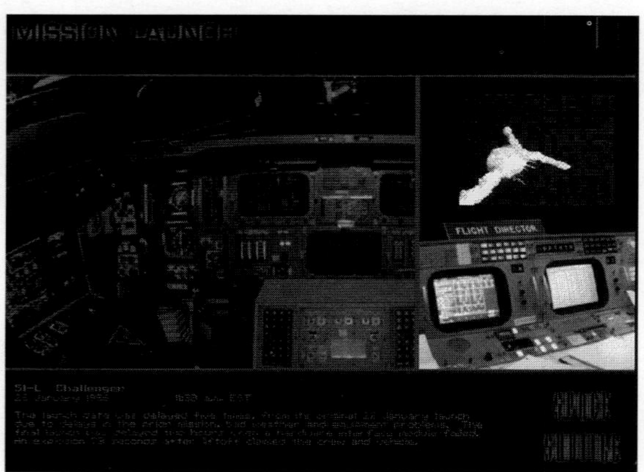

▲ View video sequences from every shuttle launch, even the fateful 25th mission.

▲ In the Company of Whales from Discovery Enterprises.

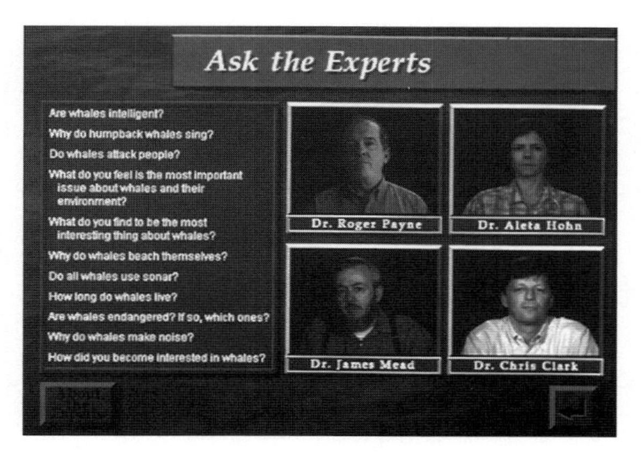

▲ Whale experts are at your beck and call with the "Ask the Experts" section.

▲ "Whales in Motion" enables you to see video sequences of whales.

Personal Enrichment

Titles in the personal enrichment category fall between simulations and research multimedia titles. While providing interactivity, they do not actually simulate anything. Though they provide volumes of data, they are not really research materials. One such title for personal enrichment is called In the Company of Whales, the first home-use multimedia release from Discovery Enterprises.

Narrated by Patrick Stewart, In the Company of Whales takes the user to top experts in the field of whale social behavior, whale intelligence, and whale songs. This title has more than 45 minutes of digital video and more than 200 still images and graphics.

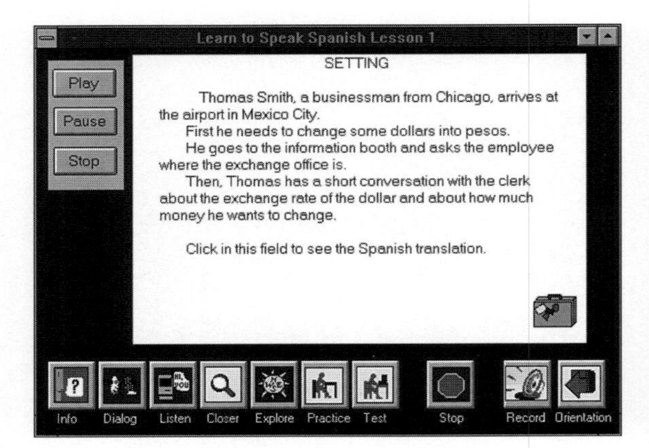

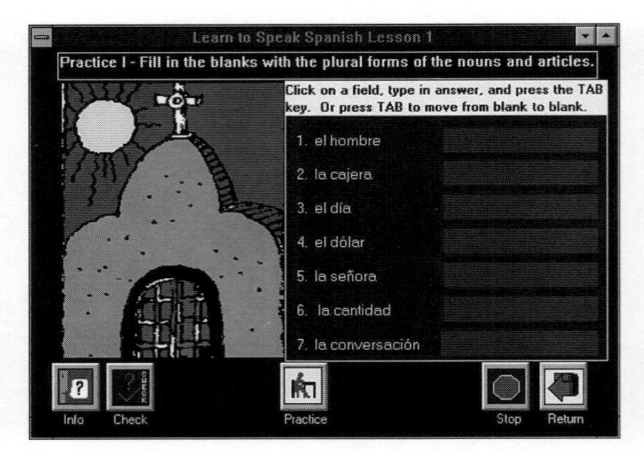

▲ Hyperglot Software's Learn to Speak Spanish CD-ROM from the Berlitz Think & Talk series.

In the Company of Whales also provides hypertext glossary words for quick answers to any whale-related question. This title is the start of Discovery's entrance into the multimedia market. In each quarter of the year, Discovery Enterprises will be releasing a new multimedia educational title similar to Whales.

Have you ever wanted to learn a foreign language? Hyperglot Software makes it easy with the multimedia Berlitz Think & Talk series. You can learn Spanish, for instance, by following a multimedia instruction course where you hear the words pronounced correctly. You, in turn, speak into your multimedia system's microphone. The software records your voice and plays it back for comparison with the correct pronunciation. The software provides 30 lessons in speaking conversational Spanish. Interactive drills in comprehension and grammar help sharpen your skills. This is a truly interactive way to learn a new language.

Another personal enrichment title is Microsoft Musical Instruments, an interactive journey into the world of musical instruments. With this multimedia title, you can explore musical instruments by geographical location, by instrument family, by ensemble grouping, or by the name of the instrument.

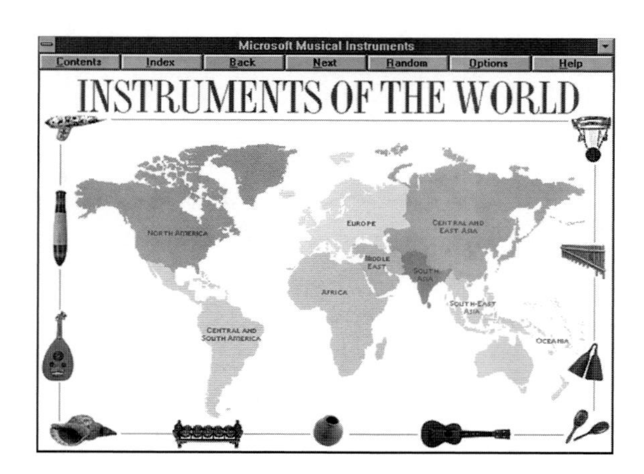

▲ Here you can choose an area of the world in which to explore the native instruments.

▲ Locate an instrument by the ensemble it is related to.

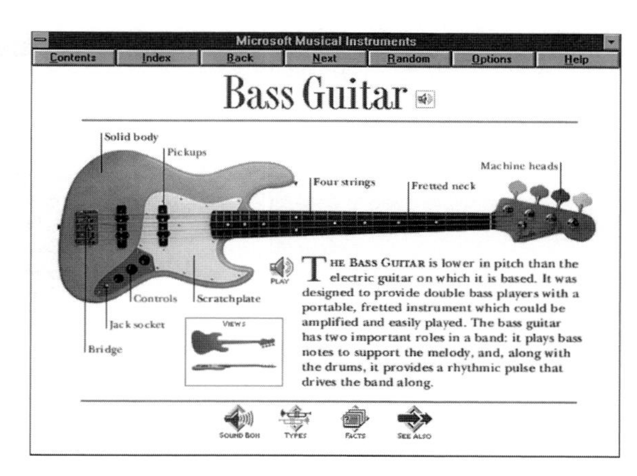

▲ Here is the detailed screen for the bass guitar.

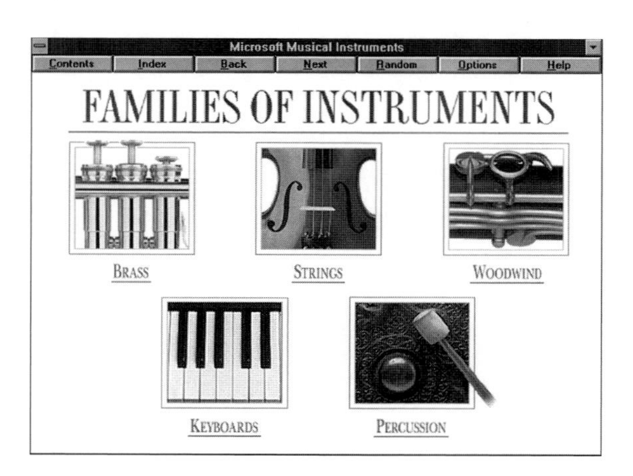

▲ Choose the family of the instrument to learn how different instruments relate to one another.

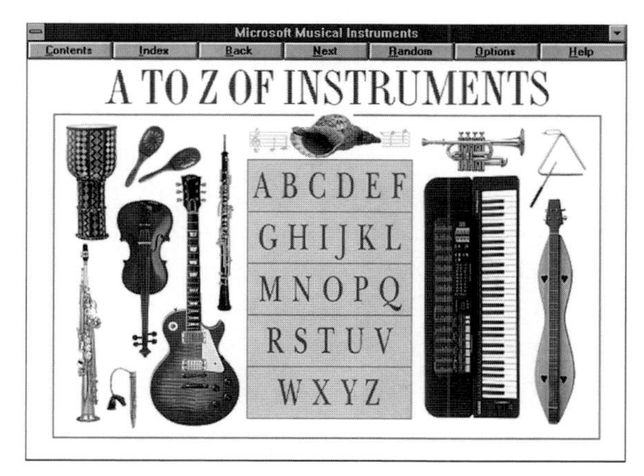

▲ Find a particular instrument by its name.

After locating a particular instrument, you can hear the correct pronunciation of its name. You can hear also a sample of music played on the instrument. You can also play the instrument yourself using the sound box, which plays back any note you choose for the current instrument.

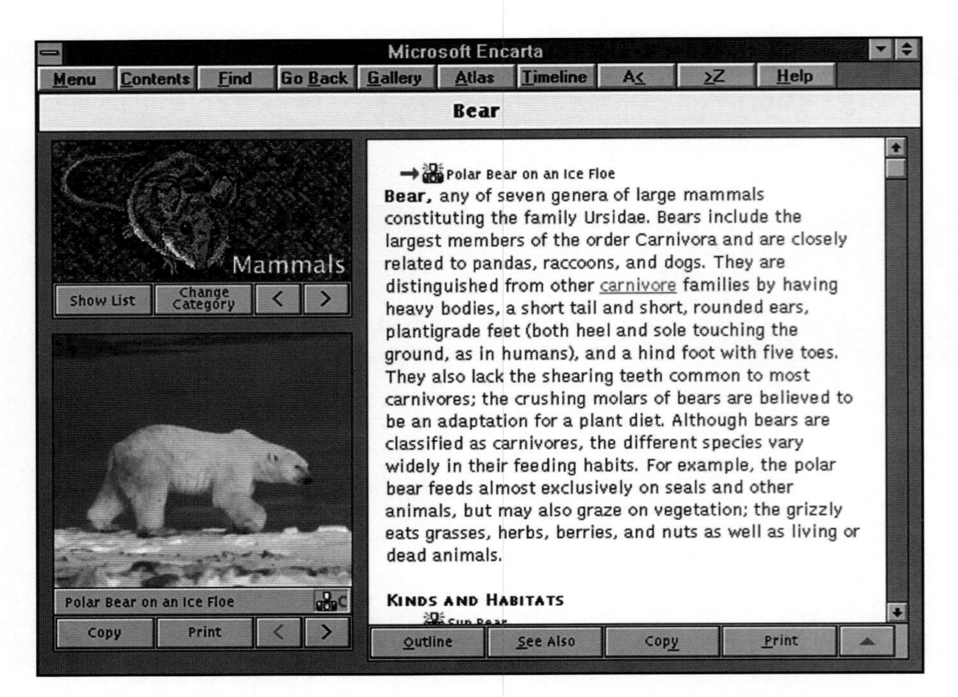

▲ Microsoft Encarta contains thousands of pictures to illustrate the text information.

▲ With the time line feature, you can access any time period and see contemporary events.

Research

The last category for multimedia titles is research. As suggested at the beginning of this chapter, you can't put an encyclopedia into video, but you can put video into an encyclopedia. This is exactly what companies like Compton's New Media have done in creating multimedia encyclopedias that offer text, audio, and graphics.

Microsoft Encarta is a multimedia encyclopedia that features the complete text of the 29-volume *Funk & Wagnalls New Encyclopedia*, with 1,000 new articles written specifically for Encarta. Encarta is rich in multimedia content, with thousands of color images and hours of sound and music.

You can use a graphical time line feature to determine when events took place in relation to each other. Some text information offers animation or digital video clips. There are also more than 250,000 hypertext links between key words, links that enable you to find related information very quickly.

Another research title is the Picture Atlas of the World from the National Geographic Society. It features more than 800 interactive maps, indexed to take you directly to the map you wish to view. Each area has political, physical, and topographic maps. As you examine each continent, you will run across some of the 50 video clips and 1,200 full-screen photographs.

Audio segments play music from around the world and samples of more than 100 different spoken languages. Vital statistics are included with each country, such as population, industries, religions, income, and climate. Narrators explain map projections, time zones, and other aspects of the atlas. Even the glossary is interactive, enabling you to jump directly to a particular item.

The merger of TIME Inc. and Warner Communications Inc. in 1990 made possible an incredible advance in the reporting of news and information. On Jan. 16, 1991, when United Nations forces started bombing Baghdad, signaling the commitment of U.S. military to a war against Iraq, top executives of TIME Magazine met to discuss a plan of action for the coming weeks and months that America would be at war. With the massive correspondence network that TIME had access to, thousands of pictures, documents, and audio tapes would soon be pouring into their offices.

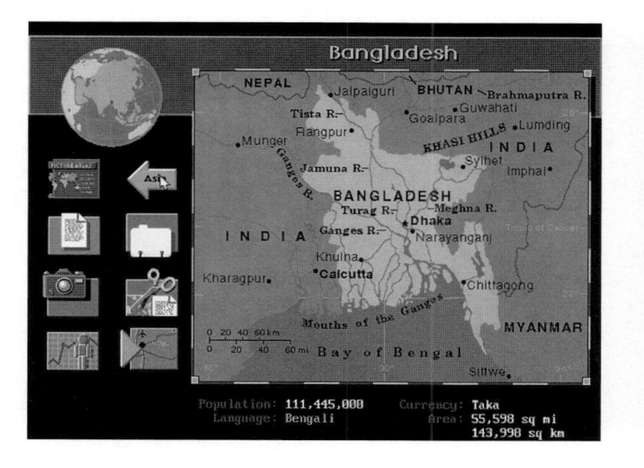

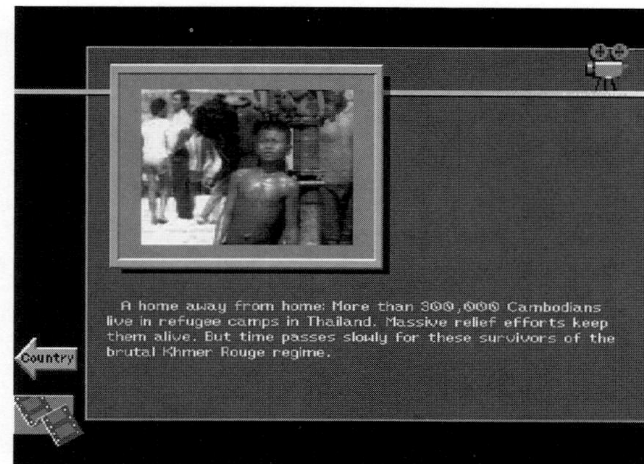

▲ Here is a video clip from the Picture Atlas of the World. *Courtesy of National Geographic.*

Dick Duncan, executive editor of TIME, called Stan Cornyn, president of Warner New Media, a California-based Time-Warner division specializing in electronic publishing. They discussed electronic publishing of TIME's textual coverage, and Cornyn recommended that all the data sources, graphics and audio, be sent to California for publishing on a CD-ROM.

In the following months, the editors of TIME in New York forwarded to California every report, audio tape, and photograph published in every issue of TIME during the Persian Gulf war. In California, the developers at Warner New Media set to work compiling the information into a navigable research product. The resulting product, called TIME: Desert Storm, serves as a standard for interactive news publishing now and perhaps even in the future under high-speed interactive cable television services.

The opening screen of TIME: Desert Storm shows a calendar, with the war divided into individual weeks. Clicking to the left of the title of a week highlights the corresponding week on the calendar.

Once you choose a week, you are taken to a menu screen with four options. You can read reports incoming directly from the field, or you can read the articles that appeared in TIME that week. You can also listen to audio reports and view narrated photographs. Choosing the photographs brings up full-screen, full-color photos from the war.

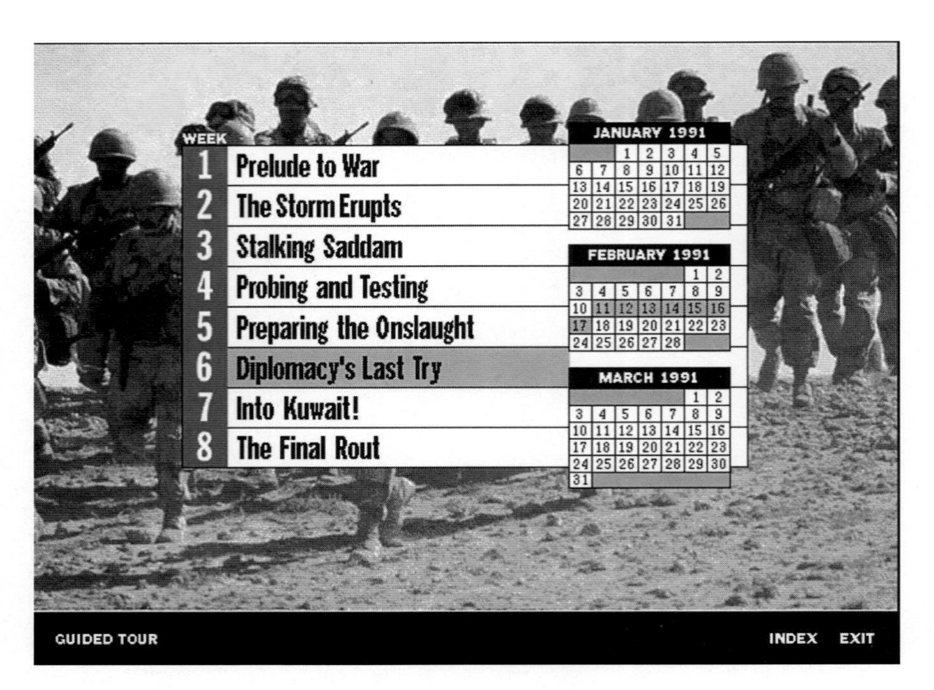

▲ Choosing the title of a week also highlights that week on the calendar.

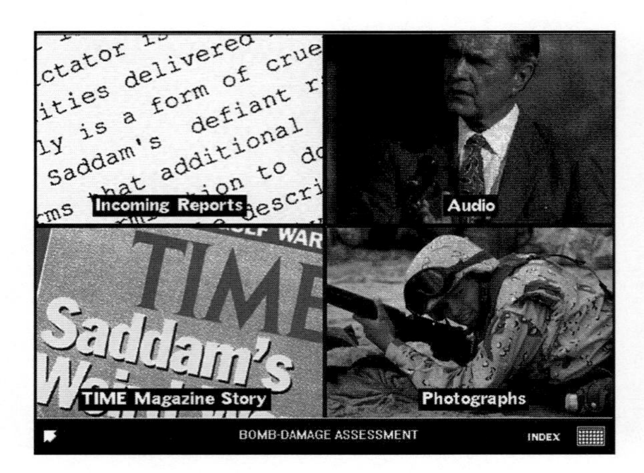

▲ The four options available within each week of Desert Storm.

▲ Here is a photograph from the "Photographs" section.

Reading through this material and listening to the audio tapes, you can gain much understanding about the war and its effect on the United States. As previously indicated, this research title sets a new standard for the multimedia delivery of news information.

This portion of the chapter has offered you a glimpse into the amazing multimedia titles that are available today. The next section presents how multimedia and CD-ROM might progress in the future.

THE FUTURE OF MULTIMEDIA

Digital video seems to be a major area into which multimedia is headed. Companies like Viacom New Media, from which comes the Dracula Unleashed product, have pioneered the use of digital video. As CD-ROM speeds increase and compression technologies advance to the point that they are easily implemented in hardware, consumers will see more and better digital video in multimedia titles.

CD-ROM technology will continue to raise the cost of producing personal computer interactive entertainment titles. Already titles like Rebel Assault from LucasArts can reach more than $3 million in production costs. Will multimedia production costs someday surpass the production costs of motion pictures? That producing a computer game could cost more than $70 million may seem unbelievable. Consider, however, the resulting entertainment value. Though motion pictures last about two hours, some CD-ROM entertainment titles have play times of 20 or 30 hours. A typical movie costs about $8 to view, and the typical CD-ROM costs about $50. Though almost 9 million people would have to see the movie to reach $70 million gross, only 1.4 million people would need to buy the CD-ROM title to gross $70 million. Keep in mind that the number of personal computers, including those capable of running multimedia titles, continues to rise. It is possible, therefore, that one day multimedia could be a bigger business than motion pictures in terms of production costs.

Perhaps the most interesting feature of the future of CD-ROM involves diskettes. Many in the industry believe that diskettes may cease to be used as a medium for software distribution. For example, a program like Windows NT, which requires about 22 high-density (1.44 megabyte) diskettes, could be easily distributed with a single CD-ROM. The savings in production costs could be passed on as discounts to those purchasing the "CD-ROM only" version of the software. In no time at all, almost every user of personal computers could justify the cost of the CD-ROM drive.

Some in the industry point to the advent of the 1.44 megabyte floppy disk drive as an example of how quickly a new technology can become popular, replacing an out-of-date technology. Bob Bates, co-founder of Legend Entertainment, states, "I think they [diskette-based games] may die a very quick death, perhaps as early as Christmas of '94. When EGA graphics died, they died fast, in one season. When 5-1/4" diskettes died they died fast. December of '92 you could still sell games on 5-1/4" disk, but by May of '93 you couldn't sell them anymore. I think that 3-1/2" games will walk off the same cliff. Hardware is coming down in price. In small quantities it is still cheaper to produce floppies, but the consumer gets so much more on a CD-ROM that the perceived value may sway the buyer. When these dynamics take place, the old format usually dies quickly. Something like CD-ROM that can deliver a lot of information will win out."

Bates continues, "First of all, CD-ROM or massive storage is going to move in very rapidly and play a big role in the games that people deliver. Generations of people have been raised on TV as the standard for graphics and pictures. People know that any graphics or video on a monitor or screen should look at least as good as television. Until computer games deliver that kind of quality they will be viewed as substandard. Games will have to look like TV for mass market appeal. I personally think that even some of the beautiful modeling and rendering as that done with 7th Guest may only survive if it can deliver TV quality performance. In the near future we are more likely to see pre-recorded video sequences.

"The next big thing is clearly the MPEG video standard for digital video compression. When it becomes possible to deliver TV-quality video in a game, people will demand it. Speed of the machines is the other big deal. The hardware must be able to handle fast enough graphics to support TV-style video. Also, voice recognition will play an important factor, even though right now it isn't very good. Our games could have used current voice technology years ago, but we have a very high vocabulary in our adventure games, and 16 words just wasn't good enough. Maybe when voice recognition reaches around 1000 words or more it will be a very powerful gaming technology. It removes the mouse and the keyboard."

The MPC Level 2 specification also tells us a little about the near future of CD-ROM titles. First, the new double-speed CD-ROMs should help increase the data transfer speed, paving the way for higher-speed graphics that fill more of the computer screen. The new video throughput specification, along with the minimum CPU of a 486SX, should likewise help with graphics titles. The 160 megabyte hard drive is an interesting requirement. Some graphics applications, for which even double-speed CD-ROMs are too slow, now can dump tens of megabytes to the user's hard disk. Also, the new requirement of 16-bit color (65,536 simultaneous colors) should help alleviate palette concerns when artists create animation or digitize video for playback on multimedia systems. This should bring better color to graphics-intensive titles.

CHAPTER SUMMARY

In conclusion, you have learned that to run multimedia titles, personal computers require stereo sound capabilities, a CD-ROM drive, a fast CPU, and graphics capabilities. Once these requirements are met, however, hundreds of multimedia titles are available for your computer. You now have a basic understanding both of how CD-ROMs are created and of their vast storage capacities.

A challenge to the domain of personal computer-based multimedia is home gaming systems. In the next chapter, you will learn what classifies a system as a home gaming system, what units are available, what their capabilities are, and what the future is for home gaming systems.

5

Multiplayers and Home Gaming Systems

"Our goal in making a video game is to make it enjoyable, regardless of graphics, regardless of multimedia, regardless of FMV. All those things add to the experience, but if it's not fun, you can forget it."

In 1983 the home video game market was devastated. Every major player—Atari, Coleco, and Mattel—was losing millions of dollars. After peaking at $3 billion in 1982, annual sales plummeted to $800 million by the end of 1984. Then in 1985, Nintendo entered the home video game market and began a resurgence that has lasted until today.

Now the home video game industry sales are topping a staggering $7 billion a year. Even more interesting is that home video game systems are surpassing personal computers in processing power. The $200 gaming machine that your child plays Mario Brothers on is probably equivalent in power to your home or office personal computer.

These same home gaming systems are now trying to leapfrog personal computers in computing power. Both Atari and Nintendo have systems that can process 64 bits of data at once. These systems run at speeds of 55 million to over 100 million instructions per second (MIPS). In contrast, a PC based on the Intel 486 microprocessor can only reach speeds of 40-50 MIPS, while Intel's fastest microprocessor, the Pentium, just barely makes it to 100 MIPS. Only the Pentium microprocessor can compute 64 bits of data simultaneously; older 486- and 386-based personal computers can only compute 32 bits of data at once. Currently, Pentium-based personal computers cost over $3,000, while the 64-bit Atari and Nintendo systems run around $200!

▲ A game console with a cartridge inserted and a game controller attached. *Courtesy of Sega of America, Inc.*

There are, however, major differences between personal computers and gaming systems. Some feel that trying to compare a game system to a personal computer is like comparing apples and oranges. Still, if you consider only raw computing power and data throughput, game systems offer impressive results.

HOME GAMING SYSTEMS AND HOW THEY WORK

The components of a video game system are fairly simple. Each system has a game console or control deck. This unit houses the microprocessor and other integrated circuits of the video game system. Connectors on the game console connect it to televisions and game controllers. A high-speed data connector allows cartridge-based games to be plugged into the console.

CONSOLE TECHNOLOGY

The brain of some game machines, the central microprocessor, is identical to the microprocessors used in some personal computers. For instance, the Sega Genesis 16-bit gaming system uses the Motorola 68000 microprocessor, which runs at a clock speed of 12.5 MHz. The 68000 was used in the original Macintosh computer, as well as the Atari ST and the original Commodore Amiga personal computers. A lot of games get started on the Amiga, and are then converted to the Sega Genesis platform because they share the same CPU. In terms of processing power, it is roughly comparable to the Intel 80286 microprocessor. Nintendo's Super Nintendo Entertainment System (SNES) uses a microprocessor known as the 65816 from Zilog. This is the same Central Processing Unit (CPU) used in the Apple II GS personal computer.

Most video games are written in the Assembly language. Sega has a version of C for the Genesis, but most programmers don't want the extra overhead of a C interpreter in their cartridge games. Programming video game systems is different from programming games on personal computers. The video game is closely tied to the display of the television. Every 60th of a second, the program switches between a graphics operation and a code operation. This is because the electron gun of a television starts at the upper-left corner of the screen, and works down to the bottom of the screen line-by-line. This occurs 30 to 60 times per second. When the electron beam gets to the bottom of the screen, there is an interval as the gun moves vertically back to the upper-left corner of the screen. This is called the *vertical retrace interval*. By human standards, this happens very quickly, but by computer standards, it is a long period of time. This vertical retrace interval is when the machine reorganizes the screen. Graphics data is moved to the screen during that interval. You must tie your program around that point. This is how game programs are organized.

What makes game system games so much more powerful than PC games? It is all the added coprocessors available in gaming systems. In the Sega Genesis for example, there are custom chips that handle high-speed graphics functions such as *sprites*. Sprites are images that can be stored in a special location of memory, then placed anywhere on the screen with simple commands to the graphics processor. Sprites can move across an existing background image without erasing the pixels they move over. Other coprocessors handle functions such as digital sound for music and sound effects. These added coprocessors enhance game systems to perform better than PCs when it comes to video games. If you play Street Fighter II on a PC and then on a Sega Genesis, the PC version will seem sluggish because the computer does not have all the extra processors.

While using commonly available microprocessors, game system manufacturers are able to produce rather inexpensive products. The downside is that these CPUs are not as efficient as they could be. Most CPUs created for personal computers have very advanced *instruction sets*. The instruction set is the language of the microprocessor. It specifies what functions are available and which commands activate those functions within the CPU. An advanced instruction set makes the programmer's job easier. Instead of writing a program to add 4 to itself 3 times, (requiring three lines of code) the programmer can simply say multiply 4 by 3 (requiring only one line of code). Although this makes programming easier, it slows down the CPU, because the CPU has to perform these extra calculations.

In addition to this problem, as CPUs advanced over the years, each succeeding generation had to be compatible with the previous generation. This meant that any instructions in the previous CPU had to be carried forward into the next generation. These types of CPUs are called *Complex Instruction Set Computer* (CISC) processors.

In contrast to the CISC processor is the RISC processor. RISC stands for *Reduced Instruction Set Computer*. As its name implies, a RISC processor has a very limited instruction set. Usually, the limited instruction sets are optimized for graphics or mathematics, which are used heavily in video games. The benefit of these simple instructions sets is that they are fast. RISC processors are also typically much faster in terms of clock speed. So even though a programmer has to write more lines of code for a RISC as opposed to a CISC, the end result is a much faster program.

The next generation of home gaming systems is moving to this advanced RISC technology. Nintendo has announced a new gaming system code named Project Reality. It is the result of a joint agreement between Nintendo and Silicon Graphics, a world leader in high-end computer graphics. The Project Reality system will use a RISC microprocessor that can compute 64 bits of data simultaneously. This enables it to exceed 100 MIPS, and offer real-time, 3-D computer graphics.

In the same vein, Atari has recently released the Jaguar home gaming system. It too uses a 64-bit RISC architecture that allows it to perform at speeds as high as 55 MIPS. Whereas the Nintendo RISC system will not be available until the end of 1995, the Jaguar is available in stores now for a suggested retail price of about $200.

Two different techniques are used in creating digital sound. These two techniques can be observed on the Nintendo Super NES and the Sega Genesis game systems. The Genesis uses FM Synthesis while the SNES uses Digital Wave Forms.

FM Synthesis is the process of using a chip that produces music by using two or four wave forms called operators. These operators modulate frequencies in order to produce musical tones. The result of this synthesis is less than realistic, so other companies, including Nintendo, have turned to Digital Wave Forms. With Digital Wave Forms you can record digital samples of sounds and then play them back. This makes the sound much more realistic.

Arnold Hendrick has been in the gaming business for more than 20 years. He got involved with the electronic gaming industry by working for Coleco. Since the mid-1980s he has been a game designer for MicroProse Software. Some of the projects he worked on include F-19, Silent Service 2, and Gunship. Hendrick has been responsible for the cartridge-based games section of MicroProse and is now in the process of reorganizing development away from 16-bit video game systems and toward 32-bit and 64-bit systems.

Developing a cartridge-based video game is very different from developing a PC-based game. Explains Hendrick, "Every machine has different hardware, which makes our work a little more difficult. This is a big difference compared to developing for PCs. Instead you are developing for a specific platform; on a Sega or SNES there is just one piece of hardware. This causes us to write our code to exploit that hardware to its greatest capability. For the Sega Genesis we try to exploit the 68000, which is a little faster than the SNES CPU. On the other hand, the SNES has digital sound and extra colors. SNES sounds use digital wave form sound instead of the FM synthesis sound found on the Sega Genesis. Each machine has different graphics modes. In general, the advantage of the SNES is that is has a few more colors, 256 different colors simultaneously. The Sega Genesis is limited to 64 simultaneous colors, but there are a tremendous number of talented artists who are able to compensate for this fact. The quality of the creative talent can easily outweigh the lack of technology in any of the systems."

CARTRIDGE TECHNOLOGY

Game cartridges plug into a data bus similar to the one used in personal computers. In the case of the Atari Jaguar, the bus runs at 26.6 MHz with a 64-bit data path; this gives a throughput of about 106 megabytes per second. Compare that to the common Industry Standard Architecture (ISA) personal computer bus that runs at 8 MHz with 16 bits of data for a total data throughput of about 16 megabytes per second.

The games are stored in the cartridges on custom chips that have the games built into them. Usually the game developer will program the game, store it on some type of magnetic medium (diskettes or tape) and 'burn' it into these special chips called *Erasable Programmable Read Only Memory* (EPROM) chips.

EPROMs are chips that can be programmed electronically by a PROM programmer. An EPROM looks just like a regular computer chip except that internally all the data bits are 1's. The PROM programmer creates the 0's in the correct patterns to form a program. Later, after the program on the chip is no longer needed, the EPROM can be erased by exposing it to ultraviolet light for 10 to 30 minutes. The benefit to using EPROMs is that developers can create their own chips in-house. The downside is that EPROMs are very expensive compared to regular manufactured chips.

Game developers have special blank game cartridges that these EPROMs can be plugged into. After they have written a game, programmers can burn a number of EPROMs with that game, and test the game on regular game consoles using these special cartridges. According to Hendrick, "These boards are the cartridge game equivalent of a floppy disk. We program the boards and give them out internally for testing. The materials cost of the board and the EPROMs, is between $60 to $80 dollars. These test boards cost significantly more than the final production line boards that go in the cartridges, which cost from $15 to $20 dollars." When all the bugs are worked out of the game, the EPROMs are sent to the manufacturer and used as Master ROMs. These Master ROMs are used to mass produce the regular chips used in the game cartridges.

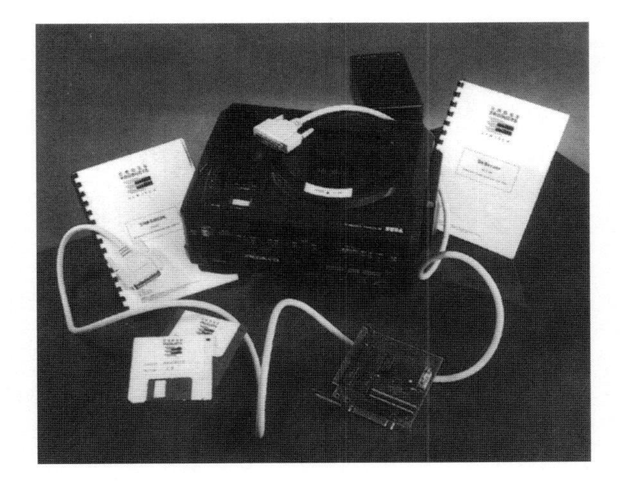

▲ A developer's cartridge into which you can plug EPROMs.

As processing power increased over the years, game capabilities also increased. Features such as digital quality stereo sound and high speed/high color graphics are now common. This means more storage is needed to hold video games. Initially the cartridges used for gaming units such as the Atari 2600 only needed about 4 kilobytes (1,000 bytes) of storage. However, modern gaming cartridges, for systems such as the Atari Jaguar, now use cartridges as large as 6,000 kilobytes (6 million bytes/megabytes). Data compression techniques can increase these cartridges to hold 50 megabytes (400 megabits). In the world of home gaming systems, the size of a game is typically referred to in terms of bits. Eight bits being in every byte, a 6 megabyte (MB) game is about 48 megabits (Mb).

Hendrick explains, "Everybody uses data compression in their cartridges. It's a standard thing today. A lot of our algorithms are based on Huffman & LZW compression techniques. We usually don't compress everything, only things that won't slow the game down. You can do that with any storage medium as long as you have the power to decompress. The savings are outstanding, up to double, triple, or even quadruple. Even PC games use compression to save diskette space and hard disk space."

CREATING A CARTRIDGE-BASED GAME

When it comes to developing games for cartridge systems, game manufacturers like Sega and Nintendo all have development systems they sell to developers. Some developers, like Absolute Entertainment, even create their own development systems. These are expensive units that plug into a personal computer on one side and into a gaming console on the other. They act like a cartridge on the gaming console. You create the game on the PC, which dumps it into the developer unit, which is plugged into the console. Then the programmer can play the game on the console.

There is also some extra hardware that enables programmers to see what's going on with the game as it runs. That way they can easily debug any errors that arise. The exact abilities of the development "debugging" software and boards vary from machine to machine. Some of the boards even replace the central CPU inside the Sega Genesis or SNES, which enables programmers to watch the processor as the game runs.

There are also small companies that provide similar hardware and software tools for cartridge development. In the case of SNES, there are two different kinds of development systems. One is from Nintendo itself, while another one comes from a different company and includes software to assist the artist. It costs between $2,000 and $5,000 to outfit a programmer with a development system. Costs are higher if a compact disc is being developed because a CD emulator, which is like a large hard disk drive, must be used. Development systems for CD-based machines can run from $8,000 to $20,000. A developer or publisher also must pay a license fee to the manufacturer, whether it be Sega, Nintendo, or some other company.

Once the game has been developed on one of these systems, the next step is to submit the game to the manufacturer (Sega or Nintendo) for quality assurance testing. A master set of EPROMs is sent along with a copy of the game on diskette. The manufacturer reviews the product, makes sure it has all the proper copyrights and trademarks, the content is not too violent, and that the game is actually fun. They do not, however, dictate the subject matter—that is completely up to the developer. The manufacturers always encourage the developers to create the best possible product. Sometimes a game has to go back and forth a little bit before everything is correct.

▲ The Philips CD-I player. *Courtesy of Philips.*

The manufacturers then send the EPROMs off to a chip manufacturing company. Turbo Technologies, Inc., for instance, sends its game EPROMs to Seiko/Epson where the chips are duplicated. After that the new chips are sent to a Mitsubishi plastic factory for the plastic parts and final assembly. From there the cartridges are sent to yet another company to be assembled into cases and boxes and shrink-wrapped. The finished product is then shipped back to TTI for distribution. This process occurs in Japan for all video game companies.

THE BIRTH OF THE MULTIPLAYER

As did the personal computer industry, the home video game industry noticed the storage advantages to compact discs. In 1992 Sega released the first CD-ROM–based game system, the SegaCD. Three years earlier however—in 1989—Matsushita, Philips, and Sony entered into an agreement to develop a new technology called Compact Disc Interactive or CD-I. In September 1989 Philips demonstrated the CD-I's capabilities, including full motion video (FMV).

The CD-I player looks like a typical audio CD player. The difference is that a CD-I player can play, not only interactive CD-I discs, but also standard audio CDs and Photo CDs. Because of its ability to play multiple types of CDs, it was given the name Multiplayer. This new category fit well, because the CD-I is not really a home gaming system; it is closer to multimedia than Mario Brothers.

Following on the heels of CD-I in 1990, Trip Hawkins of Electronic Arts formed a company called 3DO. Hawkins' goal was to create the specifications for the next-generation multiplayer called, appropriately enough, the 3DO. These specifications were then licensed to various hardware (royalty free) and software (with a comparatively small royalty structure) developers. 3DO boasts the backing of some major players in the interactive entertainment industry, including AT&T, Matsushita, Time-Warner, and MCA. Because the 3DO unit supports many CD formats, it is a true multiplayer. Now a number of manufacturers, including Panasonic and Magnavox, are producing 3DO multiplayers.

CURRENT HARDWARE

We have already discussed a number of home gaming systems and multiplayers, but it's appropriate to take a quick look at all the current models and their capabilities before discussing software.

▲ The newly redesigned 8-bit Nintendo Entertainment System. *Courtesy of Nintendo of America.*

Home Gaming Units

Home gaming units can be divided by the processing power of their microprocessors; 8-bit , 16-bit, 32-bit, and 64-bit. Surprisingly, there is still a great demand for the original 8-bit systems such as the Nintendo Entertainment System (NES).

Nintendo Entertainment System

Today one of three homes in America has an NES 8-bit system. Introduced in 1985, it has become the number one home gaming system, with total worldwide sales of 60 million units and a 99 percent share of the 8-bit U.S. market. The NES was originally released in Japan, and continues as a bestseller there under the name Family Computer (Famicom).

The NES uses an 8-bit Motorola 6502 microprocessor running at a speed of 1.79 MHz. It can display as many as 16 colors simultaneously from a palette of 52. The screen resolution is limited at only 256×240. In 1993, Nintendo released a redesigned version of the NES that featured a sleeker looking console. With a low suggested retail price of $49.95 and an existing library of almost 600 games, the NES continues to be the leader in 8-bit home gaming systems. Still, with all the excitement leading to 16-, 32-, and 64-bit machines, the days of the NES are clearly numbered.

Sega Genesis

The Sega Genesis game has the distinction of being the first 16-bit system. With over 500 colors, stereo sound, and a library of more than 350 games, the Genesis still leads the 16-bit market. In its first year (1990), 1.4 million units were sold. Sega sold 1.6 million units in 1991 and 4.5 million in 1992.

▲ The Sega Genesis 16-bit gaming system. *Courtesy of Sega of America, Inc.*

The Genesis was able to get a two-year head start on Nintendo with the 16-bit platform. High definition graphics and animation characterize the Genesis. It uses the Motorola 68000 microprocessor and runs at a speed of 7.6 MHz. The screen resolution is 320×224 with 64 colors from a palette of 512 colors. The current suggested retail price is $99.99. The low price, along with some very interesting attachments—the Sega CD, Sega VR (virtual reality helmet), and Sega Channel (see Chapter 7, "Interactive Television")—make the Genesis a very popular 16-bit system. The Sega CD system has strong adult appeal, and 60 percent of all owners are adults.

Super Nintendo Entertainment System

The SNES is Nintendo's offering to the 16-bit gaming world. Launched in 1991, the SNES offers multiple scrolling windows and digital stereo sound. Based on the Zilog 65816 microprocessor running at 3.58 MHz, the SNES offers a high

▲ The Super Nintendo Entertainment System (SNES), a 16-bit gaming system. *Courtesy of Nintendo of America.*

▲ NHL Stanley Cup for the SNES uses the Mode 7 chip for 360 degrees of rotation during gameplay. *Courtesy of Nintendo of America, Inc.*

screen resolution of 512×418. Even better is the fact that it can display 256 colors simultaneously from a palette of 32,768 colors. Yet the greatest advancements for the SNES came in the form of proprietary special effects chips that could be incorporated into SNES gaming cartridges. In 1992 Nintendo released Super Mario Kart and NCAA Basketball both of which used a new chip called Mode 7 that enables players to rotate 360 degrees during gameplay.

In 1993, Nintendo released StarFox, which used a proprietary custom chip called the Super FX. Using the Super FX chip, StarFox enables players to enter a first-person 3-D flight simulator. The Super FX chip offers RISC technology, with real-time 3-D polygon animation, software object rotation and scaling, texture-mapping, and light source shading. The SNES has a suggested retail price of $99.99.

▲ StarFox, Nintendo's first game to use the Super FX chip. *Courtesy of Nintendo of America.*

▲ The Sega Genesis with Sega CD attached. *Courtesy of Sega of America, Inc.*

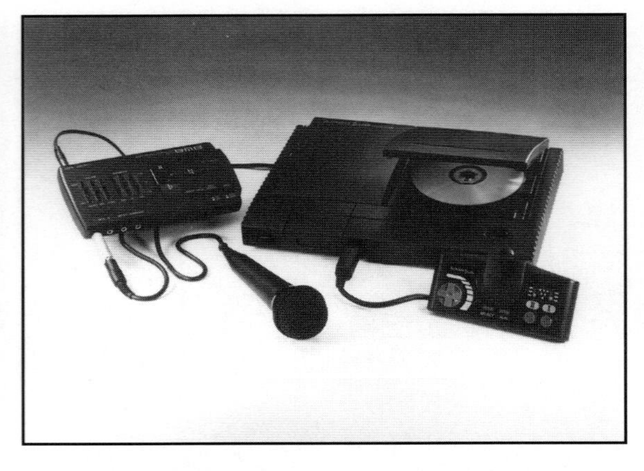

▲ Turbo Technologies Duo with an optional Karaoke add-on attached. *Courtesy of Aldrich and Associates.*

NEO•GEO

SNK Corporation is known for its popular coin-operated arcade fighting games, including Samurai Showdown and Fatal Fury. The company has taken its popular coin-op hardware and converted it to a home gaming system, called the NEO•GEO. The system uses the popular Motorola 68000 microprocessor and runs at 14 MHz with a screen resolution of 320×224. Where the system really shines, however, is by offering 4,096 simultaneous colors from a palette of 65,536. The only downside is the price—$499.99—and the fact that most of the games offered are of the fighting type.

Sega CD

In 1992 Sega released the Sega CD system, which is an add-on unit to the Sega Genesis that allowed Genesis to play CD-ROM–based games. The advantage to CD games is obvious: instead of only having about 6MB for a game (as in cartridge-based games), a CD offers 600MB. Sega CD games use this extra space for more play levels, enhanced CD quality sound, and richer graphics. The Sega CD can also play standard audio CDs, and it boosted the speed of the Genesis machine from 7.6 MHz to 12.7 MHz. Sega CD has a retail price of $229.99.

Duo

NEC Corporation and Hudson Software teamed up to create Turbo Technologies, Inc. In the area of home gaming, TTI launched the Duo (previously called the Turbo Duo), an 8-bit gaming system with a CD-ROM drive, in 1992. The Duo uses the 8-bit Motorola 6820 microprocessor and features a graphics resolution of 320×224 with 512 colors. You can use cartridges or CD-ROM–based games on the Duo, and it even plays audio CDs. An interesting aspect of the unit is that with an add-on product called the Intelligent Link, you can hook it up to a personal computer to act as an external CD-ROM drive. The Duo has a suggested retail price of $299.99, which includes five games.

Unfortunately, you'll need those games, because there seems to be a shortage of gaming titles for the Duo compared to other 16-bit systems like the Genesis and SNES. Currently there are about 50 titles, 27 cartridge games, and 30 CD and Super CD games.

Commodore Amiga CD32

Commodore has also entered the 32-bit gaming market with the Amiga CD32. Based on Motorola's 32-bit 68EC020 microprocessor running at 12.5 MHz, it also uses some advanced graphics capabilities to display 256,000 colors simultaneously from a palette of 16.7 million. It offers a screen resolution of 320×224 and a retail price of $499. It comes with a handheld 11-button controller and connectors for keyboard, mouse, and joystick. Currently popular in Europe, only about 30 games are available for the system.

Turbo Technologies' FX

Turbo Technologies has also announced a 32-bit gaming system called the FX, which will use the V810 32-bit RISC microprocessor from NEC. The system will be capable of displaying 16.7 million colors and have a built-in digital video system for playing back full motion video at 30 frames per second, full screen. It will not use cartridges but will be completely CD-ROM–based. The FX will initially be launched in Japan at the end of 1994.

▲ The Commodore Amiga CD32 gaming system. *Courtesy of Commodore.*

Atari Jaguar

The first 64-bit RISC-based system to make it to market was the Atari Jaguar. The Jaguar is a cartridge-based gaming system, with add-on CD-ROM capability. With a suggested retail price of $249.99 (with the CD-ROM attachment), the Jaguar has the best price/performance ratio of all the home gaming systems. Built by IBM in Charlotte, North Carolina, the Jaguar offers 32-bit color (16.7 million colors) at a resolution of 720×576 along with hardware-assisted 3-D graphics.

Some developers are a little leery of the Jaguar. This is because the supporting hardware is just as important as the main processor. A big concern about Jaguar is that the CD is an add-on accessory and is not included with the unit. Cartridges are far more expensive to make then CD-ROMs. A cartridge with ROM chips has a materials cost of between $15 and $20 dollars while a CD can be produced for as little as $1 or $2 dollars. However, a lot of people aren't going to put down $700 dollars to play "run and jump" style games on the 3DO, so the low price tag of the Jaguar may make it more appealing to younger audiences who like "shoot-em-up" cartridge-based games. Older audiences may opt for the more expensive 3DO unit and its more complex CD-ROM–based games.

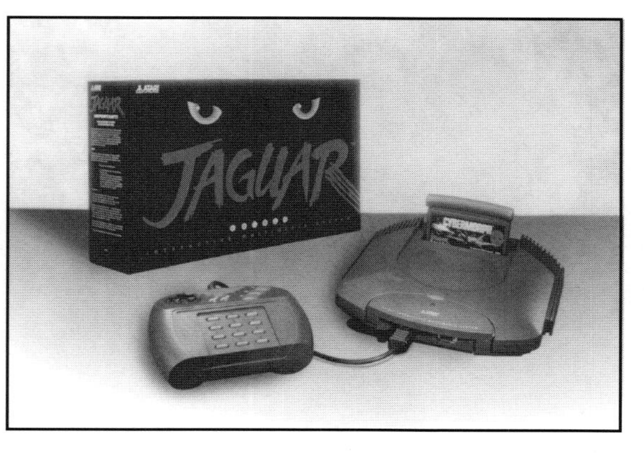

▲ The 64-bit Atari Jaguar. *Courtesy of Atari.*

Sega Saturn

Sega is currently working on the next generation system, a 64-bit CD-ROM–based unit. Code named the Sega Saturn, the system will be priced around $500. The 64-bit RISC processor will be produced by Hitachi. The Saturn system will be compatible with existing Sega CD titles as well as titles that take advantage of the Saturn's new 64-bit microprocessor. The Saturn will first be released in Japan starting in mid-1994.

Nintendo Project Reality

Finally, not to be outdone in the technology field, Nintendo has announced a joint agreement with Silicon Graphics to develop a new game system to sell for under $200. Code named Project Reality, this new system will use 64-bit RISC technology from MIPS, Incorporated. This will allow it to generate 3-D texture-mapped graphics in real-time. Nintendo plans to unveil a coin-op version of Project Reality in 1994 and a home version in 1995.

Multiplayers

Multiplayers are geared more toward multimedia titles and adult oriented entertainment. All multiplayers are CD-ROM–based and support standard audio CDs and Kodak Photo CDs.

▲ A sample of Project Reality's 3-D texture-mapping capabilities. *Courtesy of Nintendo of America.*

Compact Disc Interactive—CD-I

Two CD-I players are currently on the market, one from Magnavox (Model CDI200) and one from Philips (Model CDI220). CD-I players are true multiplayers in that they can handle audio CDs, Photo CDs, Video CDs, and CD-I titles. Both players use a 16-bit microprocessor and offer 32-bit color. The Magnavox player has a suggested retail price of $499, and the Philips unit lists at $599.

With an optional add-on cartridge ($249) both units can play full-screen full motion video from CD-ROM discs. Each disc holds up to 72 minutes of video. The Magnavox unit features a wireless remote controller pad. Since CD-I was the first multiplayer out of the chute, there are already more than 100 titles available for it.

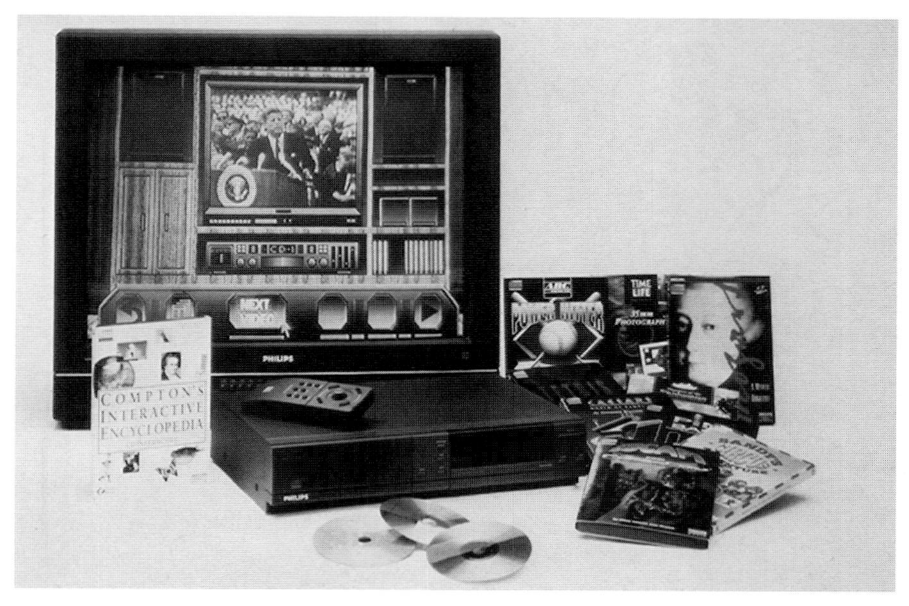

▲ The Panasonic REAL 3DO multiplayer. *Courtesy of Panasonic*.

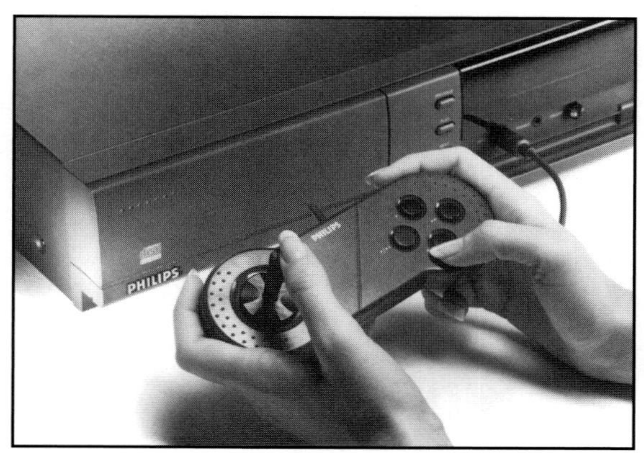

▲ The Philips CD-I player. *Courtesy of Philips*.

3DO

3DO Players are currently manufactured by Panasonic and Sanyo. The 3DO platform currently has the highest performance of any multiplayer, with a 32-bit RISC processor and custom graphics processors that can quickly fill the screen with up to 16.7 million colors at a resolution of 640×480. The 3DO also features hardware to assist the programmers in creating special effects such as image warping, texture-mapping, and transparency. The system has two drawbacks: the reluctance of game developers to create games for it and its suggested retail price—$699.99.

▲ The Pioneer LaserActive system. *Courtesy of Pioneer*.

Pioneer LaserActive

Is it a multiplayer, a video LaserDisc player, or a home gaming system? It's all of the above and more. The LaserActive system by Pioneer is the ultimate multiplayer, with the capability to play movie and concert LaserDiscs, audio CDs, Sega CD and cartridge games, Duo CD and cartridge games, a new LaserDisc ROM format (LD-ROM), and even Karaoke LaserDiscs. The only downside to the LaserActive system is its price. The base model has a retail price of $970. If you want to play Sega CD and cartridge games, you will need a $600 plug-in adapter. The Duo adapter will run another $600. LaserActive uses 16-bit micropro-cessors and 32-bit color. LaserActive is ahead of its time and most likely all other gaming systems will eventually offer adapters such as Sega and Duo.

Now that all the current gaming systems and multiplayers have been discussed, we'll take a look at the software. Let's begin by looking at the development of a title for the 3DO called Crash 'N Burn, created by Crystal Dynamics.

THE CREATION OF A PC-BASED IE TITLE: CRASH 'N BURN BY CRYSTAL DYNAMICS

In the post-holocaust year 2044, people compete in combat-style races. In these races, the drivers not only try to beat the others to the finish line, they also try to finish the other racers permanently by using lethal weapons such as 120mm guns, mines, and Gauss cannons. This is the scenario for Crash 'N Burn, a new race-combat game for the 3DO multiplayer.

As the player, you get to choose the vehicle you want to drive. Each vehicle offers different capabilities such as speed, acceleration, defenses, and stock weapons. Next a driver is chosen from among nine available. Each driver has his own personality, mannerisms, and thought patterns. The drivers are displayed in live digitized footage, and the game tracks each driver's racing and kill record.

Created by Crystal Dynamics, Crash 'N Burn comes bundled with the Panasonic REAL 3DO player. It makes the most of the 3DO by utilizing fully texture-mapped 3-D graphics in real-time. There are 30 different courses that offer steep inclines and declines, along with jumps and varying weather conditions, including ice, steam, and earthquakes. Digital voices, music, and sound effects combine to provide an exciting racing ex-perience. The best thing about Crash 'N Burn is that when you buy the 3DO player, the game is free!

▲ Here the player must fight icy roadways to stay on the road. *Courtesy of Crystal Dynamics*.

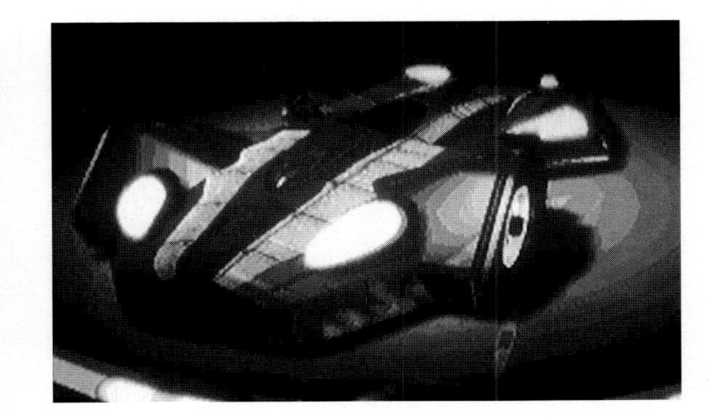

The Development of Crash 'N Burn

Crystal Dynamics was founded by three people in June 1992. Judith Lange came from Sega of America where she oversaw marketing and sales for Sega 8-bit Master System. Dave Morse was the founder of Amiga Computer and president of New Technologies Group (NTG), and Madeline Canepa came from Sega of America where she managed all phases of marketing for 16-bit video games, including the highly successful "Sonic the Hedgehog." Together these three individuals formed Crystal Dynamics, which is designed to be an advanced technology development firm focusing on high-technology software products for the next generation of gaming systems.

Lange is President of Crystal Dynamics; Canepa is the executive vice president of marketing and product development; and Morse provides strategic direction and guidance for the company.

The first step in designing Crash 'N Burn, according to Canepa, was to outline game objectives. "The objectives are critical to understand and agree upon. With Crash 'N Burn, our objective was to be available at launch so it could be bundled with the hardware. That sets the stage for the type of product one can do, to have it available at launch. Another objective was to take full advantage of the hardware capabilities the 3DO has to offer…to really showcase the power of the system."

Once the objectives were outlined, company programmers began to brainstorm various concepts for the game. After coming up with a number of concepts, they selected one, reviewed it against the objectives, and checked it against the competition. When Crash 'N Burn met these criteria, game design began. At the same time, the Art Department started developing the overall look of the game. When these steps were complete, the actual programming and artwork went into production. Once a working product was available, the project went into *alpha testing*—a major milestone when the game is first playable.

Artwork and programming continued as play testing was taking place. Finally, with the art complete and the majority of the bugs worked out, Crash 'N Burn went into beta testing. Then, with the last bugs and glitches corrected, it was released. This development occurred in just nine months, and the result has been described as "The best, first generation software product for a new hardware platform in the history of video games."

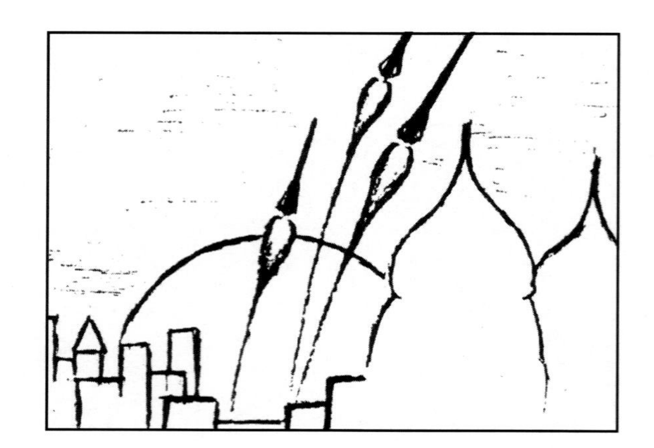

Objectives and Brainstorming

Madeline Canepa, chief technologist Mark Cerny, and producer Mark Wallace came up with the initial concept for Crash 'N Burn during a brainstorming meeting. Cerny wanted to create a racing game, Canepa wanted a combat game, and Wallace wanted to create something that took advantage of the 3DO's 3-D capabilities. That was in August 1992 when Crystal Dynamics had just six employees.

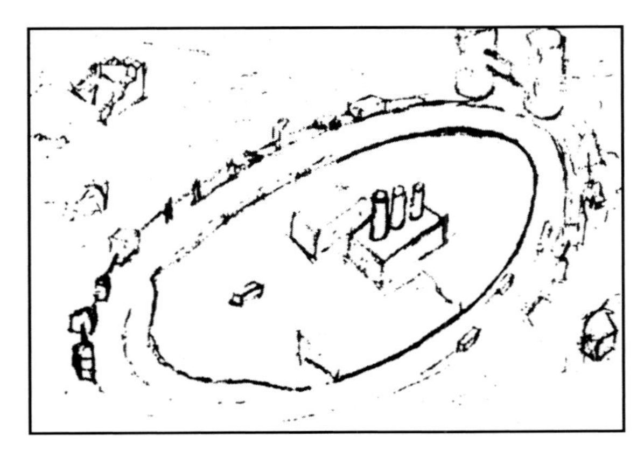

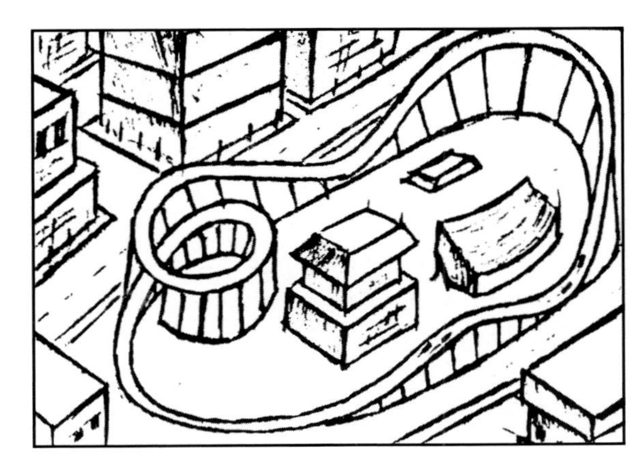

▲ Concept sketches for the two-player mode of Crash 'N Burn. *Courtesy of Crystal Dynamics.*

According to Canepa, "We had a number of different games that we wanted to create. However, since we were starting a new company using new technology on a new platform, we needed to play it safe. The safest bet was to choose a category of product that is very successful. Since both action games and racing games have been very popular over the years, that's what we went with."

There were, of course, a number of ideas that never made it into the final version of Crash 'N Burn for one reason or another. For instance, developers wanted to add a demolition mode and make Crash 'N Burn a two-player game. However, faced with a short time frame before 3DO shipped, developers had to cut these options. In July 1993, when Matsushita gave Crystal Dynamics the bundle contract, the company had two products in development. Matsushita gave Crystal the OK to use either one but also informed them the deadline would be August—the following month!

This meant development teams had to combine resources and concentrate on one product to finish it before the deadline. The product teams met and decided to move forward with Crash 'N Burn because it was the most likely product to be completed on time.

In designing the game, Crystal Dynamics wanted to take advantage of the technology but also create a fun game with good gameplay value. Crystal wanted to use 3-D texture-mapping along with full motion video. The gameplay was to include elements of combat and racing. Crystal developers weren't really interested in creating a new category of game, just in making something that was better than anything else.

Artistic Design

The Crystal Dynamics Art Department faced a lot of challenges in creating artwork for a brand new system. One of the biggest challenges the department faced was in how the art looked when it was transferred from the computer to NTSC (the standard used for television). The colors were the biggest problem. For example, vibrant reds can be created on a computer, but when those reds are displayed on a television, they blur and bleed all over the screen. The colors created on computer are not what is seen on a television. People in the computer graphics field jokingly refer to NTSC as meaning "Never The Same Color." A lot of tweaking was involved to get the artwork to look good. Developers had to develop a new tool for porting art from computer colors to NTSC colors.

To create the artwork, Crystal Dynamics used its own proprietary tools along with some commercially available tools like Autodesk's 3-D Studio, Playmation, and Alias Power Animator. Playmation is now being used for the animation and rendering of 3-D computer-generated characters in some of the Crystal Dynamics games. According to Canepa,"the output is fabulous, but the software can be very frustrating to use."

Another big issue in the Art Department was that of compression. The artists had to learn the limitations of 3DO's software compression and design their art to fit it. They designed the introduction of Crash 'N Burn long before they had a chance to work with the actual 3DO full motion video compression techniques. This caused some problems with the speed at which it was played back. "The FMV sequences have to be designed with compression in mind. It is very critical because you can create the most beautiful introduction, but if it can't be played back, then it's a waste. Panning the camera is an example of a definite no-no." says Canepa. As the camera moves in a panning sequence, every pixel on the screen must be updated between frames. This can cause playback to slow down to a crawl.

There was a little disappointment over the initial compression capabilities of the 3DO. Canepa explains, "We had hoped for more than what we were seeing with Crash 'N Burn. Now we have better 3DO compression for our next title, Total Eclipse. It's just one of the problems of being the first one out. You are not able to take full advantage of the hardware that is available. As tools improve, we have been able to make better use of the hardware."

Music and Sound Effects

The music and sound effects were contracted to another company. However, Crystal Dynamics didn't receive the sound driver for 3DO before releasing the product. As a result, Crystal had to have an external developer help them create a sound driver for the 3DO. A young company does not always have a wealth of tools at its disposal. Crystal Dynamics had to rely on the hardware manufacturer's tools—and software tools typically are not the hardware manufacturers prime concern. Crash 'N Burn was even finalized before the 3DO operating system was completed.

Programming

The programmers used the Apple Macintosh-based 3DO development kits. They wished they were IBM-compatible personal computers because the Macs were so expensive, and 3DO development requires a lot of memory.

Each production development team had 2 gigabytes (2 billion bytes) of space allocated on a network, and a 2.7 gigabyte external hard drive. Before data compression, Crash 'N Burn used 30 gigabytes of space! This was due to the tremendous amount of FMV and computer-generated Full Motion Animation (FMA). Finding enough computer memory was an incredible challenge.

The original specifications for the 3DO called for 2MB of onboard RAM. Fortunately this specification was increased to 3MB one month before the game's release. Developers thought 3MB would be plenty for future game design, but now developers are hitting the barrier with their next title, Total Eclipse.

Programming for Crash 'N Burn was done in C and Assembly Language. Crash 'N Burn was probably a 50/50 split between the two languages. As far as future projects, Crystal Dynamics will continue to use both languages depending on the game. One strategy/action game, now under development, is 100 percent programmed in C. The platform also affects the languages used. Crystal Dynamics programmers already are branching out to new platforms, such as the IBM personal computer.

Overall, Crystal designers are very pleased with the outcome of Crash 'N Burn. The 3-D texture-mapping worked great. There were many additional features that could not be fit into Crash 'N Burn because the hardware was not finalized until June 1993. Crystal Dynamics received its development systems in November 1992 and finished the game in August 1993. This time crunch caused several extra features to be discarded.

Alpha Testing

Once a working model was finished, Crash 'N Burn went into alpha testing. The game was OK but lacked the final artwork. According to Canepa, "It was very dismal looking. This was a difficult time, because it's hard to bring in a video game player, and show them the latest 32-bit game without artwork. Most alpha testing players were not that impressed. From a game play standpoint, it did fine, but for looks it wasn't that pretty. Later on, when the beta version arrived with artwork, it was a different story."

Along with in-house game testers, Crystal Dynamics brought in play testers from outside for an unbiased and fresh perspective on Crash 'N Burn. The changes play testers recommended were mostly from a game play standpoint. During this time, the game was balanced to make sure nothing was too hard or too easy.

Beta Testing

Beta testing started when most of the artwork was finished and most of the bugs had been worked out. Since 3DO titles are CD-ROM–based, Crystal Dynamics wound up making about 75 one-offs for Crash 'N Burn throughout the course of testing. This got fairly expensive, if you consider that every one-off costs about $19.

Canepa relates an amusing experience: "One night we had been testing Crash 'N Burn for about 23 hours straight. We had so many of these one-off CDs, that before we went home that night (actually about 4 a.m.) we decided to hang them from the ceiling in the testing area. After hanging up the CDs, we took off and went home to bed only to be called at about 6 a.m. by the alarm company, claiming that someone was trying to break into the office and a motion sensor had picked up the intruder. It turned out that the air conditioning system had come on and started blowing our decorative CDs around. This was picked up by the motion detectors, which triggered the alarm. Needless to say, we weren't too happy about having to get back up after only two hours of sleep, go back to work, and pull down our decorating job."

The remaining game bugs were discovered during beta testing. One bug was the result of a lack of memory. Every object on the screen takes up a certain amount of memory. The more objects on screen, the more memory is needed. On one of the game's higher levels, if a player used all the car's weaponry, the game would crash because it maxed out on memory.

Another bug developers battled turned out to be something else entirely. When developers got the first 3DO testing stations, the game worked as expected for three or four hours, then the audio and video would start to slip out of sync. This became progressively worse. They spent two days investigating it and could not figure out what was happening in the software to cause this problem. As it turned out, the testing stations were shipped without internal fans. This caused the CD itself to overheat after a period of time and start malfunctioning.

So far, no bugs have turned up in the finished product, so beta testing must have been a success. Even if a bug appears, it will be much easier to correct than a bug in a cartridge-based game. When there is a bug in the cartridge, nothing can be done about it. CDs, on the other hand, are very inexpensive, and developers can control manufacturing costs and create CDs in small quantities. Bugs can be corrected in CDs much cheaper than in cartridges.

Product Release and Consumer Reaction

Crystal Dynamics is unwilling to say how many copies of Crash 'N Burn were produced because of its confidential bundling agreement with 3DO. The game and the 3DO bundled is only shipping in the United States, and the bundle agreement is only with Panasonic. Should other electronics manufacturers such as Sanyo start making 3DO units, they may bundle a different title.

As already mentioned, consumer reactions to Crash 'N Burn have been positive, despite the $700 cost for a machine that includes only one game. There were initial fears that users might not like the access speed of the CD-ROM, but this is something inherent in CD technology. It is a double-speed drive, but it does take time to load some of the racing circuits. Canepa notes, "The CD access time is a complaint with some. We should have put some icon on the screen like the Mac clock. However, the disk never loads during game play, and this is a very small issue."

The Future of Crash 'N Burn

Crystal Dynamics is unwilling to announce a sequel to Crash 'N Burn yet, although the company is in discussion on the topic. According to Canepa, "We talk to consumers every day, and this is giving a real good idea of what they like and dislike. This will determine whether or not a sequel is created—this, along with the Crystal Dynamics internal desire to create a sequel."

CURRENT MULTIPLAYER AND HOME GAMING SYSTEM SOFTWARE

There are literally thousands of titles for both home gaming systems and multiplayers. This section discusses only a few of the more popular and technologically advanced titles. As with the other platforms, multiplayers and home gaming system titles are divided into four main categories; Action, Adventure, Simulation, and Multimedia. The first three categories are self explanatory. The fourth category—multimedia—covers some of the educational and research products available for the multiplayers such as 3DO and CD-I that don't readily fall into a game category.

Action

In the action arena, Flashback, a new title by a European company called Delphine Software, has been released in the American market by U.S. Gold. Flashback is an action/adventure game that requires a combination of hand-eye-coordination along with some reasoning to unravel the puzzles and challenges players face.

▲ Flashback for the Sega Genesis and Super NES from Delphine Software. *Animation sequence and screen captures courtesy of U. S. Gold.*

▲ The aliens have erased your memory.

You play the role of Conrad, a young scientist in the future who has discovered that Earth has been (unknowingly) overrun by aliens who can alter their shape to appear human. The aliens have discovered you know about them, so they capture you and erase your memory. Somehow you manage to escape and crash-land your vehicle in a jungle, which is where the game starts.

The beauty of Flashback is its smooth rotoscoped animation. *Rotoscoping* is the filming of live action and then scanning each frame of that video into the computer. Then when the computer plays back each frame in quick succession, the effect is just like watching the original video sequence. Delphine programmers did not use the actual colors/pixels from the original footage; instead they painted each frame to blend with the surrounding artwork. The next three pages contain frames that demonstrate the highly realistic, smoothly functioning animation of the game.

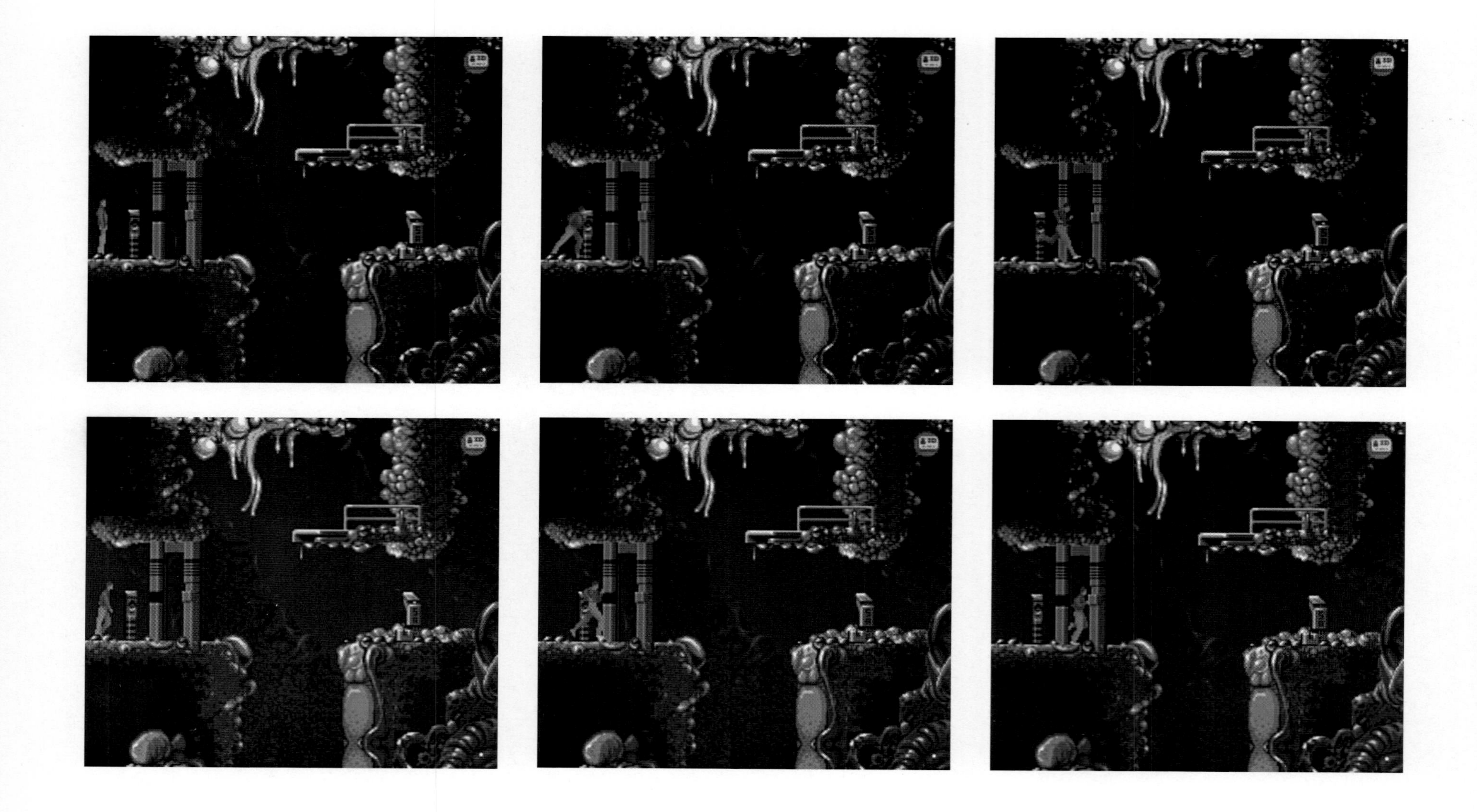

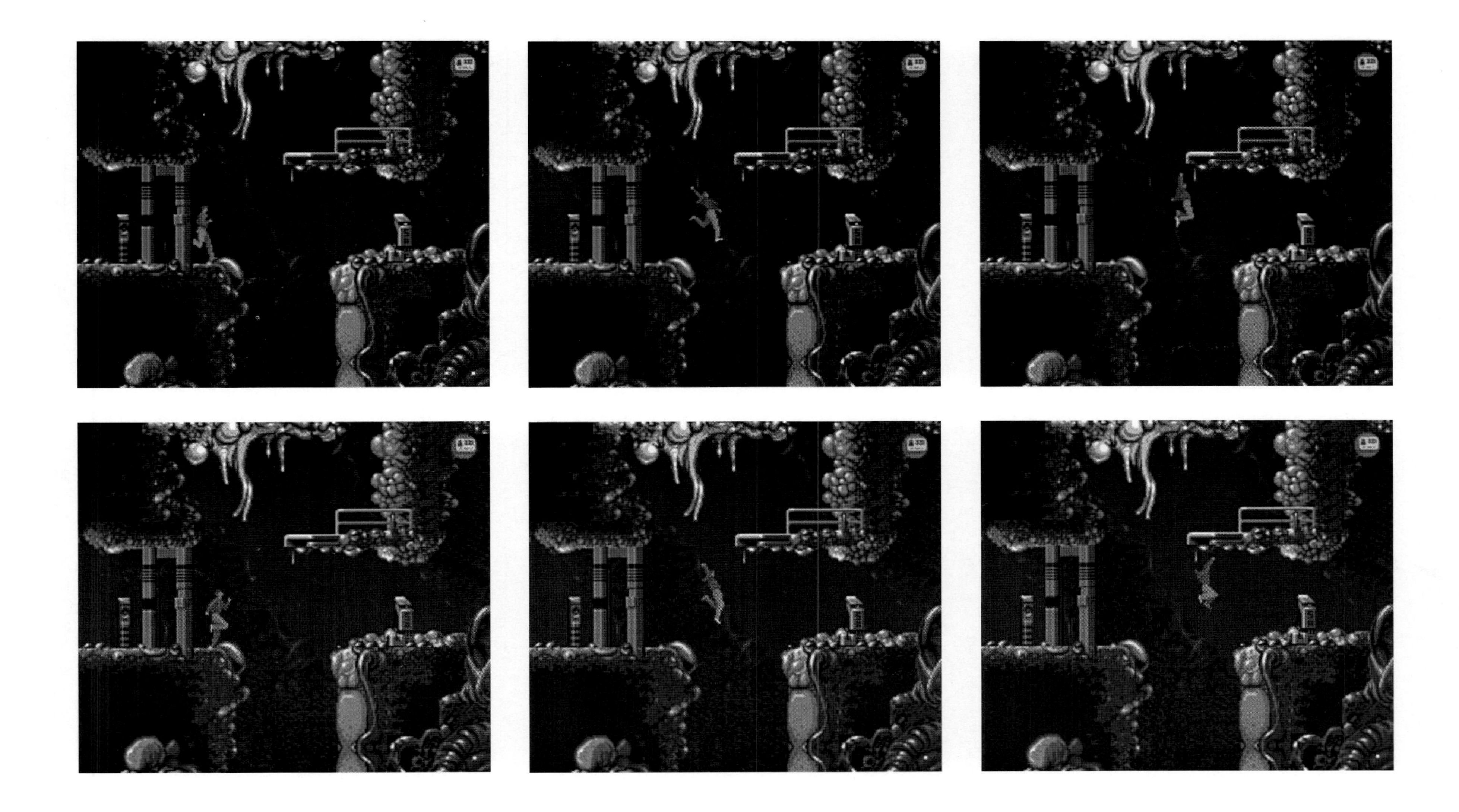

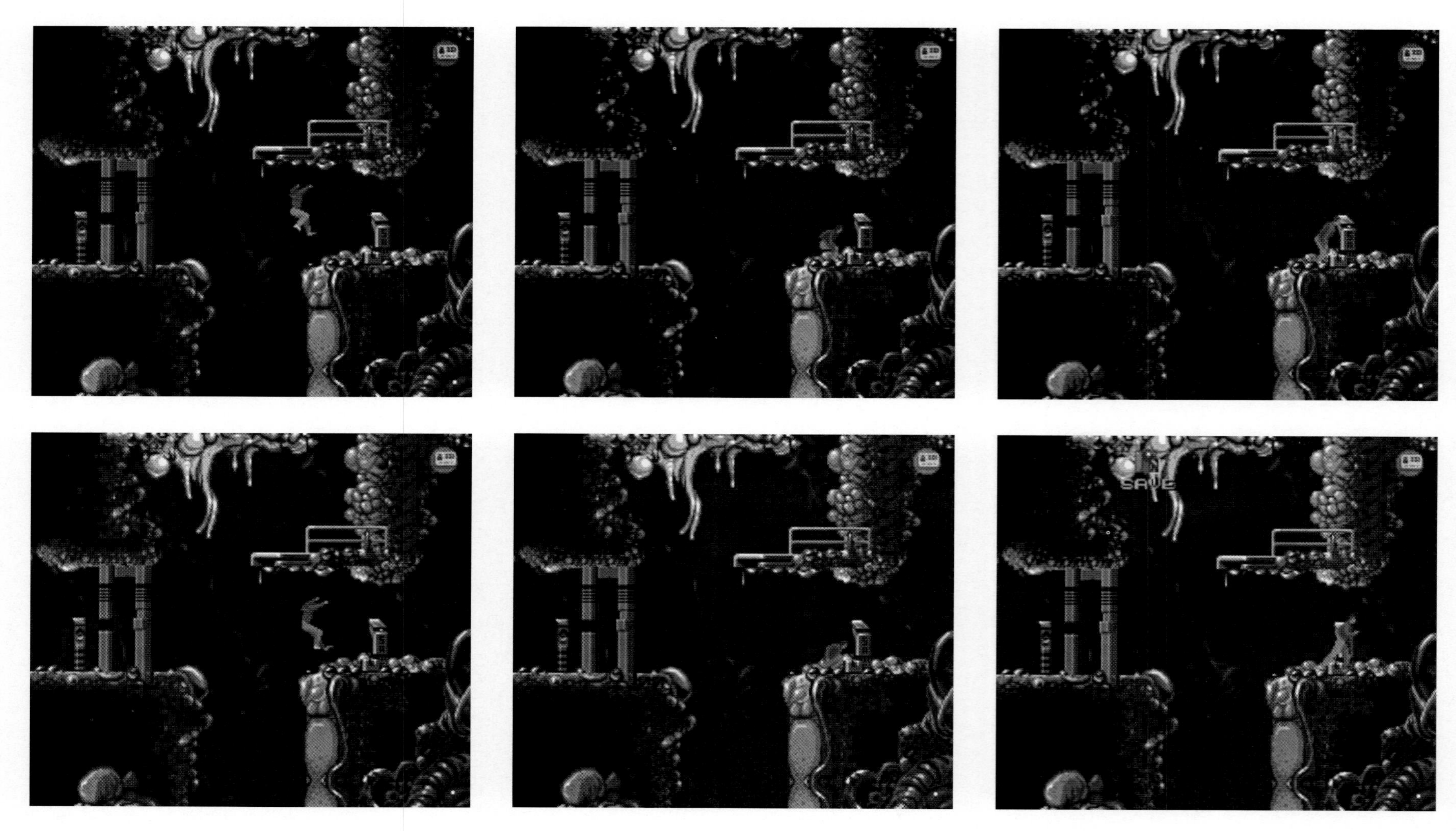

▲ An 18-frame sequence showing the smooth, realistic animation of Flashback.

▲ Animated sequences throughout Flashback carry along the storyline and plot.

▲ The password is displayed at the start of each new level.

There are 75 animated sequences that appear throughout Flashback. These sequences are all rotoscoped for smooth animation and help carry along the storyline and plot. A number of movement options, such as the running high-jump help make exciting action sequences. You can run, then duck and roll, run and jump to grab a ledge, draw your gun and shoot, or pistol whip any enemy within reach.

During the course of the game, your character travels through some 200 game screens on three different planets. Between each of 6 game levels, you are given a password that enables you to continue at the last level the next time you play the game. Within each level are save points that allow you to continue play at that point within the current gaming session.

If you restart the machine, however, you begin the game from the beginning of each level. The background art is beautifully drawn as you progress from the jungle, to a run-down mining colony, to a television game show featuring real violence, to Earth, and eventually to the alien home world.

With the aid of an old friend, your character manages to get his memories back and destroy the home world of the aliens. The authors claim the game has more than 50 hours of play time. Running in easy mode, I managed to finish it in much less time. The great sound effects and musical score add to the excitement of the game. Flashback is currently available for the Sega Genesis, the Super NES, and even MS-DOS–based personal computers.

▲ A dirty mining colony.

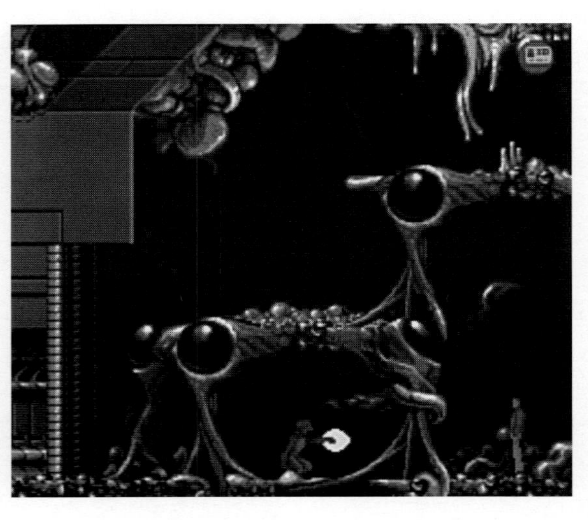

▲ The Alien homeworld where you must face shape-shifting aliens.

▲ The wild jungle.

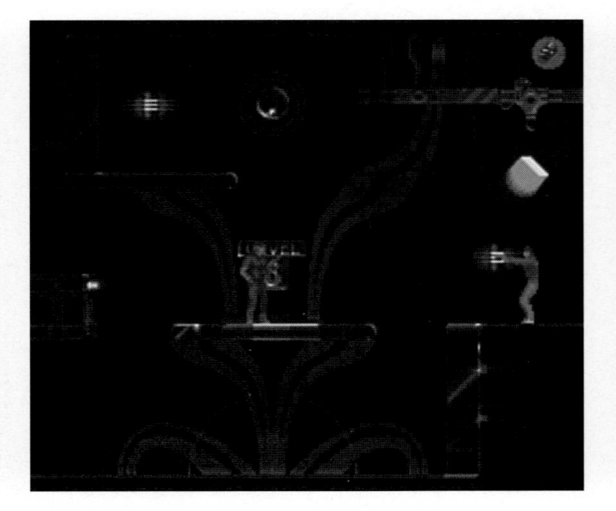

▲ The Death Tower game show forces you to compete against real people.

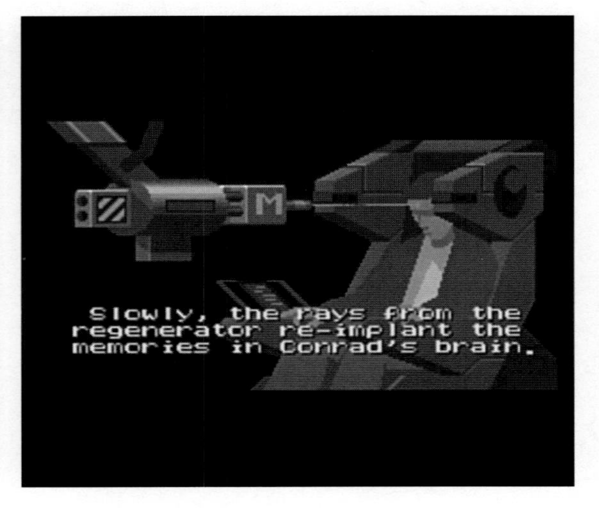

▲ A friend helps restore your memory.

Alien vs. Predator

Alien vs. Predator from Atari is a new game for the high-powered Atari Jaguar system. It features 3-D first-person perspective with real-time 3-D texture-mapped corridors and hallways. The story is a combination of the characters from two 20th Century Fox feature films—*Alien* and *Predator*—together in one game. A Space Marine is also thrown in for good measure.

As the player, you get to choose which character you want to play: Alien, Predator, or Marine. Each character has its own strengths and weaknesses. The Alien can climb walls, the Predator has superior night vision, and the Marine can use computer skills to outwit the other two. Your weapons also vary based on the character you choose.

Adventure

In the category of adventure and role playing games a number of products stand out, most notably Star Trek: The Next Generation from Spectrum Holobyte. It uses not only the latest in hardware technology but also the latest advances in software engineering to bring the hit TV series to life.

▲ Spectrum Holobyte's Star Trek: The Next Generation for the 3DO.

Star Trek: The Next Generation

Spectrum Holobyte has created a new adventure game based on America's number one syndicated hour-long TV series, *Star Trek: The Next Generation* (STNG).

Spectrum Holobyte's Star Trek: The Next Generation game involves a search for the "Fifth Scroll." You can play through any of the characters from the series, such as Captain Jean-Luc Picard, Counselor Deanna Troi, or whomever you wish. You choose where to explore in a 3-D universe filled with hundreds of star systems in the 'known' areas. Branch from the storyline and explore unknown areas of the galaxy for extra challenges. You can control all of the ship's functions from engineering to the transporter room.

▲ A dialog between characters in Star Trek: The Next Generation.

▲ This shot was chosen by the software on-the-fly to emphasize the tension of the situation.

▲ The bridge of the U.S.S. Enterprise.

Choose your own away team and beam down to any planet. The graphics feature the latest in 3-D computer animation. Versions are available for the 3DO, SNES, and even MS-DOS–based personal computers.

Project X

Project X from Park Place Systems is an interactive movie for the 3DO multiplayer. All the sets and backgrounds were created using the latest 3-D graphics techniques. Live actors were filmed against a blue screen background and composited into the Computer Generated Imagery (CGI) environment.

You are the main character, Johnny Styles. Your girlfriend's father is a scientist who created a device called the molecular sampler. This molecular sampler encodes molecular information about any object. By wearing a special suit, you can change your structure to fit the sampled structure, which enables you to morph into any object.

In this Blade Runner style future, you don't want to be some type of super hero. However, your girlfriend and her father are kidnapped, and it's up to you to save them. To make matters worse, bounty hunters are after your technology. You've got to save your skin and that of your friends, which forces the hero role onto you.

The designers at Park Place Systems understand the importance of cinematic effects. They feel strongly about keeping strong camera angles to convey feelings and moods throughout the game. Sometimes you have a first person view during the game and other times you have an omnipotent view, depending on the situation at hand.

Park Place Systems is throwing the latest technology at this project—six Silicon Graphics workstations running the latest 3-D graphics software (Alias and Soft Image), and two 3DO development systems. Written in Assembly language and C, Project X will be available in the fall of 1994.

Simulation

Simulation has become more popular on home gaming systems since simulators have started to use advanced microprocessors and accelerated graphics capabilities. We will focus on two titles that push the envelope on existing hardware platforms.

AH-3 Thunderstrike

AH-3 Thunderstrike for the Sega CD is one of the first games where you can actually turn around and go back where you came from. AH-3 is a helicopter combat simulator. You select which campaign you want to fly, from Central America, Eastern Europe, Panama Canal, South America, the Middle East, South East Asia, the South China Sea, and even Alaska.

Each campaign has 3 to 5 missions (a total of 40). Missions vary from sinking pirate ships in the South China Sea, to destroying guerrilla convoys in South America. Since the simulation is 3-D, you can rotate your helicopter 360 degrees and head back where you came from. You have a variety of weaponry to choose from, including lock-on missiles, rockets, and a cannon. After each mission, you go through debriefing to determine whether you met your primary objectives. If you did, you may be in line for a medal.

▲ AH-3 Thunderstrike, a 3-D helicopter combat simulator for the Sega CD.

▲ The debriefing screen. *Courtesy of JVC Musical Industries, Inc. ™© 1993 Core Design Ltd. © 1993 JVC Musical Industries, INC.*

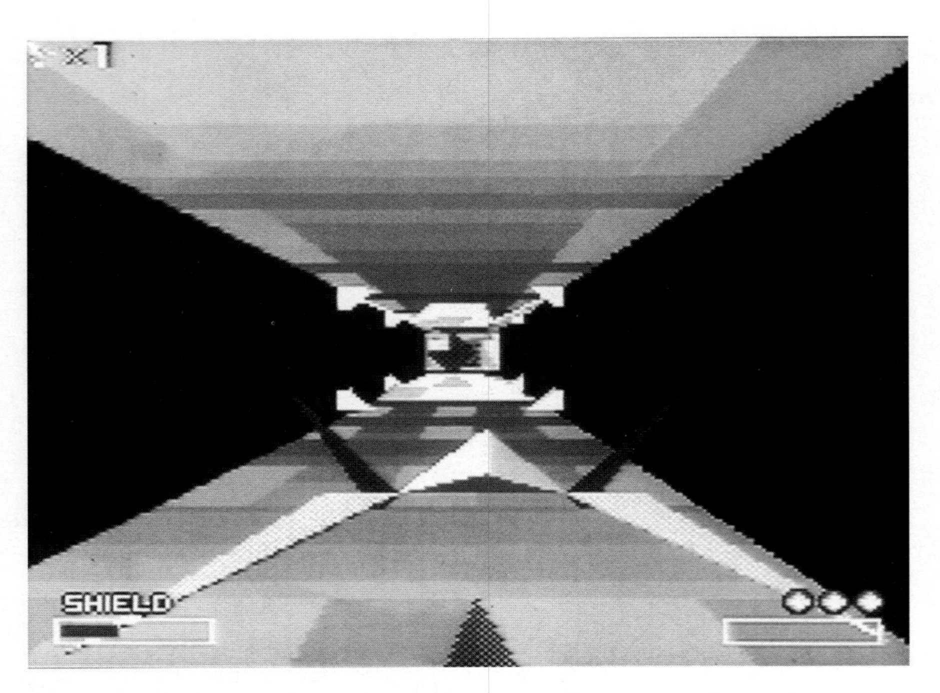

▲ The real-time, 3-D graphics of StarFox makes it an excellent space combat simulator.

▲ Low altitude combat above the planet Corneria.

StarFox

StarFox for the Super NES system was the first game to use the Super FX chip for real-time, 3-D, polygon graphics on a 16-bit gaming platform. StarFox places you in the character of Fox McCloud, who, along with his three friends, must attack an armada from the evil scientist Emperor Andross. Although it's a fairly standard plot, the game itself is an excellent space combat simulator.

Combat scenarios take you from asteroid fields in deep space to low-altitude surface combat. As you fly through the 3-D scenery, you are confronted with a variety of 3-D enemies and obstacles to overcome. There are three different paths (or difficulty levels) on the way to the final mission in the inner core of Planet Venom.

Multimedia

We come now to the area of multimedia titles for the multiplayers. Many of the titles we discussed in Chapter 4, "Interactive Entertainment and Multimedia" have been ported or converted to at least one of the multiplayers. Other titles, such as CPU Bach, have been created specifically for the multiplayer platform.

▲ CPU Bach for the 3DO composes music on-the-fly in the style of Johann Sebastian Bach. *Courtesy of MicroProse.*

CPU Bach

CPU Bach, from MicroProse Software, is truly an achievement in software engineering. A music professor, Dr. Jeffrey Briggs, along with Sid Mier, cofounder and vice president of MicroProse Software, jointly developed a multimedia title that actually composes music in the style of Johann Sebastian Bach on-the-fly as it is being played.

You might have heard synthetic music before and been disappointed by its randomness and lack of harmony, but this system is totally different. Briggs, an accomplished composer and musician, explains that CPU Bach can't be compared with computer-generated music of several years ago. According to Briggs, "The music produced is new continuously, interesting, and best of all sounds good—good enough to have the 'long hairs' turn over in their graves."

You can instruct CPU Bach to generate fugues, suites, chorales, and concerti. Some selections are played by harpsichord, some by piano, and others by flute. While the program is running, you may interact with it, controlling the tempo, mood, overall tone, and even instruments just as a conductor would. If it happens to create a composition that you particularly like, you can save it, and thus assemble a program of your favorite pieces.

Compton's Interactive Encyclopedia

Compton's Interactive Encyclopedia (CIE) for the CD-I multiplayer includes the 9 million words from the standard Compton's Encyclopedia that has been published for the past 70 years. The electronic version is complete with test, sound, pictures, and even full motion video clips.

A number of extra features make CIE interesting and entertaining. One such feature is the Timeline, which enables you to see events from the "Big Bang" up to the 1992 presidential election. You can view the Timeline in a large-scale format (millions of years), or thousands of years, or just a few years at a time. You can click on any specific event and get a more detailed view or a direct link to video, sounds, pictures, or articles.

THE FUTURE OF HOME GAMING SYSTEMS

Now that we have discussed the current state-of-the-art in hardware and software for gaming systems and multiplayers, we are in a better position to look to the future of these platforms. Industry leaders agree that a common thread seems to run through everyone's view of what drives the gaming system/multiplayer platform. This common thread is content.

Content, as in the theme, subject matter, and quality of the game, is the key issue when it comes to creating best-selling titles. Although initially there was some concern that Hollywood owned all the viable content for video games, this has proved false. If you look at the top 50 games from 1992, only three are derived from movies. This demonstrates that regardless of the subject matter, the game won't make it if the quality is not there.

Garry Kitchen, President and CEO of Absolute Entertainment, a video game developer, recently noted at the Intertainment '93 Conference in Santa Monica that the financial return per byte of program is dropping. Kitchen's first cartridge game (Donkey Kong, 1981), sold 4 million units, took five months to create, and used 4,000 lines of code. It made $100 million in sales—$25,000 a byte. Super Battle Tank for SNES did about $6 million in revenue, which comes out to about $11 dollars a byte. The Sega CD platform, with 660M, has sold 20,000 units, which means it has earned one tenth of one cent per byte.

In speaking to Kitchen about where this trend of more-data-less-money is leading, he feels that only the strong companies will survive. The high production costs will keep most smaller developers out of the market. More and more smaller developers (fewer than 10 people) will have to align themselves with larger shops. With a new gaming system coming out every few years, you have to get a title finished as soon as possible. You need a team of, designers, artists, musicians, programmers, and so forth.

"Hopefully, CD-ROM has the potential to offer far greater value on a less costly platform. You can fit much more info on a CD-ROM than you can on a semi-conductor chip for $10 dollars. Because of its much lower manufacturing cost, the volumes will go up and the quality of the product will go up," says Kitchen. "You want to hit a market place like the record industry has with $7 to $12 per record but hitting a much larger audience. If we could sell 2 or 3 million games, that would really help reverse this trend. However, it's not something that we will be seeing soon. It's still another generation beyond Sega CD or even 3DO."

According to Gilman Louie, CEO of Spectrum Holobyte, "We are working on a Star Trek property with synthetic characters, motivations, and even storylines. We have a set of algorithms that generates a character's motivation through a story. Each one of the synthetic characters has separate motivations and learns as they go along."

Louie continues, "We get voice actors involved and record fragments of conversations, and the computer glues those fragments together. What we realize is that if you have a CD-ROM and 1,000 or 1,500 different phrases for each one of the actors, which doesn't take up that much space, you can synthetically glue those dialogs together."

Not only are the character dialogs synthetically generated, but the photography is as well. The computer camera angle has preprogrammed spots and views based on a dramatic action. "It's all algorithms. If you look at *Star Trek: The Next Generation* as a television show, you know what camera angles are going to come up next. The way they shoot their show is very much formula driven. That's true of a lot of other television shows on the market. What we do is try to copy that style. Whether it's a five-second cutaway with a pan, or an over-the-shoulder shot, it's all preprogrammed...and used based on the action happening at hand," says Louie.

In looking at the advancements of the past, the software has always driven the hardware. For the Atari 2600, it was Space Invaders and Pacman—games that were not necessarily great products, but which were highly successful. Then Nintendo released the NES, which became an industry standard with more than 70 percent of the market. It was Super Mario Brothers that pushed the NES to the lead. Super Mario Brothers was a revolutionary product that is still copied by people today. Continuing on, when Sega released the 16-bit Genesis, it was Sonic Hedgehog that drove that platform (albeit just another version of Mario Brothers).

As we look to the future, it will most likely be some "Killer App" that launches one of these new platforms into the lead in terms of market share. According to Kitchen, "Processing power is a lot of marketing hype. What's equally important is the graphics chip; that is what's critical. Still, the major bottle neck is the speed of CD-ROMs. CD-ROMs are an incredible breakthrough in the amount of memory available for a game, and in five years, there will probably be no cartridge business. If it doesn't completely die out, at least no front-line software will be on cartridges. Still, CD-ROMs are not random access, so you must pull data off the disc serially. So the big technical challenge now, as I see it, is to increase the speed of CD-ROMs. There will be a large movement toward electronic delivery of software over cable, phone lines, via satellite or fiber optics."

There have been fantastic breakthroughs and advances in graphics, animation, and audio while there have only been minor breakthroughs in interactivity. "There are games on the Atari 2600 that are as fun as anything out now. CD-ROM's might not progress until play content goes up. Right now you don't see any good CD-ROM interactivity. Developers are having to take a step back in game value because of the CD-ROM's slow speed. It's a big challenge to come up with an entertaining CD-ROM–based game right now with the current platforms. I believe this is the main reason why Nintendo has lagged behind in releasing a CD-ROM system. They understand the importance of content and game play. Super Mario Brothers and The Legend of Zelda have great game play; their graphics may not be 3-D texture-mapped state-of-the-art but the game play is great. Nintendo sees the big picture," says Kitchen.

Kitchen is somewhat afraid that the industry will get overly concerned with hardware technological advances and forget the importance of game play. "The important trends involve the games being fun. We have to focus on real interactivity. Not just decision making at certain paths along a full motion video stream. Everyone talks about FMV, but FMV brings nothing to interactivity at this point. The interactivity is something that is extremely complex and extremely hard to make fun."

"Our goal in making a video game is to make it enjoyable, regardless of graphics, regardless of multimedia, regardless of FMV. All those things add to the experience, but if it's not fun, you can forget it. Tetris is a classic example; no one bought that game for the graphics. Games must be fun, so don't get wowed by all the new technology because if the games are no good, we (the video game industry) are all going to be in a lot of trouble."

Even though there is a Nintendo system in one out of three American homes, it's still not a mass market product. Look at motion pictures for instance; movies have an incredible market appeal that spans all age groups. Video games are still pretty much locked into 12- to 16-year-old boys. Still, many feel that is about to change.

Brian Fargo, president and founder of Interplay, has been in the video game business 10 years. Interplay started out as a developer and then became a publisher for cartridges and computer-based software. According to Fargo, "Software has its own beat, it's not like books, movies, or records. It's not like anything else, and we are definitely heading toward the mass market."

Fargo believes that three things will drive video games into the mass market: abstraction, diversity, and accessibility. "Consider the lack of abstraction in today's games. Twelve years ago, if you had a boat in a game, you would simply print the word 'BOAT' and have it up on the screen. Later you would have a crudely drawn picture of a boat, then a prettier drawn picture of a boat. Today, we go out on location and we film a boat out on the seas. That's a radically different way of approaching what we've done in the past."

"When we first started, a game took up about 4KB, or 4,000 bytes. Today, one sound effect is larger that an entire game was back then. Initially, there was a change over to floppy disk, which was a different way of thinking, and a lot of people didn't make the transition. Next was the transition to seven or eight high density floppies taking up 20MB to 40MB on your hard drive. A lot of people didn't make the transition, and again it was a different way of developing. The budgets went up. Now we are going over to CD-ROM, which is the biggest leap we've ever made. Now we're talking about 600MB of information. Developing games in the past, you always ran out of cartridge space or out of disk space. Now you run out of money.

"This makes the video game industry more like film in that way. Developing a game, you can spend $70 million or $700,000 or $70; the choice of quality is up to you. But the choice of platform is not, right now you have no choice but to make CD-ROM titles. Anyone that's on the fence is pretty foolish; you have to get off the fence; you have to do CD-ROM. Still, there are many differences between developing video games and creating a film. Unlike film, there are a series of trade offs, such as machine performance, and cartridge capacity, whereas a film producer can hire a consultant, spend a lot of money, and put practically anything on a film.

"All of these advancements are causing things in video games to become less abstract. In doing so, you get a level of interest that wasn't there before. I can think of times in the past that we have showed computer video to people and they weren't very excited, saying 'That's not as good as TV.' We've done things that got us very excited, but then when you show it to someone off the street, they say, 'it doesn't look as good as TV,' and that's where we need to get ahead. Getting to that point is the major key in breaking into the mass market."

Fargo also feels that many things are happening to help diversify the market. "You are going to see a lot of diversity in the product lines. Many people are coming into our business that have never even thought about it before—movie people, book people, record people, educational people. These people are all coming into this business to broaden the category and bring a level of interest that was never really there before. This will cause our products to start to appeal to more people than just the hard core gamers.

"Also the cost of CDs are starting to come down, and that will allow us to be more creative. Comparing it to the cartridge business, which has a $20 cost of goods, the CD-ROM at a $1 cost of goods for 100 times the space. There's quite a difference.

Right now we are locked in to making games for 12- to 16-year-old boys because the price of a mistake in trying something for girls or adults is too high. As the costs of goods come down we will be able to get more creative and try some different things.

"We will continue to see domination by the hardware people and the coin-op people. It's not the film people I am so concerned about. I look at the sell-through information for all the games in this country, and only three are movies. Thirty are from Nintendo and Sega, so they have 30 of the top 50 sellers in this country. They are very aggressive, and I see them moving ahead in a lot of areas, and I see them as the big influence—not the movie people."

Finally Brian focuses on accessibility: "Dealing with a personal computer is very complicated. People like 3DO are trying to fix that. Looking at the future with interactive cable TV, if there's really a simple-to-use, accessible set-top box on your TV, you will have video on demand, shopping and games on demand. People who normally would never have looked at this stuff will then take a look and get interested in the category in general."

With all the advances in home gaming systems, will they wipe out the personal computer gaming industry or will the two industries converge? Gilman Louie, CEO of Spectrum Holobyte says "A lot of people think that just because home gaming systems are now getting all this hardware 3-D geometry capabilities, that it will supplant the personal computer as an entertainment device. I don't think that is true; there are a lot of people working on hardware geometry engines for PCs. The problem, in my view, is that the computer is a lousy vehicle for entertainment. People don't go to their den for entertainment, they go to their living room. And the boxes in the living room, whether they are running some form of PC operating system or Nintendo-based operating system, are going to be a completely new kind of machine. In the next couple of years, it will probably look more like the video game machines than it will look like the PCs. I don't fundamentally believe in a large PC marketplace 10 years from now in terms of games. There's a reason why the sales today are 10 to 1 for video game machines to PCs. PCs are not built to be video game machines."

Bob Bates, cofounder of Legend Entertainment, feels differently, "There will be a PC-based entertainment market as long as people keep buying PCs. There will be games developed for PCs and games developed for home gaming systems and multiplayers. I don't see a convergence of the dedicated gaming platform and the personal computer. People will buy Nintendo to play Nintendo games and a PC to work on. But as long as they have that PC, they will probably buy games for it too."

CHAPTER SUMMARY

Home gaming systems have always provided a lot of byte for the buck. The new 64-bit machines from Sega, Atari, and Nintendo carry on that tradition. Meanwhile the new multiplayer systems appear to be bridging the gap between home gaming systems and personal computers. There are literally hundreds of games and titles for these platforms, and the market is too large to ignore.

With great high technology products like StarFox, Star Trek: The Next Generation and CPU Bach, you can move your living room entertainment system into the 21st century for as little as $200. It's a very safe bet that home gaming systems and multiplayers are here to stay.

Next, we move to portable gaming units. These are products that enable you to take computing power and interactive entertainment on the road, by the pool, or anywhere else you want to be.

6

Portable Interactive Entertainment

"The beauty of the portable units is that you can use them anywhere—at the pool while getting your tan, at the amusement park while waiting in line, at the garage while waiting for an oil change…"

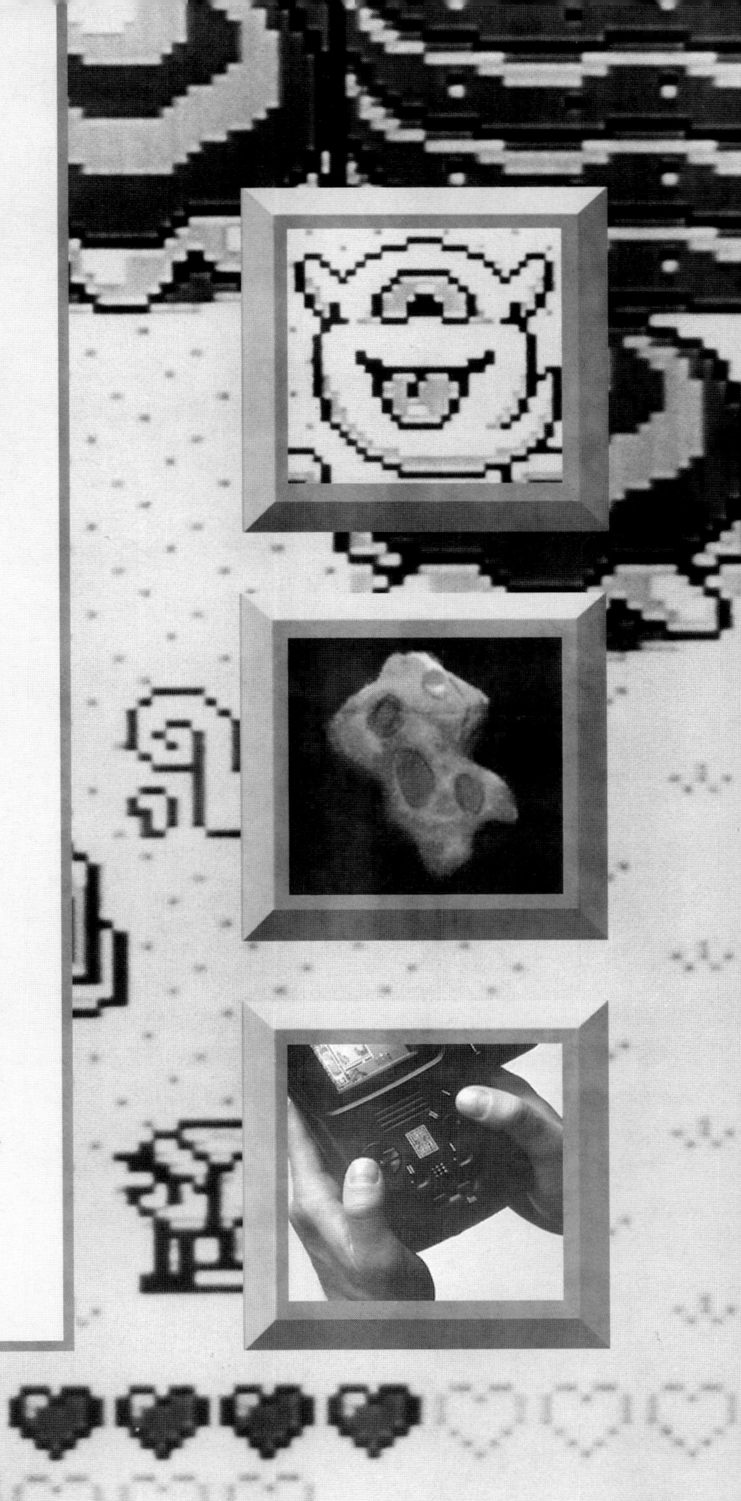

Of all the new technologies responsible for the acceptance of video games for adults, the portable game unit is perhaps the greatest. While only about 35 percent of home gaming system players are adults, more than 46 percent of portable game players are adults. Likewise, portable gaming systems appeal more to adult females, with 44 percent of adult players being women as opposed to 29 percent for home gaming systems.

Portable game systems, such as the Nintendo Game Boy, started shipping in 1989. Following closely on Game Boy's heels were the Atari Lynx, NEC Turbo Express, and the Sega Game Gear. All provide entertainment for the road with their cartridge-based games. New multiplayer systems, such as the Sony Multimedia Player and Philips portable CD-I, offer entertainment and information for adults on the go.

Anyone who has flown across the country in a plane knows that sometimes you get tired of reading. If you are by yourself with no one to talk to, your options are pretty limited when it comes to being entertained. The beauty of the portable units is that you can use them anywhere—at the pool while getting your tan, at the amusement park while waiting in line, at the garage while waiting for an oil change—practically any time or location away from home when you have to wait on something. Game developers have also noticed the trend toward older players and have responded with a variety of games geared toward the adult audience.

For example, Parker Brothers has released a cartridge for the Game Boy that allows you to play Monopoly with as many as four players. Other companies offer various adult-oriented games such as poker and chess, most of which require no hand-eye coordination whatsoever.

To increase its value as a portable system, Turbo Express from NEC offers a high-resolution color display, and even a television tuner that allows you to watch TV if you get bored playing games. Some systems offer 16-bit graphics with stereo sound, all running on AAA batteries for a street price of well under $100.

What technology is behind the portable gaming systems? What portables are available and how expensive are they? How are games developed for portables? What types of games are on the market now? These questions will be answered in this chapter.

PORTABLE GAMING SYSTEMS—HOW THEY WORK

The biggest challenge to video game manufacturers in making portable systems is the display. The first portable gaming unit, the Nintendo Game Boy, used a monochrome display capable of only four shades of gray. The screen, about 1 3/4-inch square, had a resolution of 140×102 pixels. The display technology used for the Game Boy is similar to that used in many digital watches—Liquid Crystal Display (LCD).

LCD technology was invented in the 1970s. It relies on the unusual properties of liquid crystal, which is a liquid that exhibits properties of both solid crystals and liquids at the same time. The molecules of liquid crystals can orient themselves in a specific order when exposed to magnetic or electrical fields. For example, if you shine a light through a thin layer of liquid crystal, the light waves pass straight through the liquid crystal without any effects. If you then apply a small electrical field to the liquid crystal, the orientation of the molecules in the liquid crystal will start to twist. This movement, in turn, twists the light waves as they travel through the liquid crystal.

So, by adjusting the electrical field in the liquid crystal, the light waves can be rotated to any angle required. Now, imagine that we place a mirror or reflective surface on one side of the layer of liquid crystal and then shine a light through it to the mirror. What happens? The light travels through the liquid crystal, bounces off the reflective surface, then travels back through the liquid crystal to the viewer. To the viewer, the liquid crystal does not affect the reflected light at all.

Let's take it one step further. By shining a light through a polarized filter, you can filter all of the light waves, except those oriented in a particular direction. Say we place a horizontal polarizing filter in front of the liquid crystal layer. Now when you shine a light on the filter, it blocks out all the light waves except those oriented horizontally. Those horizontal waves travel through the liquid crystal layer, bounce off the reflective layer, pass back through the liquid crystal, and back through the horizontal polarizing filter, and you see the reflected light.

If you were to apply an electrical field to the liquid crystal layer at this point, it would then twist the horizontal light waves coming through the horizontal polarizing filter. The light waves would then bounce off the reflector, go through the liquid crystal again, and twist even further—perhaps to a vertical orientation. After passing through the liquid crystal, those vertical light waves will be blocked by the horizontal polarizing filter. The end result is that you would not see the reflected light. It would appear dark, like a dark pair of sunglasses.

To turn this technology into a display screen, we need only divide the layer of liquid crystal into small segments or cells. Next we apply a small electrical current to each cell individually to make that cell block any reflected light. If we vary the amount of electrical current applied to each cell, we can carefully control the angle of the light waves. Slightly rotating the light wave causes it to be only partially blocked by the polarizing filter. This allows some of the light to escape and provides a shade between on (totally blocked) and off (totally clear).

Liquid crystal displays that twist the light 90 degrees are called *twisted nematic* (TN). The only problems are that they need a lot of ambient bright light and the viewing angle is very small. For best results, you must be directly in front of the display. The LCD technology used in the Nintendo Game Boy is called supertwist nematic (STN). *Supertwist* LCDs twist the light waves 180 degrees or more as they pass through the liquid crystal. You can recognize supertwist LCDs by their yellow and greenish color.

Supertwist LCDs use a *passive matrix* technology. That means the electric current used to twist the liquid crystal cells travels along transparent electrodes printed on the glass screen. Transistors around the edges of the display drive these electrodes. A grid-like matrix is formed from these horizontal and vertical electrodes, and a liquid crystal cell is at every intersection. Each cell then represents a pixel on the LCD. A problem with passive matrix is that, at times, the current is lost due to electrical interference as the electrodes criss-cross each other. Another problem is the slow update speed of the screen. Objects that move very quickly on the screen sometimes seem to disappear.

To solve these two problems, a new technology was developed called *active matrix*. Active matrix was developed in the early 1980s and first appeared on the market in 1985 with Seiko Epson Corporation's portable TVs with 1.9-inch diagonal screens. The active matrix LCD works in much the same way as the passive matrix LCD except that instead of the voltage being controlled by transistors along the edge of the screen, thin-film transistors are placed on every single cell in the matrix. In this way, the voltages can be altered faster, which results in faster displays.

These thin-film transistors also put out varying levels of current, which can represent different intensities or shades of gray. Another great advance was backlighting. This is where a fluorescent panel is placed behind the liquid crystal film instead of a reflective surface. This technique greatly increased the visibility and contrast of LCD panels and paved the way for color LCDs.

For color LCD, cells are divided into groups of three. Colored filters are put over each cell in the display. One cell has a red filter, another has a green filter, and one has a blue filter. When the individual cells are small enough, the human eye, just as it does with televisions and computer monitors, blends all three cells into one color.

The second biggest technical obstacle with portable systems is that of battery life. Making the display better in terms of color and resolution creates a tremendous demand on the battery. Likewise, the microprocessors used in portable systems require a lot of power.

The larger a microprocessor, the more power it requires. That fact, along with the less than $100 average price of most portable gaming systems, has resulted in 8-bit portable game systems dominating the market. While battery life varies among the current systems, you can expect batteries to run a portable system between 6 and 30 hours. This has caused a number of third-party companies to develop NiCad or rechargeable battery systems.

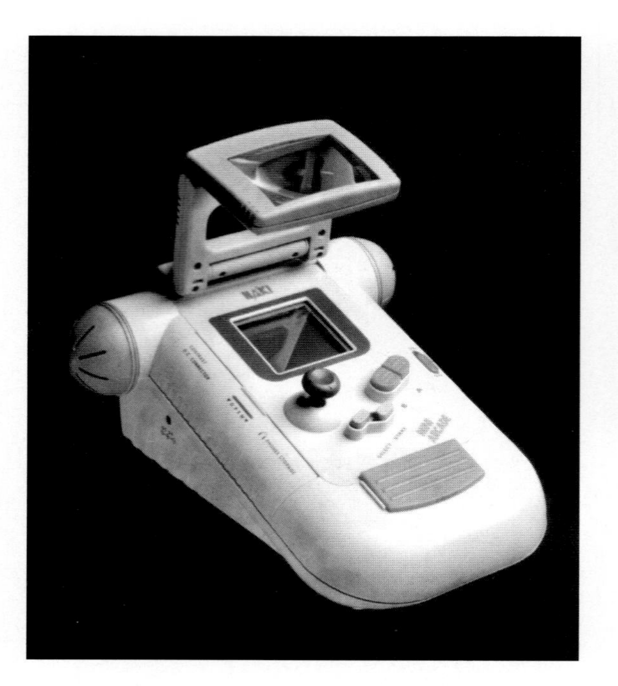

▲ A rechargeable battery system for the Sega Game Gear from NAKI. *Courtesy of NAKI Electronics, Inc.*

▲ Two Nintendo Game Boys linked with a "Head-to-Head" communications cable. The cable allows two people to play together in the same game on two different portable units. *Courtesy of Nintendo of America.*

As with their larger homebound cousins, portable gaming systems have common controller buttons to control direction, and multiple fire and select buttons. All portable systems offer stereo sound, if you plug headphones into the mini stereo jack.

An added feature of many portable systems is a communications port. Since the controller buttons are built into the unit itself and not on an external pad (as in the home gaming systems), you cannot simply plug another controller into the system to enable two people to play simultaneously. Instead, portable games offer data communications ports that enable you to hook portable units together. Data is passed from machine to machine so the players can compete against each other or work as a team and compete against the systems themselves.

Finally, we come to the games themselves. Since the cartridges for portable systems must be smaller than their home gaming system counterparts, manufacturers need the smallest possible components, so they take advantage of technologies such as large scale integration and surface mount technology.

Large scale integration (LSI) is a term that refers to the number of electronic components built into a single chip. LSI chips have from 3,000 to 100,000 transistors on a single chip. This allows the portable gaming cartridges to be very small and compact.

Surface mount technology is the process of mounting chips and other components to the surface of a printed circuit board (PCB). In the past, components were plugged into holes in the PCBs, then soldered into place on the back side of the PCB. By using surface mount technology, more components can be fitted into less space and the process is more cost-effective.

▲ The Nintendo Game Boy, the first portable gaming system on the market. *Courtesy of Nintendo of America.*

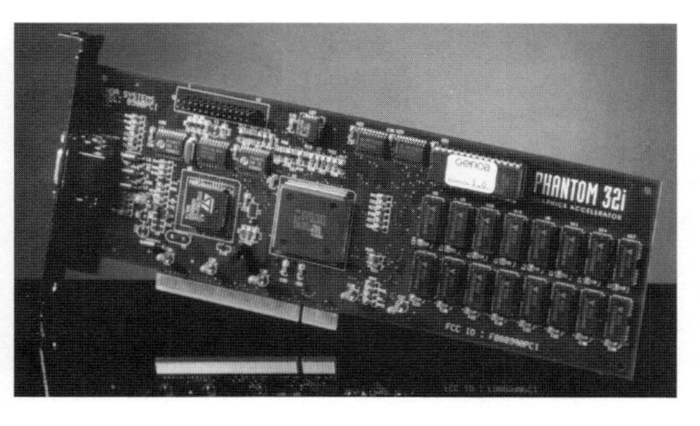

▲ Surface Mount Technology allows components to be mounted to the surface of circuit boards.

CURRENT PORTABLE GAMING SYSTEMS

As with home systems, portable systems can be divided into two areas: gaming systems and multiplayer or multimedia systems. Only four gaming systems are on the market now: Nintendo Game Boy, Sega Game Gear, Atari Lynx, and Turbo Technologies Turbo Express. In the portable multimedia player market, three products are available: Sony Discman, Sony Multimedia Player, and Philips CD-I. First, let's look at the portable game systems.

Nintendo Game Boy

The Game Boy was the first true portable gaming system on the market that used interchangeable game cartridges just like the home systems. Despite being the oldest portable system, the Game Boy is still the smallest with dimensions of 3 1/2-inches by less than 6 inches by less than 1 1/2-inches. The Game Boy weighs about 10 1/2-ounces, and has a battery life of 35 hours (on 4 AA size batteries).

Game Boy uses an 8-bit Motorola 6502 microprocessor running at a speed of 2.14 MHz. The screen resolution is 140×102, and it is capable of monochrome (one color) with four shades. A large variety of available add-ons help Game Boy's display. The unit's small, sleek design has made it very popular with adults.

Even though it has been technically surpassed by other gaming systems, the Game Boy still reigns as a bestseller, with more than 13 million units sold since its initial release. Adults are attracted to the Game Boy because it is small and discreet, and the level of concentration it demands is high. Adults view it as a good stress reliever, fun, and challenging, and an exciting way to fill downtime.

Game Boy offers a Head-to-Head cable that you can use to hook two systems together for multiplayer games. The game itself has to support this option, and each system must have its own cartridge.

There are currently more than 300 Game Boy titles, and the unit now sells for a suggested retail price of $49.95. It has the lowest price of any portable system on the market, but many feel it is getting dated, and that fewer and fewer new titles will be released for it in the future.

▲ The Sega Game Gear offers a color screen and a great variety of games. *Courtesy of Sega of America, Inc.*

Sega Game Gear

Game Gear from Sega was the first portable gaming system to offer a color screen. The screen measures slightly more than 3 inches diagonally and displays up to 32 colors (from a palette of 4,096) at a resolution of 160×146. It uses the Zilog Z-80 microprocessor, which runs at 3.6 MHz and has a suggested retail price of $99.99.

Naturally, with a color screen and high computing power, the Game Gear has a much shorter battery life than the Game Boy, even though it uses six AA batteries. As with the Game Boy, Game Gear has a unit-to-unit option that enables two players to compete by linking their systems. As an added option, a TV Tuner card plugs into the cartridge slot and turns the Game Gear into a portable TV. The TV Tuner card retails for $119.99.

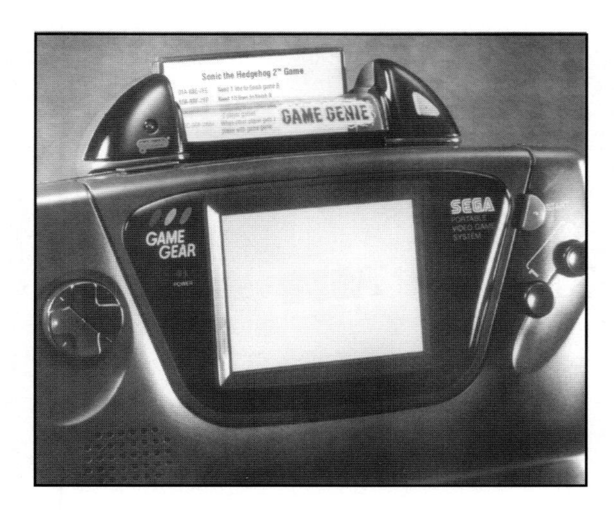

▲ The TV Tuner turns the Game Gear into a portable TV.

Game Gear is clearly the leader of the color portable systems. Currently, more than 200 titles are available, and the number is increasing. Since Game Gear is so successful, a variety of add-on products are available, from rechargeable battery packs to waterproof cases with magnifying screens (for myopic players who like to play in the rain?).

▲ The Turbo Express from Turbo Technologies. *Courtesy of Aldrich and Associates.*

Atari Lynx

Atari released the Lynx system with high hopes of it beating out Game Gear. It supports a faster microprocessor, the Motorola 65C02 running at 4 MHz. However, Lynx's color screen falls behind the capabilities of the Game Gear system. It is only capable of displaying 16 colors at a time at a resolution of 160×102. The Lynx system retails for $70, which places it between Game Boy and Game Gear.

Currently there is a severe lack of games for Lynx, and its popularity seems to be declining among both game developers and game players.

NEC Turbo Express

Finally, the Turbo Express from Turbo Technologies has perhaps the ultimate in portable gaming system performance. It is simply a scaled-down, portable version of the Turbo Technologies home gaming system, the Turbo Grafx 16. It features an 8-bit 6820 microprocessor running at 7.16 MHz.

It features the highest quality screen with 256 colors at a resolution of 400×270. The most outstanding feature is its full compatibility with cartridges for the home system. Anything that runs on the Turbo Grafx 16 will run on the Turbo Express. The only downfall is that games designed for a 21-inch television are very hard to see when displayed on a 3 1/2-inch screen. You need to strain to see the on-screen characters.

You don't get such a high-powered system without paying the price in battery life. The Turbo Express can wipe out six AA batteries in three to four hours. The price, $199.99 (twice as expensive as the leading portable system), also puts a damper on the Turbo Express. As with the Game Gear system, an optional TV tuner attachment is available.

Portable Multimedia Players

A new area of interest is portable multimedia players. Both Sony and Philips have these players, along with related software, already on the market.

Sony Multimedia Player

Sony was the first to release a portable CD-ROM–based multimedia player called the Sony PIX-100. As with PC-based multimedia, the PX-100 player uses CD-ROM XA style CDs for integration of text, sound, pictures, and animation on the same CD-ROM. It also plays standard audio CDs.

The PX-100 uses a 9.55 MHz microprocessor called the V20HL. The V20HL is software compatible with Intel 8088 microprocessors (IBM compatible personal computers). It comes with 1MB of RAM, a QWERTY-style keyboard, and an internal speaker (along with a stereo mini-jack for stereo output). The screen is a backlit, monochrome LCD with seven shades of gray and a resolution of 320×200. Extra features include a serial communications port and a video output jack for connecting to a television.

Because of its large 5-inch LCD display, full keyboard, and CD-ROM drive, battery life is limited to about two hours of continuous play. The PX-100 comes with a rechargeable battery and a programmable power-off timer. If play stops, the timer shuts off the system after a specified time.

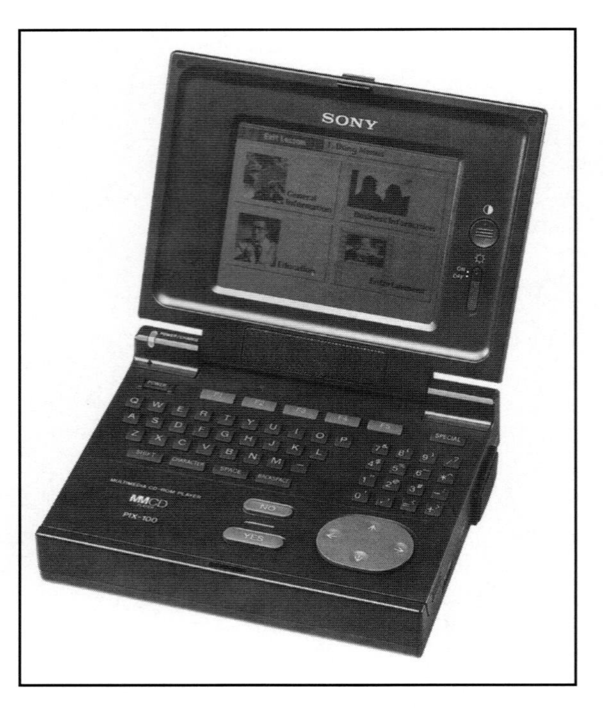

▲ The Sony Multimedia Player, PX-100. *Courtesy of Sony.*

A large variety of software is available and easily identified by the MMCD logo. More than 70 cartridges are available for the PX-100, including productivity, entertainment, educational, and reference software.

MMCD™
PLAYER

Logo for Multimedia CD-ROM Players.

MMCD™
PLAYER
SOFTWARE

Logo for Multimedia CD-ROM Player compatible software.

▲ The MMCD logo identifies a software product as compatible with Sony's Multimedia Player. *Courtesy of Sony.*

Sony Data Discman

The Data Discman products from Sony are based on the 3-inch Compact Disc format known as CD3. The Discman comes in two models: the DD-8D and DD-20B. As with the Sony Multimedia Player, more than 50 titles are available for the Discman.

▲ The Sony Data Discman model DD-20B.
Courtesy of Sony.

Both Discman models use a 4-inch LCD display with a resolution of 256×200. The 3-inch compact discs can hold about 200MB of storage, as compared to normal CD-ROMs, which hold 600MB.

Both units require four AA size batteries, which will last about three hours, slightly longer than the Multimedia Player. A complete QWERTY-style keyboard is built into each model along with an internal speaker, stereo mini-jack, and video connector.

Philips CD-I 350

The Philips CD-I model 350 is a portable version of the standard home CD-I player. It is compatible with all existing CD-I titles, Photo CDs, and standard audio CDs. The screen is perhaps the best in the entire portable market. It's an active matrix 6-inch high resolution (720×240) color LCD panel. A rechargeable battery pack is available for the CD-I 350, but the standard unit comes with an AC adapter. The CD-I 350 weighs about 4 pounds and has connectors for output to a television, as well as mini stereo jacks for headphones. It also offers built-in stereo speakers.

Now that we have discussed all the current gaming systems and multiplayers, let's take a look at the software. We will begin by looking at the development of a title for the Nintendo Game Boy called Star Trek: The Next Generation (STNG), created by Absolute Entertainment.

THE CREATION OF A PORTABLE SYSTEM TITLE: STAR TREK: THE NEXT GENERATION BY ABSOLUTE ENTERTAINMENT

Garry Kitchen started Absolute Entertainment in 1986 with four employees. Absolute has progressed through the levels of developer to publisher and now has 110 employees. Development accounts for 70 percent of the company's resources. The firm has developed more than 100 video game cartridges since 1986, and 60 titles for the Sega and Nintendo systems since 1989 (which have generated about $250 million in wholesale sales).

According to Kitchen, who is president of Absolute Entertainment, "We concentrate on cartridge games, and a lot of people don't realize what's involved in the cart (cartridge) business. We spend about 12 to 18 months to do a top quality 16-bit cart. We do about 90 percent of the development inside our own labs, and it will typically cost us somewhere between $150,000 and $300,000."

Absolute starts each project with a team that consists of a creative director and a technical director. The creative director looks at the design of the product and gets a feel for it. The technical director deals with the implementation. There is usually one lead programmer, along with one or several support programmers. An art director oversees the actual look of the product while various in-house artists specialize in background art, animation, or other aspects of the game.

An in-house technical support group handles any problems dealing with equipment and maintenance. They also get involved in creating and developing software tools. They have developed a series of tools that are platform independent, so they can create games for the 3DO, Jaguar, Sega CD, or any platform. Absolute has a multimedia studio complete with a blue screen room for filming. To create full motion video they have a video room with video digitizing equipment. The firm also has an audio recording studio, and a very extensive testing department.

According to Kitchen, "A lot of people underestimate what it takes to create a competitive video game cartridge. It's a tremendously complicated process that involves many disciplines and a lot of technology. As much as you try to schedule and predict the development process of a video game, it's really not done until it's fun."

▲ Star Trek: The Next Generation for the Nintendo Game Boy. *Courtesy of Nintendo of America. Star Trek: The Next Generation is a registered trademark of Paramount Pictures.*

Star Trek: The Next Generation

The Game Boy version of Star Trek: The Next Generation is very faithful to the TV series. The scenario is that you are a student in the Star Fleet Academy who has qualified for a special holodeck training session. Captain Jean-Luc Picard has been chosen to administer this training session in which you become the captain of the U.S.S. Enterprise while Picard sends you on a variety of missions.

You may be assigned to respond to a wide variety of problems such as dealing with a distress call to evacuate a planet, transporting valuable cargo and VIPs, or defending helpless colonies from attackers. Once your mission has been assigned, you move to the bridge of the Enterprise and the main view screen.

Colo
Galler
THRE

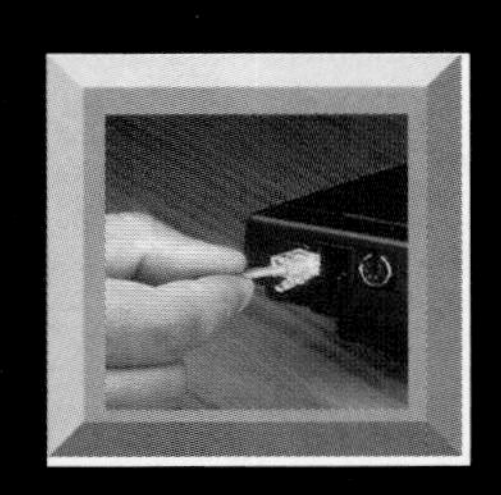

PUSH

America Online offers a variety of online action, strategy, and role-playing games. One very popular role-playing game is called Forgotten Realms. With the information superhighway just around the corner we should see multiplayer networked games becoming more popular.

Courtesy of America Online.

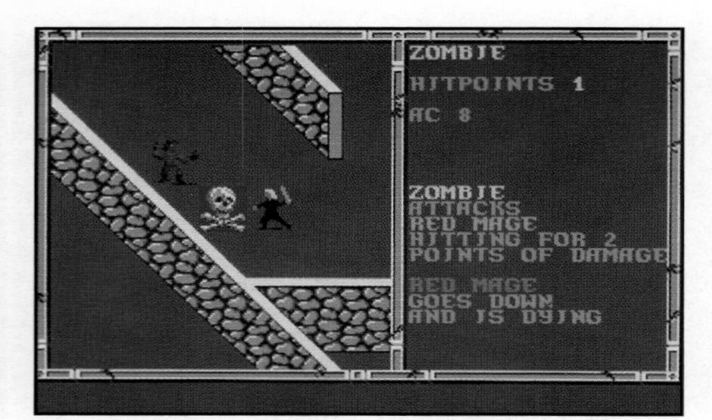

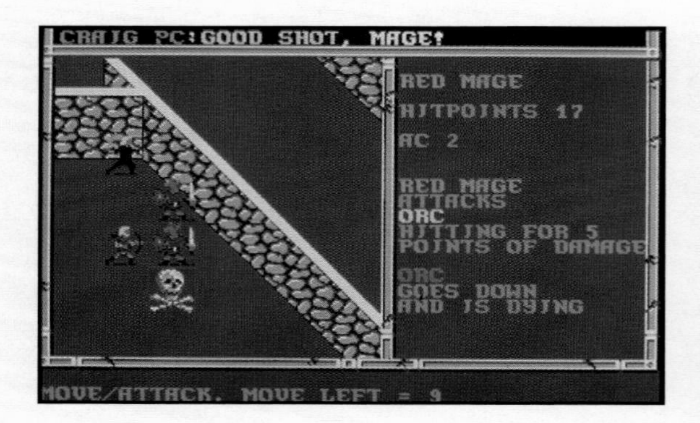

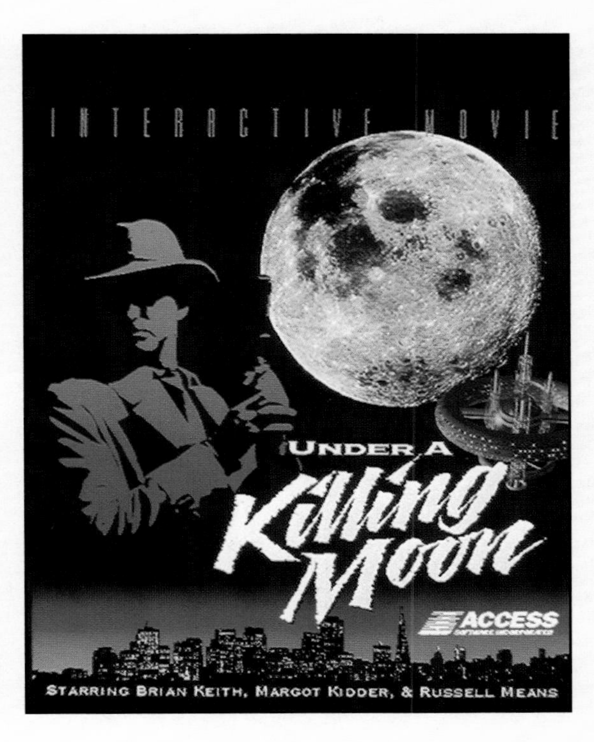

Under A Killing Moon from Access Software is a good example of how Hollywood actors are moving into the video game field. Professional actors, Margot Kidder (*Superman I, II*), Brian Keith (*Hardcastle & McCormick*, *The Parent Trap*) and Russell Means (*The Last of the Mohicans*) star in Killing Moon. Shipping on two CD-ROMs, Killing Moon offers over two hours of digital video. You can move through a 3-D world, interacting with the characters and solving your case.

Courtesy of Access Software, Inc.

Crime Patrol 2 by American Laser Games is a coin-op arcade game made for a laser disc player. With the advent of digital video, these laser disc games are finding their way into the home gaming system and personal computer market. American Laser Games has produced over seven laser disc games for the coin-op market. Of all Interactive Entertainment developers they have the most experience in creating interactive movies with branching storylines.

Courtesy of American Laser Games.

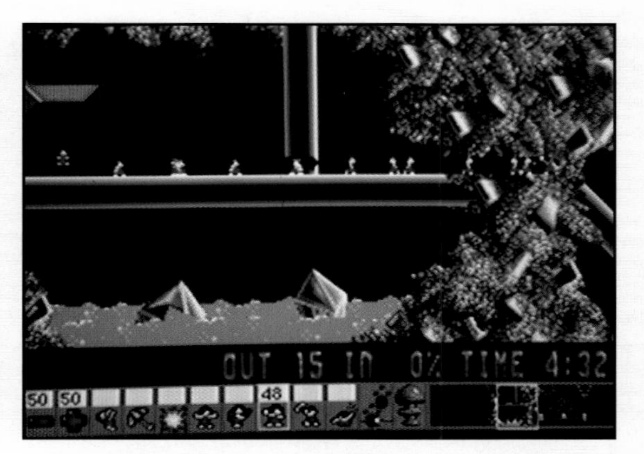

Lemmings from Psygnosis is part strategy, part action, and part animal rights activists. You take the lead in guiding bumbling lemmings safely through various hazards one level at a time. The Lemmings proceed blindly to their goal, sometimes falling to their deaths, so it's up to you to guide and direct them in building bridges, digging tunnels, and climbing. The 3DO version of Lemmings is the latest installment of this title. Originally starting out on personal computers, Lemmings has become so popular it has migrated to practically every other platform in existence from the Sega Game Gear to the Super NES and now the 3DO multiplayer. Lemmings is an excellent example of how gameplay is more information than technology. It doesn't use 3-D texture-mapped polygons, yet it's more fun than many games that do.

Courtesy of Psygnosis.

The Lost Tribe from Lawrence Products is an excellent educational game for children ages 6 to 10. In The Lost Tribe, you are the leader of a motley prehistoric tribe. After your homeland (along with your leader and hunting party) is destroyed by a volcano, you assume the role of leader to take your tribe to a new land. Good judgment must be exercised along the way as you react to unforeseen events. There are four main obstacles that you must face during the game: natural barriers, the limits of time, the need for food, and occasional surprises. Sound planning and a willingness to take risks help you survive and lead your tribe to safety. The game serves as an aid to learning decision-making and leadership skills. Lost Tribe is entertaining enough to appeal to adults.

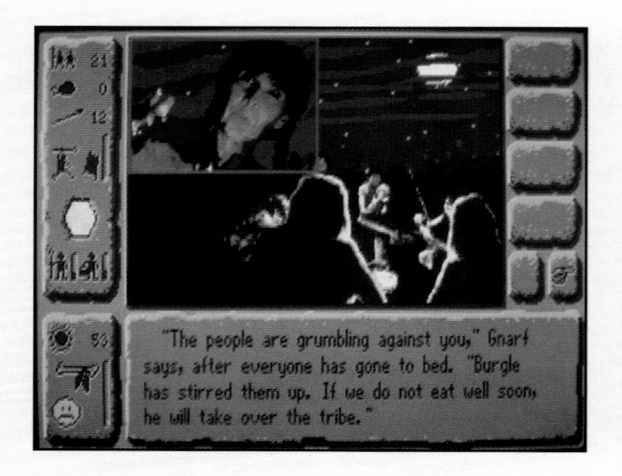

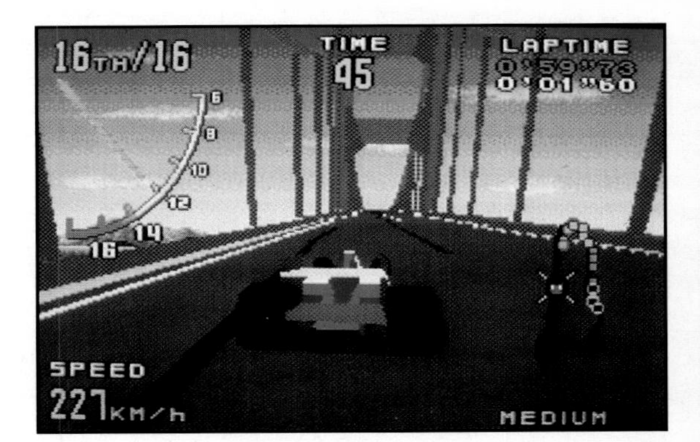

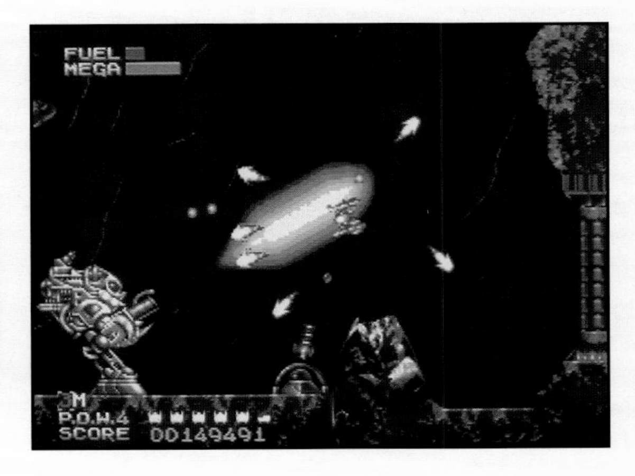

The Sega Genesis game system had the distinction of being the first 16-bit system on the market. Despite the overwhelming success of Nintendo in the 8-bit game market, Sega forged ahead and was rewarded with a full year's jump start on the SNES. With stereo sound, a CD attachment, and a library of over 350 games, the Genesis still leads the 16-bit market. Many new Sega games are coming from existing Sega Arcade games such as Virtual Racing and Sub-Terrania (pictured here).

Courtesy of Sega of America, Inc.

Developed from the Discovery Channel special, Beyond Planet Earth is a CD-ROM that explains space exploration, past, present, and future. Narrated by actor Richard Kiley, it offers beautiful NASA photography, digital video clips, stereo sound, and interviews with four top space experts including Buzz Aldrin, one of the first men on the moon. A hypertext glossary allows you to quickly locate the meaning of unfamiliar terms. Using the glossary as a reference tool, you can copy text into other applications. Beyond Planet Earth is another good example of taking existing content (in this case a video) and "repurposing" it into a multimedia title.

Courtesy of Discovery Communications, Inc.

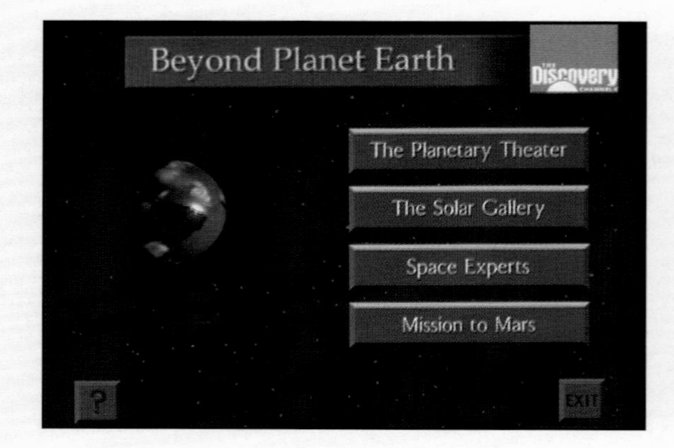

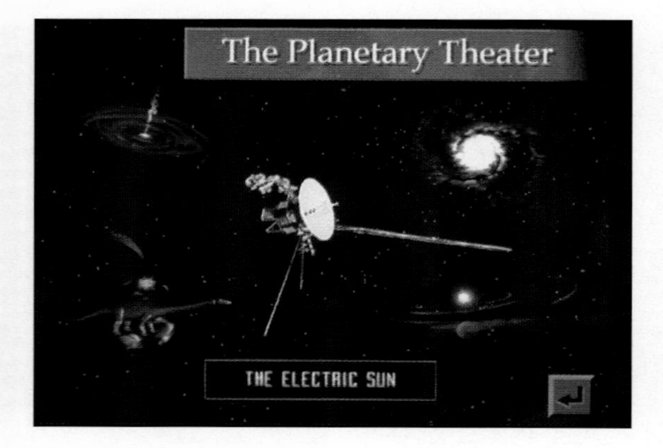

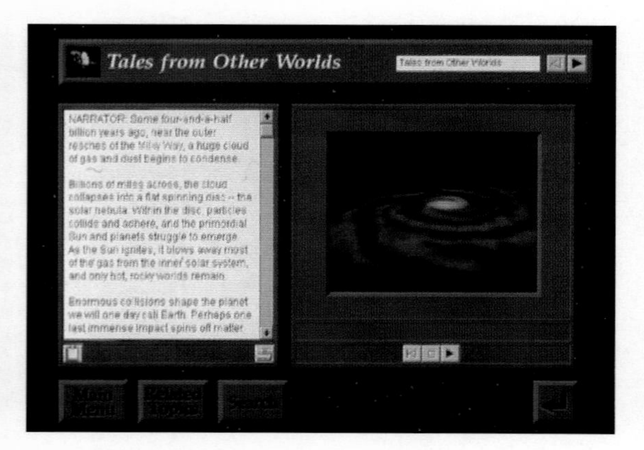

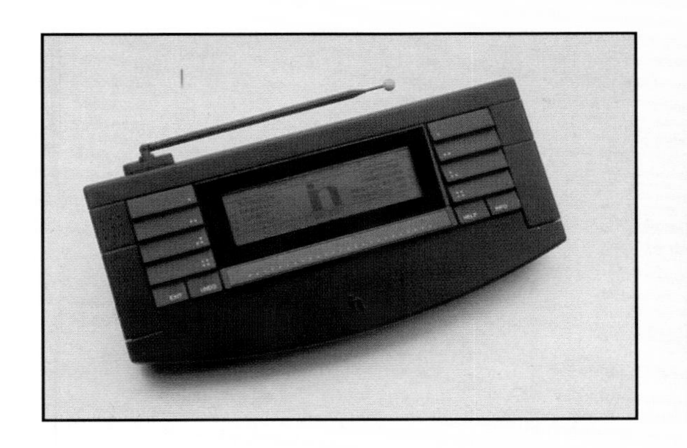

Interactive Network Television (INT) is a subscription-based interactive TV service provider that supplies over 100 interactive programs a day to its subscribers. INT uses FM broadcast to transmit data to the home network control units. The home network control unit has a suggested retail price of $199, and the monthly service charge is only $15. The subscribers at home can play along with sports, game shows, drama, news, and special events as they are happening.

Almost every televised professional sporting event is broadcast interactively. Also included are many prime time shows such as "Murder, She Wrote;" "Quantum Leap;" "Law and Order;" "L.A. Law;" "Jeopardy!;" "Wheel of Fortune;" and many others. Some of the interactive news and talk shows include "20/20," "NBC Nightly News," and "60 Minutes." Following each game or program, subscribers have the option of downloading their scores to INT headquarters for compilation and ranking.

Courtesy of Interactive Network.

Now you can star in your own game shows with Twisted for the 3DO multiplayer. Designed as a multiplayer game from Electronic Arts, Twisted features eight different TV contests. Play it with friends or compete against the six game show characters. Twisted even throws in the occasional cheesy commercial.

Courtesy of Electronic Arts.

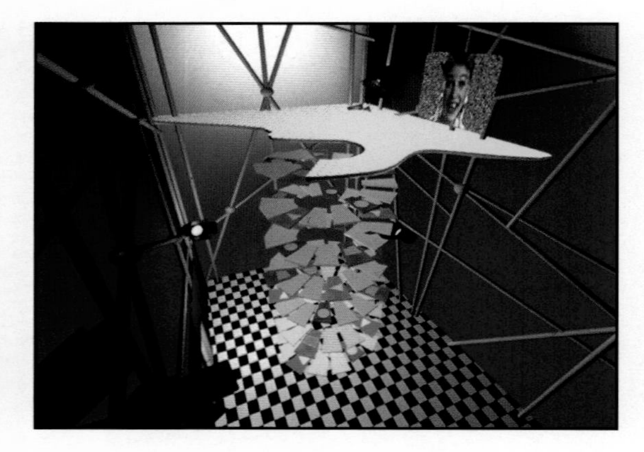

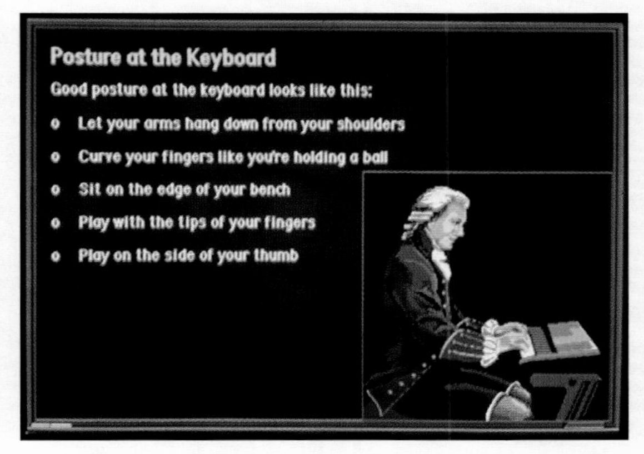

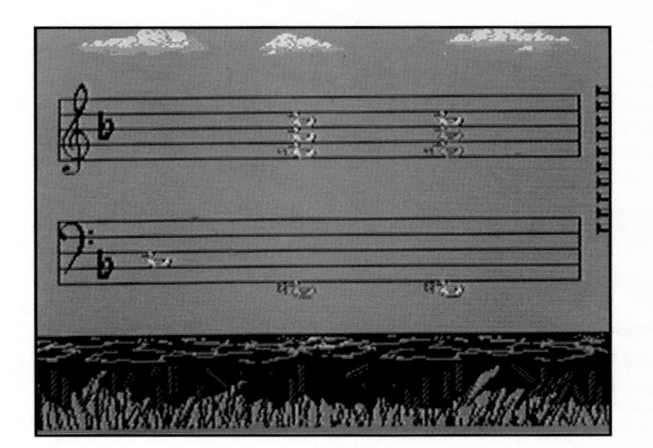

The Miracle from Software Toolworks is a combination of hardware and software that you can add to your home PC, Mac, or Nintendo system. It comes with a full function MIDI electronic keyboard, necessary cables, and software. The software comprises a year-long piano course. It can communicate to the keyboard and detect which keys you play, when you press them, how hard you press them, and when you release them. This information gets passed on to the computer, which in turn uses artificial intelligence routines to analyze the way you play. After determining the most significant errors, the software recommends and sometimes creates specific exercises to improve your playing. For younger ones, it comes with video games in which you play the piano keyboard to control the on-screen action.

Courtesy of Software Toolworks.

Launched in 1991, the SNES is Nintendo's 16-bit game system. However, it was released a full year behind the 16-bit Sega Genesis and suffers stiff competition from Sega even today. Still, Nintendo has a very large and loyal following with game developers who continue to produce 16-bit games for the SNES, some of which are pictured here. With competition rising from 32-bit and 64-bit gaming machines, Nintendo has been trying to breathe life into the SNES with advanced 3-D chips that are now included in some games such as Star Fox.

Courtesy of Nintendo of America.

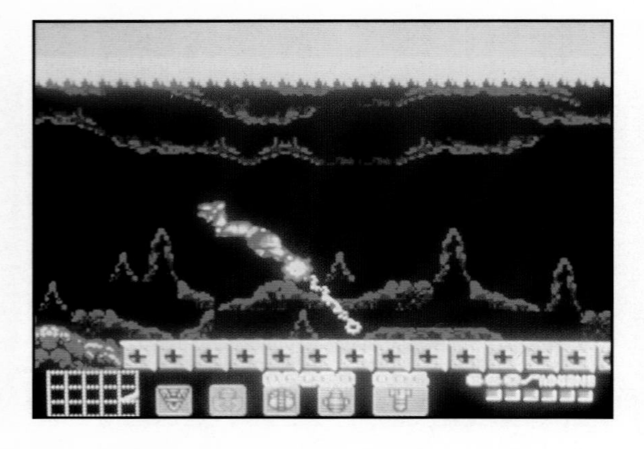

Animals and How They Grow is another CD-ROM title from National Geographic's new series, Wonders of Learning CD-ROM library. The CD-ROM includes five different books covering the main categories of animals. The speed of the narration can be varied according to the listener's preference. The narration can be switched from English to Spanish. "Animals" investigates the lives of mammals, reptiles, amphibians, birds, and insects. It also explains how these animals grow and develop.

Courtesy of National Geographic.

AH-3 Thunderstrike for the Sega CD is a helicopter combat simulator. You select which campaign you want to fly, from Central America, Eastern Europe, Panama Canal, South America, the Middle East, Southeast Asia, South China Seas, and even Alaska. Each campaign has 3 to 5 missions for a total of 40 for the entire game. Missions vary from sinking pirate ships in the South China Seas to destroying guerrilla convoys in South America. The simulator is in 3-D, so you can rotate 360 degrees and head back where you came from. You have a variety of weaponry to use such as lock-on missiles, rockets, and a Vulcan cannon. After each mission, you go through a debriefing to determine whether you made your primary objectives. If you did, you may be in line for a medal.

Courtesy of JVC Musical Industries, Inc. ™ and © 1993 Core Design Ltd. © 1993 JVC Musical Industries, Inc.

Shock Wave from Electronic Arts is the most realistic 3-D Sci-Fi flight simulator available. Created for the 3DO multiplayer, it takes full advantage of the 3DO's built-in 3-D, texture-mapped, polygon graphics. The graphics bring a new level of realism to gaming systems. with 24-bit color (16.7 million colors). Live video combines with 3-D computer rendered scenes (rendered on high-performance Silicon Graphics systems) to create a spectacular and beautiful simulation.

Courtesy of Electronic Arts.

Battle Chess from Interplay Productions is a port from the PC-based multimedia version. At first glance it simply looks like a very colorful chess program, but as soon as you make your first move, you'll quickly see what makes Battle Chess so popular. All of the chess pieces are animated. When you move a piece, it picks itself up and walks to the new location. If you take your opponent's piece, the two pieces duel it out with their respective weapons. The 3DO version offers digital sound and ten levels of difficulty.

Courtesy of Interplay Productions.

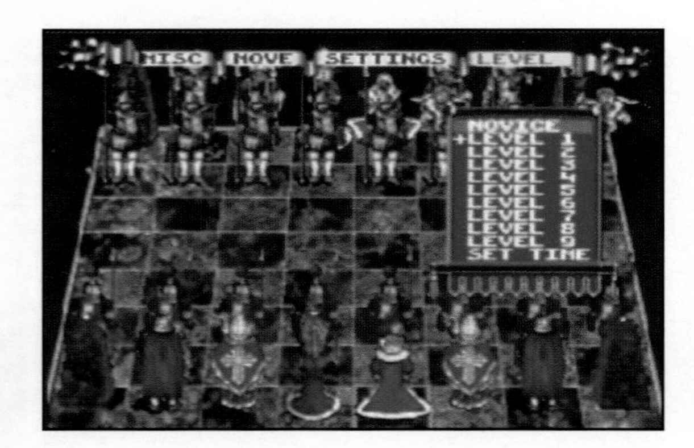

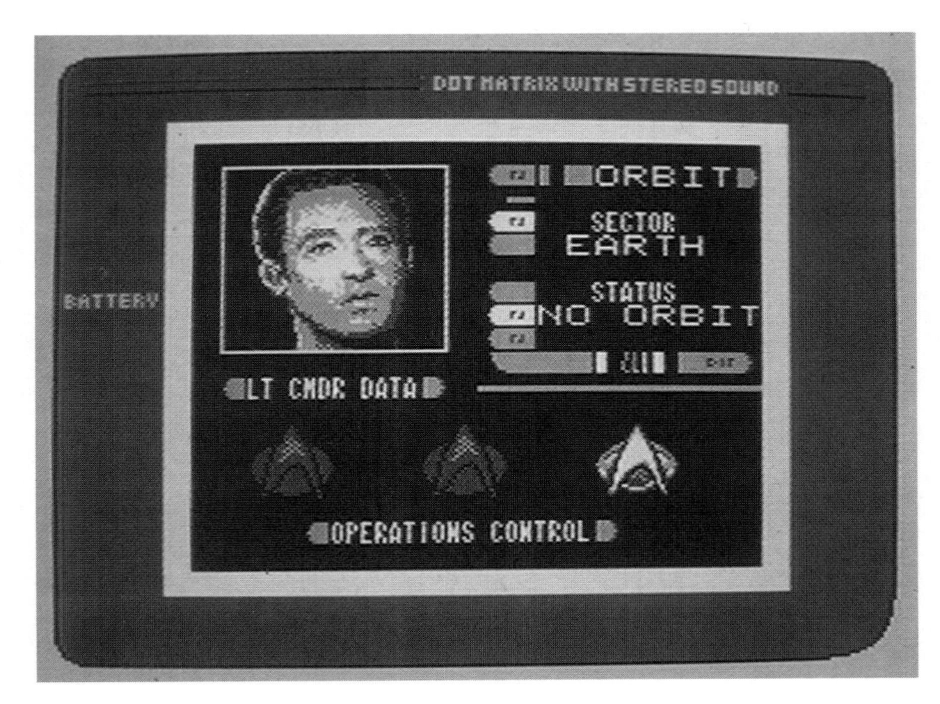

▲ The main view screen allows you to access any section or crew member of the Enterprise.

From the main view screen, you can access other crew members, and enlist their help in solving problems. For instance, if the ship comes under attack, you will need Lieutenant Worf's help in raising the shields and powering up photon torpedoes and phasers. Other crew members allow you to access operations, engineering, transporter, and mission control.

You use all of these sections while working to complete each mission. Operations helps you navigate your way through the stars by setting your course and warp speed level. Operations also provides short and long range scanners you can use to examine the current situation. You also use operations to pilot the Enterprise into a successful orbit around any planet.

Engineering controls enable you to access the damage taken in combat situations, manage repair crews, and reallocate power to urgently needed systems. With the transporter controls you can beam individuals or items on and off the Enterprise. In mission control, you can get a review of your current mission, the current star date, and the mission end date. All missions must end before a specific time or they are considered a failure. Finally, in combat you can use all of the Enterprise's weapons against an enemy. The phaser and photon torpedoes can inflict great damage on an enemy when you boost their power through engineering.

When your mission is complete, you undergo debriefing. With a series of successfully completed missions, you advance in rank and receive more challenging missions. A password is provided for each rank as you progress. This enables you to continue playing where you previously left off.

No set series of steps is required to solve the missions. Some can be solved violently or nonviolently. In other missions, timing is critical. For example, in one mission you must evacuate a small planet that is on a collision course with a wayward asteroid. If you don't get the inhabitants transported in time, they all die when the planet is destroyed.

The Making of Star Trek: The Next Generation, the Video Game

The development of STNG can be broken down into nine steps: initial concepts, gameplay design, artistic design, music composition, programming, in-house testing, quality assurance, product release, and consumer reaction.

Initial Concepts

Mark Beardsley, lead programmer and creator of the game, says that he came up with the initial concept on 1979 when he was still in college, long before a "Next Generation" television show or Nintendo Game Boy even existed. He even tried to write it on a DEC System 10 using punch cards. It never was completed, however, and Beardsley moved on with his life. Still, the desire to create a Star Trek game stayed with him.

Initially, he wanted to create a Star Trek game based on the original series. However, the handheld gaming license for the original series was not available. Still, Beardsley's basic concepts worked both with the new and the old shows. Gregory A. Faccone, the lead artist for STNG, worked with Beardsley and expanded the original game concept. They added crew members for handling each aspect of the ship, and once that structure was set, the rest of the design went smoothly. However, the technical aspects of programming a 3-D space adventure game with 125KB of memory, or the problem of creating scanned images of the crew that looked good in gray were not the biggest problems Beardsley and Faccone faced during development. The biggest difficulty arose during negotiations with Paramount, when they sought to use the Star Trek content.

Dan Kitchen, Executive Vice President of Development for Absolute Entertainment (and Garry Kitchen's younger brother), explains: "We have dealings with all the film studios. So when Mark approached us with the idea, we went directly to Paramount and inquired as to what game licenses were left. The only thing left was the license for handheld games. So that's what we asked for."

Normally, Absolute goes through a formal approval process for any new video games. This is done by a management team, which evaluates the concept and then gives it a green light. For the STNG game, there was no formal meeting; everyone knew it would be a great game.

Again, the ball went back to Paramount's side of the court. Before granting the licenses, they wanted to see a formal proposal to ensure that their intellectual property would not be abused by a terrible game.

A number of items in the initial design specification never made it to the final game. "A number of factors contributed to this such as a tight schedule, the limited ROM space of the game cartridge, and negotiations with Paramount," says Kitchen.

According to Beardsley, "One of the biggest things left out was female crew members. Originally however, female crew members were part of the team. Dr. Crusher was going to be part of the crew. If you were in a battle, a crew member could get injured, and be incapacitated until Dr. Crusher healed the person. But Paramount was very adamant about not wanting any of the Starship Enterprise's crew getting hurt, or worse yet, killed. Since crew members could never be hurt, then it didn't make sense to have Dr. Crusher standing by."

Faccone adds "We originally wanted the Cardassians as the Federation's main enemies, but Paramount did not allow us to do that. They felt

Imagineering Inc. Storyboard Form

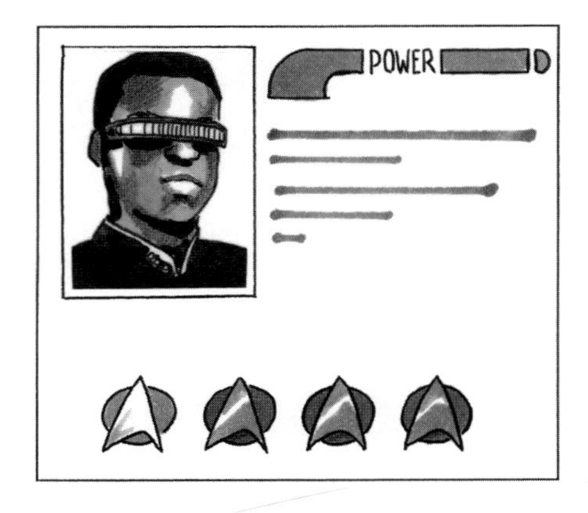

Project ____________________

Client ____________________

Screen # _____

System _____

Notes: ______________________________

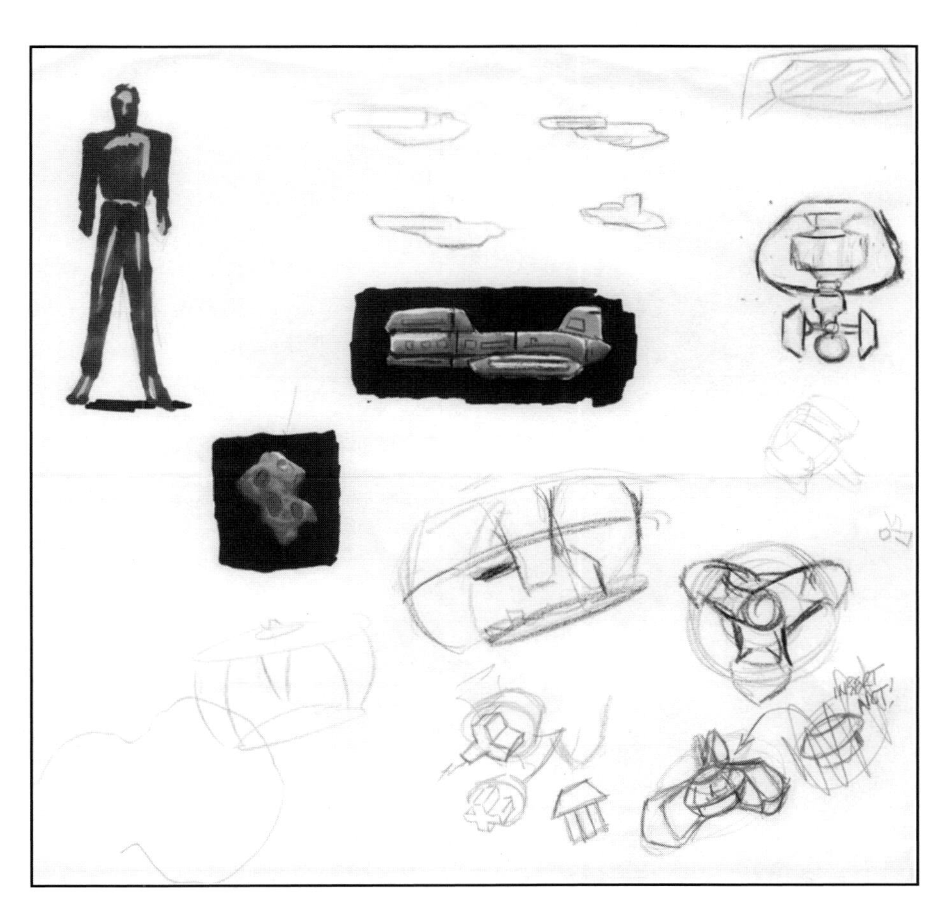

▲ Original concept sketches for STNG. *Courtesy of Absolute Entertainment, Gregory A. Faccone, artist.*

that using the alien race called the Cardassians was infringing too much on the Deep Space 9 TV series in which the Cardassians play a prominent role. Even though the Cardassians have appeared in numerous STNG episodes, they still wanted to make sure we did not dilute their character. This turned out to be a real last minute change. We had the spaceships in the game already, but were able to pull them out."

"Originally we wanted to include Deanna Troi in the game," says Faccone. As in the TV series, you (as the captain) would be able to question her about certain situations and get her help in sticky

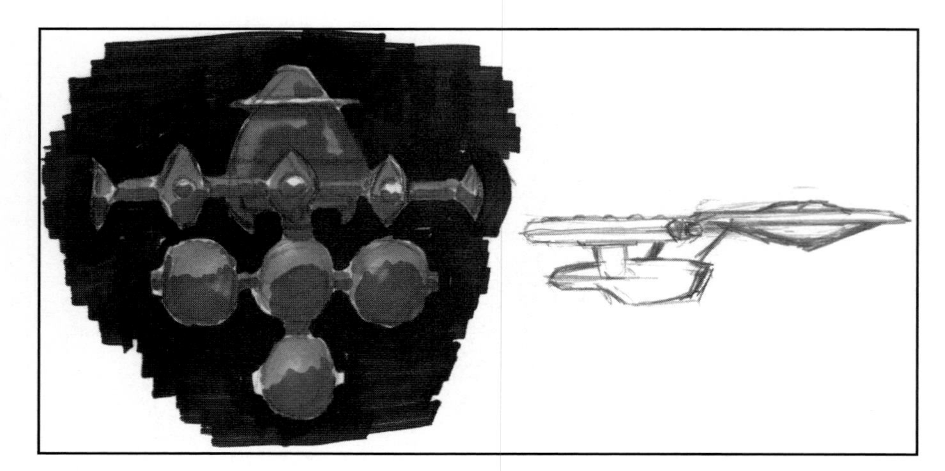

▲ Another original sketch by Faccone.

situations. "After considering this, we realized that it would require a lot of text interaction, just to ask Deanna for her opinion. Then Deanna would have to come up with some recommendations. All of this would have taken too much space, so Deanna was dropped."

Absolute finished its formal proposal and submitted it to Paramount. During this time, both Beardsley and Faccone continued with some preliminary work. But until Paramount came back with its approval, they didn't have the leeway for serious development. Paramount did not want just another shoot-em-up game based on their property, and this was their main concern. Beardsley explains: "We had to spend a fair amount of time and energy developing the overall game. At first Paramount did not even want the Enterprise making offensive maneuvers."

How could you create a STNG game that does not allow you to lock on phasers and fire? Beardsley and Faccone were not discouraged, and they found a solution. They asked Paramount, "If the Enterprise were in a simulation, could it then engage a hostile enemy?" The answer was "yes," and that opened the door and turned into a major aspect of the games design. Absolute decided to make the entire game a training simulation, supposedly taking place on a holodeck. Kitchen states, "Once we had that small wedge in the door, it made perfect sense to make the entire game a simulation. That is how we came up with the game scenario of a Starfleet Academy training session. We then added that opening page of text to the manual to carry the story along." After three weeks of negotiation, Paramount approved the licenses.

Gameplay Design

When asked "What were the main goals in the design of STNG?" Beardsley responds: "Neither I nor Greg were pleased with any of the existing Star Trek games. We wanted to involve the player in a real simulation of the Star Trek universe—something much more that just a simple shoot-em-up. We wanted to keep true to the license. After Paramount's first viewing, we knew we had hit the goal, as they said it was the finest Star Trek license software product they had seen produced. Keep in mind that this is only running on a simple black and white Game Boy, not a CD-ROM–based multimedia system."

As with any software development, some ideas wound up in the product that were not in the initial design. One example is the Temporal Rift. Initially it was a black hole, but Paramount did not like that term, so it was changed to a Temporal Rift. At random points in the game you can get caught in this Temporal Rift. To escape it, you must go through a mini game. There is also a chance of having an intruder alert, in which case you must have Chief O'Brien beam the intruder off the Enterprise.

Another change was the swapping of the Talarian aliens for the Cardassian aliens. Most of the limitations or changes were due to the amount of cartridge memory. Kitchen explains, "There were many things we wanted to add, but Game Boy games have about one-quarter the memory size of SNES cartridges. Also, the crew members blink their eyes, a feature that was added at the last minute. Someone just wandered by and said, 'why don't you make the eyes blink' so we did." It took about one and a half months to finalize the game's design.

Artistic Design

Because the game was based on an existing property, much of the artwork already existed. It was a matter of getting source material from Paramount, which was not always that easy. The developers had to rely heavily on their own collection of Star Trek paraphernalia. The faces were scanned in from photos and cleaned up by Faccone to look good in four shades of gray.

To digitize the photos, Absolute used a product called Computer Eyes, which was developed for IBM-compatible personal computers. For the artwork, Faccone used Electronic Art's Deluxe Paint II for IBM-compatible PCs. Faccone tells of how much work went into the digitized faces: "When you digitize a face, it always has too many grays. Some game developers take a digital picture and just slap it into the game. What you really need to do is take the digitized picture and then get an artist to adjust it and clean it up."

Music Composition

Mark Van Hecke created the music and sound effects for STNG. Absolute acquired the rights to the theme music, and even designed new music. They came up with music for intruder alerts and docking procedures. They asked the sound effects person to create a transporter sound. He came back with a great transporter sound effect. The only trouble was that it was the transporter sound effect from the original Star Trek series, not STNG.

Programming

Absolute has its own proprietary in-house development system. They had to face many challenges in programming such an advanced game in only 125KB of space. The biggest challenge was to simulate a true 3-D space that the player could fly his ship through. A lot of portable games try to simulate a 3-D effect but fail. If you fly past a planet for five minutes, then reverse course, you should arrive back at the planet. That is an extremely difficult task to accomplish in a 125KB program. It requires a lot of complicated 3-D mathematics. The effect was so real, that people easily got lost flying in 3-D space. To solve that problem, the programmers put limits so you can't pitch the Enterprise up too high or down too low. This was a compromise the programmers made to help out game play.

To help encourage players to progress, each rank in STNG requires a little more effort to reach than the previous one. There are five ranks through which to progress in STNG. As you complete a series of successful missions, you're promoted to the next rank. To encourage the player to get involved earlier in the game but then not finish the game too soon, the developers decided to start the number of successful missions required to advance to the next rank very low and then increase that number for each rank. The ranks are Ensign (requires 2 successful missions), Lieutenant (3 missions), Lieutenant Commander (4 missions), Commander (5 missions) and Captain (6 missions). The programming and artwork took a total of five months to produce.

In-House Testing

"We have an entire department devoted to testing although the programmers are constantly testing the game every day as they work on it. When they can no longer find any bugs or glitches, they give it out. This is done by making a master set of *Erasable Programmable Read Only Memory* (EPROM) chips, and then a limited number of people start testing it," says Kitchen.

Not only do the testers look for bugs and errors, but they also pay close attention to game play. Beardsley explains: "We went through about 20 different versions. Some versions were bug fixes, others were minor improvements to the game play, such as how hard or easy it was to destroy enemy ships."

Quality Assurance

Once all the bugs were worked out to the best of everyone's knowledge, a set of EPROMs was sent to Nintendo for their quality assurance testing. Before Nintendo allows any game to be manufactured and sold for their system, they must approve it. In this approval process, they check for excessive violence, bad language, and nudity, and they make sure that the game is somewhat fun to play. Once Nintendo approves, they give the game their little gold seal of approval, and the game goes to the manufacturer. If the game doesn't pass, it gets sent back to the developer for corrections. STNG passed the first time through.

Despite all the testing, bugs do at times slip through the cracks. As an example, in STNG, ***(Note: Don't read the rest of this paragraph if you don't want to know the game's solution)*** you eventually come face to face with the Borg. The bug is, you can fly to Earth and get the virus you need to destroy the Borg before you actually need it.

"There are always certain compromises you have to make. So it's expected that we get comments like, 'This part is not exactly like the show,' or 'That's not exactly right according to the show.' We have the responsibility to make the game fun and challenging. One example is the photons in the game—you have to aim them manually and hope for a hit," said Beardsley. "If they automatically lock on for you, then the game is not as much fun."

Product Release

Marketing and public relations are essential for the successful launch of a new product. The first step for Meredith Mansfield, the publicist, was to create and send off press releases when the product was announced. When the game was released, Mansfield sent out a second press release to alert the members of the media. According to Mansfield: "The Consumer Electronics Show (CES) provides a good launching point when the release date is close to either the winter or summer CES shows. We also produce sell sheets, individualized for each product." The resulting reviews in the video game magazines were very positive toward STNG.

Consumer Reaction

STNG was released on July 1, 1992, and all 64,000 copies immediately sold out. Another 55,000 copies were quickly produced, of which 18,000 sold by December 7, 1993. Public reaction was so positive, that an NES version was created that featured all new missions. It was released in October 1993 and has been selling well since then.

▲ The sell sheet for Star Trek: The Next Generation. *Courtesy of Absolute Entertainment. ® © 1993 Paramount Pictures. All rights reserved. Star Trek: The Next Generation is a registered trademark of Paramount Pictures.*

The Future of STNG for Game Boy

Absolute has not announced a STNG sequel yet, but Dan Kitchen said, "For Game Boy products, if we sell upwards of 80,000 to 90,000 pieces we will make a sequel. For STNG, we have already reached that mark."

PORTABLE GAMING SYSTEM SOFTWARE

There are not as many titles available for portable gaming systems as for home systems, yet there are quite a few creative and entertaining products available. This section covers a few selected titles for portable systems that are state-of-the-art in design and game play. Portable gaming system titles can be divided into three main categories: action, adventure, and simulation.

Action

There is a slang in the gaming industry to describe the different types of action games—shooters, run and jump, and fighters. *Shooters* are games where the entire objective is to shoot things. These games typically have some type of continuously scrolling terrain that you fly over while you fire at charging enemies. Most shooters use very little strategy and a lot of hand-eye coordination. *Run and jump* games, on the other hand, are not usually so hectic. Mario Brothers is a good example of a run and jump game, when you run over some type of scrolling terrain but can stop any time and make strategic decisions. Run and jump games rely on a combination of hand-eye coordination and strategy. The third type of action game is the fighter. *Fighter* games follow the genre of the classic game, Street Fighter, which simulated two people fighting each other using a variety of martial arts moves. Fighter games involve one or more characters that you control through a fist-fight.

Super Mario Land 2: The Six Golden Coins

Nintendo released Super Mario Land 2: The Six Golden Coins for the Game Boy in 1992. This is the latest portable installment of the Mario Brothers series. It features 27 different levels and the ability to save your progress on the game cartridge itself.

The game takes place in Mario Land, a large island that has been captured by the evil Wario. Wario has taken over the castle and scattered six golden coins throughout the land. Mario needs these coins to unlock the castle and defeat Wario. To collect the coins, however, Mario must make it through the many challenging levels. If you only play Super Mario Land 2 in your spare time, this can take months. This is where the save feature comes in handy. Each time you start the game, you maneuver Mario into one of three different pipes. Each pipe represents a different game in progress, which allows up to three players to use the same cartridge. At any time you can clear one of the pipes to start a new game.

Many of the levels in Super Mario Land 2 are reminiscent of an Indiana Jones movie, complete with lava pits, moving platforms, hidden passage-ways, and other challenges. From the low gravity of outer space to the depths of the ocean, each level differs greatly.

Another interesting aspect is that every level has hidden features such as secret tunnels, free lives, and invincibility stars. Even after completing a level, you will find yourself going through it again, just to explore and look for hidden features. Bonus items you find along the way will give Mario extra powers, such as a carrot, which causes Mario to sprout rabbit ears and gives him the ability to fly.

Star Wars

Star Wars, for Sega Game Gear, is an interactive version of the movie re-created as an action game. In Star Wars, you follow the original storyline and play the part of major characters Luke Skywalker, Han Solo, and Princess Leia.

There are 23 levels of play from start to finish in Star Wars, and each level is joined by use of a cinematic sequence. This, along with the original score from the film, keeps your adrenaline running. As you go through the game, you can ask other characters for advice. You are then presented with digitized sequences of the characters making suggestions. The levels range from the desert floor of Tatooine to the depths of the Death Star. The scenery in each level is beautiful.

Sonic Chaos

Perhaps the most popular game series for Sega has been Sonic the Hedgehog. Sonic is a hyperactive version of Mario, a little hedgehog with a nasty habit of spinning into a ball to mow down anything in its path. Along with Sonic is Tails, a fox with the ability to spin his tail and fly for a limited amount of time. Sonic Chaos is the third Sonic game for Sega Game Gear, and it represents the state-of-the-art in portable run and jump games.

In Chaos, you can choose to play as Sonic or Tails (each character has its own strengths and weaknesses). The artists have really worked magic with Game Gear's 32 on-screen colors. All of the characters in Sonic Chaos are shaded and have highlights for a 3-D look. The action and animation adds to the game as Sonic races around corkscrews and full 360-degree loops.

▲ Sonic Chaos for the Sega Game Gear. *Courtesy of Sega of America, Inc.*

Chaos has six massive levels in which to explore and locate green emeralds. After each level you face a "boss" character. When you have collected all the green emeralds and completed the sixth level, you face off against Sonic's arch nemesis, Robotnik.

▲ The Legend of Zelda: Link's Awakening for the Nintendo Game Boy. *Courtesy of Nintendo of America.*

Adventure

Some action games are also very close in structure to adventure games. As you will see, both Jurassic Park and Ecco the Dolphin have features from both action and adventure-style games.

Jurassic Park

Jurassic Park, for Sega Game Gear, is based on the content of the top-grossing motion picture. As with *Star Wars*, the movie *Jurassic Park* translates nicely into a video game. In Jurassic Park, you play the role of Dr. Grant, a very excited paleontologist who is trapped in a park with real-life, man-eating dinosaurs.

Grant must find his way through various dinosaur pens, paddocks, and aviaries in order to turn the park's protective electric fences back on. In the five game levels, you use a jeep to outrun dinosaurs; rely on timing and reflexes to survive forest fires, lava pits, and waterfalls; and use your wits to outsmart the dinosaurs.

The Legend of Zelda: Link's Awakening

For the Game Boy, Nintendo has released the adventure game The Legend of Zelda: Link's Awakening. In this adventure, Link (the hero) is shipwrecked on the island of Koholint. He is found by a girl named Marin, who tells him he must collect eight special musical instruments in order to escape the island.

As Link travels in search of these instruments, the island's inhabitants believe the instruments will destroy their land. Their opposition makes Link's task much more difficult. Link's Awakening is

▲ Link's Awakening uses side scrolling and top down views. *Courtesy of Nintendo of America.*

▲ Ecco the Dolphin for Sega Game Gear. *Courtesy of Sega of America, Inc.*

played from both an overhead view and a side-scrolling (Mario style) view. There are many subplots that you can get involved in by interacting with other game characters. Link's Awakening is generally considered to be one of the best adventure games available on portable systems.

Ecco the Dolphin

Another exciting action/adventure game is Ecco the Dolphin, for Sega Game Gear. Ecco is a radical departure in adventure game design. In this game you play the role of a dolphin who's trying to find his way back to his *pod* (a school of dolphins).

The adventure part is getting through all 27 levels and communicating with other sea life to get clues. The action part is getting the dolphin past all of his natural enemies, including sharks, strong currents, and sharp reefs. During the game you learn to explore undersea caves, use your speed to fight enemies, and eat dolphin-style.

Ecco is not only fun to play, it's also filled with beautiful, smooth-scrolling graphics. From the smoothly swimming killer whales to the big lumbering blue whale, to the brightly colored tropical fish and coral, the graphics really make Ecco stand out compared to other video games.

▲ Top Rank Tennis for the Nintendo Game Boy. *Courtesy of Nintendo of America.*

▲ Power Golf for the Turbo Express. *Courtesy of Aldrich and Associates.*

Simulation

In the category of simulation, we will feature two portable sports titles—Top Rank Tennis and Power Golf.

Top Rank Tennis

Top Rank Tennis for the Nintendo Game Boy is an interesting product, because it allows up to four people to play together in the same tennis match. It also features a new ranking system, in which players can advance on a player ranking ladder rather than just competing in a tournament.

Foot speed and shot power can be customized for each person. That way good players can be handicapped and still have an exciting competition. As players progress in skill, they work their way up the tennis ranking ladder.

Power Golf

Power Golf, from Hudson Software for the Turbo Technologies Turbo Express, is perhaps the best golfing simulation on a portable system. With Power Golf you can examine the course with smooth panning before you shoot. You can practice your swing, get advice on choosing a club, or adjust your form.

When you take your swing, you are provided with a view from behind the golfer looking in the direction of the shot. Before taking the shot you can turn right or left to aim around trees or obstacles. The greens are sloped in 3-D for a realistic experience.

THE FUTURE OF PORTABLE GAMING SYSTEMS

The future of portable gaming systems is a little unclear. Although all the major companies announce new, high-performance home gaming systems on an almost daily basis, they have been quiet when it comes to portable gaming systems. There have been no new announcements and no new technological breakthroughs.

One company, Nintendo, has branched out in the area of portable gaming systems by creating the Nintendo Gateway System. This will be an interactive multimedia system for airplanes, hotels, and cruise ships. The gateway will enable you to do online shopping, watch movies on demand, listen to audio CDs, play up to 10 different SNES video games, make a phone call, or check on travel and weather information. Northwest Airlines already has installed this system on 20 jetliners. The hotel and cruise ship versions will offer similar functionality. LodgeNet Entertainment Corporation has added the system to 10 hotel chains with sites around the United States, including the Sheraton, Doubletree, Embassy Suites, and others. LodgeNet Entertainment Corporation is also installing the system in cruise ships.

▲ The Nintendo Gateway System. *Courtesy of Nintendo of America.*

All of this is based on the existing Nintendo 16-bit (SNES) technology. All the circuitry for these systems—the CPU, video drivers, digital sound drivers, RAM, and multiple digital high-speed communications channels—are packed into a single small unit. The software is downloaded from a host computer via bi-directional communication. The core CPU system is the same as the SNES. The video monitor is an active matrix color LCD. The user input device is the standard Nintendo game system controller.

Will these new systems completely replace portable gaming and multimedia units? Probably not, but they will cut the portable market down a little. Stephen Muirhead, president of MicroProse Software, a developer of video games for personal computers and gaming systems, believes that the market for portable gaming systems will stay strong in the future. "These in-seat games on airlines have a great potential and it's inevitable that those systems and portable systems will get more and more sophisticated. However, I see only three platforms as surviving in the future: first, portable systems; second, semi-portable such as those on airlines; and third, home systems that are integrated into television sets, not a separate console or set-top box."

The portable market may also boost the viability of cartridge games. Portable CD players are bulky and require a lot of power to run. According to Muirhead: "There is a great installed base, and they will be around for about two more years. However, it's basically an obsolete technology. To overcome deficiencies, you have to put special purpose chips into the carts like the Super FX chip in the SNES system. This is like selling razors and blades, but every time you sell a blade you also sell a little chunk of the razor. The cost of producing these 'Super' carts is very high, and the developers take all the risk."

Kevin Lydy has worked on video games for about 10 years, and produced more than 33 games. He is currently Director of Creative Development with Leland Interactive Media (LIM). LIM is a carry-on organization from Cinemotronics, which produced a large number of successful coin-op games, including the Dragon Slayer series, Space Ace, and Super Off-Road. Now the company is focused on cartridge games and is a developer for Nintendo, Sega, Atari, and 3DO.

Lydy feels that the CD was one of the greatest advances for video games. "We are developing for the CDs even though it is still a cartridge market," he said. "Yet, I see the CD as a temporary delivery medium. What we really need is a 100-megabit cartridge because the CD is too slow. Right now the largest cartridge is 24 megabytes, but the costs of goods to go over that is just too high."

Adds Muirhead: "There are two things interesting about the video gaming market and its future. One, this industry has a tendency for companies to make 'hypothetical preemptive strikes' to announce high performance platforms, that they may or may not actually produce. I can see the logic behind this; if one company produces a product that's better than the other, all the other has to do is announce it is going to release an even better product soon. This encourages people to hold off on their purchases until this newer system arrives. The second factor is that all of this high-tech brinkmanship must be countered by economics of the existing system's installed base. When there is an installed base like the Game Boy, you just can't ignore that market. Even though the Game Boy is ancient technology, games will still sell and sell well—as was the case with Star Trek: The Next Generation."

Will home and portable gaming systems kill the personal computer gaming market? Not according to Muirhead: "They won't kill it, but it will become increasingly smaller. It reminds me of my grandfather who was totally into hi-fi. He spent thousands of dollars in woofers and tweeters and days tweaking and tuning his system. But today, I can go purchase a portable CD player that is much better than his system at its prime. What he wanted is now available for a super-cheap price. Of course you can still buy a high-end hi-fi system, and there will always be those techies out there who want the latest and greatest. I just bought a new personal computer and had all kinds of problems just getting the sound card to work correctly, spending hours of tweaking and tuning. It's the same kind of tweaking that my grandfather struggled with. Five years from now you will go out and buy a second or third generation 3DO player for a super cheap price that blows away the best personal computers we have today."

Lydy feels that with all the confusion as to these new platforms flooding the market, the PC will be the only stable platform. "PCs will probably be one of the few growth platforms. With the platform wars—in which everyone has a new machine—they are not all going to make it. It's terribly difficult for a developer to choose which machine to develop for; it must be worse for consumers trying to decide which one to buy. The PC, on the other hand, is a real blue-chipper. You won't move 10 million units, but it's a safe bet."

As LCD display technology gets better and better, the public will see great improvements in artwork and graphics. David Estus, Senior Artist for Park Place Systems (a game developer), agrees: "3-D graphics technology will keep increasing in video game artwork. It has a clean look and offers smooth animation. I look forward to future tools that will help the artist—such as motion control body suits for animating 3-D computer generated characters."

Lydy agrees: "Processing power is very valuable for the future of video games. But one of the things that will make a really big impact is motion capture because there is no real good way to do 3-D character animation right now."

According to Arnold Hendrick of MicroProse Software: "Part of the opening to Super Strike Eagle for the SNES was done with 3-D graphics and animation. We used a PC-based program called 3D Studio. As you get more storage space, the use of 3-D graphics is more valuable. On cartridge-based games like those used on portable gaming systems, you have to be careful. You can still use that 3-D technology if you are careful. We are just finishing a game called Impossible Mission 2025, and most of the characters were done in 3D Studio."

As the relationship between film and video game industries continues to build, artwork will start to cross the boundary from the film into the game. Lydy had some experience in this during the summer of 1993. "As game developers, we didn't know what we were doing. You really need to be there (during the film production) to work hand-in-hand with the production team. There will be a continued relationship between feature films and games, and, in the end, film and the interactive people will share in the production of both mediums."

As for portable gaming hardware, the technology still has far to go. Garry Kitchen of Absolute Entertainment feels the two important areas are battery life and video displays. "Batteries and displays drive portables. Right now we need a better display device that doesn't kill your battery life. The breakthroughs in portable gaming units will follow these two items."

CHAPTER SUMMARY

While viewed as a niche market by some, portable gaming units offer a variety of interactive entertainment possibilities. With hundreds of titles and many different portable units to choose from, they should continue to appeal to those who want entertainment on the run.

Because of the similarities of both portable units and home gaming systems, the development process is very similar. New games that are created for home systems are often adapted for the portable systems; likewise, when a portable game becomes a best-seller, it is ported to the home systems.

Next, we move to a new field of interactive entertainment: interactive cable television.

7

Interactive Television

"...this is starting to sound like the computer industry's dream for the future (and it is), it is also the dream that opens the doors for the television industry,..."

Interactive television (ITV) is perhaps the most publicized segment of the interactive entertainment industry. ITV easily qualifies as the most-hyped technology of 1993 and 1994. Cable companies expect ITV to increase their customer base and allow them to reach that group of consumers—called "untouchables"—who currently don't subscribe to cable TV. Advertisers are excited too, because ITV turns the television into a direct-response sales tool and allows a 30-second commercial to turn into an hour-long "infomercial" if the viewer is interested in the product. Program producers are excited about the interactive opportunities and the increased channel loyalty that interactive programs might bring. Finally, the viewers are excited, because now they can interact and participate with a medium they normally watch four hours a day anyway.

ITV is a physical expression of the national information infrastructure. It represents a vision of a widely available, affordable access to life-long educational opportunities; of better and more cost-effective health care; of universal access to the best libraries; and a way to receive other sources of information for increasing productivity and competitiveness.

This vision is based on the powerful communications and computing technologies that have emerged in the last few years. Models for the information infrastructure already exist, although none has really achieved the scale of the final product envisioned. Our universal telephone network is an example of an international communications network available to everyone.

Also, consider the vast base represented by compatible videocassette recorders available in American homes. Millions of people rent and purchase video tapes for instruction, music, exercise, and entertainment. Businesses provide tutorials and infomercials to their customers. These applications are possible because the machines are easy to use and compatible.

Further deployment of these kinds of applications is what demands a new information infrastructure. Recognition of that demand has formed among organizations a new kind of partnership never before achieved in peacetime. The partnership is making it possible for pioneering test groups to enjoy many applications, such as electronic messaging, teleconferencing, video-on-demand, distributed collaborative work, raw access to stored information, and customized information delivery.

Everyone is excited, but as industry leaders will attest, some serious questions must be answered first. How much will the new information infrastructure cost the viewer and the provider? Are viewers ready for cable television bills that may rival their car payments? Will interactivity distract people's attention from existing programming? Where is the technology today, and how long will it take to develop ITV systems that fulfill expectations? Some companies may become roadkill on the information highway, while new industries will be born. In this chapter, I will discuss these issues and provide an overview of interactive television technology as it stands today.

HOW INTERACTIVE TELEVISION WORKS

A major bottleneck in television transmission has been the lack of space on the electronic spectrum for broadcast television. Current cable systems have a similar problem and are pushed to their limit. For example, TV signals from many cable companies are routed through a system at about 100 megahertz (MHz), which breaks into 15 6-MHz channels. Newer stations running at speeds of more than 300 MHz can offer up to 50 channels. The goal for ITV, however, is to produce a 1,000-MHz or 1-GHz system with up to 160 channels.

A typical channel environment will be a system with the capacity for about 100 analog channels. The first 60 channels will remain as analog, producing the basic 60-channel world of cable TV today. That leaves 40 new channels, which are compressed at a ratio of about 10 to 1. With that compression, the 40 channels turn into 400 channels. Adding those 400 channels back to the standard 60 analog channels produces close to 500 total channels. This is where the "500-channel world" comes from. This does not mean, however, that you will receive a *TV Guide* the size of a telephone book each week.

The interesting part is that you are never going to see those 500 channels. Instead, you will have an interactive set-top cable box on your TV, with which you can choose a program from an available list. You may want to see "Victory At Sea," Episode 15, or you may want the "6:00 News" from yesterday. As soon as you make that request on an upstream channel, you are assigned a downstream channel from a neighborhood switch that handles you and your nearest 500 neighbors. That channel is one of those extra 400 channels. The neighborhood switch relays the request to a video server, and the program is routed back to you on that special channel.

You have no idea that your special channel is channel 397. The neighborhood switch simply took whatever channel was available. Considering that, at any one time, 60 percent of the people will have their TVs on—and 50 percent of those people will be watching something in the lower 60 traditional channels—there will be plenty of capacity on the cable system in a neighborhood of 500 viewers.

Instead of tuning into 500 distinct channels, you will be interacting with a system the way you interact with online services such as America Online and CompuServe today. There will be an interactivity that lets you pick and choose.

The interactive channels will initially be called *near-video-on-demand* (NVOD), a step up from normal pay-per-view in the sense that you will never have more than a 30-minute wait for the next showing to begin. This will continue to advance until television offers pure *video-on-demand,* in which you can have instant access to any program available on the video server. Video-on-demand means also that your chosen show is piped specifically to you, the viewer, and you have access to standard VCR-type controls, such as pause, fast forward, and reverse.

The Death of the VCR?

As pure video-on-demand comes online, the massive bandwidth of more than 500 channels will no longer be needed for each home, because only one to four channels will be necessary. This will mean the end of "broadcasting" and the beginning of "pointcasting," a one-to-one relationship between the cable provider and the home viewer. It's even foreseeable that VCRs will become obsolete. You wouldn't need them to record broadcast TV, because you could call up any program whenever you wanted it. You wouldn't need them to play rented videos because it would be more convenient to order a video on demand from the cable company. The only market left for VCRs would be in the home-camcorder area. However, if digital storage costs come down low enough, you could upload your home video from your "digital" camcorder to your local cable company for storage. Then you could give your friends and relatives access to it. If the latter happened, it would mean the death of the VCR.

As with other forms of interactive entertainment, interactive television has two main divisions: hardware and software. The hardware deals with the electronic components used in the communication and storage of video data. Software for ITV can be actual programmed applications just like a computer program, or it may be a television show with some level of interactivity added to it. First, I will discuss the hardware technology used for ITV. Almost all ITV systems have a set-top box that brings the interactive data into the home. These set-top boxes cost anywhere from just a few dollars to more than $500.

The data can be transmitted through a variety of sources, including cable TV wiring, satellite, FM simulcast, telephone, or even normal broadcast television. Next, the data is displayed for the home user by means of on-screen graphics or an LCD screen on the remote control unit. The viewer interacts by pressing buttons on the set-top box's remote control unit. The set-top box then displays the results of the interaction and sends the request back to the program provider by means of wireless communication, telephone line, or direct cable connection. The program provider compiles the data and transmits a response back to the viewer. The next sections present these steps in more detail and discuss the different methods used.

Sending the Data to the Home Viewer

The first step in the operation of today's interactive television systems is to send the interactive data to the home viewer. Getting data to the home is the simple part, because currently it involves a one-to-many relationship—one service provider transmits to many home viewers. On the other hand, the many-to-one relationship of the viewers giving data back to the service provider is much more difficult.

FM Sideband/Simulcast

One method of getting data to the viewers is by means of an FM simulcast. Interactive Network, an ITV provider, currently is testing a system in Chicago, the San Francisco bay area, and Sacramento, and they plan to roll it out nationally sometime next year. It uses a system that transmits the interactive data through FM simulcast. Interactive Network is able to synchronize the data being sent, so three or four interactive programs can be transmitted at once. A limitation to using FM simulcast is that it is a one-way technology. Data can be transmitted to the viewers, but it cannot be returned that way (thus, the return path must use a different technology). NTN, an interactive television provider, also uses this technology in about a dozen markets.

Vertical Blanking Interval

One of the most interesting ways of transmitting data from the program provider to the viewer was created in the mid-1980s by a company called Interactive Systems. Patented in 1987 and called *video encoded invisible light* (VEIL), the method encodes digital data directly into the television signal. The signal going to the television screen is made up of chrominance and luminance. The *chrominance* is the color information, and the *luminance* is the black and white information. The VEIL technique takes lines of luminance and modulates them, raising and lowering them. That raising and lowering is converted into a digital bitstream by a scanning device pointed at the television screen or by a set-top decoder. This type of encoding is compatible with cable, satellite, and normal broadcast transmission. This alone makes it a very appealing method of

ITV data transmission. Other companies, such as Interactive Network and NTN, use the vertical blanking interval (VBI) to transmit data to the viewer. In England, that is the only method that NTN uses. The downside is that many major cable operators have put in equipment that enables them to strip that data out. Another limitation to VBI is that errors can easily creep into the data stream, so the software needs to verify the integrity of the data as it arrives. This problem also plagues FM simulcast methods.

Telephone and Encoded Sound

Carrying this technique into the world of sound, Info Telecom, a French ITV technology provider, is working on sending digital data through the TV program's audio signal. This will allow data strings to be transmitted to the portable hand units through the existing sound track of the television broadcast. This data is inaudible to the viewer and can currently transmit data up to 128 bits-per-second (bps).

Perhaps the cheapest method getting data to the home is by use of telephone transmission. This method works the same way that computer modems do. A sound wave is modulated up and down, and this modulation is converted into data of ones and zeroes. This technique has two problems. First, it ties up the telephone line while the user is interacting. Second, the bandwidth, or data throughput, capabilities are fairly limited. For instance, without special hardware, you cannot transmit live video images through normal telephone wiring. Some companies (Bellcore, for example), are working to solve this problem, but again, the solution requires hefty investments in hardware for the service provider.

Cable

To solve the problem of tying up the telephone, some providers are sending data down the cable TV wiring. GTE Main Street currently uses existing cable wiring (along with a number of other technologies) to transmit data to the viewer. This works well, but it still has the bandwidth limitations of telephone wiring when communicating over long runs of cable. To solve this problem, many companies are turning to fiber optics.

Fiber Optics

Fiber-optic cable may look like normal cabling, but instead of transmitting electrical impulses that fade over great distances and need to be boosted periodically, fiber-optic cables transmit light. The cable itself is made of thin fibers or rods of glass or other transparent materials. A light shown into one end of the fiber reflects inside the surface all the way through until it reaches the other side. The loss rate is much lower than that of electrical-based wires.

Sent through light in pulses, a data stream can be transmitted at very high speeds. This gives fiber-optic cabling a very high bandwidth. It is easily capable of carrying computer data, digital sound, and full-motion video simultaneously. The downside is that it is expensive to install fiber-optic networks.

Initially, everyone's plan was to run fiber-optic cabling directly into every home. This, however, proved to be too costly. The plan was pulled back a little, to running fiber to the curb and then switching to standard coaxial cable to go from the curb into the home. This would probably work well, except that the light signals coming down the fiber-optic cable to the curb must be converted at the curb into electrical signals that can continue traveling down the coax into the home. These converters are known as ONUs, or *optical network units*, and they are not cheap. In fact, they are too expensive to place one at the curb of every home. Even if one ONU serviced 10 homes, it would still be too expensive.

The solution appears to be in pulling the fiber-optic cable back even further, to the point were one ONU can service somewhere between 200 and 1,000 homes. From this main juncture, the light signals are converted into electrical signals and then sent on their way through the existing coax cable. This new method is called hybrid fiber coax (HFC), or "fiber to the neighborhood." GTE Main Street also uses this HFC technique. As fiber-optic cable TV broadcasting becomes a reality (and it is becoming a reality faster than expected), you will be able to receive voice and video data in your home, without tying up your line.

Asymmetrical Digital Subscriber Line—(ADSL)

ADSL is a new standard currently being formed by the telecommunications industry. It allows existing copper phone cable to carry sound and video "downstream" (to the viewer) and at the same time carry a low-speed data channel "upstream" (to the service provider). This is where the term *asymmetric* comes from: the downstream high-speed video channel, and the upstream low-speed data channel. Currently ADSL can support a high-speed data rate of 1.544 mbps and a low-speed data rate of 64 kbps. Right now, the cost of ADSL (excluding line conditioning) is about $500 per home, but the cost of this technology is bound to drop dramatically.

ADSL is more expensive than fiber-to-the-neighborhood, but it does have one advantage for telephone companies who are trying to muscle in on existing cable TV operators; it is economical at a very low penetration. When you come into the market and are trying to grab share away from the incumbent, you have to build an entire cable network, and you might only get 5 or 10 percent penetration. You have to divide the entire cost of the network by the 5 to 10 percent of the people who actually take the service. This means the service cost for each person becomes prohibitively expensive. With ADSL, the telephone companies can pick and choose customers if the cable operator is not properly serving them.

Cellular

An ambitious technique for transmitting interactive data has come from a company called E*ON (formerly TV Answer). E*ON offers an ITV system based on a two-way wireless communication using technology similar to that of cellular telephones. This technology mixes satellite transmission and local cellular sites. With the blessing of the Federal Communications Commission (FCC), E*ON has been allocated a specific spectrum of the radio-wave bandwidth. The patented technology uses a set-top box in the home that can receive and send wireless digital data through this allocated frequency. The data originates with the providers and is transmitted by satellite to E*ON's headquarters in Reston, Virginia. From there, the data is sent back to the satellite, and local cellular sites around the country can tap into it. These cellular sites then transmit the data of the radio frequency to the homes in their local area.

Cellular networks are small versions of large radio networks. The transmitters of cellular networks, however, have a very small range—usually about two to five miles in diameter. Because they have such a small range, many transmitters, or *sites*, must be used for each city. The range of each site

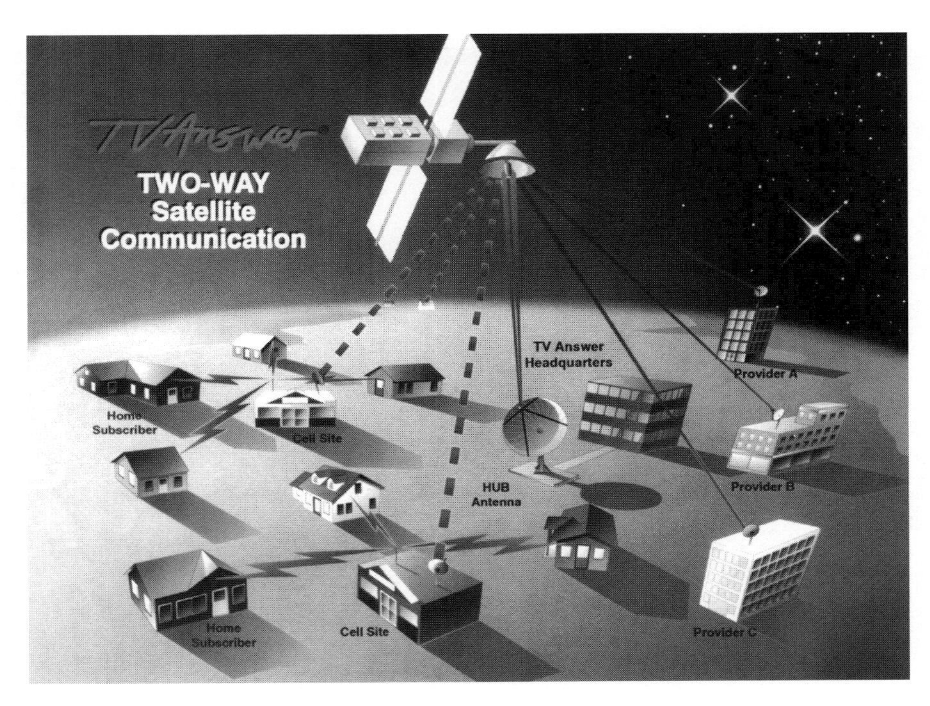

▲ The E*ON transmission technique. *Courtesy of E*ON*.

is called a *cell*; thus comes the name *cellular*. The companies are licensed by the FCC to set up a cellular network for a given area. As with cellular telephones, it is expensive to set up, but very efficient in the end, especially for the viewers. Though similar to FM broadcast, cellular's bandwidth is much more effective, and it's a two-way street. Data can be sent to and from the viewer's home.

Direct Broadcast Satellite

Direct broadcast satellite will be a major player in the future of ITV, bringing interactive services into the home. There is no return path with direct broadcast satellite, so phone line or fiber optics will comprise the return path. Still, the benefits can't be ignored. Broadcast is great for point-to-multipoint communication, and it's the cheapest way. Data can easily be piggy-backed on the broadcast signal.

Returning the Data to the ITV Service

As you can see, there are many ways to get the data out to the homes of viewers. There are, however, fewer methods of getting the data back to the interactive service provider. While reading about these different technologies, keep in mind that there is *today* and there is *tomorrow*. Today most return paths are through the phone system. It's quick, inexpensive, and easy to set up. Many providers use existing telco services such as the Tymnet network. A simple modem is used to send back data through the telephone lines.

Cellular is perhaps the second-least-expensive method of transmitting data back to the ITV provider (telephone transmission is the cheapest). E*ON claims that its return path coming out of the home costs only $1.33 per home versus nearly $1,000 or more for broadband fiber optic. Fiber is on the way, however, and it may eliminate many of the existing one-way and two-way communication technologies. As previously mentioned, ADSL is also a contender for the return path. Although it doesn't have a super-high bandwidth like fiber optic, it does have the advantage of being able to use existing telephone wiring.

ITV Technology in the Home

This section focuses on interactive television hardware as the user sees it. The hardware used on the side of the service providers is very complex and goes far beyond the scope of this book. As an overview, however, the *head-end* (service provider) has the job of getting the programming. Normally, this comes through video tape, a video server, or satellite downlink. The head-end sends the video data on fiber-optic cable through various trunks and feeders that divide a city into manageable chunks of 500 or fewer subscribers. From there, the cable switches over to standard cable TV coaxial cable as it enters the home.

As you can imagine, this is a large and terribly complex operation, and some ITV companies simply focus on one aspect of the operation, developing their own piece to the puzzle. Recently, companies have begun to band together and combine their resources, each focusing on one aspect of ITV.

Once the video data is in the home, the viewer/user accesses the network through some type of set-top box. Some of the new ITV set-top boxes currently look very similar to existing cable TV boxes; others don't. As an example, consider GTE ImagiTrek's set-top box. This box is essentially a Philips CD-I player with a cable tuner built in. As mentioned in Chapter 5, "Multiplayers and Home Gaming Systems," the CD-I player is a CD-ROM–based unit. As a subscriber to GTE ImagiTrek, you receive CD-ROM updates that include a full 4,000 page encyclopedia, along with other ImagiTrek-specific information.

Most ITV set-top boxes also include some type of modem for communicating back to the head-end. Other boxes include credit card readers, so you can slide your credit card through to do online shopping or order movies. Some systems use on-screen graphics for interaction, whereas others claim that on-screen graphics spoils interaction for multiple players in the same house. Instead, they opt for small LCD display screens on the handheld remote controls. This simplifies the electronics needed, because on-screen graphics are not needed. It also enables multiple players to compete against one another while watching the same game.

The Price of Interactive Television

The business objectives for interactive television make sense to cable TV companies—they need the channel capacity to compete with direct broadcast satellites on both quantity and content. They are also excited about unregulated revenue streams. The first step in this is the 500-channel world, using compression to increase the number of channels available to allow for NVOD programming services. Cable operators are hoping that this additional capacity will help capture a portion of the revenues generated by video stores by offering consumers a more convenient alternative.

At the same time, the cable industry sees telcos moving into their domain with ADSL and interactive video services. In defense, cable operators are exploring the possibility of providing local telephone services through the existing cable TV network. American cable companies in the United Kingdom have had very successful results doing this, and it's a strong incentive for them to pursue that direction in the United States. Also, it appears that consumers are more satisfied when they can get a large number of services from the same company. This offers an incentive to both cable operators and telcos to delve into each other's market.

According to research done at VideoWay Communications, an ITV company based in Montreal, Canada, the average amount of money spent on a monthly basis by U.S. cable subscribers to purchase discretionary services has flattened over the past 10 years. This leveling off has taken place despite the many increases in the variety and quality of entertainment services. As a percentage of the consumer's total income, discretionary spending is decreasing. Consumers therefore must make some tough choices about how to spend their limited income. This makes it difficult for any retailer to capture a growing portion of that discretionary income. Yet for ITV to exist as a reality, the price will have to be greater than that of existing cable TV services.

It's going to be very difficult for cable companies to increase their share of this discretionary income to a level that would support the investments required to offer NVOD. There are also inherent problems with ITV competing with video stores. In video stores, more than 95 percent of transactions are performed in cash, with the result that consumers usually have no record of cash spent. If you were to ask people how much they spend each month for video rentals, most would underestimate the amount. However, if they start ordering NVOD and then see an invoice at the end of every month outlining their purchases, they likely would start more closely managing or reducing their video budget. This poses a real challenge to ITV providers.

On the other hand, many feel that the cable business has matured, and it's unlikely that simply adding a greater number of channels will attract new subscribers. People who are not already signed up with a cable service are considered "untouchables." A benefit to ITV providers is that an offer of dramatically new services might trigger consumer interest and help U.S. cable companies increase market penetration.

Most set-top boxes for ITV carry a fairly large price tag, anywhere from $100 to $700. To finance these bi-directional boxes, some ITV providers are going into partnerships with other organizations that are interested in providing interactive services through the system. When a number of these companies get together and share in the capital cost of the set-top boxes, the cost is less daunting. Each organization can use the electronic highway linking every home to improve its business while only paying for a portion of the costs associated with setting it up. Each partner gets to keep the benefits it can derive for its business.

An added benefit to getting these partners involved early is that the consumer can start to see the added benefit to having an ITV system. This allows ITV to tap into existing budgets and even save money, because corporations and government organizations doing business with the consumer will save money using electronic transactions and perhaps pass on the savings to promote the system. This helps move the budget for ITV out of the discretionary income bracket.

Exactly how expensive will interactive television be? Robert Alexander, president of Alexander & Associates, of Austin, Texas, is currently completing a profile of the major consumer ITV trials. He is looking at the operating system, network interface cards, drivers, how these networks are being assembled, and what the cost is.

Not surprisingly, the cost per subscriber in the trials today is quite high, around $6,000 each. That is higher than most services quote, and yet it might be a little conservative. The video server is $1,000 per subscriber. It's only one piece of the overall network. However, if you take the $6,000 per subscriber and follow it along a computer-cost curve (a 50-percent decline every 18 months), you start to see some reasonable prices. Starting at the beginning of 1994, the systems are $6,000. Cutting that by 50 percent in 18 months would bring it down to $3,000. In another 18 months (by 1996), it would be down to $1,500. Carrying this forward, the next stops are $750 and, finally, $375 by the year 2000.

Once the price gets under $500 per subscriber, the technology will really take off. The set-top boxes won't roll out fast until then. Right now, there's no cheap way to do it. The equipment, set-tops, switches, routers, and other hardware are not cheap. Furthermore, this is add-on equipment to the wiring already in place. If you look at that kind of time frame, it also happens to be the time frame that Bill Gates and Microsoft are looking toward. Gates in the long term is looking toward the end of the decade.

Gary Lauder, chairman of ICTV, a company that focuses on providing interactive cable television networks to cable system operators, agrees. "Many new entrants to the market," he says, "have mistaken a clear view for an easy path. Anyone who has tried to make reasonable financial models for cable operators to make money with this technology quickly learns that these systems have to be very inexpensive. At the same time, they need to be able to support many applications reliably. They also have to be easy to use, fun, and inexpensive."

"The $500 set-top boxes just don't cut it for mass-market deployment," Lauder continues. "We believe that to be on TV you have to look like TV. That requires a degree of multimedia that really costs. Remember, to get beyond a trial, the CFO of a cable company has to agree, and economics tends to get left behind amid the media hysteria. There's a small pay-per-view exercise to illustrate.

"Let's say that you are a cable operator trying to make some money on a digital decompression box. The primary way is through pay-per-view. You charge $4 per movie for a recent-release hit movie. Now, 55 percent of that goes back to the copyright holder and packager, 5 percent to the local franchise authority, and 5 percent was probably spent on marketing. If automatic number identification for telephone is used, another 4 percent goes to that. The bottom line is that you have about 33 percent of the top line. This equates to about $1.30. Let's say that this new box costs $100, plus $25 for installation. Cable operators look for a four-year payback. That means that they need $2.60 per month of contribution margin. So, to break even, they need to sell two movies per month, a rate known in the cable industry as a 200-percent buy rate. Unfortunately, that's about an order of magnitude higher than today's buy rates, but it may be achievable for a segment of the population. The goal, however, is to make a profit, not break even. So what happens to the incremental costs if these digital boxes don't hit their cost-target of only $100 more than existing boxes? The profits become even more elusive. But what about all the extra equipment at the head-end, all the servers and switches and things like that? It puts profits even further out into the future," Lauder concludes.

The general consensus is that ITV applications must be competitive with what people are paying now for the services. No one thinks that somehow services are going to be so compelling that people will be willing to pay twice what they pay for one-way cable TV.

THE CREATION OF AN INTERACTIVE CABLE PROGRAM, QB1 BY NTN

QB1 (Quarterback One) was the first and is the longest running interactive television program in the United States. Running simultaneously with live-televised football games, QB1 lets you predict the plays that the quarterback on the field will call during the course of the game. For example, you

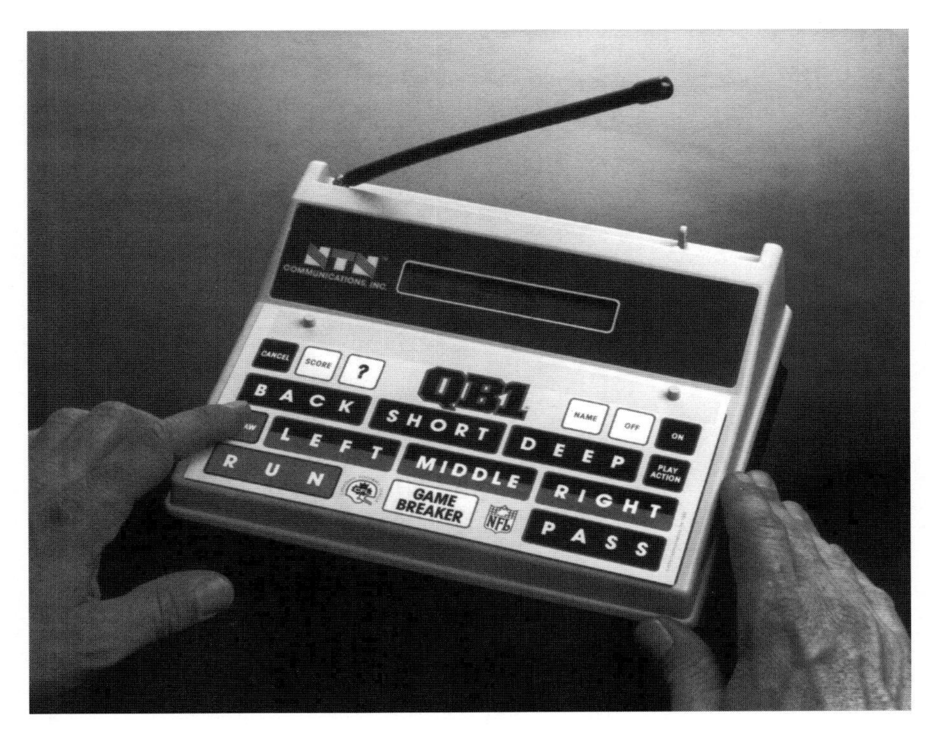

▲ NTN's wireless playmaker for QB1. *Courtesy of NTN Communications, Inc.*

might predict that the quarterback is going to call for a pass. You simply hit the pass key. For more points, you can also choose which side of the field he is going to throw to: left, middle, or right. For even more points, you can choose a long or short pass. As the play begins, you watch the live action, and you are awarded points based on how accurate your prediction was. You can enter your prediction until just seconds before the snap.

This makes QB1 a game of skill, and thus it is licensed by the NFL. It's also played in conjunction with live-televised college games. Some players are so good they can correctly predict plays 87 percent of the time. Scores are tabulated instantaneously and displayed throughout the bar after each play. During halftime and at the end of the game, scores are transmitted back to NTN for national rankings. This allows players to see how they stack up against players across the country.

Currently, NTN supplies QB1 to a number of interactive television services such as Zing, GTE Main Street, GTE Imagitrek, GE's GEnie, ImagiNation network, Interactive Network, and E*ON. In the future, NTN is making plans to provide QB1 to Prodigy; Microsoft; Time-Warner in Orlando, Florida; Bell South in Omaha, Nebraska; ICTV; Viacom in Castro Valley, California; and Bell Atlantic.

The system you play QB1 on determines the hardware you use. The most common installation for QB1 is in the hospitality industry, including restaurants, pubs, and bars. In hospitality locations, electronic wireless playmakers are available for the players. Each location has between 10 and 20 playmakers; this allows for team competition. During the 1993–1994 football season, QB1 was played by more than 1.5 million people during more than 400 football games.

The Development of QB1

The initial concept was developed in 1967 by Daniel Downs, stadium manager of the Houston Oilers, along with Donald Klosterman, general manager of the Houston Oilers. Says Downs, "We were sitting there enjoying a game in Rice Stadium, while the new Astro Dome was going up across the street. We thought it would be great if football were more active for the spectators. That's where we came up with the idea of an interactive football game. So we started the first one in 1967 and then copyrighted it in 1969 under the name of Armchair Quarterback, and that's where we gave birth to it, back with the Houston Oilers football team."

Initially, they wanted to wire up the stadium so the spectators could play as they watched the game. This proved to be too expensive. Next, they considered using an IBM mainframe, programming the system with punch cards. This too was not practical, and their interest cooled down for a little while. Down's brother, Pat, came up with the name QB1, but the game was originally called Armchair Quarterback. During the years it was being developed, another company grabbed the rights to that name because NTN hadn't preserved it. Still, the name QB1 has worked quite well, and it is recognized industry-wide as one of the first true interactive television products.

In 1978 and 1979, Daniel Downs and Klosterman started working on Armchair Quarterback again, getting more serious about it and looking into what technology was available. In 1982, Klosterman and the two Downses decided to form a company. Klosterman went on to become the chairman of the board of directors, Daniel Downs the executive vice-president and COO, and Pat Downs became the president and CEO. The company was started in 1983, and with funding they started looking for additional investors.

The goal was to take their first product, QB1, to be the catalyst to create an interactive network. That was their business plan during the 1982–1983 time frame. It was during this time that NTN hired Don Shula, Hank Stram, and Bill Walsh. These individuals, along with the founders, brought the game to life. They also hired a professor at the University of Stanford who specialized in statistical data. They also brought on board a game psychologist, Gary Shirts. They spent from the first part of 1983 until the end of 1985, testing and modifying the game until it appeared as it is today.

There have been, of course, many updates and changes to QB1 since then, but the foundation of the game has remained the same. Initially there was a game for adults and a different one for kids. "Originally NTN had a Pop Warner division for the kids," Downs explains. "They also had George Halas and Vince Lombardi divisions. As we worked with our game psychologist and statistical people and even our coaches, we then realized we could incorporate it all into one game. So someone could play, and play easily just by calling 'run' or 'pass.' However, if they were more advanced players, they could earn more points by getting more specific." NTN went from an offensive game to a defensive game. Downs continues, "We went through a lot of things to come up with the game we have today. It took three years of development. This, however, paid off in that we developed an expertise for creating interactive programming. This allowed us to create new games much faster."

NTN received a temporary NFL license in 1985. The NFL granted only a temporary license because they wanted to make sure the game did not involve gambling.

Gameplay Design

Initially, the game play design was done on IBM-compatible personal computers. "We ran thousands of people through our labs here in San Diego at night," says Downs. "We used live games and taped games, and had people play. Then we would do question and answer sessions. It also lead us to an understanding of what has now become the interactive industry. We don't care whether it's a telephone keypad, a remote control, a PC keyboard, or a wireless device. We don't care what the input device is; our game stays the same. This is one of the principles we came up with. So whether you play on a cable-based system or a satellite-based system or an online system, we don't care. You are competing against everybody wherever they are. That is one of the things that has distinguished our company and set us apart, and all of this came out of our early testing with QB1. We tried a lot of different devices, tried a lot of different systems, and then we just all woke up one day and realized that it isn't going to be one system, and one set-up box. We decided that we didn't want to be in that business; we didn't want to build a box."

NTN filled itself with good games people. This allowed them to recognize early some of the social aspect that is critical to interactive games. For example, they realized that there is a "critical mass" needed for playing QB1 in a bar. What goes on with QB1 in a bar when 11 or more people are there is very different when fewer are there. It's a different situation with seven to 11 individuals playing. Five people or fewer have a different experience.

From the beginning, NTN's first game was definitely going to be the football title. The first interactive game was played during the Super Bowl of January, 1984. NTN set QB1 up and played it in a Harbor Island hotel in San Diego with executives from HBO and some members of the public. While NTN was being pressured to do baseball as its second game, the company chose game shows and trivia-based games. These gaming areas offered a broader entry into the market. It freed the network from being tied only to sporting games and enabled NTN to kick off a year-round network.

As each play is made during a football game, an NTN employee serves as the referee, entering the final play into the network. It's this final play that everyone gets scored on. In the early days, NTN referees actually went to the games and sat in the press boxes in stadiums around the country. Today it is all done off television feeds to NTN headquarters. When CBS and NBC are doing six or seven games in the morning, NTN is doing them all simultaneously. In the early days, NTN worked with the NFL and USFL and actually had someone in the press box on a phone line communicating back to their headquarters.

It was still a major concern to create a game of skill that the NFL would recognize as such. It's not a guessing game. This was important because in some cases where the game was wired into a home and people were charged to play, the game could be construed as gambling. The NFL was very aggressive in making certain that NTN didn't come up with a gambling game. So NTN worked hand-in-hand with the NFL itself, and people within the NFL played it during the early days and provided feedback. Because of concerns about gambling, NTN worked very closely with them.

NTN was on a three-year test license before finally getting enough data and statistical information to prove to the NFL that QB1 was a game of skill and not a gambling game (or even promoted as gambling). This was very tricky because it was all breaking new ground. Being a two-way service, it was easy for the programmers to collect data from QB1's inception. The statistics specialist helped analyze the data. In an effort to create a game of skill, the score system was developed that awarded you for a series of consecutive correct answers. If you don't know the play, you can sit it out and not be penalized.

Artistic Design

Initially NTN was limited by what they could do artistically. The cosmetics were important, but the key focus was on displaying the names of all players and giving recognition to the players. It was basically a text-based service at first. However, the way NTN entertains changes each year. The company has a panel that sits down and evaluates input from the players and then recommends changes on that input. Today, because of changes in graphics and video cards, and with the ability to transmit pictures, focus has started to shift to the

▲ Early versions of QB1 were text-based. *Courtesy of NTN Communications, Inc.*

cosmetics of the game. NTN is constantly changing the cosmetics, and the game today looks very different from just 18 months ago. All of NTN's games are revamped from time to time.

As Daniel Downs explains, "We give them more information than they ever had before, and the way we provide it is quite good. As a result, we now attract some pretty good sponsors since we can now run a commercial as opposed to text-based messages. We've seen QB1 evolve over the years, and if the ITV industry evolves, QB1 is a great example of that, both in terms of the game itself and then how you can present it cosmetically. As we got onto new platforms and systems, we found that they could do more, so we took advantage of it. We have a tendency now to take a system like GTE Main Street and exploit that system beyond where the designers intended it to go."

Back in 1987, ads were sold to Winston Cigarettes (R.G. Reynolds) and Molson beer. These ads, however, were very limited. During that time, NTN had a video laser disc player in each bar. This allowed them to take the video commercial ads and store them on the laser disc. The problem was control. Some bars would turn off the laser disc; others would take out the laser disc because they didn't want a tobacco commercial running. NTN had little or no control over this, so as graphics technology advanced over the years, the laser disc was phased out. Greater graphics capabilities were added to the system, and with advances in graphics performance they will only get better. NTN's goal is to have full-motion video (FMV) in the future.

Music

Initially, NTN had sound in bars and restaurants. The technology is there, and it's easy to send audio into bars. The bars, however, didn't want it. It would be intrusive if NTN tried to force audio into the system. The reason is that each bar likes its own ambiance, and one of the ways they create their own ambiance is through music. Some QB1 players, for example, might be at a country and western bar, while others are at an easy listening bar. Some bars even program their music for different parts of the day and different audiences. NTN found that the audio for their games was intrusive; it didn't go with the ambiance. NTN had to adjust the system to fit the environment. On other systems, this is not a problem for QB1. For example, on GTE Main Street, QB1 has audio. In 1994, NTN will enter some new systems and include audio on those.

Programming

Everything NTN developed was created on IBM-compatible personal computers. The very first QB1 was played in January, 1984 on a group of Kaypro computers. At that Harbor Island hotel, they used a room full of Kaypro PCs that were linked together. The software was written in a mixture of C and assembly language for the hospitality installations. However, NTN has to develop in many different languages for the various systems they run on. They have experts who can program in various languages for these various platforms.

Testing

When the players saw QB1 for the first time, they thought it was great but that it needed many changes. At that early stage, it was still a very rudimentary game. There were a number of important ingredients for QB1 today that came out of that very first playing. After the game was played, NTN conducted a three-hour meeting with everyone who played. NTN's game psychologist then walked them through the game, getting input and suggestions. This process continued for another three years.

"Somehow in our naive way back in 1983 to 1986," says Downs, "we did some right things without realizing they were so right at the time, bringing in a statistical analyzer, a gambling expert, a game psychologist, and three coaches, including Don Klosterman. We really put together an interesting development team. In 1984 and 1985, we went to great lengths to have 6-year olds play and 80-year olds play..., people who were football fanatics and people who couldn't care less about football. We really went to great lengths in developing QB1. We felt that we could reach out to different levels of expertise and still get them hooked on the game itself. The best proof was that whatever it was we did, we did right and we continued to do right. We never set QB1 in stone and said it could never be changed."

This formula seems to work for NTN. The proof is that since 1984—when the company started with just 20 or 30 people playing at that hotel—QB1 has progressed to more than 5 million players today, with 1.5 million added in 1993 alone. The numbers are really starting to escalate. Next year, another 2 million or more players are expected to start. QB1 has stood the test of time. Sustaining interest was something many people wondered about, including those at NTN. Employees wondered if it was just a fad, something here today and gone tomorrow. However, they don't think so anymore, and neither does the rest of the industry.

An important principle to NTN was not to compete with the telecast. Instead, NTN only wanted to enhance it. Enhancing the viewing enjoyment of the broadcast was a major goal. If certain people feel that QB1 is too much work, then they can just sit it out and watch the game.

Product Release

The QB1 hardware wasn't to NTN's satisfaction, so the game release was delayed until August, 1986. After NTN released QB1, the company began marketing it to the hospitality industry. While the company was waiting for the hardware to advance, developers worked on improving the game itself.

Trying to sell interactive television to the hospitality industry in 1986 was difficult. Since NTN is free to the players, it was difficult to explain to the hospitality industry that they had to pay for something and then turn around and provide it free to customers. "People looked at you like you dropped off the moon," Downs explains. "It wasn't that easy, but Holiday Inn was one of our earliest supporters and first big contracts with more than 30 locations. Today in North America, we are in upwards of about 1,500 locations. We are doing around 5 million participants a month. We doubled the network size since last year. We've never had the money or financial wherewithall to go and blow this thing where and when we wanted to. But very likely the product wasn't as good as it should have been, had we had the money. Now in recent years, the product is so much better; so when we got the money we were ready for it. We had a much better product. We have a very good chance of doubling the network again in 1994, with well over 2,000 locations."

The Future of QB1

NTN is now working on other interactive games involving football that are designed to be different. These games put you in a different mode. Instead of being the quarterback, you might be the general manager or president of a team. In other cases you might be the middle linebacker. These new games haven't been released yet.

NTN has also been doing the fantasy football programs for a while. The company doesn't believe it has cornered the market on creating interactive sports games, so it is constantly looking for new products created by talented people and for ideas that are fresh, innovative, and proved. For example, NTN recently acquired the programs of a company called Replica out of Boston, Massachusetts. Replica has been producing fantasy sports programming in the Boston area for some years. They are head and shoulders above other companies, so NTN took an interest in them. They have a financial game, as well as baseball, basketball, and football games. NTN acquires the electronic rights to those games and brings them up to their standards for delivery across NTN's different platforms. There will be a complete TV show just for that product. The TV show created just for that product will air on one of two major sports networks that currently want it. It is not a play-along game, but it's definitely a sports game.

Issues in Converting Game Shows into ITV Games

Interactive Network Television (INT) makes interactive games and was founded five years ago by Lawrence Taymor. Taymor started the company as a joint venture with Interactive Network and brought together a number of people with broadcast TV game show experience. The basic company produces interactive programming: about 110 shows a month, totaling about 3,500 to date, all from original software. The key shows that INT does are the most popular shows in the TV game category: for example "Wheel of Fortune" and "Jeopardy!" They also do "Murder She Wrote," "L.A. Law," and "Law & Order." Whodunit shows lend themselves to interactive programs quite well.

NOTE

Taymor describes some of the issues facing ITV program creators: "We had to think twice about some of the assumptions we initially had. At first we thought we needed some type of on-screen display. That was something we tried but were not really sure that it was the best solution. One of the things that is very important in designing interactive games is to make it incredibly easy to play and incredibly intuitive."

For example, people who are watching a football game are very involved in that football game. If they have to think, 'press one for pass, two for run, three for this,' you will lose them. The play must be simple and right in front of them. NTN solved this problem by creating overlays that fit over the keypad of their playmakers. INT, on the other hand, created a handheld device with an LCD screen and programmable dot keys so the buttons are right next to the available commands. The feedback is immediate, and it's right in the user's lap. It does not force the user to look at a remote control and at the screen.

INT made their navigation very easy due to various menu levels. The whole system is programmable. Software is downloaded into the box every day, so if you want to make a change, it's easy to do. There's no resident software except an operating system. The operating system is also programmable and is updated periodically, all without the user being aware of it.

Initially, INT thought it could just use dot keys and offer multiple choice letters for "Wheel of Fortune," but that didn't work at all. So INT added a full keyboard to the set-top box. Having a keyboard and typing letters turned out to be really important in playing board games. Board games are probably the most popular games on television right now.

"When designing an interactive television game," explains Taymor, "you have two models, the video game and the TV show. You think through how is it different and how is it the same. Compared to a TV game show, you have to make a game that works for lots of other players. You have thousands, hundreds of thousands, and perhaps some day, millions competing against each other. How do they compete? How do you achieve ranking and scoring? What's the sense of competition? When does the home player have a turn? Do they play at the same time as the on-screen players, or do they have their own turn? These are questions that you have to ask yourself."[1]

Another challenge is in dealing with different skill levels. When a TV game show is designed, they can basically hand-pick their players: they can all be good, they can all be bad, or they can all be mediocre. With an interactive version, anyone can play and they need to feel like they can participate in it. Compared to doing a video game, television interactive games are very different.

It's also very different from creating video games. Video games may have one or two players who will play very intensely for hours on end. It's a highly focused activity and usually has very complex rules and complex game activity. Video games tend to be very competitive, not social.

Creating "Wheel of Fortune" Interactive

"Wheel of Fortune" is one of the first games developed at INT. It has simple rules, but it's a very complex game when you analyze it, Taymor points out. "We had to figure out, Does the home player have their own wheel? When does the home player play? What happens after the home player solves (which may happen before the studio players solve)? We designed and tested a dozen variations."

▲ The interactive version of "Wheel of Fortune." *Courtesy of Interactive Network.*

"Our end result was a game that used the following rules," Taymor continues. "We use the studio players' wheel because we wanted to make it a game of skill rather than a game of luck, so it wouldn't violate lottery laws. That way we could award prizes. We also wanted the players to play on every spin; otherwise, they get bored. We wanted some special strategy for them, so what we came up with was that the home player can guess the letters before the studio player does. If they guess a letter that's in the puzzle, they get the points that are on the wheel, just like the studio player does. They also get the studio player's points if they guess a different letter from the studio player. This gives you a double challenge not to pick necessarily the most obvious letter. We allow you to buy vowels, and on any spin, you get to solve. You can only solve once, however, because when the home player solves, we have to give them some feedback as to whether they got it right or wrong. Of course, you would have to choose or type in a letter, and this would give it away. So players could just choose to solve all the time, until they guessed it."

"After the player solves the puzzle," Taymor adds, "we let them continue playing with the use of pop-up questions. Our pop-up questions are puzzles just like the normal puzzles on 'Wheel of Fortune.' These puzzles are unique to our system, the reason being that people can cheat by watching the show via satellite in an earlier time zone and know all the answers. That's a problem in creating interactive games that are synchronous with broadcast programming. This is a problem that you don't have on dedicated cable networks like the Family Channel, where you have one time zone for the whole country."

"If you were to design an original version of 'Wheel of Fortune,' just forgetting the TV show that exists now (and some time in the future there may be enough interactive viewers to justify creating something just for them), this is where it gets interesting," Taymor concludes. "You are going to have a different competitive environment and a whole new set of rules. You may even want the host to turn to the camera and say, 'Now it's your turn,' or somehow acknowledge the players at home. Some wonder, 'Won't there be studio players? Players that you will compete against? Or is it going to be more like a video game, where everyone has their own game that they are playing at home, and everyone's game is different. You could put out a Sega cartridge version of "Wheel of Fortune" on a network.' This is something you will have to decide at some point when you create interactive games."

Creating "Jeopardy!" Interactive

INT found "Jeopardy!" much easier to design. Their only real challenge was how to enter the answers. Initially, they thought typing the answers would be one possible way to go, but it was much too time-consuming. Merv Griffin liked the idea of putting the first letter in. For instance, if the answer was *aardvark*, you would type A. But they found that it was too hard, because the questions were so difficult, and many players would end up with negative scores. Instead, they decided to make "Jeopardy!" a multiple-choice game, for which they would create three plausible questions for each answer. Thus they could control the degree of difficulty.

One thing they couldn't control, however, was the speed of the game. One of the attractions of "Jeopardy!" is that it is very fast, about seven seconds per question. That is twice as fast as most other question-and-answer game shows prior to "Jeopardy!" This could be one of the secrets to its success. Even watching it on (non-interactive) TV, if you don't know the answer to the question or are not interested in the category, you don't have to wait very long until something else happens. But that means that most of the home players are just buried in their home control units playing their interactive game, and they don't really have time to watch or participate in the broadcast game.

Creating "Family Feud" Interactive

There was a game that INT came up with that was perfect for interactivity, "Family Feud." All the viewer has to do is guess whether the player gives a good answer or a bad answer. If it's a good answer, they can predict where the survey occurred for more points, whether it was in the first tier or second tier. As a result, players can actually watch the game. It's a personality-based game, so they can root for their favorite player on the screen. They can also take in the game as a linear broadcast program as they normally do, but at the same time play along with it. The game has a very nice feature—it's based on accumulative knowledge: anyone can win and you don't have to be very smart to win. As a result, the interactive version out-performs the broadcast versions rating.

The elements of any great game are skill, luck, strategy, and rewards. Those combine in a very interesting way if you want to award prizes, because the lottery laws forbid you to charge an entry fee for a game in which winning is based on luck and the reward is a prize. Having two out of three of those things is, however, acceptable; doing so doesn't violate the lottery laws. Many ITV providers run into trouble because they want to charge an entry fee to make money until some point in time when the network gets large enough to be advertiser-supported, but at the same time they want to award prizes. The law is different in every state but the basic concept is the same: skill must be the deciding factor in determining the winner. So ITV game designers have to analyze their games carefully.

It's interesting that many game shows probably wouldn't make it if the same laws applied to them. "Wheel of Fortune" has a wheel or roulette that definitely wouldn't pass. "Jeopardy!" *might* be considered a game of skill. Chess is definitely a game of skill. Now you may think that "Jeopardy!" is a game of skill, according to the producers of the show; the winner is often determined by the categories that come up. If they have very bright people on the show, they might know much more about presidents or wine, and those might be the categories that come up in Double Jeopardy and so forth.

The challenge in any of these games is in keeping the same players from winning all the time. ITV has the same problem. There will always be people who are drawn to an interactive game system who are very good at a particular game of skill. The lottery in Las Vegas has figured out how to make it fun; they will let you win one out of 11 times. If you buy 11 scratchers, you are guaranteed to win at least $1, and you'll come back and buy some more. ITV game designers have to be a little more creative.

At INT, they created a competitive membership group with leagues, such as a novice league, an intermediate league, and an advanced league. There are always targets and special events coinciding with holidays and seasonal events. INT also comes up with new games or variations on games all the time. According to Taymor, "This is the greatest challenge, because just creating an interactive game like 'Jeopardy!' seems like it is real easy; but when you actually try to build it into a business and test it for game play, you will discover that there are a bunch of little traps that you can fall into that will create games that don't work."

CURRENT INTERACTIVE TELEVISION SYSTEMS

Looking at some of the interactive television systems and the programming currently available, you'll see that many television-based products existing right now use the word *interactive*. These vary from audio-text to scratching off a number on a lottery card. Much depends on how the word *interactive* is defined. This section will discuss only products and services that offer two-way communication using the television and some type of set-top box or handheld unit.

VideoWay Communications

VideoWay Communications is a supplier of both hardware and software for ITV. Based in Montreal, Canada, VideoWay is Quebec's largest cable company, with more than 1 million subscribers in Canada alone. It has 300,000 paying subscribers to its VideoWay ITV service. It owns a U.S. cable company called Transworld Wireless Cable in Tampa Bay, Florida. VideoWay also has formed joint agreements with a number of U.S. cable companies, such as Transworld Telecommunications of Salt Lake City and Omnivision of Las Vegas. These networks give VideoWay access to another 1 million subscribers in the United States.

Three main divisions within VideoWay Communications deal with interactive television. One is TV Interactively (TVI), which provides the shows and programs and produces them. The second is the VideoWay division, which provides the software and hardware contained in the set-top boxes. The third is Videotron Plus, which handles all the downloaded software, videotext, and audiotext commercial applications, including lottery games and electronic mail.

VideoWay's strategy is to offer new interactive services aimed at unsatisfied cable customers and the "untouchables," at the same time offering a more efficient and effective way for organizations to do business with consumers. These organizations include governments, consumer product companies, financial and educational institutions, and catalog firms.

Many attempts have been made to provide services such as educational and financial information, video games, home shopping, classified ads, and banking, and most of them have failed. Those that did not fail required massive financial commitments. VideoWay hopes to avoid that situation. VideoWay sees two basic problems associated with the failed ventures. First, the systems were not user-friendly; they were aimed at computer-literate people. Secondly, they used dedicated terminals, and the consumers' need to purchase dedicated terminals obviously slowed down penetration. These things combined to produce an environment more associated with work than with entertainment and fun.

NOTE

"Since the beginning," says Sylvie Lelande, president of VideoWay, "our approach has been dramatically different. We use TV sets as terminals. They are available in every home, and each member of the household spends an average of 24 hours a week in front of one. We introduced our interactive services through entertainment so that it would be fun for people to use it. More importantly, they do not have to master all the applications at once, but rather can learn gradually as they feel more comfortable using a disguised computer."[1]

VideoWay has found that its exclusive services are very popular, and are used an average of 13 hours per week per household. This compares to 1.2 hours for the Prodigy online service and 24 minutes for Minitel in France (a national video text system). Plans already exist at VideoWay to provide more geographically oriented applications, such as electronic flyers, lotteries, coupons, and classified ads. These services, of course, will require or greatly benefit from deployment into every home in a given territory. This requires that VideoWay's system reach at least 80 percent penetration in a given area. This, however, demands very significant funding and presents a potentially serious technology challenge.

By being in the field for the last three years in Canada and the United Kingdom, VideoWay has reduced its technology risk. In these two market places, it has approximately 300,000 paying subscribers every month, and the technology definitely does work. From there, two important principles guided the development of the service. The service has limited capabilities. It is meant to perform functions for basic interactive services that tend to gain high subscriber usability: simple video games, mass-appeal databanks, and two-way transactions such as ordering goods and paying bills.

VideoWay's set-top box does not have the capability to store very large amounts of information, and it does not offer video-on-demand. Furthermore, it doesn't have the processing power to accommodate sophisticated video games. The set-top box and its related software are meant to be a platform for a gateway link to other hardware that offers more sophisticated functions.

For instance, the VideoWay set-top box has the capabilities of downloading software into Nintendo or Sega home gaming systems and linking personal computers, printers, and fax machines to the network. It can connect to security systems and home-automation peripherals. VideoWay avoids the high risk of sophisticated peripherals that rapidly become obsolete. Instead, VideoWay leaves it to the customers to decide which peripheral they want to buy. VideoWay thus pushes the investment over to the consumers.

Interactive Systems

In 1986, Merv Griffin Productions and Mattel Toys formed an alliance to create interactive television programming. As a company, Interactive Systems knew ITV was coming, but they wanted to make money on it right away, utilizing current technology. So they decided to make some products for niche markets that used current technology, not the promised technology of the future.

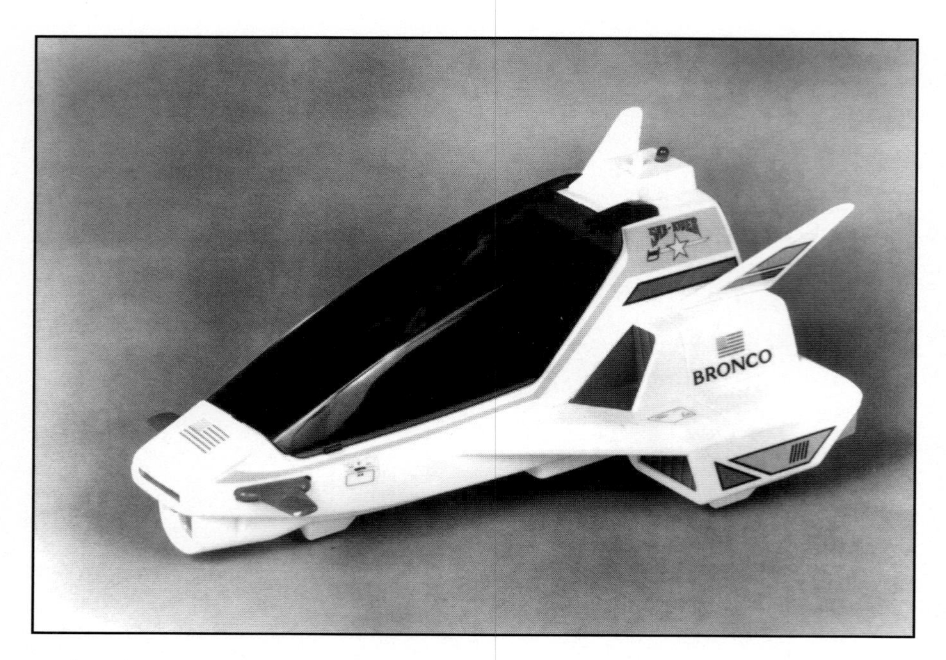

▲ The Saber Rider action toy used the patented VEIL™ technology. *Courtesy of Interactive Systems.*

In 1987, they produced the first animated interactive show, called Saber Rider. Using their patented video encoded invisible light (VEIL) system, the Saber Rider show was run in conjunction with the sale of a toy that enabled children to interact with the cartoon. The toy had an optical scanner, so that when it was pointed at the television screen, it would pick up the coded data with the vertical retrace interval. During the cartoon, there would be situations where the home player had to shoot the screen. If the player was not fast enough, the Saber Rider gun blew up and the toy pilot was ejected. The program was on the air for 1 1/2 years on more than 200 stations in the U.S. and Canada. More than 250,000 toys were sold with the optical scanner.

Since then, Interactive Systems has also taken the optical scanner and put it into exercise products: a stepper, a cycle machine, and a cross-country ski machine called Ski Vision. The optical scanner on the front of the ski machine, for example, reads the terrain from data encoded in the video. As you're skiing and the terrain goes down, the scanner reads that and reduces the tension on the ski machine. As the terrain goes up, the tension gets greater.

A recent interactive TV product was Toby Terrier and his Video Pals. Introduced in February, 1993, it is based on the same optical scanner technique and geared toward children. More than 700,000 toys have been ordered by Walmart, Toys R Us, K-Mart, Target, and others. On Toby's collar is the scanner that reads the data. The dog interacts with both videos and broadcast programs. As long as the show has the data encoded in the VBI, Toby will react. The retail price for Toby is $49.95.

As technology has progressed, Interactive Systems moved into the ITV industry. Before releasing anything to the United States, the company took their products overseas. Paul McKellips, director of corporate communications, explains: "Going overseas, it was much easier to get an ITV system started. For example, here in the U.S. on December 13th of 1993, we started an Alpha system test in Portland, Oregon, with KGW, the NBC affiliate. As we went to market-test, we had to deal with the three local affiliate broadcasters, Fox, and the independents. Then we had to deal with the

▲ Toby Terrier and his Video Pals, an interactive television product for children. *Courtesy of Interactive Systems*.

national parent companies. We had to deal with the programmers, the producers, the guilds. We also had to deal with four telephone companies, three cable companies, and quite a few other people. When we launched in Spain, we dealt with two organizations, the National Telephone Company and the National Broadcasters (RTVE); and when we got the *yes*, it was quick, and that was it."

▲ The System 1 set-top box, called Telepick, currently used in Spain.

Interactive Systems ITV is licensed in more than 19 countries. Currently, it has four different ITV systems. Of those four systems, System 1 is installed in Spain, System 2 in the Netherlands, System 3 in the U.S., and System 4 in Australia.

System 1 in Spain uses a set-top decoder box. The box uses an Intel 80286 microprocessor, and it has a modem on the back. The modem has a store-and-forward feature so it doesn't tie up the phone. The box also has a graphics printer that uses colored paper. That way, if McDonald's wants to offer a coupon in their interactive commercial, the printer can print the McDonald's golden arches logo on the coupon. The printer has been an incredible success with their advertisers. For example, McDonald's ran a two-for-one hamburger promotion. At the end of that 24-hour promotion, Interactive Systems could tell McDonald's that 89 percent of the homes viewed the commercial, 62 percent of the homes printed a coupon, and 39 percent of the homes redeemed a coupon. An added feature is that on the coupon is a bar code of addressability; should it decide to do so, McDonald's could use the address to show up at homes the next day to deliver hamburgers.

System 2 in the Netherlands uses simple on-screen graphics like the graphics common VCR players use today. One example is a sports trivia question that pops up before a commercial. During the commercial, you enter your answer, and at the end of the commercial, the correct answer is given. If you have selected the correct answer, the printer prints a coupon for a free sports souvenir mug that the viewer can redeem at K-Mart. K-Mart gets the traffic, and the advertiser and sports team get the promotion.

System 3—to be launched here in the United States—uses a completely different approach. It will look like, feel like, and act like an Apple

Macintosh computer. The system will use on-screen icons and a floating cursor, with a thumbstick on your remote control. It will be interesting to see the results of this system, because so many people in the United States are not computer literate and probably qualify as computer-phobic.

System 4 in Australia will launch with 250,000 units that will be placed into the market at a subscription fee of $7.95 a month. There the biggest potential market is off-track wagering.

McKellips feels that entertainment is not tied to interactivity. "When we are talking about training, games, services, and TV programs," he says, "those are all the things that are lumped under ITV. Entertainment can stand alone; interactivity cannot. Nobody in the world wants to buy interactivity. In Spain, we've launched our ITV service, and we put right on the box the words *interactive television* because everybody in Spain is hearing all the Americans talk about ITV, and they want it right away. We just released a product that's an interactive toy, and we keep the word *interactive* off the box because in the U.S., John and Mary consumer are pretty intimidated by the word. Interactivity cannot stand alone. In our opinion, don't put interactivity in the showcase. Put it in the warehouse. The creative community needs to view interactivity as a tool, like scripting, lighting and special effects, costuming, and staging. It's a tool, a tool to enhance whatever your creative entertainment or information is. Interactivity is not the thing we really need to focus on. What we need to focus on is the creativity that Hollywood uses."

"In my opinion," McKellips continues, "if interactive television is left to the merger folks, and the media pundits, and all of the forecasters, ITV has the power and probability to exceed Orwell's worst nightmare. But interactive television left in the hands of creative people, producers, directors, writers, all the people that know what the customer wants, then I think ITV has the ability to exceed even Shakespeare's wildest dreams. It's going to be one or the other."

GTE ImagiTrek

In Cerritos, California, GTE has been providing an advanced ITV system to 60 homes for a little over a year. Called GTE ImagiTrek, this system is done in conjunction with the Discovery Channel and World Book Encyclopedia. It is a joint venture with Philips to use the Philips CD-I players as an ITV set-top box.

The word *ImagiTrek* comes from the two keywords, *imagination* and *trek*, representing "content" and "transport." Says Mark Dillion, director of interactive publishing, "When ITV reaches the hype and popularity of where we want it to be, we will not be using most of the technologies that we are using today. When we instituted this test, we recognized that we were trying to duplicate an experience. We were trying to get some sense of what people wanted to do or could do with interactive television, so we cut out a niche a little differently than some people. There were already interactive shopping channels, interactive games, so we took a slightly different approach. We said, 'let's just make television interactive. What can be done with television programming on a more generalized basis and still give it an interactive element?' And that's quite a challenge because, as you know, television, almost by definition, is pretty linear. It's broadcasting one-to-many, and to take that one-to-many experience and make it interactive is quite challenging."

Dillon offers the illustration of an airplane flight: "There is a way to take even linear experiences and make them different for each person. The analogy I like to use is a little like a plane flight. If a group of people got in an airplane and flew from the West Coast to the East Coast, while everyone would be having the same linear experience, one would watch a movie, one would read a book, one would sleep. It would be a very different experience for everyone, although based on the same linear pathway. In a way, that's the approach we have taken."

Some ITV creators feel that *more* always means *better*, so they are planning to remove channels in order to offer more video on demand (VOD) services. The problem is there will probably not be enough material for that to happen. There is a limited budget in the home for entertainment or for discretionary spending. If people are using pay-per-view movies, their funds will be taken away from the premium channels, causing a robbing-Peter-to-pay-Paul phenomenon. One of the goals at GTE ImagiTrek, therefore, was to find a way to provide more interactivity, more programming, and not have the consumers look at their phone or cable bill and mistake it for their car payment.

Dillon feels that one of the most critical things, is that you can't get lost in the pursuit of technology to the point of forgetting the economics of what interactivity is about. People tend to look at it as a pay-per-view or pay-to-own experience like movies or software. Yet for television, that doesn't work. Consider, if all the network television and all the cable television that you see had no commercials, and all of that television that is free now had to be produced based on subscription dollars or on pay-per-view basis, we would end up with about three channels in about a week. Because the economics just don't allow the ITV provider to go out and grab the money from the viewers in advance or to depend upon them buying a given program. Any form of television requires sufficient commercials so it will be advertiser-supported.

That became another goal of GTE ImagiTrek: to add commercials to the interactive experience. "We felt that for this to be really successful," Dillon explains, "there had to be a way for the sponsors to support the interactivity so you can afford not to have to pay for it. This turned out to be one of the most exciting parts of the test, because when you start doing interactive commercials, you move from a broadcast environment to a direct response environment."

GTE ImagiTrek understands the importance of not trying to replace the television viewing habits of people. They just want to make the experience a little more interactive. The goal isn't to turn the Discovery Channel into a Nintendo game. Instead they simply want to give the viewer a little extra value. Each set-top box (a modified Philips CD-I unit) has a CD-ROM drive with about 4,000 articles on each CD.

The interactive advertising simply locates the geographical location of the viewer and then adds information pertinent to the view, such as local telephone numbers or local specials. Another lesson learned at ImagiTrek was that people respond to high quality graphics, visuals, and motion.

Providing the extra information on CD-ROM for the viewer to access at any time during the program turned out to have an unexpected benefit. People will typically switch channels when they start getting bored. With the research CD-ROM, when a person starts to get a little itchy, and they want to switch channels, before they do, they tend to check out the menu and pull up the globe, look at a map, or call up an article on the current subject. The whole idea here is to maintain channel loyalty. So the programmer benefits by increased channel loyalty. The advertiser benefits because they've increased a 30-second spot to a 4- or 5-minute infomercial. The viewer benefits because it is a more enjoyable experience. Dillon concludes, "They are not being forced into something but are on the plane and get to decide whether to watch the movie or read a magazine."

GTE Main Street

Main Street is an ITV service currently being used on three cable systems in the U.S. in upwards of 4,000 homes. It has also been in businesses for about a year providing news and stock information. At a reasonable price of $9.95 a month, Main Street provides a lot of bang for the buck. You don't have to buy a piece of hardware and you still get a full range of services from shopping to banking, stock portfolio management including buying and selling stocks, practice SAT tests, airlines, community calendars, and more. The entertainment programming comes from NTN Communications.

Of all the services being marketed today, Main Street is considered to have the best balance and service for the price. The network was designed to work with fiber, but also works with coaxial cable and telephone lines. The negative side is that the return path requires the phone to be off the hook. Once the fiber is in place, it can do everything simultaneously on the fiber line, and customers won't have to change the set-top box to switch over to fiber.

The Main Street system provides two types of customers: the subscriber and the direct-access user. The subscriber interacts with Main Street via a set-top box. The direct access user has access to a subset of the full Main Street system by using his dial tone telephone and a regular television set. Data is sent to the home through the TV's VBI, the telephone, or both.

GTE Main Street is currently on three cable systems: Daniel's, Apollo, and Continental Cable. In 1994 GTE Main Street will expand into two or three more very large cable systems. By the end of 1994, GTE expects to have more than 20,000 people on Main Street.

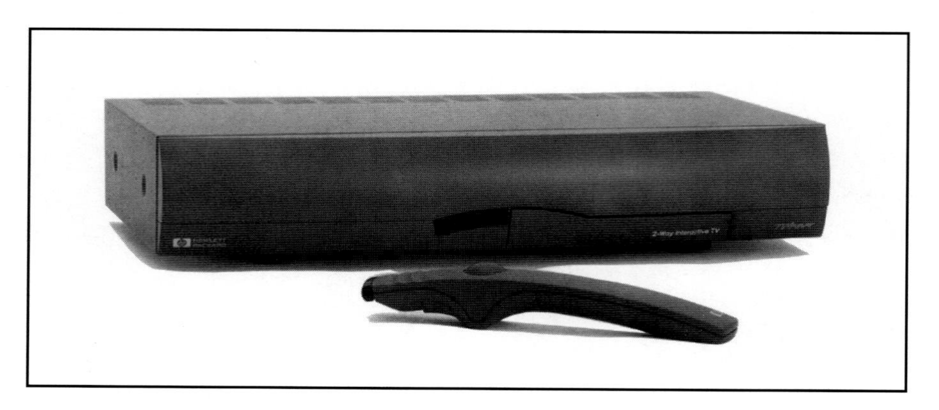

▲ The E*ON set-top box. *Courtesy of E*ON.*

E*ON

IVDS (Interactive Video Data Service) is a two-way wireless ITV system using an FCC-allocated spectrum to mix satellite technology and local cellular sites. IVDS networking offers an inexpensive return path coming out of the home. E*ON signals synchronize with any local program delivery by means of a stand-alone piece of equipment that is either a set-top box or a box built into a cable converter. Channel mapping maps the cellular interactivity with a particular program received on your TV set.

In September 1993, the FCC finally selected 18 winners from over 4,100 applications for the top nine cities in the country. The more than 700 markets remaining will be auctioned within a year.

E*ON has cell sites operational now near Washington D.C. and will be expanding early in 1994 to two more market trials in Los Angeles and Philadelphia. During the tests of E*ON they will roll out both the stand-alone unit and the cable platform box. This means going to the consumer directly through infomercials and retail stores as well as cable operators. Currently the platform is based on an Intel 80486 microprocessor. It includes an RF modem and some extra goodies, which together put the initial cost at around $500.

The home unit displays E*ON services as graphics and text on the TV screen. In the future, when fiber optics do come to the home, E*ON will migrate their cellular network to fiber with their existing services. Then, to keep the cellular license from going to waste, they will re-deploy the network for mobile devices. That way you can take your portable TV and control unit to the beach and tape a movie at home, or grab news content on a particular topic while you are away from home.

E*ON has three operating modes. *Navigation control* channels you among applications and serves as an advanced program guide. It also activates your VCR to record programs. *Synchronized overlay* delivers simulcast applications, such as play-along games and polling, and off-channel applications like retrieving messages, shopping on-screen catalogs, and conducting home banking. *Impulse pay-per-view* lets you click a movie trailer and then tune into the next exhibition of that movie on a pay-per-view channel.

There will be three marketing growth phases for the IVDS category. First, equipment roll-out, which is getting the boxes off the shelf and making the service available. Second is service sampling, which is an acceptance of the more winning applications. Third is an optimization period where we will see combinations. During this time, E*ON hopes to see their theory that the ITV market will be driven by a combination of applications, not just a single "killer app."

How do consumers feel about all of this? E*ON and Hewlett Packard have been involved in a joint effort, three-year research program. In their statistics among average consumers, two-thirds of those surveyed agreed that TV should be more interactive; three out of five people surveyed find the whole concept exciting; and 75 percent conclude that this approach (of bringing together a number of services) has many useful features. These people are strongly inclined to try the service. Among electronics enthusiasts, the interest is even higher. The most interesting group is a combination of early adapters and interactive fans that comprise a core market of a projected 14 million households in the United States. There is a second utilitarian market that is almost as large; it is accessible if we can prove how this will clearly save time and money.

NOTE

Says Marty Lafferty, vice-president of E*ON, "We also have learned that people need a full menu of applications in five areas. *Entertainment*—and it might be QB1 off of Monday Night Football for Dad, and play-along Jeopardy! for Mom. *Distance—Learning* so we can keep the kids more competitive. *Health*—interactivity in the 90s has to be perceived as a 'green' service. *Home banking*—virtual shopping malls are absolutely expected, and the information delivered will be more personalized and faster than any alternative."

"Now the way this is delivered is also a key," continues Lafferty. "We have the four C's of consumer marketing for interactivity. *Control* means that nothing gets by me that I want, and I control the outcome of events that are interactive. *Convenience*—the system responds quickly, and it's always available, 24 hours. It's *customized*. I can personalize my service and make it more of my own; and it's *comprehensive*. If I want a particular game, E*ON delivers that game. It's a quest for the killer combo, and it will rejuvenate your life as a TV viewer."[1]

E*ON has found some unique applications of ITV. For instance, some country music artists want to use E*ON to sell cassettes to people who shun the noise of the "long-hair courts" and record stores. Broadcasters such as ABC want to launch pay-per-service to be like cable services with two revenue streams, and be paid directly from consumers for interactions as well as by advertisers. Hallmark Cards is interested in using E*ON to send reminders when Aunt Jane's birthday is coming and to allow for custom greetings. Mannings Baseball wants to run a quick-buy option for the pennant or cap, just at the moment the Blue Jays have won another game. L.L. Bean wants its free-order entry. A Santa Monica savings and loan wants to get rid of its store-front teller operations and have customers do banking from their homes.

Everybody wants to play, and the most obvious place to start is in interactively assisted commercial airtime: Click to order the pair of Nikes shown in the commercial right now, click to get a sample of Crystal Pepsi, or click to get more information on a Lexus. If the local Lexus dealer wants, John would get a 48-page full-color brochure, whereas Larry would get a postcard, and Eddy would get a phone call from the leading salesman of the dealer to come down for a test drive that afternoon, all based on the demographics of these viewers.

E*ON has plans to "de-risk" all of this for the advertiser by using a variation on per-inquiry so that they only have to pay for the transaction generated. That's very interesting for existing broadcasters to make that same airtime with existing viewers more valuable than it has ever been before. There are also avenues to direct revenue or new revenue streams, for example ideas like, "Pay a small amount to be counted in an opinion poll, pay more and have your opinion conveyed to a leader of your choice." Its entertainment applications allow you to guess who might be the murderer, based on the clues of "Murder She Wrote." ESPN wants to make sure that they are the center for all the sports applications on E*ON. Comedy Central will start a new program "Nuke the Comic" live on Wednesday night. You can click to applaud, or click to hiss (and the comedian gets the electronic hook). High profile shows like that will gain a lot of interactive on-air promotion.

Lafferty feels there is one key pitfall that must be avoided at all cost, "the temptation to use IVDS to reach into the viewers' homes without providing real value. This means entertainment, with a capital 'F' (fun), and information that is really timely and proprietary, personalized, and very valuable to the consumer. I'm always amazed at how quickly providers grasp this concept. It's like starting broadcasting all over again and saying, 'Gee, we can do advertising, but why bother doing programming?' We have to be careful there and provide real value from the start with ITV."

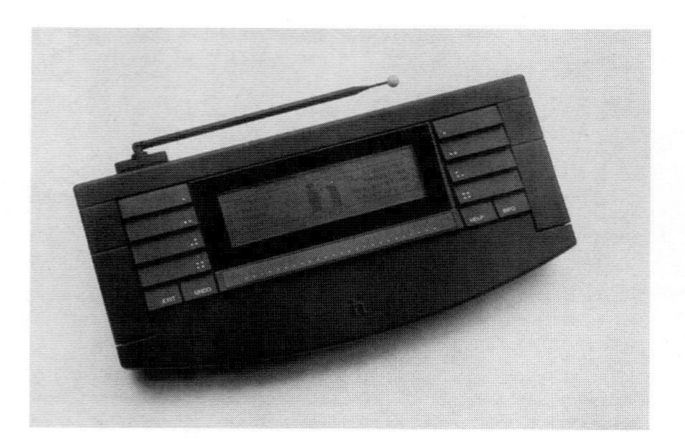

▲ The Interactive Network control unit receives data through FM broadcast. *Courtesy of Interactive Network.*

Interactive Network

Interactive Network (IN) is a subscription-based ITV provider for the San Francisco Bay area, Sacramento Valley, and Chicago. The service is based on FM broadcasts that are received by network control units, which in turn are sold through standard electronics retail channels such as Circuit City, Macy's, and Sears. The home network control unit has a suggested retail price of $199, and the monthly service charge is only $15. Many in the industry feel that this price is much too high for the consumer, and yet the units are selling.

▲ The Interactive Network production studio.

▲ An Interactive Network subscriber plays along with interactive football.

▲ By plugging into your phone jack for 20 seconds, you can have your score ranked with all other players. *Courtesy of Interactive Network*.

As with the NTN system, sporting games are monitored by "data jockeys" back at IN's production studio. The data jockeys input plays and commentary, and they lock-out signals in real time. This lock-out prevents predictions and answers from being changed. Once the ball is pitched or snapped, or once a contestant gives an answer, it is too late to play from home. The data is then broadcast over the air through FM broadcast and simulcast with the television signal arriving at the homes of IN subscribers. In areas of poor reception, the vertical blanking interrupt is used to transmit the data.

The control unit receives from IN the data that allows the subscribers at home to play along with sports, game shows, drama, news, and special events as they happen. Almost every televised professional sporting event is broadcast interactively. Also included are many prime-time shows, such as "Murder She Wrote," "Quantum Leap," "Law & Order," "L.A. Law," "Jeopardy!," "Wheel of Fortune," and many others. Some of the interactive news and talk shows include "20/20," "NBC Nightly News," and "60 Minutes."

Following each game or program, subscribers have the option of downloading their scores to IN headquarters for compilation and ranking. Subscribers simply plug their telephones into the back of the control units for 20 seconds. Within 4 to 5 minutes, results appear on the control unit. The results include the highest score of all those who played, the score of the individual subscriber, and a percentile ranking of everyone's score.

Founded by David Lockton in January 1988, IN continues to supply more than 100 interactive programs per day to its subscribers. On Dec. 7, 1993, IN signed an agreement with Sony Pictures to jointly produce interactive programming for the new *Game Show Channel* premiering in 1994. This agreement gives IN access to more than 41,000 episodes of the most popular game shows in television history.

Interactive Network Television

Interactive Network Television (INT) is an interactive games producer that was founded in 1988 by Lawrence Taymor. Taymor started the company as a joint venture with Interactive Network and brought together a number of people with broadcast TV game show experience.

The focus of INT is on electronic parlor games. Their concept is that the market potential is far greater for parlor games than it is for Nintendo-style interactive television games. Nintendo has very narrow demographics: 13- to 18-year-old males. Taymor explains, "We started using existing broadcast shows rather than trying to make something from scratch for the same simple reason why people rob banks, because that's where the money is. "Jeopardy!" and "Wheel of Fortune" will net about $300 million a year. The production cost is essentially nil and distribution costs are very low."

When INT creates a new ITV game, they keep three elements in mind: skill, luck and strategy. The way those three items interact with prizes and legal issues become very important, just as it was for NTN and QB1. INT started looking at platforms five years ago. They explored 900 phone lines by dialing in using your home telephone. They decided to pass on that route, because it wasn't fun enough and it was too expensive at $1 a minute. "And I just don't think it delivers enough value in the long run to consumers. In the short run, if you promote it enough you can drive the phone to ring. Certainly "Jeopardy!" and "Wheel" have done one-shot promotions with huge call counts. The Family channel is doing a very interesting 900 game now with "Trivial Pursuit." But there is a tremendous burn-out and fall-out factor in 900 games." says Taymor.

Currently, INT's system works with all video, cable interactive shows and broadcast interactive shows. The system rides on today's digital highway by sending the data out over FM simulcast, and bringing it back over the Tymnet network via modem. The biggest trick to using FM simulcast is making it synchronize well enough to transmit three or four interactive programs in sync. Currently, INT is operating in several markets—Chicago, the San Francisco Bay area, and Sacramento—and they expect to roll it out nationally sometime next year.

Zing Systems

There are two key components in the Zing system. The Zing Blaster sits on top of your television set and plugs into the video-out of your cable box. It reads the *vertical blanking interrupt* (VBI) of the video signal, a technology very similar to closed-captioning. VBI is an in-band technology, so when you turn on the television set, no matter which channel you are watching, you will receive an interactive signal with that channel. Most people watch TV and surf through a lot of channels. Zing wanted to make sure that people won't have to make an appointment to play a game or get an interactive application. This also enables you to tune in late to a show because you can pick up the messages as they happen.

The second device is a handheld wireless remote unit that has a small LCD screen on it. Right now it doesn't include any on-screen graphics. As with other companies that don't produce on-screen graphics systems, Zing feels it hampers multiplayer capabilities and clutters up the screen too much. Zing takes it a step further, however, and allows multiple players to communicate individually with each of the viewers.

NOTE

Based in Denver, Colorado, Zing Systems has a very single-focused mission. Their goal (like the goal of so many other ITV providers) is to enhance television. As Eddy Polon, director of creative services, explains, "We are not trying to turn the television set into a computer screen. So if you want financial services, the computer is probably a better place for it. We are not trying to turn the television into a game player. Right now, television is a very powerful medium, and people can come to it and get what they want out of it. We don't want to change that. We are just adding something new to it."[1]

Also available is the Zing Dialer, an infrared device that allows you to return a score, purchase items, or participate in a poll. You just use the handheld device, and in a 30-second blast, it sends down all the information about the player and what they've played. It goes back to the back office where we get a computer printout. If it's a live show, then a prize may be awarded on the air, or if it's a call-in show or talk show where they want to get the Zing viewers opinion instantaneously, or for an advertiser so they can add the customer on their mailing list. All three pieces are available for a list price of $100.

Zing works through cable, broadcast, or satellite transmissions. If you can get the picture in your home, you can get the Zing information, because it uses VBI technology. Eventually, the Zing blaster will migrate into the cable box, and the consumer will be purchasing the handheld unit only. The system is very easy to use. You turn the television set on, and the Zing will beep to you when it has information for you to interact with or participate in.

NOTE

Polon says, "Our research has told us that there is a certain key-point that all interactive television has to have. One is it needs to be fun. It obviously has to be entertaining. It has to be mindless and simple and look like television. That's something we believe the consumer will latch on to. It needs to be approachable, and if you look at our handheld device, it's something easy to pick up. It doesn't look like a piece of technology. Even though there is a computer inside of it, it looks much more like a toy or a game, and it's easier to get into. The final point is that it is affordable. The unit will be available for approximately $100. This puts it at a price point much lower than that of other interactive services, and at a price that's acceptable to our focus groups, and this will allow people to experiment with interactive television."[1]

One interesting aspect of the Zing strategy is that it encourages the producers of the programming to control what they want their interactive games to be like for their interactive shows. They feel that it's important because each program has its own feel, its own vocabulary, its own pacing, and Zing doesn't want to usurp that from the creative community. They have created an authoring toolkit, that runs on any IBM-compatible computer with simple point-and-click functions. It's disguised to look like a word processing program; the producers simply decide what they want the text of their messages to be and the style of the game. Then Zing's program will actually create all the mathematics and the encoding that sends the game over the satellites. This is something that Polon feels strongly about, "This is a very key ingredient that you don't want to take away from producers. There is really no incentive for producers to turn control of their program to an outside party."

Zing, like other ITV providers believes that there will not be just one "Killer App;" instead it will be a collection of applications. There may be a genre such as game shows, sports, education, or information that may interest you, but there needs to be a lot of widely available applications to let you really enjoy and see the value to it. Polon concludes, "For interactivity to keep growing and draw consumers into it, there will need to be a large variety out there. The people that are already creating shows right now that are reaching a mass audience are probably the best people to handle that."

NTN Communications

NTN is one of the oldest companies in the interactive television business. NTN was formed in 1982 long before the media hype regarding ITV. NTN also has the distinction of being one of the few companies that are actually in business and making money today doing interactive television. They produce 14 hours of interactive programming a day, most of it original programming. For interactive sports, they do about 500 college and NFL football games a year. NTN also produces interactive versions of hockey, baseball and basketball, and other games such as "Trivia."

The primary market for NTN is in the hospitality industry: restaurants, hotels, and bars. However, they are also now in homes and are actively participating in a number of ITV tests being conducted around the U.S. Original programs are transmitted from the NTN control center in Carlsbad, California, through an uplink to a satellite above the equator. The programs are then transmitted to the Hospitality Entertainment Network, cable homes, gateway services companies, schools, and corporations. The entire process takes less than one second. Transmissions can be sent point-to-point or point-to-multipoint. The return path is an 800 telephone number.

Currently, NTN is tracking about 5 million participants a month internationally. That 5 million is based on 1.75 million playmakers in use every month, with an average of three people sitting with a single play maker. NTN is now part of the LodgeNet system in more than 10,000 hotel rooms. NTN also supplies interactive training to the corporate world with clients such as General Motors, Hughes Pet Foods and Goodyear. They also have educational programming for college preparation.

NTN is in the home, providing services to at least six different platforms. NTN provides interactive programming to GTE's Main Street in Newton, Massachusetts; Daniel's Cable in Carlsbad, California; and Apollo Cable in Cerritos, California; and a number of other home cable systems. Online services carry NTN, such as GE's GEnie and Sierra On-line's ImagiNation network. For online services, you must connect with your personal computer through a modem, and then watch the video program on a television.

When NTN goes into hospitality businesses or classrooms, they provide their own hardware. On the home side, they simply feed their interactive programming to other companies. NTN offers the same games for all platforms. They have become a production house, syndicator, and distributor, which opens the door to work with ESPN and other networks for one-shop ITV shopping.

Although gaming aspects will definitely be a part of the interactive landscape in the future, NTN is also known for its educational ITV. They provide hardware and software technology to KET, which is delivering distance learning programs in 19 states to more than 600 classrooms. They also broadcast educational programs to about a dozen schools in four different countries and on a paid test to many different school districts in California. According to Downs, "We think this is going to lead to some tremendous advances in education and we are very optimistic in being a major player in that. We are also bidding for a major contract in Mexico with the Mexican government to provide our system to over 3,000 schools."

NTN is spending a great deal of money to bring on programming that was created and designed to be interactive. Up until now, most ITV providers had to contend with taking programming that is already on television and trying to make it interactive. That puts tremendous limitations and restrictions on interactive program designs. Some products were great fits like QB1, horse racing, game shows and trivia games. In many cases, however, like "Jeopardy!" or "Wheel Of Fortune," which are syndicated shows played at different times across the country, the shows are very difficult to do interactively with national competitions. "Everyone thinks of "Jeopardy!" as being a great program for interactive television. But those people are screaming out those answers so fast that, unless we turned to a multiple choice format, it's difficult to really make that program come alive from an interactive standpoint," explains Downs.

"What we like to do is enhance a program, not compete with it...not try to put something on the air interactively to compete with the show. As a program provider, this is one of our main challenges, to enhance the program without competing with it for the viewer's attention. As the hardware side of ITV gets more complicated and varied we expect some companies to dump their hardware and get into our business—that of providing ITV programming."

Info Telecom

Four years ago, Info Telecom started developing an ITV product in the French city of Strasbourg. What they came up with is a $20 controller that is now available in a number of different European countries. Info Telecom specializes in the development and manufacturing of portable consumer electronics. So when they started designing out ITV products and concepts, they looked at the problem from the users side, not from the technical side. What they found out at that time was that the TV entertainment field in Europe was not ready for highly sophisticated applications.

So they started designing a product that was very simple to use, inexpensive, and has a real play value to allow users to play with TV shows and win prizes. The product needed to allow people to play and validate their winnings from home without having to move outside. For those reasons, Info Telecom came out with a simple, totally autonomous and portable product named LUDICS that doesn't require a sophisticated TV network or equipment.

It is easy to use, and it has a very user-friendly keyboard. The EPAT, a world-wide patented technology, stores the game answers within the LUDICS as the player enters them. Thus, no running score is available, but it avoids expensive radio or optical transmission systems. The EPAT technology allows the identification of the player and the validation of his score by acoustical transmission through any common telephone.

When you buy the LUDICS at any electronics store, you write your name and address (as well as the serial number located on the back of your LUDICS and also engraved in its chip) on the registration card and mail it in. From then on, you just turn on the LUDICS and answer questions. If you reach a required number of points, you win. To receive your prizes and find out your score, you call the server, and the LUDICS transmits your serial number and answers. The server automatically processes your transaction and tells you what prize you have won.

It looks simple but if you look at it a little bit closer you find out that it is a little more sophisticated than expected. There are some security devices inside the product to avoid cheating problems because people could phone in and win a Mercedes car. The product will play up to 16 games every day. That comes from the fact that the functioning and the way the LUDICS reacts are determined by a few parameters that are injected into the product during the manufacturing process. So using exactly the same electronics base, Info Telecom can use the product for the requirements of the TV game managers in any country.

The LUDICS generates a number of different incomes for the game managers. First, there is the selling of the product itself, in department stores, and any other type of distribution channel. Then the revenues generated by the telephone calls of the players on the premium rate networks. Then comes what is related to indirect promotion because this product is seen on TV every day by a few million viewers. Then comes the merchandising of all the sub-license products that use the image and cosmetics of LUDICS. Finally, you have the player database that contains 600,000 TV viewers.

Now LUDICS has been launched in three different countries: Spain, France, and Italy, under three different brand names. On the marketing side, 1.3 million units have been brought to market to date. It's pretty interesting to notice that in Italy part of the success of LUDICS comes from the fact that winners get to go on TV to get their prizes right during "Wheel of Fortune."

Currently, Info Telecom is working on two new technological developments. One is to allow data strings to be transmitted to the portable hand units via the existing sound track of the television broadcast. This data will be inaudible to the viewer and reach transmissions rates of up to 128 bps and higher. The second is an acoustic coupler for the telephone in the home for transmitting data back and forth. This will work with existing LUDICS units and give them bi-directional communication.

ICTV

ICTV (Interactive Cable Television) has been in business three years and currently has about 40 employees and subcontractors. "We create complete interactive TV systems for cable operators. Our applications are video-on-demand, electronic yellow pages, games, and other interactive multimedia applications and ANTOY (anything not thought of yet)," according to Gary Lauder, chairman of ICTV.

ICTV creates these systems by combining what they can buy or license along with their own hardware and software. ICTV currently has some big name partners such as IBM, and at the National Cable Television Association Expo, ICTV demonstrated a full service network platform that combined video servers from IBM, a billing system from another partner, New Century Communications, and ICTV's own interactive services exchange (ISX).

ICTV is not trying to establish itself as a multimedia ITV standard the way 3DO, Kalida, Silicon Graphics, Microsoft, and others are. "We use standards like this in our unique architecture. In fact, one of the nice things about standards is that there are so many to choose from," explains Lauder.

"We think that the hybrid fiber coax will win the broadband plant bake-off. And Bell Atlantic appears to think so as well. Of the various ITV architectures for hybrid fiber coax, we think that our architecture will prevail due to its high production values, low cost, and ease of authoring for it. Our goal is to pave the information highway without becoming road-kill on it." says Lauder.

Mark Goodson Productions

Mark Goodson Productions is the producer of more than 20 half-hour television shows a week, including such popular shows as "The Price is Right," and "Family Feud." Currently, they are actively pursuing interactive television programming and are about to release new interactive versions of their shows.

NOTE

Jonathan Goodson, President and CEO, who supervises the production of "The Price is Right," "Family Feud," and "Classic Concentration," sees the importance of ITV but feels that it should not be over-hyped. "The extraordinary hype over interactive television has created sort of a modern day alchemy. Add the word *interactive* to your product and it turns to gold. I don't believe that adding interactivity necessarily improves every product."

All of the ITV system providers such as Zing, GTE Main Street, Interactive Systems, Interactive Network, E*ON, NTN, and others are tied to ongoing mass entertainment—entertainment that would be there even if the set-top device did not exist. These are technologies that let you play along with the TV game show as it is being telecast.

"The fact is that most TV game shows are already interactive—in the sense that their play-along elements invite the viewer to mentally compete with the on-screen contestants. Since viewers can already play interactively with their favorite game shows, the role of the set-top interactive device is principally to objectify the mental play-along so that different at-home players can have a reliable record of their scores when they compete among themselves. If the technology is to be appealing, it must enhance the ability to compete over and above whatever players can improvise at home. Above all, the process of interactive play must be transparent, and unobtrusive to the viewing and enjoyment of the TV show." says Goodman.[1]

How transparent and unobtrusive are set-top interactive devices? Imagine trying to play "The Price is Right" interactively. Things happen so quickly that when players try to play it interactively, most of them mentally lose track of what is happening to the show's real contestants. Something about the interactivity itself is a distraction to the show's content. Because viewers traditionally play along mentally and still follow the program, the problem must arise when the viewer is asked to enter data manually during actual play. This is one of the most surprising aspects of set-top interactivity.

It appears as if you have to make a choice, either play interactively on TV or ultimately watch what's happening on the screen. But once the viewer becomes an interactive player, they seem to stop paying attention to the rest of the program. Unlike a one-on-one Nintendo game, a TV game show is created to entertain the passive viewer by making the person care about the outcome of someone else's game. "What happens if an interactive device makes the viewer lose track of the contestant, lose track of the prizes, and lose track of the outcome? Why should they continue to watch the rest of the show once their own interactive role is over? The answer to those questions has significant implications for the content of mass market interactive programming. It also suggest that making commercials interactive would have to be approached with great caution," warns Goodman.

Another problem is the speed or pacing of existing TV game shows. "The Price is Right" for instance has many aspects that simply happen too fast for hand-eye coordination. The only thing fast enough is verbal responses, like those the contestants use. According to Goodman, "I call this the 'Off the Rack Fallacy'; for example, when you buy a suit at a department store, if you know your size, you can pull any ready-made suit off your section of the rack and reasonably expect it to fit with only minor alterations. Marketers of TV set-top devices make the analogous assumption that any TV game show can be pulled off the rack after broadcast and used with the interactive set-top devices. Yet as you know, some games do not lend themselves to interactivity."

One of the chief reasons for this incompatibility is timing and pace. TV game shows go at a rapid clip. Anything slower, and the viewer would be bored and tune out. Interactive set-top devices are, however, inherently slower because they require you to enter data manually instead of verbally. The set-top devices are thus, by definition, married to the TV shows' fast rate of play. "The result is a mismatch, forcing the interactive player to play an entirely different game or no game at all. Now, there is one aspect of the 'Off the Rack Fallacy'; there's a subtler, more important nuance called the 'Same Game Fallacy'."

NOTE

"Consider the game of 'Family Feud,' in the part where family members try to come up with a popular answer to the question, and then that answer is compared to the survey. How would you make that game interactive and still keep it as the same game?" asks Goodman. "I'll tell you that the interactive versions of 'Family Feud' that I've seen have challenged the player to do one of the following things. In some versions, the home player listens to the family's answer and then guesses whether or not the answer really is on the survey. In other versions, the home player listens to the family's answer and guesses how popular that answer is; that is, how high up on the survey it appears. What's important is that in none of the cases is the home player playing the same game as the TV player."

The home player is always engaged in a game that is materially different from the TV show. "This is true not just in 'Family Feud,' but also 'The Price is Right,' 'Wheel of Fortune,' 'Jeopardy!' and every other game show I've examined. This is what I call, the Same Game Fallacy, that set-top interactivity allows the home player to play the same game as the TV player he is watching. Still, these devices are marketed as enabling the viewer to play along with his favorite TV game show," complains Goodman.

Unlike the problem of matching the fast pace of TV game shows, this problem (the Same Game Fallacy) doesn't seem to have been caused by the failure of technology. Moreover, it doesn't seem to be remediable by a leap in technology. Goodman continues: "For example, imagine that there is a voice-recognition package placed inside every set-top device. Now, does that mean the player can play the real game of 'Family Feud' simply by saying aloud that answer he thinks is on the survey? Well, no, it's not that easy. Remember, the family in the studio is going to be guessing different answers than the at-home player, but the home player can hear what the studio family guesses. What happens if the studio player knocks off a good answer before the home player guesses it? And if the home player and the studio player give different answers, which answer do we keep track of on-screen? Which score do we show on-screen?"

"If your solution is, 'OK, keep the home player from hearing the studio player's answers; show the home player's answers on-screen and feature his score,' then congratulations! You have just reinvented solo-play on the PC. Let's put that another way. The only way that I can figure out to let the home player play the exact same game as the TV player is to completely insulate him from the TV program itself. Just create a purely electronic one-on-one game. Now, if *that* is the goal of the set-top device, it's the same as play on the PC, but the PC uses more versatile technology, superior play features, and allows play-on-demand," argues Goodman.

"Now suppose we try a different solution and simply admit the home viewer can never play the same game as the TV player. Now, when I say the home game is different, I must admit that I'm generally saying the home game is usually a pale version of the studio game. Let me ask you, Which you think would be more fun? Guessing the answer to a 'Jeopardy!' question, or guessing whether somebody else's answer is correct or not?"

"Those are what I consider the shortcomings of interactive set-top devices," Goodman concludes. "Where does that leave us? I would say it's up to the next generation of TV game shows to address and solve these problems, if indeed they can be solved. If the public has not been or does not get discouraged by the limitations of current set-top devices, we will have the opportunity to build game shows from the ground up to accommodate these problems and these potentials. Our challenge for the future, as programmers, is to find a way to reconcile the inconsistent requirements of half viewers and half interactive players, and somehow integrate them into a single entertainment vehicle."[1]

THE FUTURE OF INTERACTIVE TELEVISION

What is the future of interactive television? The biggest concern of ITV providers now is getting a large bandwidth of communication into homes at a reasonable price. Pursuing this problem is the Applied Research Division of Bellcore Labs. There, Eric Addeo, director of research, is charting the future of interactive entertainment as it relates to ITV. Addeo joined Bellcore Labs 10 years ago and is also vice-president of the IEEE Data Communications Systems Committee.

Addeo believes that, in the future, computing and color displays will be integrated into every aspect of life. The kitchen of the future will include "smart" networked appliances, integrated multimedia computing, and screen-based telephones. An era of emerging applications will open up, applications like home shopping, how-to videos, home security, and remote monitoring of appliances. The family room of the future will have a large-screen, digital TV, with interactive communications and integrated multimedia computing, which will make possible a whole collection of applications, including video-on-demand and music-on-demand.

You will be able to use game-specific hardware and software as you can today, but these will be coupled synergistically with the audio and video communications that enable people to really talk to and see each other while sharing a game on a network. In a productive environment, in the home office of the future, you will see multimedia workstations, large-screen displays, faxes, and screen-based telephones to support applications such as computer-supported collaborative work at a distance, an electronic white board, and multimedia information retrieval.

The composite of all these services will be available to the home through a collection of access capabilities. "I don't believe there will be just one access, but multiple accesses to information, or access to receiving information through satellites, the telephone, and even cable TV. The applied research area of Bellcore is contributing to this vision of networked interactive video applications through prototyping efforts," explains Addeo.

True Video-on-Demand and Electronic Panning Cameras

At Bellcore, they see two families of applications for ITV, and they have prototypes of both. The first is video-on-demand, which includes three major components: the broadband backbone network (fiber optic); the wideband access network that includes ADSL (analog digital subscribed line), ADMSL (analog digital microwave subscribed line), HDSL (high-bit-rate digital subscribed line) for two-way access; and the network file servers that serve as information warehouses. The information warehouses will benefit directly from subscribing to the broadband network.

Information travels down the high-speed broadband backbone to the wideband access network that feeds directly to the homes. In order to support the broadband backbone network and the slower local access of—for example—ADSL, there must be some mediations or "bit-rate mapping." That's done at the sites of the cable companies on devices called *service circuits*. The applications can take advantage of the broadband backbone network, which offers flexible, on-demand switch transport for accessing remote databases and communicating with other users.

Dr. Alex Galemon of Bellcore, the principle architect of the video-on-demand prototype, explains: "We are working on a joint project between Bellcore and Philips. We have created a prototype Networked CD-I player (compact disc interactive) designed to retrieve graphics and audio from a compact disc. Normal CD-I units equipped with FMV (full-motion video) capabilities can retrieve movies from a compact disc. Networked CD-I, which can connect to Bellcore's video-on-demand prototype, can retrieve movies, games, and educational multimedia from a server."

One 8-mm videotape can contain five full-length movies if they are digitally compressed. At the information warehouse, there are "stacker" units that can hold up to 10 tapes, or 50 full-length movies. There are boxes available that can hold 600 movies, and an electronic video-rental store can purchase multiple boxes for its system.

When a movie is requested by a viewer at home, the movie is downloaded under computer control from a tape drive into the online disk array. A typical disk array can hold up to 12 full-length movies, and up to 64 independent users can retrieve the movies with full VCR-like controls: stop, pause, fast forward, reverse, and so on. Bellcore designed a network interface card that can retrieve the information from the online hard drive, connect the information to data "packets," and send the information on its way through fiber-optic cabling on the network to the cable company.

Packets of video arrive at the cable operator through a fiber-optic line. They are received by a network interface card and then distributed among intelligent line cards. The intelligent line card buffers these packets of video and then sends them over ordinary telephone wires to the user's home.

At the home, the user simply requests the menu from a network and makes a selection by pressing an icon. Various features are available with Network CD-I; for example, slow motion, regular play, forward advancing, and moving to a new position. You can change the selection at any time. In addition to full-motion video, various editing features are available to the system. A window of FMV can be moved around or changed in size. A multilingual audio track enables you to change between the English, Japanese, or Dutch languages.

This joint development of Bellcore and Philips demonstrates the capabilities of Networked CD-I. At the press of a button, a world of information can be available right in your living room. The trick for the service provider is to convert the high-speed data coming from the information warehouse down to the slower-speed data going from the cable company to the viewer's home. The information warehouse transmits at about 150 megabits per second (mbs), whereas the cable company transmits to the homes at about 1.5 mbs. This means that the service circuits at the cable company must buffer the data as it comes through, usually about five seconds worth of video in two separate buffers. When the buffers run out, a request is sent upstream to the information warehouse for more data. At that point, the information warehouse bursts data down to the service circuit at 150 mbs again; so there is a 10:1 ratio between the home/cable company and the information warehouse.

The second application that Bellcore has prototyped is the electronic-panning camera. Imagine watching a football event where electronic-panning cameras are used instead of mechanical cameras. The electronic camera takes in a huge field of view, much larger than can be displayed on a television set. Within this field of view, however, you can pan your own personal view electronically, through the associated service circuits. Hundreds, thousands, or even millions of end-users could access these circuits and customize their view of the football event.

The electronic-panning camera enables you, the viewer, to change your perspective at will. The system also has features such as touch-sensitive screens, remote controls, and a capability that lets you track people across the field of view. Networking the electronic-panning camera would create further capabilities for users. For example, participants in video conferencing could focus on a single person in the room or a student in one state could follow a teacher's every movement in another state.

Changing the Industry

Howard Postley of Ideal Point, a software and technology development company, believes that ITV has little to do with television. "What it has to do with is communication," says Postley. "There's a lot of talk about Al Gore's information superhighway. Interactive television and the information superhighway are one and the same. ITV will be a technology where people communicate so fundamentally that entire industries will become unrecognizable."

The network that has the capability to select a movie from a video server and deliver it into a home also has the capability to request that a section of text be checked for spelling or the standard deviation of a series of numbers be calculated. The only similarity between all these services is that none of them needs to exist in the user's equipment. Each can be handled by a machine on the network that provides the service.

NOTE

Postley gives the example of the London Stock Exchange: "Shortly after the London Stock Exchange's computer network was updated a few years ago, all of the traders from the trading floor disappeared. The exchange has been vacant ever since. Rather than this being a story of a haunted stock exchange, it's a story of technology changing an industry. The new trading network eliminated the need for the traders to be present, by allowing them to conduct their business electronically."

Right now, we live in a country where it takes at least thousands of dollars worth of equipment to make a word processor, an electronic spreadsheet, and a simple picture-drawing tool usable by more than just 25 percent of the population. The machines and software are too expensive or too hard to use, or both, for the remaining 75 percent of the population. The tremendous potential of the equipment is mostly wasted.

You can contrast the 25 percent of the U.S. population that uses computers with the more than 98 percent that uses television and telephones. "The problem," complains Postley, "is that the personal computer of today is too expensive and a jack-of-all-trades, master of none. These general purpose machines try to be all things to all people, and manage to frustrate almost everyone with the effort.

"The technology and infrastructure that is necessary to allow interactive television to exist is substantial. However, once it is in place, we will begin to see a major shift in the way we view computers. The general-purpose personal computers that we use day after day will cease to exist. They will be completely unnecessary. The 'television devices' that attach to the network will be designed solely to assist their users in finding services. These services may be movies, sitcoms, news, clothing, or restaurant reservations, but they also may be spell checkers and statistical functions."[1]

"Once the 'little empire' model of computing is broken," continues Postley, "the new structure will pave the way for a new type of business to provide services for the 'television' user. A user needs to purchase only the simple equipment that is necessary to access the network. The actual task to be performed will be handled elsewhere. The need for users to buy new and improved hardware and software and the incumbent configuration headaches will disappear, because the functionality will be available somewhere on the network, accessed on demand and billed at a fraction of a cent for use."[1]

Computer and hardware vendors will thrive because the demand for equipment by service providers will grow, but the public won't even know the names of those vendors. Software vendors will see huge increases in revenues resulting from greatly simplified distribution and the elimination of software piracy, coupled with huge growth in the user base. As the technology for delivering interactive television improves, wireless devices that communicate with the network will become possible. In the future, the portable device not only will act as a telephone and pager, but also will provide books and music on demand, with numerous selections available. Radio stations, print publishers, and the music industry are as much involved in this interactive revolution as anyone else. Although this is starting to sound like the computer industry's dream for the future (and it is), it is also the dream that opens the doors for the television industry, the music industry, print, advertising, and real estate. The list of industries with an economic interest in ITV is very long.

If all of this seems a little far-fetched, keep in mind that direct TV will be capable of broadcasting 150 TV channels to every home in the country in 1994. Motorola will soon ring the planet with low-orbit satellites that will allow a signal to be sent to and from anywhere in the world. Time-Warner is today using as a TV tuner a piece of equipment that would have cost more than $10,000 two years ago.

Navigating the Information Highway of the Future

Postley feels that the problem of the future with ITV has much more to do with finding the services on the network than how the technology will put the services out there. "Technology problems tend to solve themselves," he says. "I agree that the costs have to be inexpensive, but I don't necessarily believe that they have to be near-free, because what we are going to see is not so much a service scavenging from other areas, such as video stores and other places where consumers spend money. We are going to see a whole new set of industries providing services that don't exist. Those industries are going to bring with them a lot of users. The fact is that most of the people in this country are not cable users. They are not pay-per-view users. They are not information network users, and that's going to change. It's going to change by necessity."

"The problem is that—as we get hundreds, then thousands, then tens of thousands of servers on the network—it's going to be very difficult to find them," continues Postley. "Menus won't work. Room organizations with pictures of virtual malls won't work; it will be too big. The technology problem is really, 'How do you solve the navigation problem for people who are arguably not computer users?' given that, in the environment that we live in, most VCRs flash 12:00. I spend most of my day dealing with that problem, and I don't have an absolute answer to it and have not seen one. I'm looking forward to having people like Bellcore and ICTV put out networks that can carry the information that we will need, but I look at that as just the paving on the road to the future, because the service itself is not going to look like anything we've ever seen before."

In the long term, the challenge will be making the navigation friendly and easy to use. How do consumers get what they want, when they want it, in a friendly, accessible way? Without a doubt, there will be multiple boxes from many services around the world, but there should be a standardized method of navigation. It might be a set-top box from anybody, but most of the services will be much the same.

In this regard, Microsoft Corporation is making an operating system called Modular Windows for set-top boxes. The Modular Windows user interface is optimized for use on television screens, which means low resolution, but high colors. Viewers sit much farther away from TVs (usually five to 10 feet). A set-top controller usually offers fewer controls (two to eight) than does a computer keyboard and mouse. The memory requirements of Windows have been greatly reduced for Modular Windows. It fits on a 1 megabyte ROM chip and uses only 1 megabyte of RAM. Even with the modification, Modular Windows still uses 75 percent of all the APIs (application programming interfaces) that Windows for personal computers uses. This means that it will be easy for PC developers to port their software to the set-top box. Although Modular Windows does have some navigational capabilities, it will probably be a new application running under Modular Windows that gives full access to the ITV network.

Steven Muirhead agrees: "There is a great opportunity to provide an interface for the upcoming ITV environment. An intelligent interface is needed to process the huge volume of entertainment available. There is more than enough entertainment already. For example, I have 60 channels and have a great deal of trouble picking which program to watch. You have to channel surf or wade through *TV Guide* with the mass-market problems of figuring out what national program is on what local station. An intelligent interface is needed to enable the consumer to choose or perhaps even sample or see what is available. The next step will be to enable the interface to form a profile of its users and monitor the programs they like. It would automatically record those for them and offer a choice of episodes it recorded."

Person-to-Person Interactivity

To what extent will people be interacting with other people and not with the network? History has shown that people like to interact with other people, not computers. This has been true with 1-900 numbers, HAM radios, Minitel, Prodigy, and ImagiNation. ITV has enormous potential for helping people interact with other people, whether through video dating services, teleconferencing, or other ANTOY.

Some form of multiperson communication will probably be the biggest profit center in the whole system, whether through a point-to-point system or something like a multiuser game. Inevitably, multiple users are going to be the prevalent environment. An ITV system can certainly be built to circumvent person-to-person interactivity, but hopefully that won't happen. Fiber optic, ADSL, and hybrid fiber coaxial all allow it, but much depends on how the switches are installed and how they pass data back, as well as what bandwidth backchannel (upstream channel) is put in the system. Most ITV providers recognize that it will be worthwhile; but the trick is to put enough bandwidth in now, despite the costs of doing so, even though the costs seem to be justified. Even today, people are willing to pay more for person-to-person interactivity, as they do with video dial tone.

True Interactive Programming

When it comes to creating true interactive content, no one is more experienced than the video game industry. Says Steven Muirhead, president of the video game developer MicroProse Software, "Interactivity is a major challenge. I think that most entertainment is storytelling. People want to *watch* "Murder She Wrote," just like storytelling. It has a tradition of thousands of years, people sitting around a fire while someone tells a story, but adding interactivity is difficult. Most people don't want to participate; they want to be passively entertained. The potential to have interactive theater has been around over 2,000 years, and yet no one does it. Why not? The majority of people don't want to do it. It's very hard to do so that the audience participation is not overbearing. I personally do not believe that we are going to have in the next 10 years a successful mass-market interactive product, because a significant number of people don't actually want to interact with the programming. What they want is more good TV, and the intelligent interface will simply provide more of what they want: fishing shows, soaps, game shows, and movies.

"There is a minority market that wants 100 percent interactive," Muirhead continues, "and a significant market that wants 100 percent passive. What is interesting is the middle ground, to somehow allow the user to select the degree of interactivity. It needs to be indistinguishable. You have the option of jumping into it and becoming a character, jump in and out, or totally interactive. Basically what you're looking at is the other characters being endowed with AI, with a relatively scripted path to follow. People will start off at a low level of participation and slowly build up, rather than total control like video games."

Security and Privacy Issues

Security and privacy relate to each other but do not necessarily overlap. Security concerns issues of whether your neighbors can see your interactive TV set, or can your 6-year-old gamble on a horse race at Del Mar, or whether someone can tap into your financial transactions. Privacy concerns the questions both of the ITV provider knowing everything about you and of what the ITV provider can do with that information.

For security issues, a number of commercial products are available: for example, public key cryptography systems. With these, not only can you encrypt downstream information coming from the ITV provider, but also you can authenticate the end-user before the service is delivered.

Bellcore is looking at collections of Publi-Key Crypto systems for interactive video services and other applications. Protecting the security and privacy of end-users in shopping situations and in access to movies is fundamental. The trick is being able to do it at a very low cost.

At NTN, security is a big concern, especially with wagering aspects. It will be a bigger concern when more financial capabilities come online and access by minors becomes an issue. One option is to put card readers on the set-top box and require a PIN number. End-users must have a card and a secure PIN number to access the system. This raises the security to the level that ATM machines have today. The good thing is that, in this new environment, the ITV provider will know for each transaction the address, who owns the house, and who accessed the box.

For wagering programs, NTN has been dealing with encryption methods such as DES, the Data Encryption Standard, created by the National Institute of Standards and Technology for public and government encryption of nonclassified data. It uses a binary number as the key and scrambles the data into one of 72 quadrillion possible combinations. The number, which can be random, is used on both ends of the transmission to encrypt and decrypt the data. Federal banking laws require DES encryption in ATMs.

NOTE

Lawrence Taymor, of Interactive Network Television, brings up another security issue: "What happens when you take a TV game show and combine it with a computer game? Because the technology to do that is coming, game channels are starting to look at that; their challenge is how to get enough good interactive games on the air. They will all wind up using reruns up the wazoo for the first few years, then that will decline. Obviously, you have a security issue. You can't take the same show and rerun it any time, the way you can take the same episode of "The Simpsons" and load it onto a video server, and just make it available any time anyone pushes the button during the week. You can't do that with a game show, because people will know the answers to the questions."

"Another related problem," Taymor continues, "is that people are going to expect to have the game they want on demand. They will want to watch their game show when they want and their movie when they want, and they are going to want to play games that they like. Some people are going to want to play trivia, and they might want to play all day. Other people are going to want to play war games all day, and the successful network is going to have to deal with that problem."[1]

INT has a concept called the Virtual Game Channel. What it does is take the concept of computer-generated games and combine that with the "look and feel" of a live studio game. This is becoming possible now with the new hardware that's available. 3DO and photorealistic games are in their infancy, but when you look at a TV game show, it's not too hard to imagine a virtual game show with virtual characters. It's not a very complicated digital environment to re-create. As a result, you can come up with an unlimited number of original games, and each of those games could be optimized for an interactive audience.

Here is where the issue of privacy arises. As you can imagine, the ITV provider will, over time, know practically everything about you, one of their customers. They will know what size your clothes are, based on your online shopping. They will know how often you wear your shirts out, and what color and style of shirts you like. They will know where you like to go for vacation, based on your airline reservations. In general, they will know what products you like, and which commercials you watch and which ones you ignore. They will know when you are home, and what your interests and hobbies are. By monitoring your shopping, entertainment, education, research, financial transactions, and other ITV services over a period of a year or so, the ITV provider will know more about you than your own mother, and there's not much you could do about it. The question is, What will the ITV provider do with that information? How will consumers be protected from marketing abuse?

Concerning what the cable operator does with the information, the Video Services Privacy Act—enacted in 1988 after Judge Bork's video rentals were made public—does preclude the sale of specific information, for example about video rentals. The Cable Act, passed in 1992, also has privacy provisions in it, and a number of pre-existing privacy constraints generally preclude people from selling, without your approval, much information that is specific to you.

What can be done, however, is the sale of aggregate information, for example, characteristics of everybody in a certain neighborhood. There are no restrictions on that kind of information. The broadband plant operators could take the information that they gather, and if they see that you happen to like to watch many electronics-related shows, they could send you an electronics catalog. They could use specific information on you within the same organization, but they are not allowed to sell that information outside their organization.

From a marketing point of view, you could get more junk mail. Many moves are afoot, however, to have people self-disqualify from that. The Direct Marketing Association (DMA) allows you to remove yourself from any junk mail list, and you can probably expect more of the same in the future. This is a public issue that needs to be dealt with, and consumers need to make it obvious to service providers that the consumers will be very unhappy about having their information used by anyone, including a service provider.

Single Purpose Televisions

One view of the future of ITV that few people have is that televisions will cease to be general purpose machines. Mark Dillon, of GTE ImagiTrek, explains: "Going back to radio, you can use it as an analogy to show how it evolved differently than the original pictures showing a happy family sitting around a piece of mahogany. We feel that, based on our experience, we can use this to make some projections about how ITV will evolve."

"First of all, I have intentionally or unintentionally positioned radios all throughout my day. I've got one in the bedroom that wakes me up; it has a function. I have one in my car; it has a function. I've got one in my office; it has a function. I've got a walkman and a boom box I take outside. I use them on airplanes, and they all have different functions. My car radio is for news; my walkman is for rock 'n roll; my office radio is for wallpaper music, and my tuner is for concerts and things like that. I don't listen to news in the office. I don't listen to rock 'n roll in the office. I tend to specialize my listening according to where I am in the day, what I am doing, and I pick my device to do it."

"I think that is what's going to happen with interactive television. We are going to find that we are not going to be locked into one venue. We are going to be spread out over a couple. That has economic basis, too. For this to be successful, the product has to reach high-quantity pricing levels. That means they have to be ubiquitous and cheap. When you have one big thing that does everything, it's not cheap. You've got to have lots of little things to do one thing very well to make them cheap."

To support this idea, consider that there are already three different venues in the home for viewing. Looking at the three most popular ITV applications and attaching them to those three venues will show us that what has already happened in radio is happening in television.

The first is the entertainment center venue. That's where groups of people, two or more, tend to watch movies or sports together. Next is the home office; that is more individual, has higher transactional capabilities, and has more upstream communications. Then there is the game set, where game viewing goes on. As with radios you experience during the day, you have different monitors you use at different times of the day for different experiences, interactive or not. Each one of these venues has a different demographic breakdown, different age group, and different functions. ITV providers trying to put all this interactivity into one set may find that, over time, it will be broken up into these different venues.

What Will Make or Break Interactive Television?

Even though the ITV market is projected to reach approximately $3 billion to $8 billion by the year 2002, the biggest danger today seems to be overhyping the technology. We need to separate fact from fiction and be careful not to promise or expect too much too soon. The expectations of people are getting too high, prompted by unrealistic numbers and time frames. This overhype of the technology is bound to lead to a cooling-off period. I hope that won't affect the market place or the investors, although it probably will. When things start to cool off, we will probably see some failures. In the short term, that seems to be the main danger to ITV. Despite what many people say, it will probably be seven to 10 years before there's a good, solid penetration of 20 million to 30 million homes.

The other big challenge is that the cost must come down greatly. It must be under $200, and under $100 would be the best shot. Consider the razor and blade illustration: you've got to get the razors into people's homes so they can start using the blades.

How will you react when your first interactive television service bill arrives and it rivals the size of your car payment? Initially, consumers will look at ITV service as entertainment. In reality, however, the cost of ITV should come out of many different household budgets, including shopping, utilities, and transportation. There are also intangible benefits to ITV, such as convenience, time savings, and ease of use. These things will save money in the long term, but when those first bills come in, there will be sticker shock.

As is the case with every other interactive entertainment platform, it is not technology that makes the products, but the software or applications. For ITV, the applications are there in our everyday lives, but it's up to the program providers to harness them and make them simple to use. Again, it won't be the killer app that makes or breaks ITV; it will be a full lineup of applications that will make consumers want to purchase the system. The killer app is a collection of applications.

Marty Lafferty, vice-president of E*ON, agrees: "Over time, we will see the information expand beyond the initial applications. The real growth will come through combining applications. Say you're watching 'Good Morning America,' and Joan Lunden is interviewing Denzel Washington about the movie *The Pelican Brief*. You like the interview, you click and see where *The Pelican Brief* is playing near you, and you can then order and pre-pay for reserved tickets. Click for directions; click for a restaurant recommendation where movie patrons for that theater get a discount. This is where the real explosion will come from when we get creative consumer-driven combinations of all these applications put together into a routine for consumers."

"Ultimately," Lafferty continues, "the overlays will become their own advertising medium with their own rate cards. Interactive billboards will appear on play-along sports. All of TV will become sort of an infomercial opportunity. This product placement concept will literally blow up, where you can click on items all over the screen and buy them or zap to a channel with product information."

CHAPTER SUMMARY

In conclusion, interactive television is here. It may not be in your neighborhood yet, but it is available in many places around the world. The rumors of the death of the home video game system and the VCR are greatly exaggerated. Interactive television does offer, however, some very exciting and practical applications of interactive entertainment.

Next I will present a look at the role of education in interactive entertainment. Can children and adults be "tricked" into learning by having fun? What can you expect from educational software today? Is educational software available only on personal computer platforms? What considerations go into creating an educational software product? Can any form of education be made entertaining? What is the right mix of entertainment and education? Can they be mixed at all? These are a few of the questions and issues that will be covered in the next chapter, "Education and Interactive Entertainment."

1. Quotes taken from speakers at the Intertainment '93 Conference held in Santa Monica, California, on November 3-5, 1993.

8

Education and Interactive Entertainment

"We should see a new level of educational software that perhaps even rivals experiences of everyday life."

Educational software is one of the fastest-growing software markets in the interactive entertainment industry. According to the Software Publishers Association, educational software is a $125 million market and is growing some 35 percent to 40 percent each year. Today you can walk into a software store and find educational products for ages 2 to 102. For preschoolers to adults, an ever-increasing variety of educational software is becoming available.

What is helping educational software achieve such outstanding success? In part, the increasing number of educational titles is drawing people's attention to the category. Another aspect is the broadening of that category to include adult education. A third factor is that the quality of new educational software has increased greatly since the advent of multimedia. Along with multimedia, educational software has become one of the main reasons people can justify to themselves the purchase of $500 multimedia upgrade kits.

There are plenty of buzzwords to describe educational software. One such word is "edutainment software," which Electronic Arts defines as "entertainment software with an educational twist." They define "infotainment software" as "entertainment software with an informational twist." Another term used to describe this category of software is "creative learning software."

What can you expect from educational software today? Is it only available on personal computer platforms? What considerations go into creating an educational software product? Can any form of education be made entertaining? Who are the consumers of educational software? What is the correct mix of entertainment and education—or can they be mixed at all? These are a few of the questions and issues that will be covered in this chapter.

EDUCATION AND ENTERTAINMENT—CAN THEY BE COMBINED?

Before discussing the relationship between education and interactive entertainment, it would be useful to look at the science of education itself. Educational psychology, the application of scientific methods to the study of people in instructional settings, is a relatively new field. Within the past 100 years very little has been learned about how people take in knowledge and retain it. Only since the late 1800s has it been pursued. Even until the 1940s, only a few people were doing scientific research in the field of learning. World War II however, changed that.

The History of Learning Science

During World War II, a great deal of thought was given to finding ways of teaching soldiers to master specific skills quickly. Army psychologists working in this field learned how to determine whether a certain individual would make a good radio repairperson or a good pilot. At the same time, these psychologists learned how to teach certain skills, such as cooking and aircraft gunnery, very quickly. When the war ended, those psychologists turned their attention to the field of education.

Following World War II, the postwar baby boom filled U.S. schools, and educational psychologists were needed to evaluate and create new educational material. In the late 1950s, with the Cold War running at full steam, there was added pressure for the United States to keep its curriculum in step with that of the USSR. Millions of dollars were funneled into this field in the 1960s to help disadvantaged students. These factors led to an explosion in educational psychology by the late 1960s. Today there are more than 3,000 educational psychologists working in the field, and thousands of other educators researching how to improve education.

The study of education encompasses many different aspects, and naturally must cover an extremely wide range of people. Currently there is no one theory to cover all of education. The field is broken into many categories, but this chapter focuses on the field of learning.

What Is Learning?

Simply put, learning is the accumulation of knowledge and useful skills or methods of doing things, which results from some sort of useful interaction with your environment. You are learning all the time, being bombarded constantly by all kinds of information, experiences, knowledge, and so forth. So much data is coming in that your brain dissipates most of it extremely quickly. The only way to make any of that data stay in your brain is to be able to put it to some practical use.

Researchers believe that different storage mechanisms exist for short-term memory and for long-term memory. If a piece of data is not placed in long-term memory, then it will dissipate very quickly. Some feel that even short-term memory can be divided into two parts: immediate and short term. Immediate memory stores information that lasts only long enough to keep a train of thought or perform a simple task. Short-term memory stores information from a few minutes until long-term memory kicks in. Part of getting data into long-term memory is to use the data in a practical way, so it becomes part of your "knowledge base."

David Traud, a new media analyst who has worked on a large variety of educational products and who is one of the few people educated in both computer science and education (he has a Master's degree in education), shared at a recent conference some information on the learning process:

"There are actually five types of learning that go on. One type of learning is attitude. This is something that you develop from a technology, as through television, but only over a long period of time. Attitude is probably one of the least useful ways of learning if you are looking at giving people life skills or helping them realize some sort of use in their environment. There are other types of learning that are much more useful to everyday survival.

"One such type is problem solving, which is obviously very important," Traud continues. "Higher-order learning is where you learn from yourself, or learn from your own experience of problem solving. There's motor skills, and then there's verbal skills, which are actually the accumulation of data and knowledge that you can apply to communication. These are some of the types of learning that you can apply to games. And there are many types of learning that technology doesn't address."

Everyone goes through a series of processes in learning. The first process is data acquisition. As receivers, people gather data in many ways—through reading, television, games, and the environment in general. You have to do something with that knowledge to make it useful; you have to get it out of those temporary storage areas. Your brain evaluates data to determine whether it will have a life beyond that initial receipt.

The next process is known as social discovery, or social learning, which is a form of interaction. Interaction between people is the most common form of social discovery: People exchange information, and they assume each other's perspectives to ensure that they've understood one another. This is the fastest way for knowledge to be assimilated. As you talk with somebody about something, your knowledge of the topic is used as a tool, and thus moves into your long-term memory.

The third process is that as these disjointed pieces of data reside in your memory, you reflect on the data. You ask yourself questions such as Are these things useful tools to me? and What is the practical application of this data to myself? Now, how do these different processes relate to entertainment?

Education and Entertainment

Entertainment is an engagement, an interaction, of sorts. With television or film, you suspend your disbelief; you identify with the characters so much that you are no longer aware of your immediate circumstances. With games, you have a stimulus/response experience. An ideal engagement, in terms of gaming or interactive technology, is where you have suspension of disbelief as well as a stimulus/response experience. In this elusive area, the technology starts to replicate what life itself is like.

Of course, the best way of learning is through life experiences. As computer graphics and games become more photo-realistic and more real-time, their interfaces become less obtrusive and more natural. People learn even more, and more quickly, than they've ever done before.

Computers are used in many ways today. They are commonly used for drills, tutorials, and testing. These are methods that obviously help move data from temporary storage into long-term storage, by fooling the brain into thinking that the data is actually playing some useful role. However, for more complex learning processes, computer simulations and video games can be very powerful devices in the educational world.

An interesting point regarding video games, whether or not we realize it, is that every video game is an educational medium, and every video game is an entertainment medium. Because a video game has rules and requires fairly complex thought processes, and because you must use that data constantly to play a video game, the data is finding its way into your long-term memory. You can test yourself on this by locating an old video arcade that has some of the ancient video games, perhaps some of the first you ever played—maybe up to 10 or 15 years ago. As soon as you put a quarter in the machine, you'll see how effective video games are at moving data into long-term storage areas of your brain.

So if every video game is an educational product, the question is: What are you being educated with? Those who are developing interactive media are responsible for monitoring their message, the data that will find its way into the long-term memory of millions of people. Whether they like it or not, they are teaching.

Creating Educational Software Titles

Educational software as a high-growth field is a new occurrence, and many existing entertainment companies are starting to add educational products to their lines. In the process of moving over however, they are also learning some interesting aspects of educational software.

Electronic Arts (EA) is one of the biggest and oldest video game developers, and it has made inroads into the educational software market. Stewart Bonn, executive vice president of the Advanced Entertainment Group at Electronic Arts, explains, "The genesis of the success of Electronic Arts is really founded on one key thing; that is, we've always hired people who are passionate about interactive entertainment. Our strategy is to start with products that have entertainment value and then add the appropriate educational value so the parents would recognize and appreciate what they were paying for." Content is also an important issue in children's educational software. In 1993, Electronic Arts signed an agreement with Children's Television Workshop to be its exclusive development partner for products in the interactive media.

EA learned that the design is the most important part of a product. The message that you are trying to deliver is more important than the technology with which you deliver it. According to Bonn, "We initially minimized the importance of the school market. We made a conscious effort not to pay too much attention to it because several of us were convinced that teachers think one way, and consumers and parents think a different way. That turned out to be wrong. Thankfully, there are many wonderfully talented teachers in the world. One of the things that we did to better understand the schools is that we created an advisory board. We pulled in educators and all different kinds of people on a regular basis to play with our software, and many have offered a lot of great advice."

Color Gallery FOUR

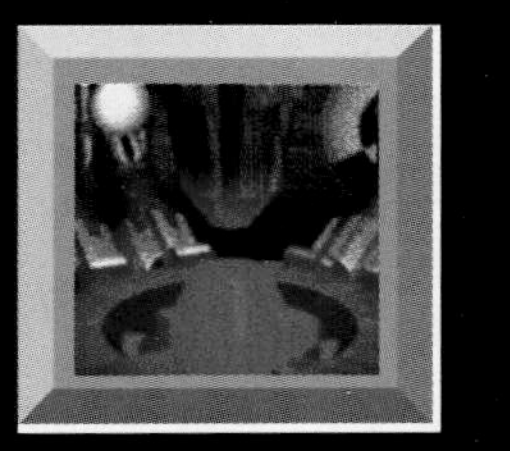

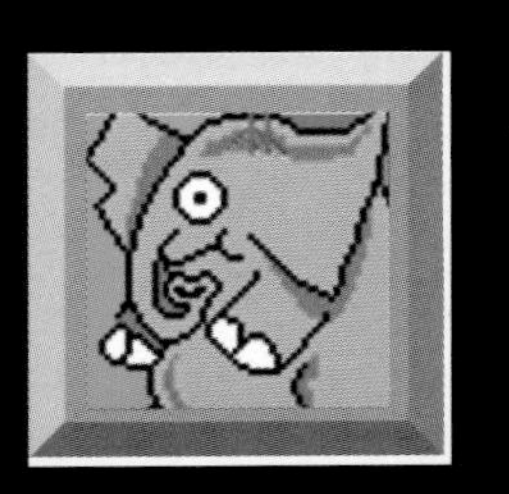

Knowledge Adventure is pioneering the use of true stereo 3-D for educational multimedia titles. 3-D Dinosaur Adventure is a good example; it's an extremely rich and in-depth look at dinosaurs. You can wear 3-D glasses and actually see depth in your computer screen. Created almost entirely with 3-D computer graphics, Dinosaur Adventure boasts over 10,000 computer-generated images. It also features more than 30 digital movie clips with digital sound effects and an original musical sound track.

Note: Use the 3-D Glasses included with the book to view these images.

3-D Dinosaur Adventure is a good educational tool because it appeals to children of all ages. It's a talking storybook for the very young, an interactive 3-D environment for older children, and an online Dinosaur encyclopedia for adults. In the encyclopedia, you can explore any location on Earth at any time to see whether dinosaurs lived there at a particular time. Dinosaur Adventure even teaches you a little bit about 3-D computer graphics with the Create-A-Saurus game. In Create-A-Saurus, you are presented with a 3-D wireframe version of the selected dinosaur. This wireframe model can be rotated in real-time, because it is simply playing back pre-rendered animation. Still, the effect is quite stunning. You can also apply a surface material to the wireframe dinosaur and look at it from any angle.

Who Wants Arthur? from Media Vision is a new multimedia title based on a children's book. It not only reads the book to the child, but also allows the child to read along with on-screen text and to interact with the story to learn more about the words and language used. As an aid to parents, Arthur provides management functions to display information about the child's progress. You can see which sections have been completed along with the individual words that the child has chosen or missed during each lesson. Multimedia is the perfect platform for children's books. We can expect more successful children's books to find their way onto CD-ROMs in the future.

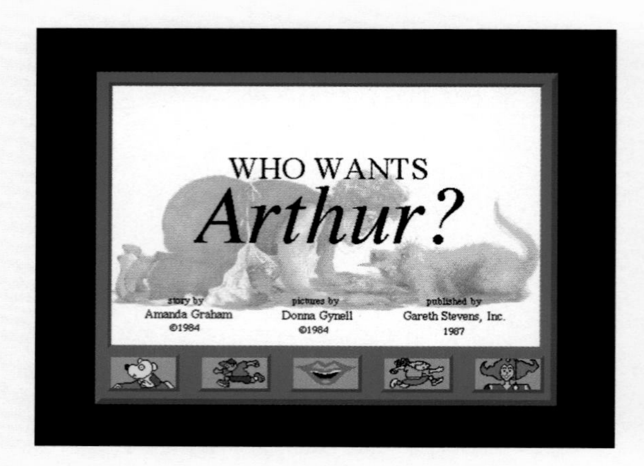

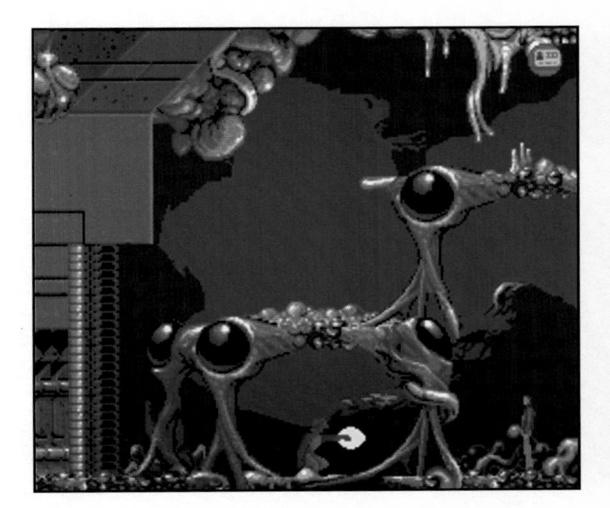

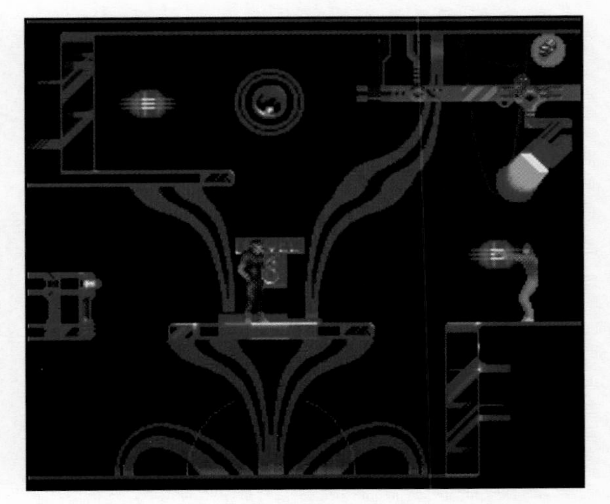

Sometimes actors and props are filmed for video games, yet the actual footage is never used in the game. Flashback from Delphine Software/U.S. Gold is an action adventure game that uses smooth rotoscoped animation. Rotoscoping is the filming of live action and then scanning each frame of that video into the computer. From there, the artists at Delphine painted over each frame. When the hand-painted frames were played back, the result was highly realistic, smooth animation throughout the game.

Flashback contains a total of 75 animated cinematic sequences (such as the ones on the next two pages) that appear throughout the game. These sequences, which help with plot development and storyline, were rotoscoped for smooth animation. During the course of the game, you travel through some 200 game screens on three different planets.

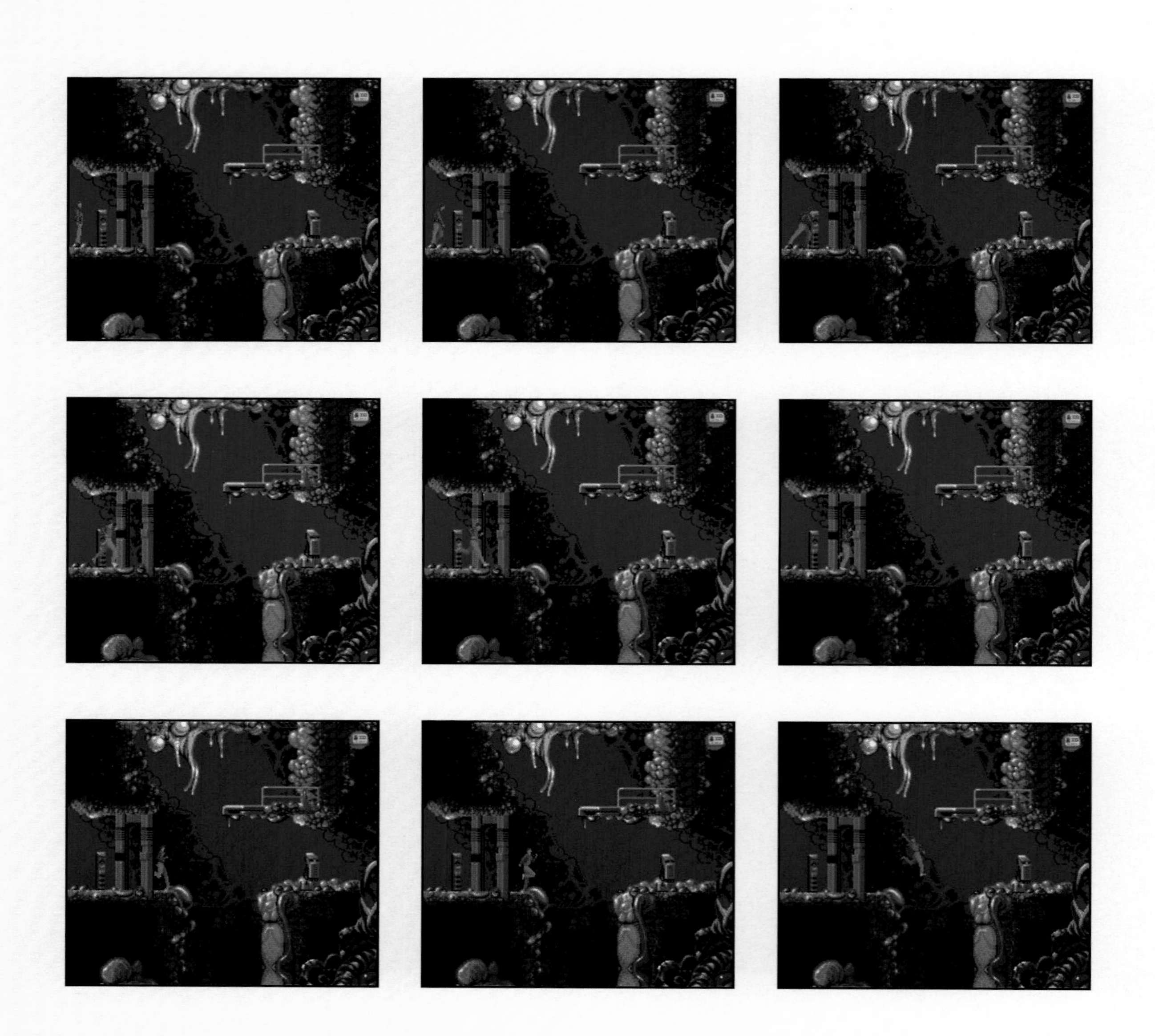

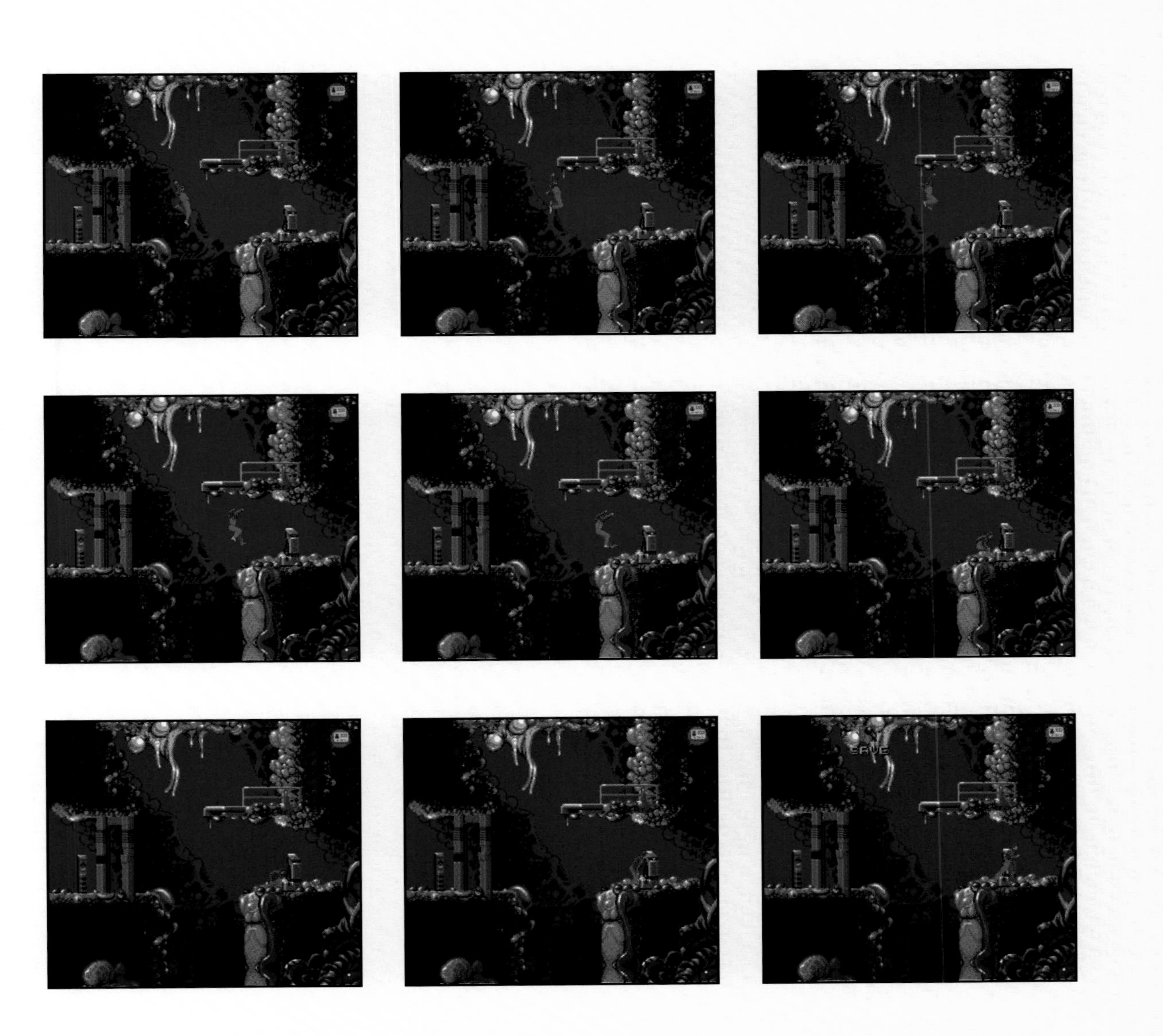
SAVE

Comanche Maximum Overkill from Nova Logic is a helicopter simulator for personal computers. The graphics are without a doubt the best that have ever been seen on a PC-based flight simulator. This method of generating 3-D graphics is called *Voxel* (volume pixel) Graphics. This technique was borrowed from professional flight simulators and scientific visualization systems costing millions of dollars. Commanche offers unmatched realism by including fractal-based terrain with shadows, trees, reflective water, and more.

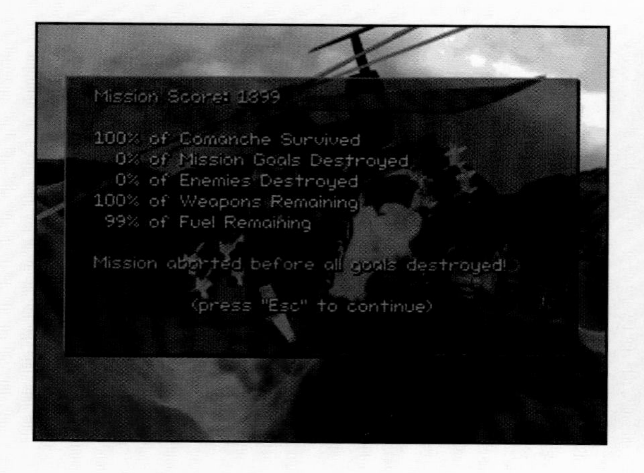

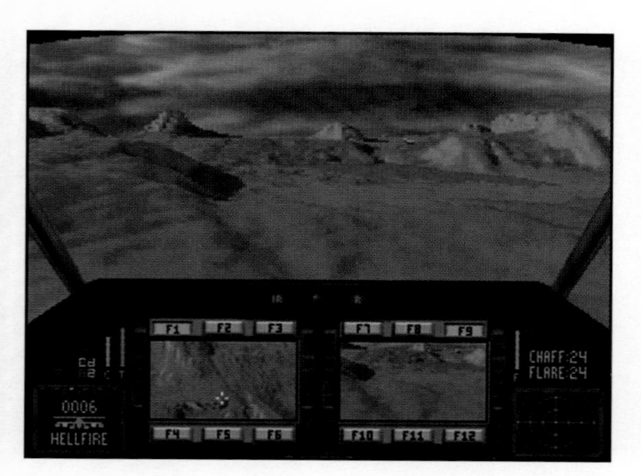

The Learning Company has released Treasure Cove!. Treasure Cove! is another multidiscipline educational title that covers topics relating to science, reading, math, and thinking problems. Treasure Cove! is similar in design to side-scrolling arcade games. You can move your diver left and right over the ocean floor while various fish come and go on the screen. The goal of the game is to find gems, but to do this, you need hints, which you must get from starfish. To catch a starfish, you shoot your bubble gun, which causes the starfish to either disappear or provide you with a question. When you answer a question correctly, you get a clue to the location of the gems. Finding the gems is more of an arcade game, but the search for hints, which involves answering questions, is more educational. The product is fun, and children enjoy the challenge of the questions while searching for sunken treasure.

Fly the Grand Canyon by Hyacinth software is the first flight simulator to offer 3-D stereoscopic graphics on the PC. It contains satellite scanned elevation data of the main section of the Grand Canyon. As a simplified flight simulator, it lets you fly through a 3-D wireframe representation of the canyon. While the 3-D graphics themselves may not be cutting-edge technology, they are very effective because they appear in stereo. With glasses, you can see in true stereo 3-D, which makes your monitor look as if it's about five feet deep. The fascinating thing is that, thanks to satellite scanned data, you could theoretically explore areas of the Grand Canyon that no one has ever seen before.

Note: Use the 3-D Glasses included with the book to view these images.

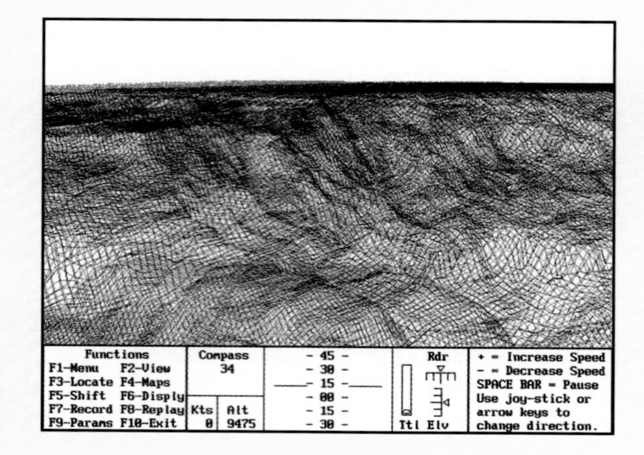

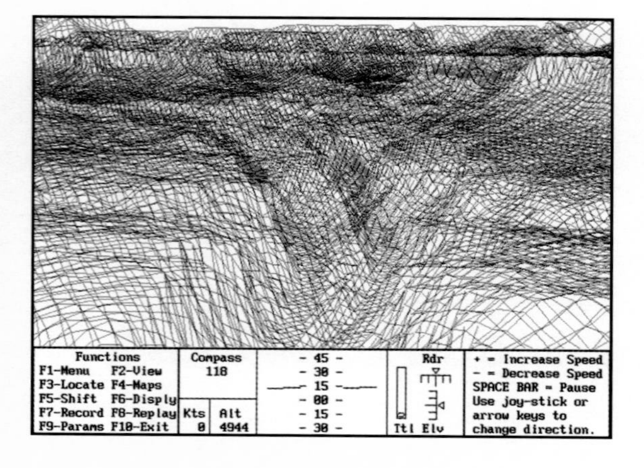

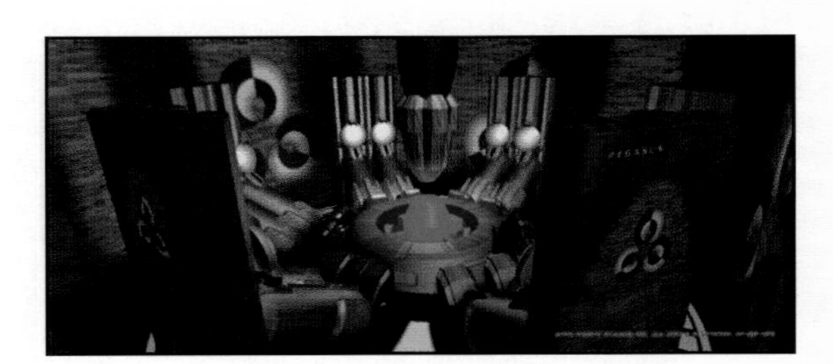

The Journeyman Project is a multimedia 3-D adventure game for both PC and Macintosh platforms. With beautifully rendered scenes you can explore the underground tunnels of a Mars colony to the NORAD center at the bottom of the Atlantic ocean. There are multiple solutions to the problems and puzzles in the game. You receive more credit for finding nonviolent solutions, but these are much more difficult than the easy, violent solutions you discover. The game offers more than 30 minutes of digital video sequences shot with professional actors to enhance the realism of the game. It's a good example of the use of 3-D rendering and animation in interactive entertainment.

Microsoft Arcade is the result of a licensing agreement between Microsoft and Atari, which allowed Microsoft to create personal computer versions of classic Atari arcade games. Arcade runs under Microsoft Windows, and comes with five different arcade games: Asteroids, Battle Zone, Centipede, Missile Command, and Tempest. Microsoft went to great pains to perfectly duplicate the original coin-op games; its versions are so accurate that even the subtle strategies players used in the original coin-op games work with Microsoft's versions. Microsoft even digitally recorded the sound effects from the original games. This is a trend we will no doubt continue to see as game developers license and convert successful coin-op games to the personal computer platform.

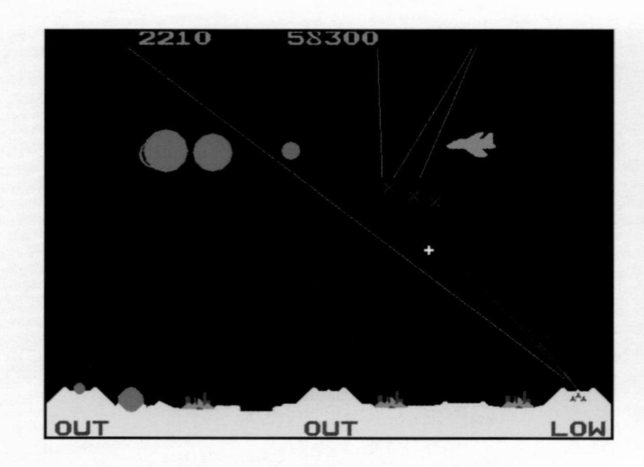

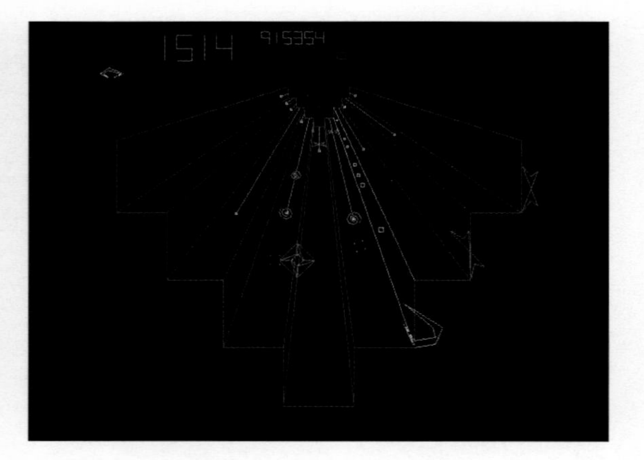

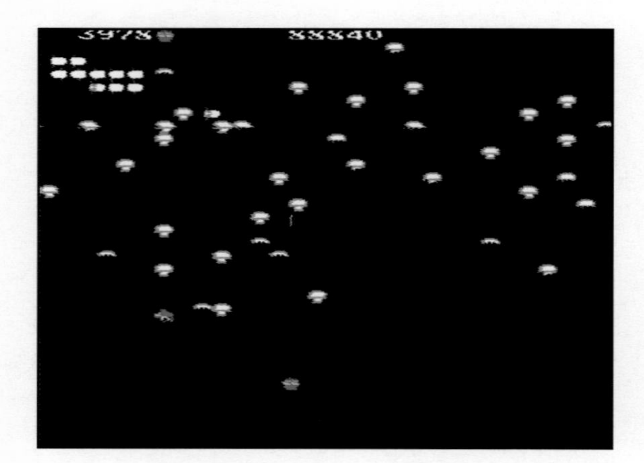

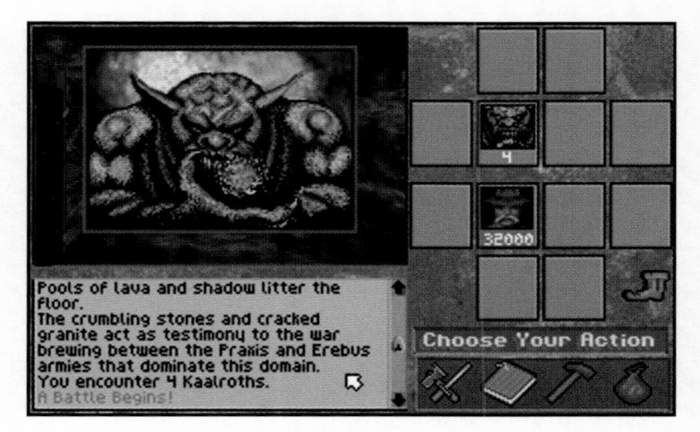

The ImagiNation Network from Sierra On-Line Systems is one of the most popular online systems dedicated to computer games. Over the past four years it has grown to more than 25,000 subscribers. When you connect to ImagiNation with your personal computer (through a modem), you are presented with a graphical picture that looks like a fairy tale. The picture represents all the areas available within the ImagiNation software. By simply moving and clicking with the mouse, you can select any location on the map, which joins you into the game in progress, starts a new game, or enables you to communicate with other online users. Online services are also making close ties with interactive television. The ImagiNation Network, for instance, carries NTN's QB1 interactive football game.

Courtesy of Sierra On-line, Inc.

Oceans Below from Software Toolworks is a simulation that enables you to explore the world of SCUBA diving. You are taught about diving gear, dive sites around the world, and the varied sea life you encounter in your simulated dives. The first-person perspective allows you to perform dives in various parts of the world…choose the Caribbean ocean and dive down 70 feet to feed an eel…dive the northern coast of California to get a close-up view of the Great White Shark. Each dive you experience gives you access to more than 100 high resolution underwater photographs and more than 200 digital video sequences. While diving, you can discover lost treasure or sunken plane and ship wrecks.

Courtesy of Software Toolworks, Inc.

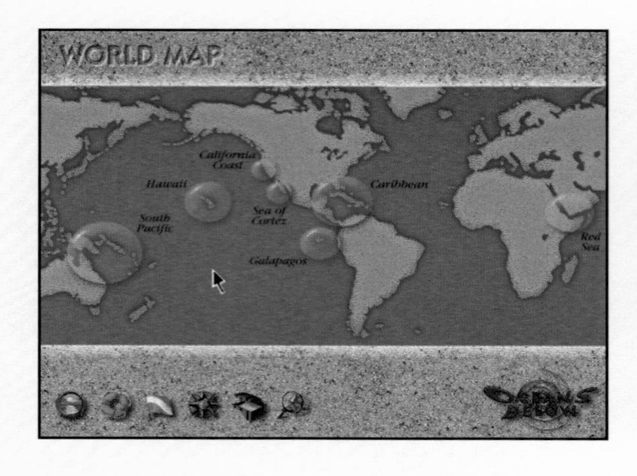

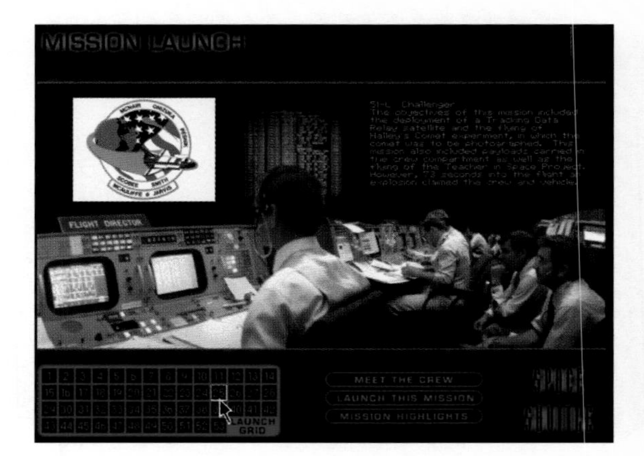

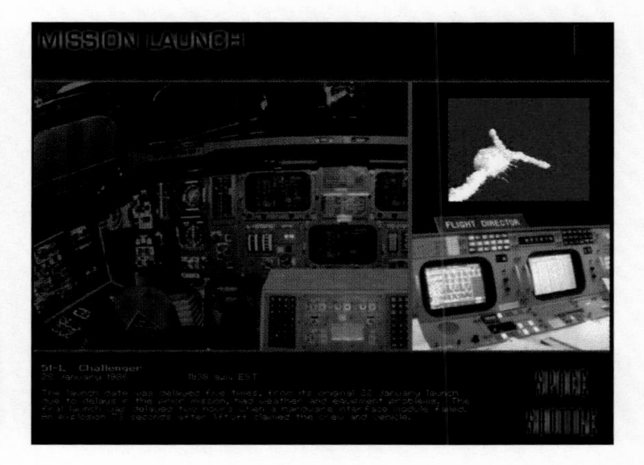

Space Shuttle, also from Software Toolworks, is an advanced simulator for NASA's space shuttle program. It allows you to experience NASA's training program firsthand and follow along with any of NASA's 53 shuttle missions. Each shuttle mission is complete with video sequences of the launch and landing. This even includes the horrifying video sequence from the Challenger's final launch (Mission 25) in which all the astronauts lost their lives. For nonclassified missions, you can even view video from aspects of the mission such as satellite deployment, maintenance, and science experiments.

Chuck Yeager's flight simulator by Electronic Arts has successfully integrated an American legend with a quality flight simulator. The result is that it has been one of the best selling games ever produced by Electronic Arts. In this game, Chuck Yeager offers his own flying tips and guides you through various flying lessons. You can also match wits against Yeager himself by trying to follow his plane through maneuvers that he recorded himself on the simulator. If you crash or get shot down, Yeager comes on the screen and chides you. This makes crashing almost as much fun as flying!

Courtesy of Electronic Arts.

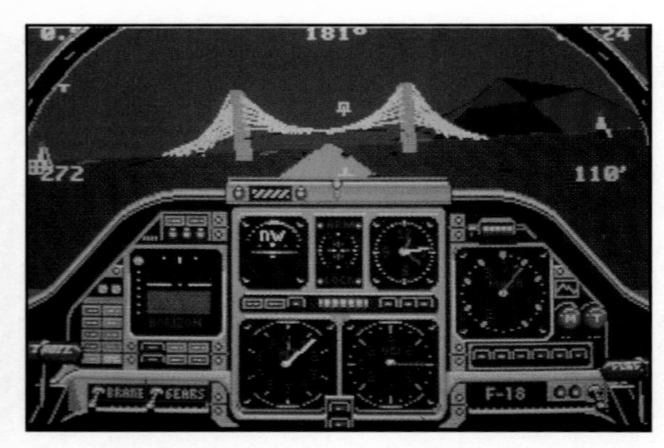

Bonn continues, "We also learned that there is a real technology involving how people learn. There was a certain amount of learning that we had to go through to improve the quality of our products. You can see that as the products have evolved, it's more apparent that we're actually getting this part of the equation as well. Now we have very targeted programs for the schools. We are creating school packs and doing all kinds of things because it's important for us not only to have the approval of the teachers, because that feedback is very valuable in the end to the consumer. But the other extraordinary thing about schools is that you can actually give the software to them for free, and if you do the math right, you end up making more money than if you didn't. Obviously one reason is because schools are huge billboards for children."

There's another key aspect that EA understands: These products have to appeal to the child as well as to the parent. Many educational products communicate a wonderful message to the parent, but unfortunately they are competing with an incredible number of things that are much more entertaining to a seven- or nine-year-old child than sitting down and playing an educational product.

Bonn concludes, "That's really where the entertainment part of our products comes in, where playability is an important component in what we are doing. We have a set of guidelines about how much value a child ought to get out of a product. One of the things that we set up early on is that we wanted to over-deliver on entertainment, we wanted to bring much higher-quality graphics. All of our products use 256 colors. They tend to take the medium to high ground in the PC area in terms of configuration. We just said that if entertainment clearly was one of our primary objectives, there was really no point for us to do anything other than the highest entertainment value."

A good example of this in action is an EA product called Peter Pan, A Story Painting Adventure. Peter Pan is a product for which EA hired some great animators to create an interactive cartoon. It combines interaction with reading, comprehension, and cognitive thinking. It's definitely not a replacement for school, but kids certainly find it entertaining.

Joyce Hakansson, president and creative director of Berkeley Learning Technologies (BLT), has been in the software business since 1976. She started the computer division at the Children's Television Workshop in 1979. Hakansson is a designer and producer of children's media, and her company produces educational and edutainment titles for museums, games, and schools.

Hakansson has noted two key areas in the creation of educational products that need attention: "One of the problems is that there is not a large enough base of really good software to make this market grow effectively. I think there needs to be a whole lot more of it out there. People are buying too many things that are failing for them, and they're getting turned off. I think we better do something about the quality issue quickly, and get it out there much faster than we have in the past."

In developing software for children, BLT believes it has two markets: children and parents. The parent will have to take that box off the shelf and purchase it. Like every other software developer, BLT already does a lot of on-the-box selling. Much of the success of a sale is based on what the box says. "Does it say that it's going to make your

▲ Peter Pan, A Story Painting Adventure, from Electronic Arts. *Courtesy of Electronic Arts.*

kid smarter in 30 days? Does it say that it will get your kid into Harvard immediately? All of that stuff that goes on the box—that sells it," Hakansson explains.

Children, the second market, must be interested in the product. That's where BLT puts a great deal of energy and where their focus groups point them. "We are developing for children who are moving from Barney to Beavis and Butt-Head, and we've got to satisfy them as they go along that journey. Children are beginning to make much more of a marketing choice, and there is this 'network,' or underground, that goes on in preschool, where kids say, 'have you tried?' and 'do you do?' Guess? jeans are big in the preschool set. And in software, children talk about it, and influence the purchase, so it really does have to work for children," says Hakansson.

"The hardest part I think of all of this is putting together the qualities of entertainment that will appeal to children. Children go from Barney to Beavis and Butt-Head in two years, and it is very difficult to make something that is really interesting to them. Making sure that it has developmentally appropriate activities, things that are sound and are really going to work for kids. Making it something that is interesting and engaging. Making it something that works on a moving target of technology. And doing it within a reasonable budget and a short period of time," Hakansson continues.

Putting together the people who can do that can be a difficult challenge. BLT works with educators, artists, programmers, sound design engineers, designers of interactive media, and many others. BLT usually starts from a concept rather than from the entertainment, but it very quickly looks at entertainment as the overriding goal. So it is blending those two things—entertainment value and educational value—and making them work together that is really the creative challenge.

Currently, BLT is facing one of its most challenging projects when it comes to making educational products fun: a spreadsheet for kids. The idea is to create a tool for children. BLT works at not talking down to children; they try very hard to make products that are not condescending. "We were asked if we could work on a spreadsheet for kids. My first question was 'Why do kids want to use a spreadsheet?' and I'm not sure we've got the answer yet, and I'm not sure kids do yet either. So this one is still up for grabs," Hakansson explains.

The first thing BLT wanted to teach was how a spreadsheet works. A spreadsheet works, as you know, with horizontal and vertical adding and accumulating cells. BLT did an excellent job of creating a simple and fun explanation. An on-screen character by the name of Sheba (who screams at you whenever she comes by, much like the actress Charo) plays the leading role. Sheba is building an aquarium. She puts a fish in the first cell, and it gets added horizontally to the right, and those are added to more empty cells down vertically. Finally, the fish die in an empty cell because there is no water or fish tank.

Your job or activity is to build an aquarium with Sheba. You do this by adding the aquarium parts—the glass fish tank, the water, and the plants—to the spreadsheet. When you place all the needed objects in the empty cells, they combine to function as a spreadsheet. You thus begin to understand the way a spreadsheet works. The program has six tutorials. Each is more like a spreadsheet than the fish tank. As you go through the tutorials, you get closer to working with a real spreadsheet. The last tutorial is very much like a real spreadsheet. Going through the tutorials enables you to learn how to use a spreadsheet.

The BLT spreadsheet itself is a powerful tool. It will import from and export to Excel, Works, and other major spreadsheets. It works very much like a regular spreadsheet. It allows you to do all the things you could normally do in a spreadsheet, except that instead of having 20,000 ways to put in the date, you've only got two. Instead of having 10 ways to find an average, you've got two. BLT tried to simplify the process of making and using a spreadsheet. They talked to many children before they started working on the spreadsheet. They took it into schools and asked, "What would you like? What would make this more interesting and appealing to you?" The response was, "Graphics! We really like programs with graphics and sound."

BLT went to the drawing board and developed a tool called the Sticker Picker. With the Sticker Picker, you can select graphics, and place them anywhere in your spreadsheet. You can collect any one of a number of graphics that the program comes with, and you can import new pictures. A variety of different frames can be chosen, and the finished picture with its frame goes immediately into your spreadsheet. The stickers float, so they can be moved around without affecting the text and numbers. Some of the stickers are animated stickers, which are exciting to kids because they come alive when you click them. Any of the stickers can be erased immediately.

Hakansson says, "We added other things, such as a notebook down at the bottom that allows you to take notes, to put in your assumptions, to write whatever you need to. One of the things that's going on in the math community now is a lot of integration with writing, and we gave kids an opportunity to do that. This also works in the schools, so that teachers can write in notes, put in ideas, and the kids can respond."

The program also has a charting function that makes charting understandable for kids. You can see what you are going to get before you actually put the chart together. You can see whether the data is going to be calculated on columns or rows. The finished chart comes up as a sticker, which can be moved anywhere on the spreadsheet, sized, or put into the notebook. Stickers are also dynamically linked to the spreadsheet so as you change a value in the spreadsheet it will show up in the chart.

"Essentially this is the kind of thing we are trying to create for kids. We are working with kids and educators, and we are just trying to create some things that will make it worthwhile for people to think about software for their children," Hakansson concludes.

Purchasing an Educational Product

If you are in the market for good educational software, there are a few things to keep in mind. First, look for products with the appropriate mix of education and fun. They should have been developed by a qualified team of learning experts, and tested by both parents and children. Finding products that support the latest technology in graphics and sound with contemporary artwork is important, too. Another feature to watch for is options for customization, so that the game can be played many times in many different ways, perhaps even allowing parents to enter lessons.

Try to find out if a program will be fun for your child. Ask yourself "Will my child enjoy playing it?" An easy-to-use design is a must. A product should offer progressive levels of play, so a child remains challenged once he or she masters a game element. The right environment can make a big difference in a child's learning; good software uses exciting game environments and intriguing characters to motivate young people and stimulate their natural curiosity.

Good software offers many benefits in the long run for your child. In addition to developing basic learning skills, good educational software enhances your child's problem-solving abilities and thinking, which will build self-esteem and confidence. This paves the way to future learning success. Furthermore, your child will become more familiar and comfortable with computers.

A number of companies are qualified to produce good educational software. Most offer a line of products that covers your child's critical learning needs and offers a progressive path from one age and grade to the next. Once your child is familiar with one product, he or she can easily use others in the series. Finally, make sure the company guarantees the product.

Following the discussion on the creation of Forever Growing Garden, this chapter reviews and discusses 11 popular educational products. Also see Appendix A, "Resources for a Listing of Entertainment Software Developers."

THE CREATION OF AN EDUTAINMENT TITLE: FOREVER GROWING GARDEN, BY C-WAVE

Media Vision has released a unique educational title for multimedia personal computers called Forever Growing Garden. Garden allows children to experience the fun of planting flower or vegetable gardens, even if they live in the city.

▲ Forever Growing Garden, from Media Vision.

▲ The starting screen of Forever Growing Garden allows you to choose the type of garden you want.

This 256-color, animated program simulates all aspects of growing gardens, including choosing the seeds, trapping gophers, planting, watering, harvesting, and even selling the vegetables or flowers.

The plants' growth is simulated by the computer at any speed you choose, from real-time growth up to where one real second equals one simulated day. As time passes, Garden animates each individual plant's growth. It also monitors the actual time you spend cultivating your garden, so you can turn off your computer, come back a week later, and find that your plants have grown during the week.

The game starts by enabling you to choose the location of your garden. You can choose a home location for a flower garden, a farm location for a vegetable patch, or a castle for a shrubbery and ground cover garden.

▲ The almanac provides useful information about your seeds.

▲ In Forever Growing Garden, you can plant a flower bed in front of your house.

The first time you choose a garden type, you are taken to the hardware store, where you can purchase seeds for your garden as well as helpful insects and animals to rid your garden of infesting pests, such as aphids, caterpillars, and snails. You can look at the almanac in the hardware store. It provides background information on the various plant types, such as how, when, and where to plant them.

One feature of Forever Growing Garden is that you can click just about anywhere on the screen, and something will happen. For instance, in the hardware store, clicking on the wooden planks of the floor produces musical tones. Clicking on a feed bag in the hardware store causes it to change into the shape of a hippopotamus head. When you are next to a house, you can click on its walls to change the color or pattern. Clicking on the tree in the country garden causes an owl to appear and look around.

Another fun feature is the fantasy plants that are sprinkled throughout the gardens. You can plant Monster Squash, which sprout and grow miniature Godzillas. Snap Dragon flowers grow dragon heads that breathe fire. The game also has TomaToes (tomatoes with toes), FireWork flowers (which you can make explode by clicking the mouse once they're grown), and many other fantasy plants.

If you choose to plant a flower bed at your suburban home, you will be taken to the front of your house. Here, there is an area where you can plant your seeds and bulbs. Planting is accomplished by simply dragging the seeds or bulbs from their packages, and dropping them into the ground. After all the seeds are planted, you must water them by clicking the water bucket and dragging it over the newly planted seeds.

Once the seeds and bulbs are planted and watered, it's time to sit back and watch them grow. You can wait as the plants slowly mature in a realistic time frame (months), or you can adjust the timer and speed up the growth of your virtual garden. Forever Growing Garden lives up to its name in that it keeps track of the date you planted the garden, and each time you run the program, it updates its growth according to the current date. You can tell your kids that their garden is still growing even though the computer is turned off. If you are impatient, you can set the timer so that one virtual day passes during every real second—you can watch the plants grow right before your eyes.

Once the flowers are fully developed, you can cut them with the shears. (However, you can't cut or harvest any fantasy plants.) After you cut or harvest a plant, you can use the trowel to dig up

▲ Plants in Forever Growing Garden are animated to grow realistically.

▲ In the flower shop, you can create many sorts of flower arrangements.

▲ Growing vegetables in the country.

the remaining roots, so you can use that section of ground for a new plant. Once you cut flowers, you can go to the flower shop, where you have an opportunity to look around and create your own flower arrangements.

If you decide you want to be a farmer rather than a florist, you can plant vegetables in the country. The process is the same, except that instead of cutting the flowers, you harvest the vegetables. Once you harvest the vegetables, you can take them to the farmers' market, where you can place each one on a scale to weigh it, and you can attach prices to the vegetables. Passersby make amusing comments about the pricing of your produce, ranging from disbelief at how cheap you've priced a piece of produce to outrage at the fact that you've overpriced something.

Finally, you can choose to plant ground cover and hedges at a castle. When the plants are mature, you can try your hand at creative hedge trimming.

In each of the three gardens, there is a gopher hole. When you least expect it, the gopher will hop out and make off with one of your prized vegetables. Clicking on this hole takes you to the

Gopher Game, in which a squirrelly gopher runs through his house, and you have to try to catch him with the mouse. You have to be careful, however, because the gopher's friend happens to be a skunk, and if you grab the skunk by mistake, you lose the game.

▲ The gopher game requires you to catch the gopher and avoid the skunk.

CREATING FOREVER GROWING GARDEN

C-Wave is the company that created Forever Growing Garden for Media Vision. C-Wave was founded by Chris Krueger, Tyler Peppel, and Amy Pertschuk. Peppel was manager of new product development in the Multimedia and Personal Electronics divisions of Apple Computer. Pertschuk and Krueger had previously developed a multimedia kiosk system for the California Academy of Sciences Natural History Museum. Based on this kiosk system, Krueger, Peppel, and Pertschuk produced a series of CDs called Life Man, which is published by Time-Warner Interactive Group in Burbank, California. Based on three CDs that discuss science topics related to life on Earth, Life Man is a high school- or college-level science education product.

"We don't think of [Forever Growing] Garden as a game. We don't even think of ourselves as a game developer, mainly because other 'real' developers might laugh at us if we did," Peppel says. Instead the developers prefer to look at Garden as a toy. Peppel explains, "We think of the product as a software toy. Just as if it were a doll or truck or any other toy. Before children are really ready to drive a truck, for instance, they have the toy. This is a really good introduction to gardening in a way that a child can grasp quickly and find to be fun. It may prepare them for growing real gardens."

Initial Concepts

Krueger, Peppel, and Pertschuk initially developed the concepts for Forever Growing Garden during a brainstorming effort. They are constantly developing ideas for multimedia titles, and at any time they may have 30 or 40 ideas at various stages of development. Some of those ideas are only a paragraph or even sentence; others are fully developed and ready for production. C-Wave is always nurturing ideas.

This brainstorming process for the three of them is extremely informal; they throw ideas out and build on them in a free-form way. They go with a gut feeling about what they think would be entertaining or inspiring to people. They also look at titles on the market, and spend a lot of time with those products. Sometimes C-Wave gives its publishers a list of title ideas, and other times they verbally describe concepts. The company's relationship with Media Vision is likewise very informal. Of the ideas that C-Wave has brainstormed, Garden is the one it chose for presentation to Media Vision. Stan Cornyn, a producer at Media Vision, is always interested in hearing new ideas from C-Wave. In early 1993, C-Wave informally presented the idea for Forever Growing Garden, along with several other ideas, to Cornyn.

Media Vision immediately liked the idea of Garden, and accepted it. Once it was decided to go ahead with the product, Media Vision decided to come up with a final features list, which they did, in a collaborative way, with C-Wave. At that time they also put together the final schedule, milestones, budget, and so on. The project went into effect July 1, 1993.

A major factor in the selection of Garden was that Media Vision wanted a product that could ship in 1993, and that put a lot of constraints on C-Wave. They had many good ideas, but there was no way that most of them could be completed in the time allotted. Many of the ideas C-Wave would have liked to implement were disqualified simply because they would have taken too long to carry out.

Gameplay Design

Peppel explains the ideas behind Garden's design: "I think the motivation was that we were looking for concepts that take the audience beyond just browsing a CD-ROM database of fixed information. To allow the audience to create something original, start a process that had a life of its own, something that is activity oriented where you could get unexpected results from the process. So we started to think about things that have a natural life of their own. One of the ideas we threw out was the Garden, along with many other ideas, which I'll keep under my hat because we may go on to develop them. It was starting with this notion of developing a product that would be more dynamic and more activity oriented than looking at a database of unchanging information. I really think there is a place for that kind of product, where you browse a database. A multimedia encyclopedia is a good example. We felt it would be better if we made a product that allowed users to create unique results each time they used it.

"This notion of activities and creating something new and unique each time you use the program was perhaps our main goal," Peppel continues. "You can go in and build dozens of configurations, and they all look a little different each time. Even in the development and testing of the product, we didn't make and test every kind of garden that could be made. This idea of activity oriented software, where you create something unique, is really a different angle on gameplay than your typical game, where you play for a high score." From the start, Garden was perceived to be a children's product. Although they weren't exactly sure of the age group, the matter of the target age group was discussed quite often over the course of developing the product.

There were many initial ideas as well as new ideas that didn't make it into Garden in the final cut. This often happens when you are creating and producing a product at the same time. Furthermore, when you are designing and developing a product at the same time, the temptation is there to add more and more to the product.

Peppel explains, "We came up with a lot of features that we actually liked quite a bit, but it became a matter of time. We pushed very hard to make the deadline. We liked some of the initial features that we came up with, and Media Vision liked some of the initial features, but we had made a commitment to try to get the product out by the end of the year, and that's what we stuck to. We had originally hoped to have more of everything in the product—more seeds, more gardens, and so on. We had originally hoped to have the almanac section of the product be much more extensive. We thought it would be fun to include information about growing real plants. It's those painful creative or artistic trade-offs that you always make in any creative endeavor. It's tough deciding what you can fit in or what you can include and what you can't."

The package includes a packet of real seeds that children can plant and take care of themselves. The seeds were C-Wave's idea, and Media Vision did a good job picking up on it and following through.

A lot of the gameplay came about when the developers were actually putting the product together. As they saw how the elements were coming together and how the program behaved, a lot of the best stuff in the way of additional features came about. Some of the features made it in, and some didn't. Some that did make it in, for example, are the changeability of the color of the house, and the monster swimming in the swimming pool. These ideas didn't occur to the developers until they had the house and the background in place. That's when they started thinking about what it would be fun to include. Most of the ideas that didn't make it into the program were removed during development. C-Wave pushed hard to get everything in they could.

During Garden's development, Media Vision gave C-Wave many ideas and suggestions; they didn't sit passively, looking at C-Wave's ideas and nodding yes or no. Instead, Media Vision took an active roll in listening and giving their thoughts about features or other items that could be added or improved.

Artistic Design

Many issues arose during the artistic design period. A lot of thinking and discussion went on about whether the program should be photographically realistic or cartoonish. If it were cartoonish, how cartoonish should it be? Krueger did a lot of the background layouts, many of which were inspired by the paintings of Grant Wood. If you look at Grant Wood's paintings, you'll see a similar kind of rolling landscape (for example, the initial birds-eye view).

All of the creative development was done on a Mac. C-Wave used Adobe Photoshop as the primary workhorse. They had to do the creative development on the Macs, thinking about the palette and file format issues involved with running the end product on a PC as well. The same pictures, animations, and sound were used for both the Mac and PC versions. The contract specified that both versions were due at the same time. The product that's shipping now has both products on one CD-ROM. Because their deadline was tight—less than six months—it became a major factor in the project.

A small amount of 3-D computer graphics and animation was used, created with Infini-D for the Mac. However, the 3-D graphics had to be toned down a bit, and adjusted to match the other artwork. "It's an interesting talent to get the output of these different tools to harmonize on a single screen. So for the artistic side of development, Photoshop and Infini-D were the two main tools. It was our first Windows or MPC-based CD, so it was a challenge to learn what we needed to know to put out a Windows product. Media Vision was very helpful in assisting us with that challenge," Peppel says.

Music and Sound Effects

C-Wave used two freelancers to produce sound effects and the music sound track. Jeff Essex performed the sound effects and Dennis Hysom created the music. Hysom had cut a series of CDs of natural sounds integrated with music for the Nature Company. Those CDs had been very popular, and his work seemed just right for the Garden. Previously, the people at C-Wave had heard some of his music. Krueger and Pertschuk knew him personally, and were very happy with his music. Peppel explains, "It's not all that easy to find a composer to sit down with and say, 'now we need music for a computer garden simulation for kids,' and then have them come up with something that fits as well as Dennis's music fits. We were very happy with his end result."

Programming

Garden was put together with the Apple Media Tool. It's a Mac-based development tool that has a visual editor allowing you to assemble programs without writing any code. It also has its own scripting language with support for extensions written in C. (C-Wave only used about 10 lines of C code.)

The Apple Toolkit is divided into two pieces: the Apple Media Tool (AMT) and the Apple Media Language (AML). AMT is the visual scripting component, and AML is the scripting component. A lot of AML scripting was done by a software programmer at C-Wave. In the future, C-Wave plans to use that custom software to develop other products along the same theme as Garden. The Apple Media Tool enables you to compile a runtime version for MPC as well as one for the Mac.

Because Apple had just shipped a new version of Media Tool, C-Wave found themselves working with practically new software. The bugs that frequently appear in new software versions made C-Wave's development more challenging. Peppel explains, "We found a couple of bugs in the program in the process and were able to work them out with Apple. We were very happy with that. The tool itself was not that new, but many new features had just been added to it, particularly the cross-platform capabilities. That was essential to us, because Media Vision is very much focused on the MPC market."

Testing

Once C-Wave got together an alpha test, they sent it to Media Vision. "We did some very basic testing, but Media Vision did the bulk of the testing since it was in our agreement that they would do the testing. They have an entire software testing group in Fremont, California. They did the primary testing for the product," Peppel explains.

The initial reactions from the testers were positive. They liked Garden because it is simple and different from other products. Peppel says, "They told us that they really liked it, but they probably tell all the pretty developers that. They made a lot of good suggestions, both technical and feature-wise, for improvements to the product. We really felt that Media Vision was pulling with us to make the product as good as it possible could be. They did all the testing, since it was their responsibility in the contract."

Product Release

Alan Thygesen, marketing director for Garden, set up a number of press events that led to the successful launch of the product, "We had an event at the Tech Museum in San Jose. We developed a video news release that featured footage from, among other titles, Forever Growing Garden. It aired on a variety of shows, and I was actually on CNN with Forever Growing Garden on their 'Showbiz Today' segment." In all, 50,000 copies of Garden were produced.

On the merchandising side, C-Wave developed a distinctive packaging that is very playful and whimsical, in keeping with the nature of the product. It features a front flap that gives more information about the product before you buy it. They also developed an interactive kiosk, and placed one in each of more than 200 Super Computer Stores. It's a computer with a CD-ROM drive, that runs demos of Media Vision titles as well as hardware infomercials. The customer can choose which demos the kiosk plays, and the computer randomizes when the consumer is not using it. C-Wave also created a software-only cardboard point-of-purchase display for Garden and their other recent titles.

According to Thygesen, "We are also doing a variety of national trade promotions and participating in retailer mailings, etc. We have done some advertising for the product, but not a very substantial amount, mainly because we weren't sure how to reach the target audience. We didn't feel like we had good vehicles for that. It's hard with any multimedia title, but for this one in particular it was not easy to find a good vehicle."

"We were a little late with the product, and as a result, review copies didn't go out until early to mid-December. Because at this point...reviewers will not write a review without having a copy of the retail product. We had numerous press mentions about the product, including TV, radio, and print. In print, for example, it was mentioned in *Multimedia World*, *Computer Gaming World*, and *New Media*," Thygesen continues.

Consumer Reaction

According to Peppel, "I haven't heard much yet. The little consumer response so far has been very positive. People seem to appreciate that [Garden is] different, it's not quite like any other product that's out there. The product was shown at Comdex in November of 1993, and we got a lot of good feedback from people who saw it at the Media Vision booth there. We did enter it in a CD-ROM contest sponsored by Apple and another company called Impress. We got a Judges' Special Award in that contest, which included about 209 other CD-ROM titles that had been entered in that contest. That happened before the product was released."

Thygesen likewise feels that it is too early to tell whether Garden will be successful. "It's a product that's not easy to explain. It begs to be demonstrated—which is why we had four TV stations do coverage of us at Comdex. Every single one of them showed footage of Forever Growing Garden. In the absence of an actual demo, we are having a little harder time communicating what Garden is to the user.

The Future of Forever Growing Garden

C-Wave is interested in doing a sequel, according to Peppel. "We've already talked to Media Vision about Garden's future. We are going to see what kind of reaction the marketplace is going to show. We are ready to do some sequels, and we have already talked about that with Media Vision. Many people have told us since then that we should do an adult version of the product, for those long winter nights, so people can plan their summer gardens. We are not really sure if we are going to do an adult version or not."

CURRENT EDUCATIONAL ENTERTAINMENT PRODUCTS

The following edutainment products are grouped according to the age of the consumer for whom they were developed. Products on the market are for children as young as two years old all the way through to adults. Some products note the age group they are geared for (such as ages two through five). Other products do not mention an age group. Keep in mind that despite what some products claim, many cross age group boundaries.

Another aspect is mentioned by Jan Davidson, president and founder of Davidson & Associates, an educational software developer. Davidson feels that it's not always so easy to match a child to a software package by age alone, "A six-year-old may not have learning skills that correspond to his or her age. You may need to choose software that is geared to four year olds, or perhaps eight-year-olds. Generally, children exposed to computers at early ages, three and under, pick up computer skills earlier, more quickly, and more easily than those who haven't." This review of some current products starts with those geared toward younger children, and advance to those geared toward adults.

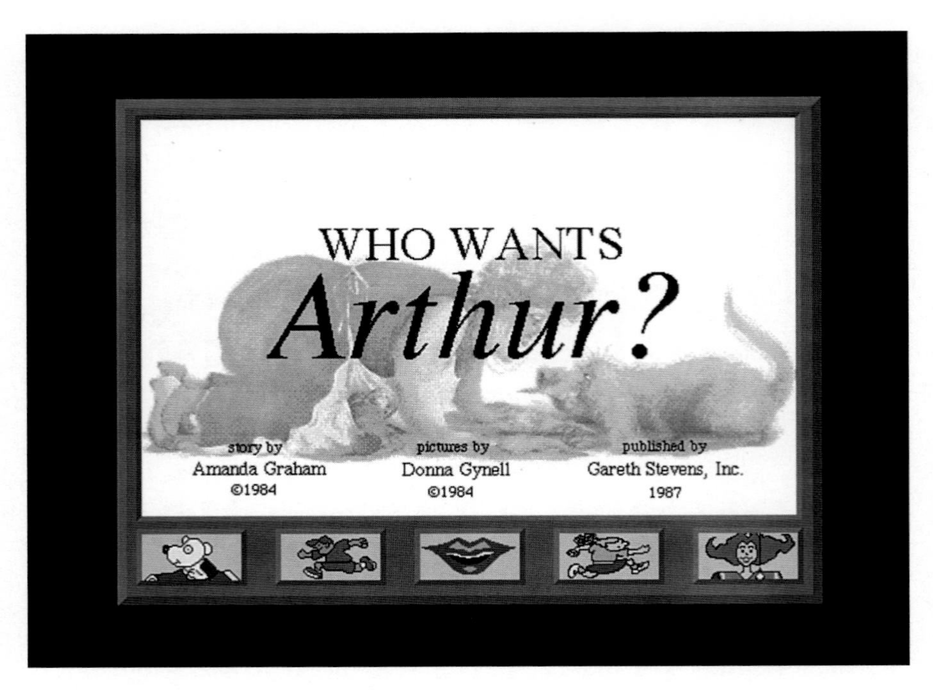

▲ Who Wants Arthur?, an edutainment title from Media Vision.

Who Wants Arthur?

Media Vision, along with Imagination Pilots and Taylor Associates, has released a new reading multimedia product called Who Wants Arthur?. Arthur is a children's book that has been converted into a multimedia educational program. It not only reads the book to the child, but it also allows the child to read along with on-screen text and interact with the story to learn more about the words and language used.

The story is about an "ordinary brown dog" who finds himself stuck in a pet store because no one wants to take him home. In an attempt to be more appealing to pet store shoppers, he learns how to act like a snake, a rabbit, a fish, a bird, and many other animals that are finding homes. Finally, he gives up trying to act like other animals, and he just acts like himself, an ordinary brown dog. Of course, right then a little girl comes in looking for an ordinary brown dog, and Arthur finds a home.

Media Vision knows that the first years spent learning to read are the most critical. Educators say that successful beginning reading experiences influence all areas of learning as the child progresses. They also feel that making reading enjoyable, stimulating, and enriching are important.

Arthur is one of the first Professor Gooseberry's I Can Read Club products. These are multimedia adaptations of popular children's books that are based on scientifically proven techniques for learning. All the titles are not just game-based reading programs, but they are based on pedagogic (teaching) principles. These titles combine viewing, read-along, learning, and independent reading activities with books that have already been praised for their literary and artistic merit.

▲ Arthur's beginning screen allows the child to take a tour or go to the main menu.

▲ The Who Wants Arthur? main menu.

The first step in Arthur is to log in; you type your name, so the software can interact more personally later on. The beginning screen allows you to take a tour or go to the main menu. The guided tour quickly walks you through Arthur's capabilities and navigation.

After you are finished with the tour, you are taken to the main menu. From the menu, you can access any area of the program, or you can replay any section you've already read. Pop-up help boxes make it easy for children to choose the right options. The main menu offers four different choices; Look & Listen, Read with Me, Think About the Story, and You Read. When you choose an item from the main menu, a little dog named Blooper drives a car to the selected option.

The Look and Listen section reads the entire story to you without showing you any text. Pictures are displayed along with background music, accompanying the narrator's voice. In the Read Along section, the narrator reads the story to you, and at the same time, you see the text of the story on the screen. The Think About the Story section helps children grasp the ideas of the book and explains unfamiliar terms interactively. Finally, the You Read section enables the child to read the entire story, and click any unfamiliar words to get a verbal explanation.

To help children navigate through Arthur, friendly icons appear at the bottom of the screen. Instead of using graphic symbols, such as fast forward and play buttons, Arthur uses pictures that describe the actions available. To turn to the next page, you click the button with a little girl running to the right. To go back to the previous page, you click the button showing a little boy running to

▲ Blooper is friendly and helpful in guiding you along your way.

▲ In this scanned color image from the book, Arthur works on his rabbit impersonation.

the left. To hear the page read, click the button with a pair of lips on it. To return to the main menu, click the button that shows Blooper in his car. For extra help, click the button with Professor Gooseberry's picture on it. If you seem to be delaying, and don't know which button to press, Blooper is likely to pop up and point to the button you should press.

In Look and Listen mode, you sit back and watch as the story is read to you and as scanned color images from the book are displayed on the screen. When text is used, as in the other three sections, the color pictures fade slightly and text is laid on top. As the narrator starts to read, the text (initially in a small size) enlarges to help prevent children from being distracted. The narrator speaks slowly and deliberately in the Read Along sessions so that you follow along.

In the Think About the Story section, you are quizzed on various aspects of the story. The story is displayed and read; however, certain words are missing, and you have to choose which of three words is missing. This helps develop vocabulary recognition as well as an understanding of use and meaning. If you choose the wrong word, the narrator helpfully explains why the chosen word is not correct.

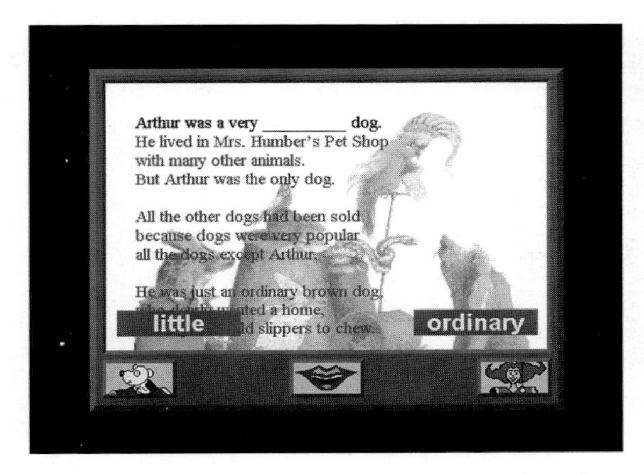

▲ The child has to click the word that is missing from the story.

▲ The Fairy Tale Factory allows young children to create pictures and speaking cartoons.

▲ A picture created by six-year-old Anastasia Nikoulina using Fairy Tale Factory.

As an aid to the parents, Arthur provides management functions that are available by pressing Ctrl+A. The management screen displays the child's progress information. You can see which sections the child has completed, along with the words the child has chosen or missed during each lesson. The manual supplied with Arthur also gives helpful suggestions to the parents, in the Parent Guide section. The book supplies some Do's and Don'ts for parents; for example, "Do discuss the story with your child, and share your ideas and things you liked most about it.", "Don't correct your child during mistakes in their reading that might change the meaning of a section. Instead, let the error surface naturally in your discussion of the story. Remember, the focus is always on the enjoyment of the story and the pleasure of reading."

Who Wants Arthur? is an excellent product for teaching children how to read.

The Little Mermaid & Beauty and the Beast Fairy Tale Factory

Hi-Tech Expressions, a producer of educational and entertainment programs for personal computers and home gaming systems has an interesting program for very young children, called The Little Mermaid & Beauty and the Beast Fairy Tale Factory. The Fairy Tale Factory enables children to create their own pictures by arranging predrawn images any way they want on the screen. The resulting picture can then be saved to disk or even printed. Programs like this, in which you only have to press the space bar and move the mouse, are appealing to very young children.

Millie's Math House

Intended for three- to six-year-olds, Millie's Math House, created by BLT, won a number of awards in 1993 for early childhood programs. Millie won the Eddy award for being the best early learning product, and also the SPA award for early learning.

Millie is a much smaller program than many of the new educational products on the market. BLT decided that they wanted to stay within four megabytes, and that to take any more than that from the hard disk would be difficult to get from the parents, so they kept their size low. They also had a limited budget, which limited the amount of animation they were able to include.

According to Joyce Hakansson, president and creative director of BLT, "Another thing we look at when we develop is that we try to keep things within the child's control. There are two ways the educators talk about this. They talk about it in terms of convergent versus divergent learning. We try and blend the two so that in divergent, children are creating their own things. In convergent, they are learning some skills or gaining some process that will allow them to be building things."

In the game, Millie is a cow, and as you move the cursor on the screen, her eyes follow it. If you click on her, she tells you that she is Millie, and she invites you to come play in her math house.

One of the activities in Millie's Math House is Build-A-Bug, in which children learn quantities and are able to use them to make an appealing creature. In Build-A-Bug, you get to make a bug by indicating how many of a particular bug part you want. Those parts are then placed on the bug, and you can move them anywhere on the screen or change the number and put in more parts. It's the kind of activity that has a construction-like base to it that kids enjoy . When you choose a number, it actually says that number (for example, "four"), and when you choose a body part, it says the number and the name of the part (for example, "four eyes"). The program builds vocabulary and gives kids empowerment, not forcing it down their throats through drilled practice and quizzes, but rather teaching through an engaging activity.

In another aspect of the game, you learn the attributes, small, medium, and large, as well as how to organize by those attributes. You have three different sizes of characters (small, medium, and large) and three different sizes of shoes. The goal is to place the shoes on the correct characters. At first if you place the wrong-sized shoe on a character, the character gives you a funny look, but it doesn't voice the concern. Later, the character will give you the message that he wants some shoes. He will give you clues along the way. If you put the wrong shoes on him, he will say, "those are too small," and give you a forlorn look.

"One of the things we wanted to have happen is that we wanted the learning that takes place to go beyond the video screen. We want kids to take away with them some knowledge that they can use in the real world. One of the really exciting things that happens is that kids who play with the program start learning and applying what they learn immediately," Hakansson explains.

Hakansson continues, "As an example, one of the parts to Millie's Math House is a number machine in which kids do simple counting at a cash register. We have children who have played with it, and as the numbers come up, it says, 'One, two, three, four...Four worms!' they join in. One little boy went off to play with his trucks and he was organizing them, putting them into categories and was saying, 'One, Two, Three, Four...Four Trucks!' and that's what we are looking for. That's the greatest success I can imagine. This is the kind of transfer from the visual screen to the real world we are hoping and trying to promote."

Treasure Cove!

The Learning Company has been producing educational software since 1980. Now, with more than 14 years of experience, they are releasing true state-if-the-art edutainment titles. One of their popular titles is Treasure Cove! Treasure Cove! is another multidiscipline educational title that covers topics relating to science, reading, math, and thinking problems.

Treasure Cove! is a fantasy world filled with gold, treasures, and colorful sea creatures. A villain by the name of Morty Maxwell tries to upset the happiness of Treasure Cove by polluting the ocean with his experiments. Morty, the "Master of Mischief," has destroyed the Rainbow Bridge. It's up to you, the Super Seeker, to find the shining gems that lie hidden at the bottom of Treasure Cove. You can use your science, math, and reading skills to stop Morty's pollution and locate the lost gems so the Rainbow Bridge can be rebuilt.

Treasure Cove! is similar in design to side-scrolling arcade games. You can move your diver left and right over the ocean floor, while various fish come and go on the screen.

The goal of the game is to find the gems. To do this, you will need hints from starfish, which are abundant. If you shoot your bubble gun at a starfish, the starfish either disappears or it asks you a question. By answering questions correctly, you get clues to the location of the gems. The actual finding of the gems is more of an arcade game rather than an educational game. Still, the product is fun, and children will put up with countless questions just for a chance to swim around in search of sunken treasure.

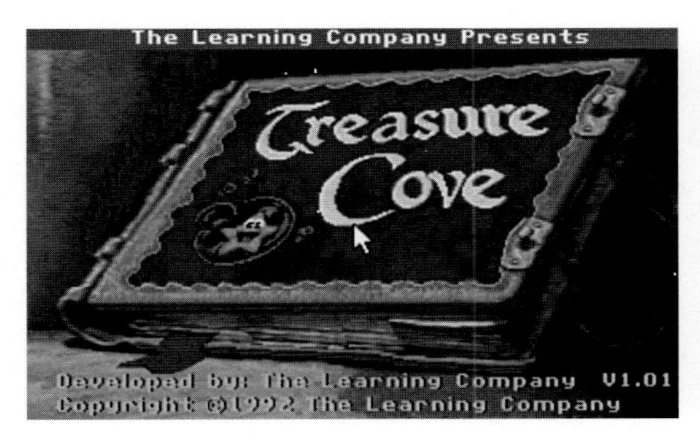

▲ Treasure Cove! from The Learning Company teaches children about science, reading, math, and thinking problems.

▲ Treasure Cove! has disguised itself as a harmless arcade game.

▲ A view of Treasure Cove from the shore.

▲ The starfish asks the player a mathematics question.

▲ The Wonders of Learning CD-ROM products from National Geographic.

▲ The Animals and How They Grow CD-ROM.

▲ You can click a word to hear its pronunciation.

Animals and How They Grow

Baby animals are always a hit with kids, and National Geographic realizes this. Animals is just one CD-ROM title out of a new series called the National Geographic Wonders of Learning CD-ROM library. Each product has narration, sound effects, and music that go along with the pictures. All the products include word and syllable pronunciations, explanations of words in context, and parts of speech to help develop a child's language skills.

There are many ways to customize the software to suit your needs. The speed of the narrations can be varied according to the listener's preference. The narration can be switched from English to Spanish. You can even choose the font, size, style, and line spacing of the type that's displayed. The Animals and How They Grow CD-ROM investigates the lives of mammals, reptiles, amphibians, birds, and insects. It also explains how these animals grow and develop.

The CD-ROM includes five different books covering the main categories of animals. At any time during the story, you can click a word to hear it pronounced. Those chosen words are then stored in a special recall menu for later review. While you are reading the books, you can place a bookmark to save your place.

Images on this page courtesy of National Geographic.

▲ The Main Menu of 3-D Dinosaur Adventure.

▲ Here you are presented with all 30 movie clips. By clicking on one, you can start it.

3-D Dinosaur Adventure

Some educational programs run the entire age spectrum. 3-D Dinosaur Adventure from Knowledge Adventure, a privately held company with about 80 employees, is a good example. Boxes for their products say, "Ages 3-103." Dinosaur Adventure is an extremely rich and in-depth look at 1993's most popular animal: the dinosaur. Created almost entirely in 3-D computer graphics, Dinosaur Adventure boasts more than 10,000 computer-generated images!

The product also features more than 30 digital movie clips (6 on the diskette version), with digital sound effects and original musical sound tracks. Another unique aspect of Dinosaur Adventure is that it is in true stereoscopic 3-D. By wearing special blue and red 3-D glasses that come with the game, you can see depth in your computer screen. This, combined with the photo-realistic and smoothly animated 3-D computer graphics, makes for a very exciting experience.

As an educational tool, 3-D Dinosaur Adventure appeals to children from 3 to 8 years of age because it features a talking storybook. The storybook walks you through the different types of dinosaurs as it speaks text to you from the screen. You can click any dinosaur pictured in the storybook and hear its name pronounced, or you can click a word in the text to hear it spoken.

▲ This is a 3-D computer-generated movie from computer graphics firm HD/CG of New York.

▲ The storybook reads simple stories about dinosaurs.

▲ To save the dinosaurs, you need to learn what time period each dinosaur lived in.

The interactive environment helps older children, ages 7 to 10, to learn about dinosaurs. One of the games in the program is Save the Dinosaurs, in which you travel back in time and are given a limited amount of time to navigate through a 3-D world and locate specific dinosaurs. Quizzes, such as Name-A-Saurus, Dinosaur Safari, and Who Am I?, help teach children the names, habitats, attributes, and other details about dinosaurs.

For the 10 years-to-adult age group, Dinosaur Adventure is an online Dinosaur encyclopedia. Explore any location on the earth in any time period to see when dinosaurs lived there. Within the picture window, you can click on a particular dinosaur to get more information. You can also rotate the globe while zooming in and out. You can perform keyword searches on the database. View dinosaurs by length, weight, or time by scrolling the data line beneath the picture window.

Dinosaur Adventure even teaches you a little bit about 3-D computer graphics, with the Create-A-Saurus game. In Create-A-Saurus, you are presented with a 3-D wire-frame version of the selected dinosaur. This wire-frame model can be rotated in real time because it simply plays back prerendered animation. Still, the effect is quite stunning. You call apply a surface material to the dinosaur, and then look at the creature from any angle.

▲ In the Name-A-Saurus game, you have to match the name of a dinosaur with its picture.

▲ The Who Am I? game shows you an enlarged close-up of a dinosaur, and then it asks you to match a complete view with the close-up view of the same dinosaur.

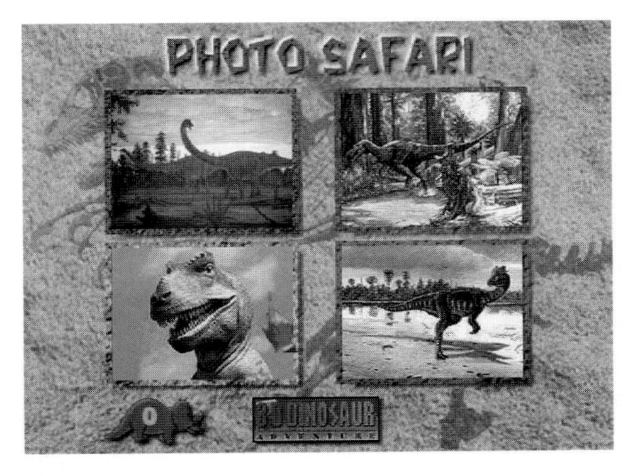

▲ While you take a Dinosaur Safari, the narrator will quiz you on the different aspects of dinosaurs.

▲ The Dinosaur Reference area enables you to zoom in to any location on earth and see local dinosaur happenings.

According to Rob Turner, president and CEO of Knowledge Adventure, "The difference between us and other educational software developers is that we are a multimedia technology shop that makes creative use of our own technology. Some people believe that success in this field is all about content, and if you have a fantastic character or cartoon, or if you have a *Jurassic Park* license, then you can do well. Others believe that it's all technology. Still others feel it's a matter of creativity. In truth, you have to have all of the above."

Turner explains, "There are some interactive products on the market right now which aren't very good and they aren't selling too well. They have a great name, neat concepts. Dinosaurs are very popular, as we all know, but you've got to have all three components. We are trying to get a balance of all three. I've seen some really neat products put together with some very extravagant, or very worthwhile, licenses of famous characters that kids know and are immediately attracted to where the product is not good enough; it's just an OK product and those products don't do well in the marketplace. You've got to have all the aspects together.

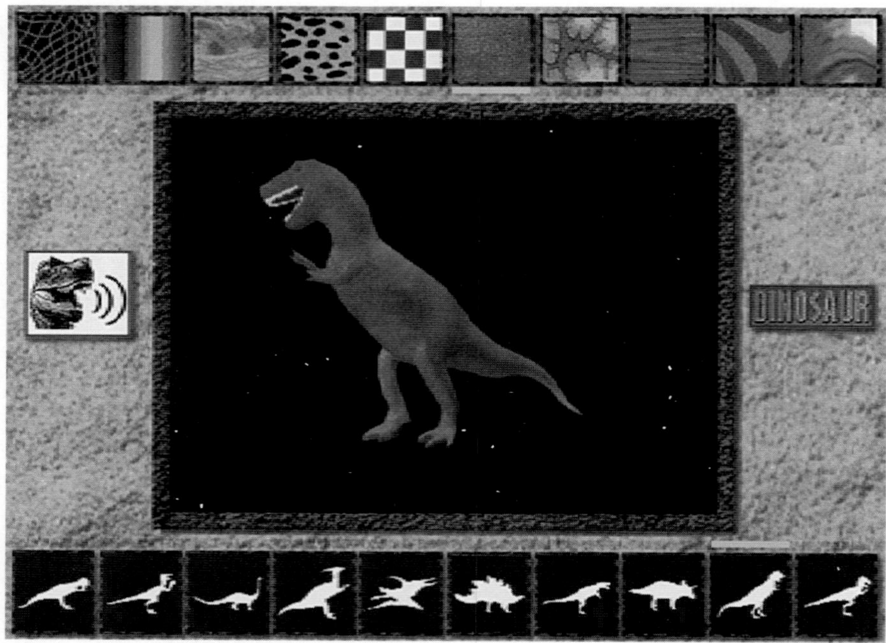

▲ The Create-A-Saurus game enables you to experiment with 3-D computer graphics.

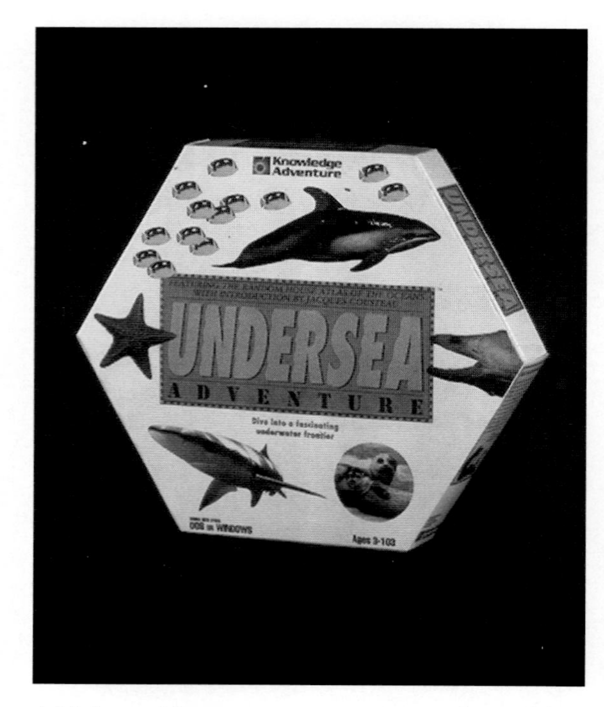

▲ Undersea Adventure covers many aspects of ocean life, as 3-D Dinosaur Adventure covers dinosaurs.

"What we believe we're doing is developing leading edge multimedia technology which allows us to do things that other people can't do, to push the envelope and redefine what multimedia is. If we are successful in making creative use of that technology, we can do products and do really neat, creative things and make experiences for kids that no one else can," Turner concludes.

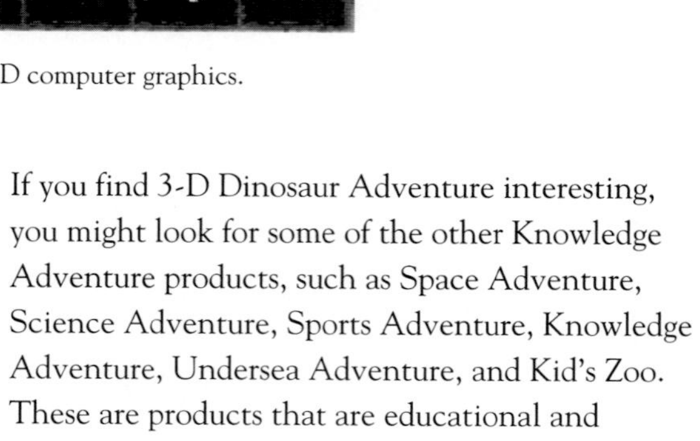

If you find 3-D Dinosaur Adventure interesting, you might look for some of the other Knowledge Adventure products, such as Space Adventure, Science Adventure, Sports Adventure, Knowledge Adventure, Undersea Adventure, and Kid's Zoo. These are products that are educational and exciting, and they focus on subjects that kids like.

Use the 3-D glasses included with this book to view the dinosaur images in Color Insert 4.

▲ A scene from a full motion video clip on whales.

▲ The Castle of Doctor Brain, from Sierra On-Line.

▲ The front door of the castle in The Castle of Doctor Brain.

The Castle of Doctor Brain

The Castle of Doctor Brain, from Sierra On-Line, is a very difficult program to classify. It's not just a logic or problem-solving program. Nor is it simply a math, history, or science educational program. It's also a puzzle-oriented program that teaches not only MENSA-style problems, but also how to count in binary, solve 3-D mazes, learn spelling basics, and even how to write a program for controlling robots. The game is written for ages 12 to adult, and even adults will find the captivating puzzles very addicting.

The object of the game is to make your way through Doctor Brain's Castle. You are applying to Doctor Brain for the job of lab assistant. He tests his applicants by making them find their way through his castle. Along the way, you must overcome his various tricks, traps, and puzzles. To start your journey, you begin at the front door. If you ring the door bell, the bricks over the doorway light up in various colors and play different sounds. By clicking on the bricks in the correct order, you gain entrance to the castle.

Once inside the castle, things get worse. The first hallway is where the mathematics puzzles are. Moving the cursor to the top of the screen reveals an icon-based menu bar. Using this menu bar, you can switch your current action between "look" and "touch," move backward through the castle, and adjust your settings (for example, sound and difficulty levels).

Every doorway or object that you click brings forth some type of mathematics puzzle. With puzzles from magic squares to simple number-slider games, practically anyone will be challenged. The deeper you get into the castle, the more challenging the puzzles become. Some puzzles require you to discern patterns.

Elia Nikoulina, a nine-year-old friend of mine from Moscow, is a big fan of Doctor Brain. He says, "I like the Castle of Doctor Brain because it's a very good game, and you need to think about the things you are making. I like to program robots. Even if it's too hard, it's still interesting, and you can really learn something." Apparently the gameplay value for children (even under 12) is very good.

The Castle of Doctor Brain is an excellent edutainment product. It's so much fun that you forget you're actually learning something. It's very engaging and can teach valuable skills that are useful for everyday life. In addition, the game stimulates curiosity in the topics that it teaches, encouraging you to explore other games, books, and activities.

▲ The first hallway inside Doctor Brain's castle—the icon bar at the top of the screen is visible.

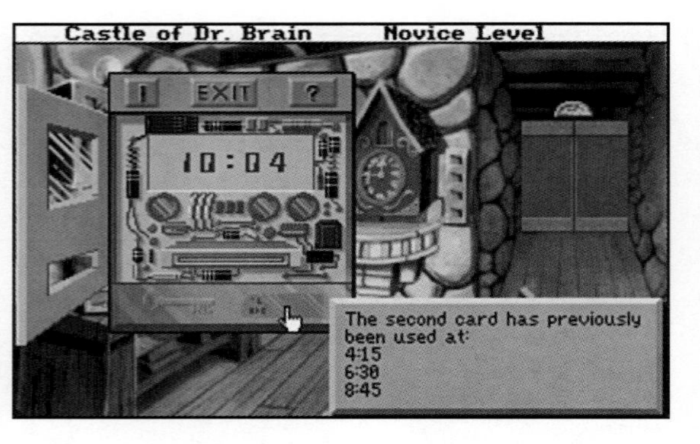

▲ In this scene, the player must figure out the next time needed on the time card.

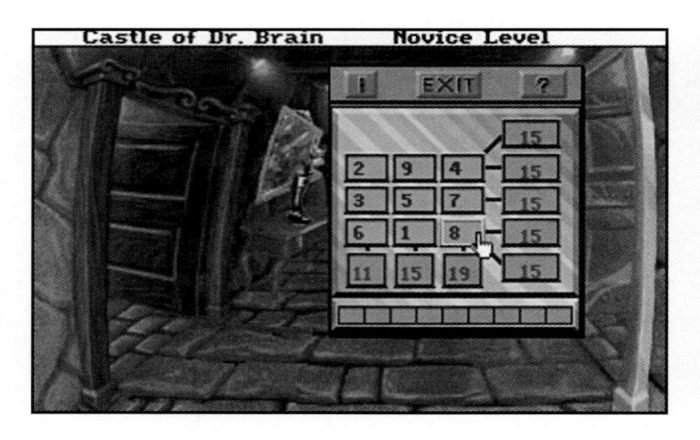

▲ This is a magic cube puzzle, in which all directions must equal 15.

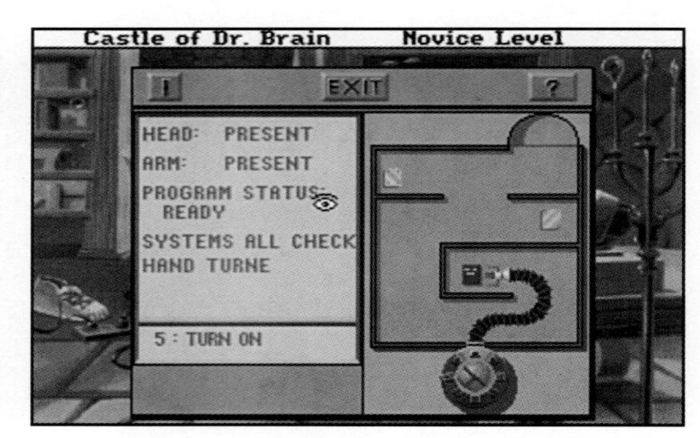

▲ A robot tries to run your program to retrieve objects from a maze.

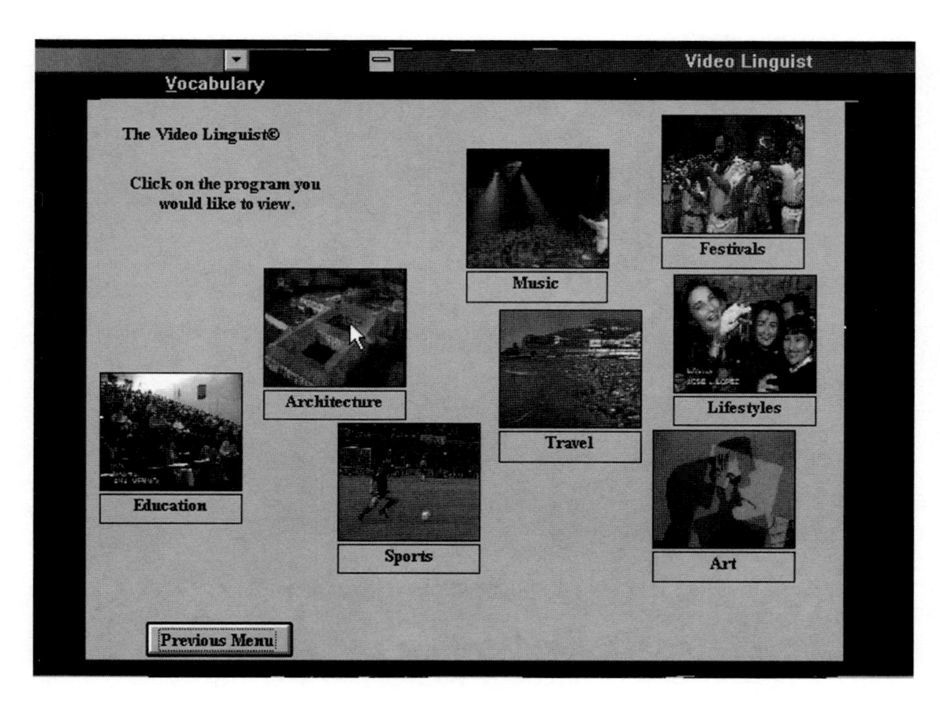

▲ Choosing the topic "Architecture" from the main menu of Video Linguist Spanish.

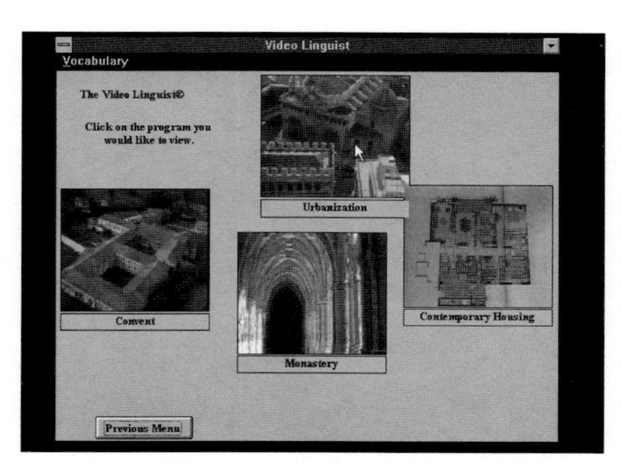

▲ Choosing the lesson discussing "Urbanization" from the "Architecture" menu of Video Linguist Spanish.

Video Linguist: Spanish

For those who are interested in learning another language, there are a number of educational programs designed to teach you. One series of language tutors is the Video Linguist, from Cubic Media. Currently, they offer software for learning Spanish, French, and a number of other languages. Video Linguist shows videos about the country whose language you want to learn.

Video Linguist's 44 interactive video lessons span more than 30 hours of study time. You start by choosing a category, such as education, architecture, sports, or music. After choosing a main category, you are presented a lesson relating to that topic.

Next you are taken to the lesson screen, which is divided into a controls section on the left and a workspace on the right. As a video sequence plays in the video window, you can pause, fast forward, or reverse it. Any phrase or sentence can be replayed instantly by pressing the Repeat Phrase button. If the narrator of the video seems to speak too fast, you can press the Slow Play button. This will cause the speaker's voice to slow down to an easily understandable pace.

The Record and Play buttons are perhaps the most interesting. Because almost all multimedia computers (IBM-compatible and Macintosh) have microphones, you can record your attempts at speaking Spanish. If you click the Play button, the computer will play back your voice. You can then listen to the narrator again, by clicking Repeat Phrase, and compare the two. This allows you to listen to yourself carefully, and work on getting the pronunciation and accent just right.

Two additional buttons are located at the bottom of the screen: Original Language Text and Native Language Text. Turning on the Original Language Text will cause subtitles to appear in the upper-right corner of the workspace. Likewise, choosing Native Language Text causes the English translation of the spoken word to appear. You can also print a copy of the text so you can study it.

At any time, you may click on a word in the Spanish text to pull up a Spanish-to-English dictionary. The 3,000-word dictionary indicates whether a noun is masculine or feminine, and it shows the masculine and feminine forms of adjectives, as well as the plural forms of irregular nouns. If the word you choose is part of a compound verb or an idiom, the dictionary will display the complete verb or phrase, and point out other helpful information.

Once you look up a word in the dictionary, Video Linguist remembers that word and the video clip with which it was associated. Then if you ever look that word up again, the same video clip will run to remind you how the word was used the last time you looked it up.

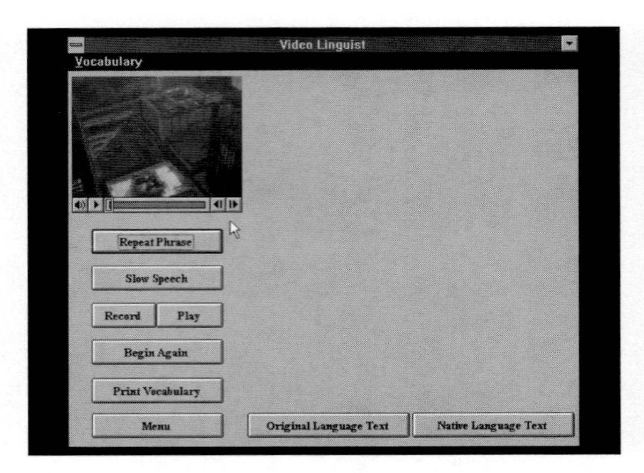

▲ The lesson screen offers special features, such as slow speech, to help you understand the video.

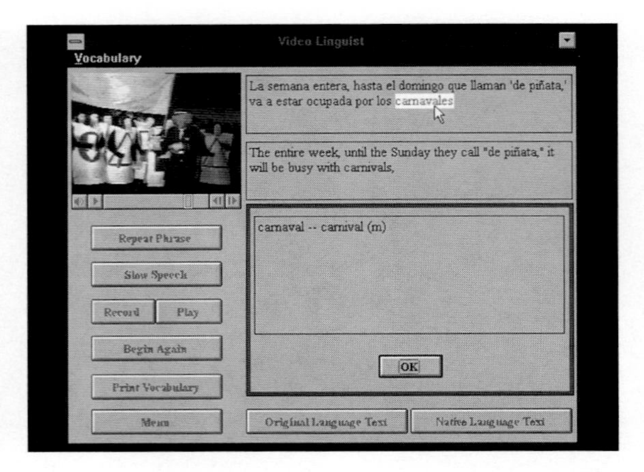

▲ Calling up the Spanish-to-English dictionary is as simple as clicking the mouse on a Spanish word.

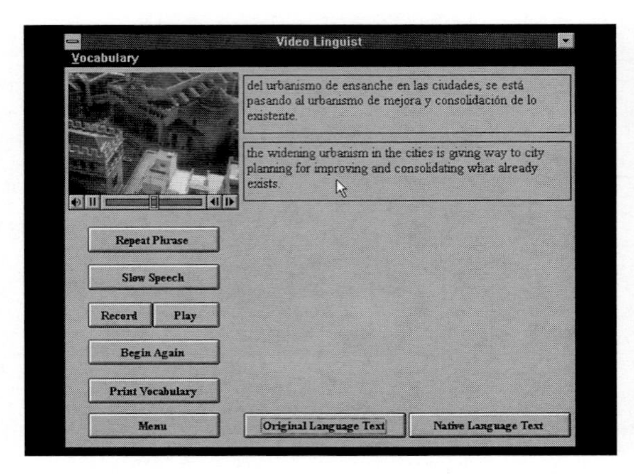

▲ Subtitles are available to help your pronunciation and clarify the phrases.

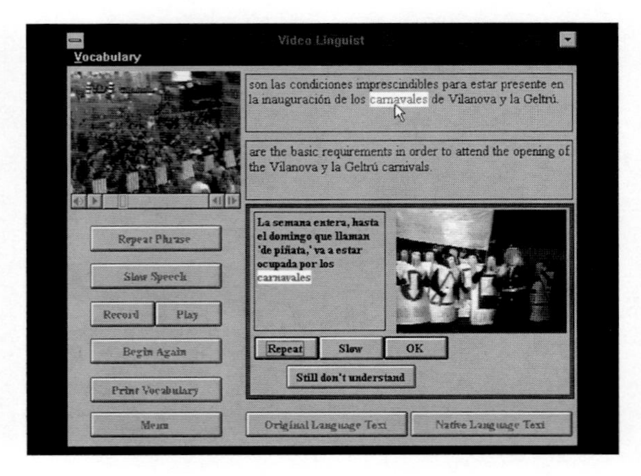

▲ Video Linguist plays a video clip to remind you how *carnavales* was used last time.

▲ Musicware's Piano enables you to learn to play the piano at home at your own pace.

Piano

Musicware offers a different type of educational program, called Piano, the first piano instruction software for Microsoft Windows. It teaches you how to play the piano with a year's worth of piano lessons created by a professional music instructor. Piano requires that you have an IBM-compatible personal computer and a MIDI (Musical Instrument Digital Interface) piano keyboard. MIDI cables are supplied with the software. Piano can work with any MIDI piano keyboard, unlike other piano instruction software, such as The Miracle.

The software keeps track of individual students so all the members of a household can have private lessons. The key areas of instruction are sight-reading, ear-training, rhythm, and music theory. As you play through the lessons, the software provides immediate feedback if you make a mistake.

To help you learn the piano keyboard, the software displays a piano on the screen. The package includes special labels that you can attach to your MIDI piano keyboard. These labels allow you to answer all the on-screen prompts and quizzes directly from your piano keyboard. Another way the software makes use of your keyboard is by outputting the music to it via the MIDI connection. So as it plays a sample piece of music for you, you hear that music being played on your own electronic keyboard.

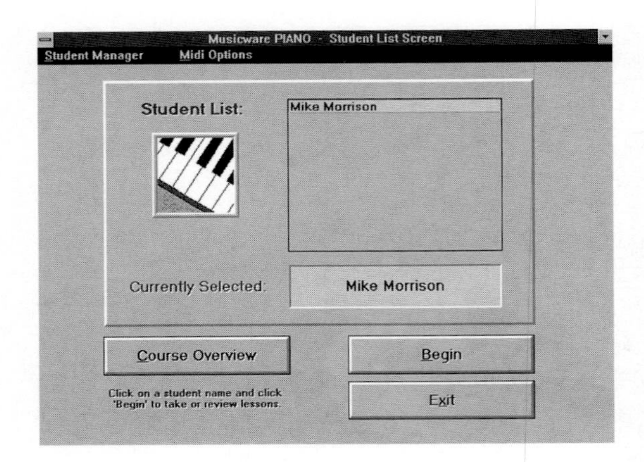

▲ Multiple students can keep track of their progress independently with Musicware's Piano.

Musicware PIANO - Unit Review Screen

Student Name: Mike Morrison

Unit Title: Course One - Unit 1

	Lesson Titles	Date Taken
1	Unit 1 - Lesson 1	Jan 04
2	Unit 1 - Lesson 2	Jan 04
3	Unit 1 - Lesson 3	Jan 04
4	Unit 1 - Lesson 4	Jan 04
5	Unit 1 - Lesson 5	Jan 04
6	Unit 1 - Lesson 6	Jan 04
7	Unit 1 - Lesson 7	Jan 04
8	Unit 1 - Lesson 8	Jan 04
9	Unit 1 - Lesson 9	Jan 04
10	Unit 1 - Lesson 10	Jan 04

Exit Review

6	QUESTION	Correct Answer: 1	Your Answer: 1		Right
7	QUESTION	Correct Answer: 3	Your Answer: 3		Right
8	QUESTION	Correct Answer: 4	Your Answer: 4		Right
9	RHYTHM	Total Notes: 6	Correct: 5	Played: 6	83%
10	RHYTHM	Total Notes: 5	Correct: 4	Played: 5	80%
11	RHYTHM	Total Notes: 6	Correct: 2	Played: 6	33%
12	RHYTHM	Total Notes: 6	Correct: 3	Played: 6	50%
13	RHYTHM	Total Notes: 6	Correct: 6	Played: 6	100%
14	RHYTHM	Total Notes: 5	Correct: 1	Played: 5	20%
15	Comment / Demonstration				

▲ The Unit Review screen allows you to view your progress.

Flash cards are the basis for the instruction. Piano offers three types; Keyboard, Music, and Interval. The Keyboard flash cards use a picture of the keyboard, whereas the Music flash cards use actual music notation. The Interval flash cards use the music notation, but only show you certain notes. All of the notes (hidden and visible) are played for you, and you must play back the correct notes, even the hidden ones. This is how Piano accomplishes ear training.

The flash card lessons are backed up with multiple-choice questions, music exercises, and rhythm exercises. A songbook with 50 songs is provided. It has music ranging in difficulty from novice to first-year student (the range of the music lessons in this course). If you send in your registration card, a second songbook will be sent to you. Additional courses for advanced students are also available. Musicware plans to offer courses through the fifth- to sixth-year student level.

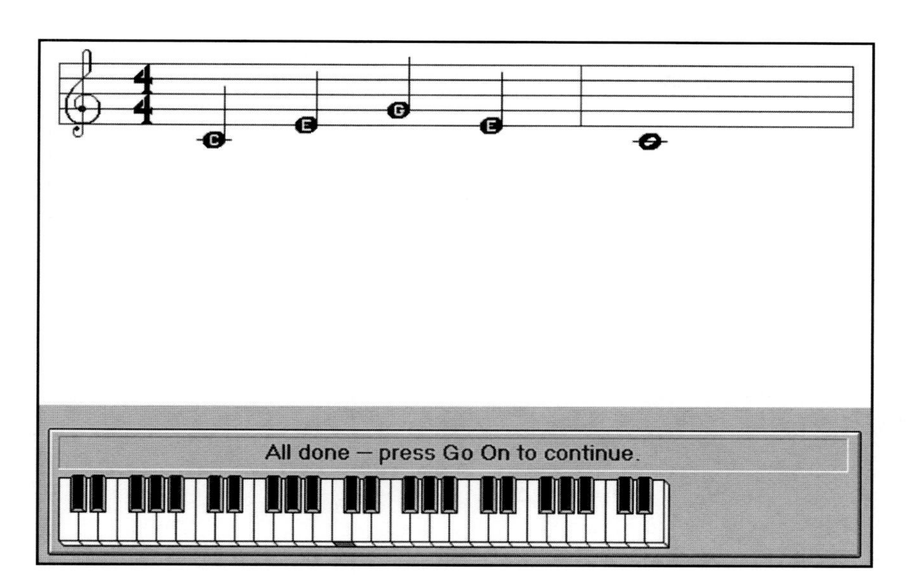

▲ An on-screen piano helps you locate the correct keys on your MIDI piano keyboard.

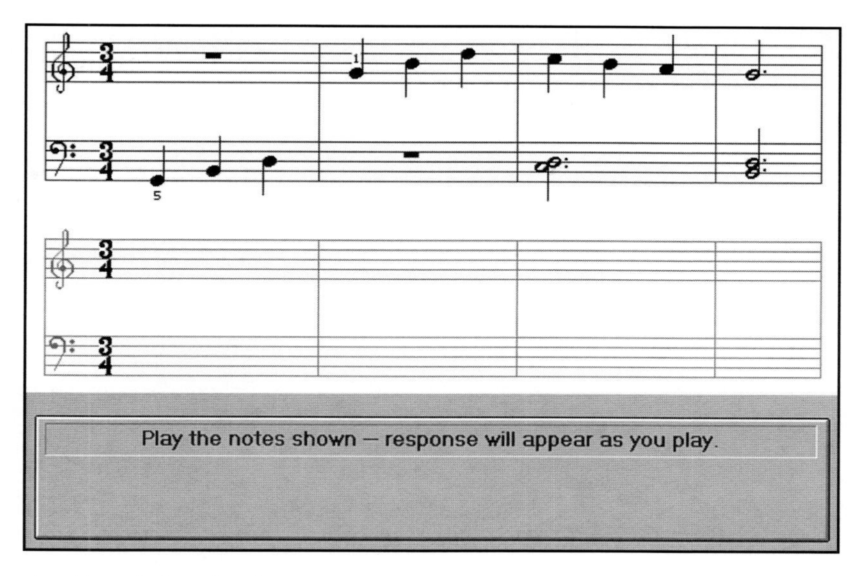

▲ A Music flash card with music notation.

Piano has units with more than 200 lessons, and as you progress through these lessons, the software keeps track of your progress. You can review your progress at any time by calling up the Unit Review Screen. It offers a breakdown of each lesson in the unit. Musicware's Piano is an excellent way to blow the dust off your electronic keyboard.

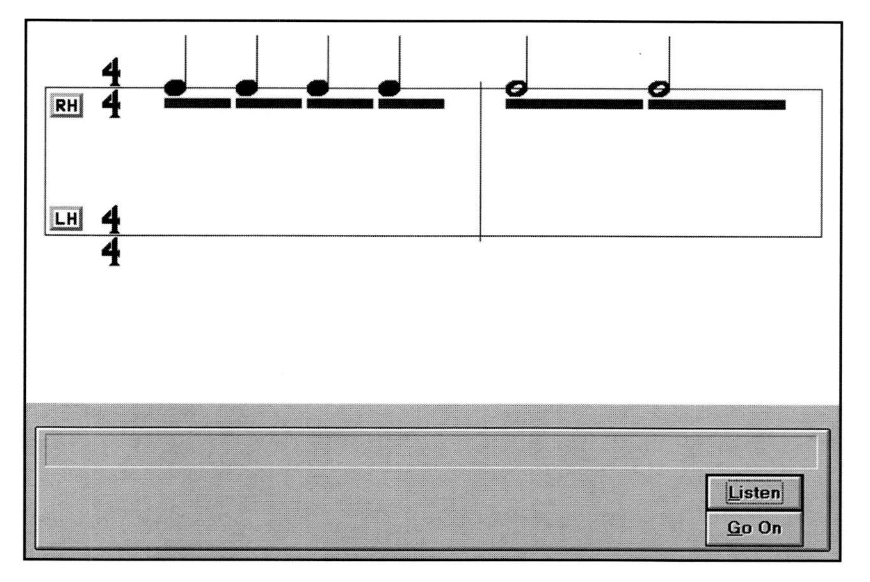

▲ A Rhythm flash card draws lines under the musical notation as you play.

▲ The Miracle, from Software Toolworks.

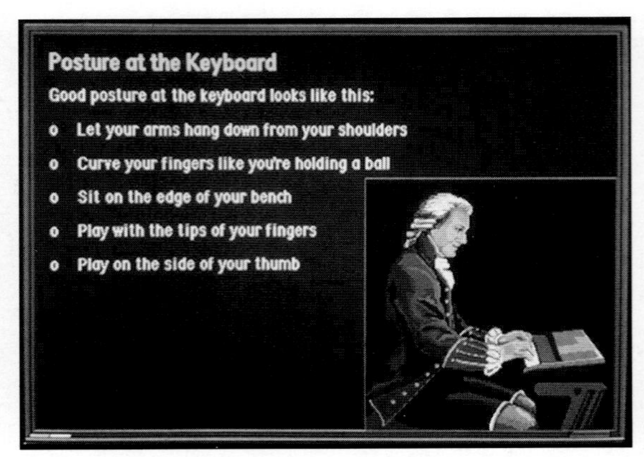

▲ A lesson on posture is illustrated by a graphic.

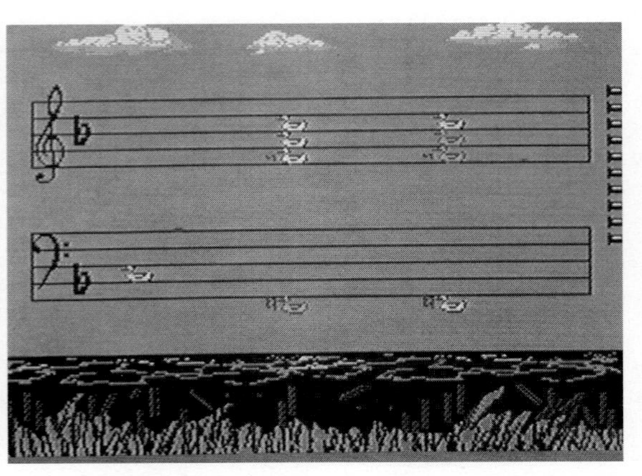
▲ The game Ducks that is included in The Miracle.

The Miracle

If you think it may take a miracle to get your child from in front of the Nintendo to the front of a piano, you may be right. A second musical educational package is The Miracle, from Software Toolworks. The Miracle is a combination of hardware and software that you can add to your home PC. It comes with a full-function MIDI electronic keyboard, the necessary cables, and software. Although the Miracle software only works with the Miracle keyboard, its advantage is that it is available for IBM-compatible personal computers, Macintosh personal computers, and even Nintendo Entertainment Systems.

The software comprises a year-long piano course that teaches how to read music notation, play with two hands using chords and common rhythms, learn new pieces of music on your own, and even perform with other musicians. All the lessons feature easy-to-follow instructions, and many of them offer graphics for easy explanation.

The software can communicate to the keyboard and detect which keys you play, when you press them, how hard you press them, and when you release them. This information is passed on to the computer, which in turn uses artificial intelligence routines to analyze the way you play. After determining the most significant errors, the software recommends and sometimes creates specific exercises to improve your playing.

For younger ones (and those young at heart), video games are included. These video games are not played with joysticks, however. They are controlled by playing the piano keyboard. One of the games, Ducks, shows empty music bars in the sky. Instead of notes, ducks appear on music bars. You have to play the corresponding notes on the piano keyboard to shoot the ducks.

Images on this page courtesy of Software Toolworks.

▲ Unforeseen occurrences require that you make snap decisions in The Lost Tribe.

▲ The Lost Tribe offers digital video sequences.

The Lost Tribe

As an aid to learning decision making and leadership skills, The Lost Tribe, from Lawrence Products is one of the best educational games available. It was recently the winner of the National Parenting Publication Award as an outstanding program for children ages 6 to 10. The game is so fun that adults are purchasing it for themselves.

In The Lost Tribe, you are the leader of a motley prehistoric tribe. After your homeland (along with your leader and hunting party) is destroyed by a volcano, you assume the role of leader to take your people to a new land. Good judgment must be exercised as you react to unforeseen events.

There are four main obstacles that you face during the game: natural barriers, the limits of time, the need for food, and occasional surprises. Sound planning and a willingness to take risks help you survive and lead your tribe to safety.

THE FUTURE OF EDUTAINMENT

The future of educational software certainly looks bright. As more developers move into the market, edutainment will enjoy higher consumer awareness. As interactive television becomes more of a reality, there may be closer integration between schools and educational software at home. Perhaps one day, a child who stays home sick will be able to complete assignments electronically.

A largely untapped market is in educational software for cartridge-based video game systems. Currently, only a handful of developers are in the cartridge market with educational titles. One such company is Software Toolworks. According to Software Toolworks Public Relations Specialist Tracy Egan, "At Software Toolworks we have been creating advanced artificial intelligence software since back in 1985 when we first released Chessmaster. Now we're using those skills to track and develop customized courseware for educational titles. These will be both on the personal computer side and the cartridge side." Currently Software Toolworks produces Mario is Missing for personal computers and Nintendo Entertainment Systems. Geared for four- to six-year-olds, it teaches children letters, numbers, and preschool activities.

Stewart Bonn of Electronic Arts agrees that the trend for the near future is going to be in advanced software technology, "We certainly learned that our original idea of putting the entertainment in first, and then adding the educational value may be the right way to do it. The key for us is trying to find creative relationships (game designers and educators with the design talent). I think that this is absolutely the main thing that is limiting the growth, certainly of our group, and perhaps the industry. There just aren't enough good products out there. We've had good initial success in terms of critical feedback and sales results, in terms of our product that clearly says that customers recognize value and we've priced the products below where a lot of the competition was and have delivered a lot more play value, so that seems to be an important component as well. And I think the challenge for us going forward is more creative experiments in order to create new ways of creating interactive entertainment with an educational value. That's the direction we are headed at Electronic Arts."

Another aspect is that when the graphics and input devices get good enough, you are no longer encumbered by keyboards and mice. We should see a new level of educational software that perhaps even rivals experiences of everyday life.

CHAPTER SUMMARY

This chapter explores the current theories and research on education and learning. It also discusses current theories on how the brain stores and recalls information. It examines the development of Forever Growing Garden, by Media Vision/C-Wave. It looks at 11 of the educational software packages currently on the market, and at the future of educational software.

Right now there are a number of good educational interactive entertainment products on the market. That number will only increase. Now you can locate educational software for any platform from the IBM-compatible personal computer to the Super Nintendo Entertainment System. In the way of software, from preschool learning to adult education, you can find something to fit any age group.

G

Glossary

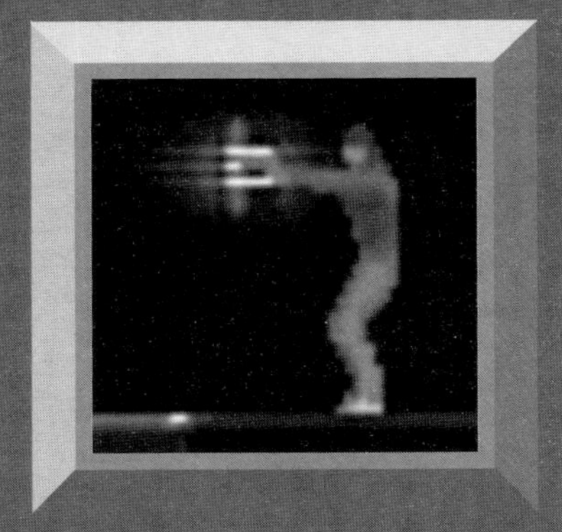

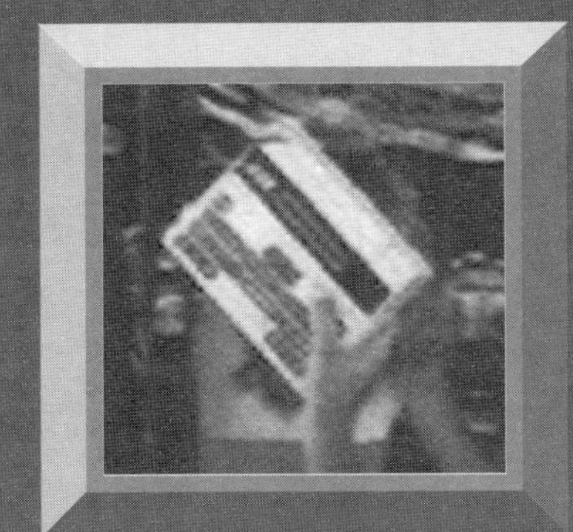

1-bit color The number of colors per pixel that a graphics file can store. With 1-bit color, each pixel is represented by one bit which has only one of two colors. A 1-bit pixel is either black or white. (*See also:* **Color depth.**)

8-bit A designation of capacity for CPUs and Graphics. An 8-bit CPU can process eight bits of data at once. (*See also:* **CPU, bit, NES, and Gameboy.**)

8-bit color/grayscale 8-bit color means that each pixel is represented by eight bits which can have 256 colors or shades of gray as in a grayscale image (see also **Color depth.**)

16-bit A designation of capacity for CPUs and Graphics. A 16-bit CPU can process 16 bits of data at once. (*See also:* **CPU, bit, Genesis, and SNES.**)

24-bit color 24-bit color provides 16.7 million colors per pixel. The 24 bits are divided into three bytes—one each for the red, green, and blue components of a pixel. (*See also:* **Color depth, True color**)

32-bit A designation of capacity for CPUs and Graphics. A 32-bit CPU can process 32 bits of data at once. (*See also:* **CPU, bit, 3DO, and Amiga CD32.**)

64-bit A designation of capacity for CPUs. A 64-bit CPU can process 64 bits of data at once. (*See also:* **CPU, bit, Saturn, Jaguar, and Project Reality.**)

3-D graphics The process of creating three-dimensional models within a computer's memory—that is, setting up lights and applying textures. After you tell the computer from which angle you want to view the 3-D scene, it will generate an image that simulates the conditions you have defined for the scene. 3-D animation involves the same steps, but it also sets the choreography or movement of the 3-D objects, lights, or cameras. (*See also:* **Texture mapping, Ray tracing, and Realtime.**)

3DO 3D Optics. A multiplayer standard created and licensed by the 3DO company. Currently Panasonic, Sanyo and AT&T are manufacturing 3DO units.

ADC See Analog-to-Digital Converter.

Anaglyph A technique for producing stereoscopic images. Right and left eye views of the image are printed in red and blue colors. The viewer then wears 3-D glasses, which have a red filter on one eye and a blue filter on the other. As a result, each eye sees a different image, and the mind builds a three-dimensional scene. (*See also:* **Stereoscopic.**)

Analog A form of measurement in which the indicator has no fixed state such as ON or OFF. *Analog* measurements are variable, like the up-and-down motion of a cork floating on the ocean. Broadcast video, consumer audio and videotape formats, and videodisc are all examples of analog media. (*See also:* **Digital.**)

Analog-to-Digital Converter (ADC) An electronic device that converts analog signals to digital patterns. (*See also:* **Analog, Digital, and Digital-to-Analog Converter.**)

Animation The illusion of movement caused by the rapid display of a series of still images. When each image differs slightly and the images are viewed in a series of more than 10 per second, they appear to be in motion to the human eye.

Amiga CD32 A CD-ROM-based home gaming machine from Commodore that uses a 32-bit CPU. (*See also:* **CPU, 32-bit, CD-ROM.**)

Artificial intelligence (AI) A field of computer science that attempts to create software that emulates the characteristics of human intelligence. (*See also:* **Expert system.**)

ASCII American Standard Code for Information Interchange. A standard code that assigns a unique binary number to each character in the English alphabet, numerals and other common characters.

Authoring software Software used to create multimedia titles. This software enables you to simply specify graphics, animation, video sequences, and text to play at specific times or in response to user input. (*See also:* **Multimedia.**)

Back-End processing An ITV technology used to process an ITV viewer's requests for information, movies, goods, or services. (*See also:* **ITV.**)

Bandwidth The amount of data that a channel can hold while transmitting from source to destination. A channel with a wide bandwidth can carry a complete TV signal, or 1,200 voice telephone channels.

Binary Having only two states—ON or OFF, or 0 and 1. A light switch is an example of a binary switch, because it is either ON or OFF and there are no other possible settings.

Bit A binary unit of storage that can represent only one of two values—ON or OFF or 0 and 1. Bit is an abbreviation for binary digit.

Bitmap A bitmap is a visual picture stored in the computer as a series of pixels. If the bitmap is applied to a 3-D surface, it gives the appearance of a real-life texture on that surface. (*See also:* **Pixel, 3-D graphics, and Texture mapping.**)

Blanking The time period that an electron beam in a video display is turned off and reset to the starting position of the next scan line.

Boss An enemy character in a video game that is very difficult to beat. Bosses usually guard the conclusion of a game level.

Byte A unit of storage composed of eight bits. It can store a numeric value from 0 to 255 (decimal) or one letter. (*See also:* **Bit.**)

CD-DA Compact Disc—Digital Audio. The standard format of compact discs that store music or any other form of audio. (*See also:* **Compact disc.**)

CD-I A compact disc format for storing graphics, audio, and text data. CD-I is also a multiplayer platform from Philips that features two 16-bit CPUs for playing video games and multimedia titles. The CD-I format can hold up to one hour of stereo digital audio or one hour of full-screen video (including sound). (*See also:* **Compact disc, Multiplayer, CPU, 16-bit, Multimedia, Digital video.**)

CD-ROM Compact Disk—Read Only Memory. It is identical in size and shape to an audio/music CD, but is organized to store computer data instead of sound. A single CD-ROM can hold more than 600M—equivalent to 428 floppy disks. (*See also:* **Compact disc, Photo CD, Multisession CD-ROM, CD-ROM XA, and CD-WO.**)

CD-ROM XA Compact Disc—Read Only Memory eXtended Architecture. This CD format was created by Microsoft to allow the interleaving of audio with data. Not all CD-ROM drives recognize the extensions. (*See also:* **CD-ROM, Photo CD, Multisession CD-ROM, and CD WO.**)

CD-WO Compact Disc—Write Once. These CD-ROMs (also called One-Off discs) can be written to one time. They are commonly used for creating test discs before sending the master to be manufactured. CD-WO discs conform to ISO 9669 standards and can be played in CD-ROM drives. (*See also:* **Compact disc, Photo CD, Multisession CD-ROM, and CD-ROM XA.**)

CD+Graphics A CD format that includes video data along with audio data. These CDs can be played by most CD-ROM-based game systems and multiplayers.

Cell site A local radio transceiver for relaying ITV viewer requests to and from the home. (*See also:* **ITV.**)

Cellular A radio transmision technology in which a geographical area is broken down into "cells" that are handled by a single transmitter/receiver antenna. Commonly used for wireless telephones and ITV. (*See also:* **ITV, Cell site.**)

CGI Computer Generated Imagery. A term used to describe motion picture and television special effects that are created on computers.

Chrominance The color component of NTSC television broadcast. (*See also:* **NTSC, Luminance.**)

Circuit board An electronic board in which computer chips have been laminated. Often called a printed circuit board (PCB).

CISC Complex Instruction Set Chip. The most common type of CPU, the CISC has a large number of complex instructions that are available to the programmer. (*See also:* **CPU, RISC.**)

Color depth The amount of color stored in an image expressed in *bits*. An image with a 24-bit color depth can have 16.7 million colors. An image with 8-bit color depth can only have 256 colors or shades of gray. (*See also:* **1-bit color, 8-bit, and 24-bit color.**)

Compact disc A plastic disk, 4.75 inches in diameter, that uses optical storage techniques to store up to 72 minutes of music (CD-DA) or approximately 650 megabytes of computer data (CD-ROM). The information is stored in the form of microscopic pits manufacturered into the surface of the disc. A laser light reads these pits and a CD player coverts the pattern back into music or data. (*See also:* **Megabyte, CD-ROM, and CD-DA.**)

Compression A means by which to reduce the amount of data required to store a computer file. (*See also:* **Huffman compression, Run Length Encoding, and LZW.**)

Computer-generated 1. Created on or by the computer. 2. Any image that was not scanned from an existing original.

CPU Central Processing Unit. This computer chip is the brains of the computer. It controls all other functions and processes information fed to it by programs.

Cursor A small blinking character on the computer screen that indicates where the next typed character will appear. Often controlled by a mouse. A cursor is sometimes called a pointer.

DAC See Digital-to-Analog Converter.

Data Any type of information that is stored in a computer. All data must be in a digital format.

Data processing The manipulation of data by a computer.

Dialog box Any type of screen in a graphical user interface that displays or requests information from the user. (*See also:* **Graphical User Interface.**)

Digital A form of representation in which information or objects—in other words, digits—are broken into separate pieces. Numbers are examples of digital information. Digital information is the the opposite of analog information, such as sound and light waves.

Digital painting Creating artwork directly on a computer, as opposed to using traditional media and scanning the artwork.

Digital sound Audio sound waves that have been recorded digitally. (*See also:* **Digital, Digitizing, and Digital-to-Analog Converter.**)

Digital-to-Analog Converter (DAC) A device that converts digital data into analog data. For example, a DAC would convert digitally recorded sound into analog patterns a speaker can project. (*See also:* **Digital, Analog, and ADC.**)

Digital video A video sequence recorded digitally. (*See also:* **Digital, Digitizing, and Digital-to-Analog Converter.**)

Digital wave forms A method of producing electronic music from pre-recorded digital samples of sounds. These short samples are played back in a long sequence, producing the sound of the original instrument. Digital wave forms produce more realistic sound than FM Synthesis. (*See also:* **Digital, FM synthesis.**)

Digitizing The process of converting analog information into a digital format. Recording sound into a computer is a form of digitizing, as is capturing video or pictures on a computer. (*See also:* **Scanner.**)

Directories An electronic area on a computer disk for storing data files. Similar to storing letters in a folder. A directory can be considered an electronic folder. (*See also:* **File.**)

Distortion morphing A method of morphing that distorts only a single image or sequence without fading into another image. (*See also:* **Morphing, Transition morphing.**)

DMA Direct Memory Access. A procedure used to transfer data directly from a peripherial device (such as a sound card) to memory without going through the CPU. (*See also:* **CPU, Memory.**)

Double-spin A CD-ROM drive in which the data access speeds are twice as fast as standard CD-ROMs. The same applies to triple-spin and quadruple-spin.

Editing The process of changing or manipulating data.

Edutainment Software or video games that combine education and entertainment.

Encryption The process of converting information into codes that cannot be deciphered.

EPROM Erasable Programmable Read Only Memory chip. A memory chip that can be erased with ultraviolet light and reprogrammed.

Expert system A computer program that simulates the knowledge and experience of an expert in a given field. The simulated intelligence is accomplished by very large "IF...THEN" lists. By the process of elimination, the computer attempts to narrow down possible solutions to questions posed to it. If the expert list is large enough, the computer will likely find the correct solution.

FCC The Federal Communications Commission. The federal government agency that regulates telecommunications services in the United States.

Fiber optics A data transmission technology in which short pulses of light are sent through very thin glass or plastic fibers. The pulses of light are converted to digital data by the use of an Optical Network Unit (ONU). (*See also:* **ONU.**)

File A collection of data organized onto a storage medium, such as a hard or floppy disk.

File format The specific type of organization a given file uses. Some file formats are strictly for word processing documents, others are for graphics/images. Most file formats support some form of data compression to save storage space. (*See also:* **Compression.**)

Floppy disk A small circular piece of mylar with a metallic coating inside a plastic cover. Used by computers to store *data*. (*See also:* **Hard disk.**)

FM synthesis The process of using a chip that produces music by using two or four wave forms called operators. Each operator modulates a frequency in order to produce musical tones. The result of this synthesis is less realistic than Digital wave forms. (*See also:* **Digital wave forms.**)

FMV See Full Motion Video.

Format Any method of arranging data for storage or display.

Fractal graphics A term coined by Benoit Mandelbrot in 1975 to describe certain types of geometry. Commonly used to describe irregular organic shapes that occur in nature, such as coastlines, mountain ranges, and plants.

Full Motion Video Continuous motion digital video that can be played back on a computer or gaming system. Sometimes called FMV. A minimum of 12 frames-per-second are needed to simulate smooth motion. (*See also:* **Digital video.**)

FX A special 3-D graphics chip designed for use in SNES cartridges. It gives games the ability to generate realtime 3-D graphics. (*See also:* **SNES, 3-D graphics.**)

Game Gear A portable cartridge-based gaming unit from Sega. The Game Gear features an 8-bit CPU and a color LCD display. (*See also:* **8-bit, CPU, LCD.**)

Gameboy A portable cartridge-based game unit created by Nintendo. The Gameboy was the first portable cartridge-game system and uses an 8-bit CPU and black-and-white LCD display. (*See also:* **8-bit, CPU, LCD.**)

Genesis The first 16-bit cartridge-based video game system. Created by Sega, Genesis has a large library of game titles. (*See also:* **16-bit, CPU, SegaCD.**)

Gigabyte A unit of computer storage representing 1 billion *bytes*. (*See also:* **Byte.**)

Graphical User Interface (GUI) A graphics-based interface between a user and the computer. GUIs usually require a mouse-type pointing device. All programs within a GUI look similar, and generally feature pull-down menus and scroll bars.

Hard disk A computer memory storage device similar to a floppy disk, except that the disk itself is made with a rigid material. Located within a computer, hard disks spin much faster and have higher operating tolerances; therefore they can store much more information than floppy disks.

HMD Head Mounted Display. These are helmets used for virtual reality that contain built-in miniature display screens.

Huffman compression A method of compressing data developed by David Huffman in 1952. Commonly used to compress graphics files. (*See also:* **Compression.**)

Icons Small graphics symbols used to represent programs, data, or other functions within a graphical user interface. (*See also:* **Graphical User Interface.**)

IFR Infrared—a portion of the electromagnetic spectrum. Commonly used for fiber optics and air transmission over short distances.

Image processing The capture and manipulation of images in order to enhance or extract information.

Input The process of entering information into a computer.

Interface The connection between two hardware devices that enables the devices to exchange data.

Interpolation The calculation of smooth transitions from one value to the next.

ISO International Standards Organization. The ISO is responsible for setting data communications standards nationally and internationally.

ITV Interactive Television. ITV is an enhancement to standard television broadcast, which allows viewers to communicate with broadcasters or vendors, or access other services through their television sets.

Jaguar A 64-bit gaming system from Atari Corporation. Jaguar offers 24-bit graphics, along with realtime 3-D graphics and texture mapping. (*See also:* **64-bit, 24-bit color, 3-D graphics, and Texture mapping.**)

Kilobyte A unit of storage that represents 1,000 bytes. Often referred to as "K" as in 640K. (*See also:* **Byte.**)

LCD Liquid Crystal Display. A device that takes advantage of the unusual properties of liquid crystal to display graphics. By increasing the density of the pixels, and adding backlighting and color filters, LCDs can project color images. (*See also:* **Pixel.**)

LSI Large Scale Integration. LSI is a technology used in integrated circuits. LSI is the fabrication, on one chip, of up to 100,000 transistors. (*See also:* **VLSI.**)

Luminance The part of the video signal for televisions that determines the brightness level of the resulting image. NTSC television signal is made up of two Luminance signals and one Chrominance signal. (*See also:* **Chrominance, NTSC.**)

Lynx A portable cartridge-based gaming system from Atari Corporation. It has a high-resolution LCD color display and uses an 8-bit microprocessor.

LZW Lempel Ziv Welch. A compression algorithm based on work done by Abraham Lempel, Jacob Ziv, and Terry Welch. The algorithm is commonly used for compressing graphics files. (*See also:* **Compression.**)

Megabyte A unit of storage that represents 1 million bytes. Often referred to as a Meg or M. (*See also:* **Byte.**)

Memory Electronic chips that store patterns which the CPU can decipher into letters and numbers.(*See also:* **CPU, RAM.**)

Menu bar Menu bars are used in graphical user interfaces to organize groups of commands in menus along the top of a programs window. (*See also:* **Menus, Graphical User Interface.**)

Menus A group of related commands provided on a list that drops down from a menu bar. Menus are used in graphical user interfaces (*See also:* **Menu bar, Graphical User Interface.**)

Microprocessor See CPU.

MIDI Musical Instrument Digital Interface. MIDI is an industry standard protocol for the electronic exchange of information between musical synthesizers and computers.

MIT The Massachusetts Institute of Technology.

Morph points Points placed on an image which can be moved to warp or distort the image during a morphing sequence. (*See also:* **Morphing.**)

Morphing A method of distorting images or sequences from one state to another. Two types of morphing exist—transition morphing and distortion morphing. Transition morphing transforms one scene into a different one. Distortion morphing manipulates a single scene by warping it. Sometimes called warping. (*See also:* **Distortion morphing, Transition morphing.**)

Mouse A common input device used to move a cursor around on the computer screen. Usually a small hand-sized plastic device with one or more buttons on the top and a roller ball underneath that detects movement as it is pushed across a desktop.

MPC The Multimedia Personal Computer standard set by the MPC council for IBM-compatible personal computers. (*See also:* **Multimedia.**)

MPEG A standard developed by the Motion Picture Expert Group for compressing and storing digital video sequences. The standard allows for high enough compression to provide for CD-ROM playback. (*See also:* **Digital video, FMV, CD-ROM.**)

Multimedia A software program (or game) that makes use of multiple media, such as sound, graphics, text, and video. (*See also:* **MPC.**)

Multiplayer A home CD player capable of playing multiple types of CDs, such as multimedia, audio, CD+Graphics, and Photo CDs. (*See also:* **Multimedia, 3DO, CD-I, CD-ROM.**)

Multisession CD-ROM A new type of CD-ROM and CD-ROM drive technology that allows CD-ROMs to be recorded during multiple sessions or at different times. A standard record could be considered single session, since it is created in one pass. If a record were multisession, an audio store could continue adding more songs to it until it was full. Photo CDs are multisession because you can continue to add images to them until they are full. (*See also:* **CD-ROM, Photo CD, and CD-ROM XA.**)

NES The Nintendo Entertainment System. An 8-bit home gaming system that uses cartridges. (*See also:* **8-bit, CPU.**)

NTSC The National Television Standards Committee. NTSC also stands for the standard the committee created for broadcast television in the 1950s. The NTSC standard is used by all televisions, videodisc players, VCRs, broadcast, and cable TV in the U.S. and some foreign countries.

NVOD Near Video On Demand. NVOD, an early step in interactive television, enables viewers to watch pay-per-view movies that start at very frequent intervals—15 to 30 minutes, for example. This is an advantage over current pay-per-view methods, in which viewers must wait until a current movie ends before watching the next one. (*See also:* **VOD.**)

On-screen controls/On-screen graphics ITV controls/graphics that appear on the television screen as opposed to being included on a separate or hand-held unit. These graphics might be an electronic TV guide or electronic ATM machine. (*See also:* **ITV.**)

One-Off disc See CD-WO.

ONU Optical Network Unit. ONU is a device that converts the optical signals of fiber optic cabling into electrical signals of today's common copper-based cabling. (*See also:* **Fiber optics.**)

Output The process of getting data out of a computer. Printing is one form of output, sending images or pictures to a computer screen is another. The opposite of Input.

Password Special codes that are given to players to allow them to resume playing at their previous stopping point. When the player resumes a game, and enters the correct password, they begin play at the level corresponding with that password.

PDP-1 Programmed Data Processor. The PDP was the first computer created by Digital Equipment Corp. (DEC) in 1959. It had an 18-bit CPU and cost $120,000.

Photo CD A new technology developed by Eastman Kodak to scan high resolution 35mm or professional quality images and write them to a CD-ROM. The resulting PCD (Photo CD) can be viewed with consumer players that attach to televisions. They can also be viewed on personal computers that have multisession compatible CD-ROM drives. (*See also:* **CD-ROM, Multisession CD-ROM.**)

Pixel A picture element. The smallest element of an image that has been digitized into a computer. The more pixels per square inch, the higher the resolution of the image will be.

Pixellization The effect when the pixels that make up an image are so large that they are visible.

Polygon In computer graphics, a multisided object that can be moved around the screen and scaled (simulating movement in 3-D space). Ploygons can be filled with a solid color or wallpapered with a bitmap in the case of texture mapping. (*See also:* **3-D graphics, Bitmap, and Texture mapping.**)

Project Reality An announced venture by Nintendo and Silicon Graphics to jointly develop a very high-performance gaming system with 64-bit CPU capabilities and realtime 3-D graphics with texture mapping. (*See also:* **64-bit, 3-D graphics and Texture mapping.**)

QWERTY The acronym used to describe the standard typwriter and computer keyboard used today. The phrase QWERTY is derived from the first six letters as read from left to right across the top of the keyboard.

Random Access Memory (RAM) The working memory of a computer into which the computer stores programs and data so that the CPU can access them directly. RAM can be written to and erased over and over again. (*See also:* **CPU, Memory.**)

Raster Graphics Computer graphics in which the images are stored as groups of pixels as opposed to vector graphics which are stored as groups of lines. (*See also:* **File format, Vector graphics.**)

Ray tracing A technique of tracing how rays of light would bounce and reflect around a 3-D model within computer memory. Ray tracing produces very realistic shadows and reflections, as well as transparent objects. (*See also:* **3-D graphics.**)

Read Only Memory (ROM) Identical to Random Access Memory except that Read Only Memory can only be written to once. ROM usually stores programs vital to the operation of personal computer. (*See also:* **Memory, RAM.**)

Realtime A definition of speed, in which data or graphics is processed on-the-fly as it enters the computer or is generated by the computer. Realtime 3-D graphics enables a user to rotate or move 3-D objects while the screen is instantaneously updated. (*See also:* **3-D graphics.**)

Render To create a new image based on a transformation of an existing one- or three-dimensional scene. (*See also:* **Morphing.**)

Resolution 1. For computer displays, their height and width in pixels. 2. For images, the height and width in pixels. 3. For output devices, the dots-per-inch the devices can produce.

Retrace The return of the electron beam (inside a computer display) back to the upper-left corner after making one pass. It can also refer to the return to the left side of the screen from the right.

RGB (Red, Green, Blue) A color model that describes color based on percentages of red, green, and blue present in an image. RGB is commonly used by computers and television to produce simulated color. (*See also:* **Color.**)

RISC Reduced Instruction Set Chip. RISC is a special CPU that has fewer instructions and runs at a higher frequency. It is able to perform many more computations that CISC based CPUs. (*See also:* **CPU, CISC.**)

RPG Role Playing Game. RPG is any game where the player acts out a real-life situation and the computer character has attributes such as strength, dexterity, wisdom, and so forth. RPGs are commonly based on medieval themes.

Run Length Encoding (RLE) A method of compressing data by replacing long consecutive runs of numbers with the number and a count of how many times it repeats. (*See also:* **Compression.**)

Saturn An announced Sega video game system with 64-bit CPU capabilities and realtime 3-D graphics with texture mapping. (*See also:* **64-bit, 3-D graphics and Texture mapping.**)

Scanline A single line of pixels displayed on a computer monitor or scanned in by a scanner. (*See also:* **Scanner.**)

Scan rate 1. A measurement of how many times per second a scanner samples an image. 2. A measurement for the speed that a monitor's electron beam scans from left to right and top to bottom.

Scanner A hardware device that converts light from a source picture or transparency into a digital representation.

Scroll The direction of movement in a game, sometimes called scroller. Games can be side-scrollers (moving left and right), vertical-scrollers (moving up and down) or multi-scrolling (up and down as well as left and right).

SegaCD An upgrade package to the Sega Genesis game system that allows it to play CD-ROM–based games and CD-DAs. (*See also:* **Genesis, CD-ROM, CD-DA.**)

Selection An area of computer data that is currently chosen to perform some type of operation.

Selection border An option used to select only the border of the current selection. (*See also:* **Selection.**)

Service providers Companies that offer services, goods, or products over ITV networks. These may include restaurants, merchants, schools, broadcasters, banks, and so forth. (*See also:* **ITV.**)

Set-top box The electronic device that sits on top of a television set and decodes cable television signals. In the case of ITV, the set-top box also encodes a viewer request for transmission back to the broadcasters. (*See also:* **ITV.**)

Shareware Computer software that is copyrighted but still made available to anyone on a trial basis. Persons who keep and use the software are expected to pay a registration fee to the author.

Shooter A video game with a continuously scrolling background in which the main objective is to shoot wave after wave of enemies.

Slider A method of entering numeric values used in graphical user interfaces. By moving the slider back and forth, numeric values can be adjusted.

SNES The Super Nintendo Entertainment System. A 16-bit home gaming system from Nintendo. (*See also:* **16-bit, CPU.**)

Speech recognition The use of a computer to input and analyze the sound from a human voice. The words spoken are then detected and stored or acted upon.

Status bar An information bar common in graphical user interfaces. Status bars display important information about the current status of the document you are working on. (*See also:* **Graphical User Interface.**)

Stereoscopic An image or viewing system that appears to produce a three-dimensional scene that gives the illusion of depth. Anaglyphs are stereoscopic. (*See also:* **Anaglyphs.**)

STN Super Twist Nematic. STN is an LCD technology that makes color LCDs possible by increasing the density of pixels on the display screen. (*See also:* **LCD.**)

Supercomputers Very high-speed, high-capacity computers. Supercomputers are the fastest computers in the world.

Texture mapping The process of applying a two-dimensional image to a 3-D object defined within the computer. Similar to wrapping wall paper around the object. This enables computer artists to simulate items like wood by scanning in an image of wood grain and having the computer texture map the wood to a 3-D model of a board. (*See also:* **3-D graphics and Polygon.**)

Title Bar The top bar across any window in a graphical user interface. The title bar usually includes the name of the program or data file that you are currently working with. By clicking and dragging a title bar you can move the active window. (*See also:* **Graphical User Interface.**)

Transistor An electronic switch or gate. When many transistors are used together, information can be encoded in the patterns of open and closed gates. (*See also:* **Bit, Byte.**)

Transition morphing Cross-fading from one image or sequence to another while warping the two images to appear as if they are transforming into one another. (*See also:* **Distortion morphing, Morphing.**)

True color Color that has a color depth of 24-bits (16.7 million colors). (*See also:* **Color Depth, 24-bit color.**)

Turbo Duo A CD-ROM–based home gaming machine from Turbo Technologies that also supports cartridges. It uses an 8-bit CPU. (*See also:* **CPU, 8-bit, CD-ROM.**)

Turbo Express Turbo Technologies' portable cartridge-based gaming unit. It uses an 8-bit CPU and offers a high-resolution color LCD display. (*See also:* **CPU, 8-bit, LCD.**)

Undo Option A command that undoes the last operation performed.

Vector Graphics Graphics that are based on individual lines from point A to point B. Vector graphics represent line drawing well, but cannot represent a photograph. For photographs you need to use *raster graphics* (*See also:* **File Format, Raster Graphics.**)

VESA Video Electronics Standard Association. VESA is an organization that sets standards for IBM-compatible personal computer systems.

VLSI Very Large Scale Integration. VLSI is the fabrication of more that 100,000 transitors on a single integrated circuit chip. (*See also:* **LSI.**)

VOD Video On Demand. VOD is an ITV technology where the viewer can request a movie from his set-top box and then watch it. Full VCR functionality is available with stop, rewind, fast forward, pause, and so forth. (*See also:* **NVOD, ITV.**)

Voxel Volume pixel. Voxel is similar to a pixel but instead represents a color in 3-D space as opposed to 2-D space. Voxels are used in flight simulators to represent 3-D objects. (*See also:* **Pixel, 3-D graphics.**)

WIMP Windows, Icon, Menus, and Pointing device, a derogatory reference to GUIs. (*See also:* **Graphical User Interface.**)

Windows The graphical user interface standard for IBM PCs and compatibles.

X The common reference for the width of an image.

Y The common reference for the height of an image.

Z The common reference for the depth of a three-dimensional scene.

R

Resources

The following resource appendix includes information on related companies, books, magazines, trade shows, and software developers. This list of resources is by no means exhaustive, but will help you get more information about the world of interactive entertainment.

BOOKS

The following books provide valuable historical information as well as insight into the interactive entertainment industry.

Brand, Stewart. *The MIT Media Lab*. New York: Penguin, 1987.

Cohen, Scott. *Zap! The Rise and Fall of Atari*. New York: McGraw Hill, 1984.

Levy, Steven. *Hackers: Heroes of the Computer Revolution*. New York: Bantam Doubleday Dell, 1984.

Sheff, David. *Game Over: How Nintendo Zapped an American Industry, Captured Your Dollars, and Enslaved Your Children*. New York: Random House, 1993.

MAGAZINES

Below is a list of magazines that cover the field of interactive entertainment.

CD-I World
Parker Taylor & Company
49 Bayview St., Suite 200
Camden, ME 04843
(207) 236-8524
Fax (207) 236-6452

CD-ROM Today
GP Publications, Inc.
300-A S. Westgate Drive
Greensboro, NC 27407
(919) 852-6711
Fax (919) 632-1165

CD-ROM World
Meckler Corporation
11 Ferry Lane West
Westport, CT 06880
(203) 226-6967

Computer Game Review
Sendia Publishing Group, Inc.
1920 Highland Avenue, Suite 222
Lombard, IL 60148

Computer Games Strategy Plus
Strategy Plus Inc.
P.O. Box 21
Hancock, VT 05748
(800) 283-3542

Computer Gaming World
Ziff-Davis Publishing Company
130 Chaparral Ct., Suite 260
Anaheim Hills, CA 92808
(714) 283-3000
Fax (714) 283-3444

Computer Player
L.F.P. Inc.
9171 Wilshire Blvd., Suite 300
Beverly Hills, CA 90210
(310) 858-7100

Diehard Game Fan
18612 Ventura Blvd.
Tarzana, CA 91356

Electronic Entertainment
Infotainment World, Inc.
951 Mariner's Island Blvd., Suite 700
San Mateo, CA 94404

Electronic Games
Decker Publications, Inc.
1920 Highland Ave., Suite 222
Lombard, IL 60148

Electronic Gaming Monthly
Sendai Publishing Group, Inc.
1920 Highland Ave., Suite 222
Lombard, IL 60148

Electronic Gaming Retail News
Sendai Publishing Group, Inc.
1920 Highland Ave., Suite 222
Lombard, IL 60148

Full Throttle
9420 Bunsen Parkway, Suite 300
Louisville, KY 40220
(800) 223-8720
Fax (502) 491-8050

Game Informer
Sunrise Publications
10120 W. 76th Street
Eden Prairie, MN 55344
(612) 946-7245

Game Players
GP Publications, Inc.
300-A South Westgate Drive
Greensboro, NC 27407
(919) 852-6711
Fax (919) 632-1165

Game Pro
Infotainment World, Inc.
951 Mariner's Island Blvd., Suite 700
San Mateo, CA 94404
(800) 337-PLAY

InterAction
Sierra On-Line, Inc.
P.O. Box 485
Coarsegold, CA 93614
(209) 683-4468

Interactive Television Report
Intercor, Inc.
575 Anton Blvd., Suite 450
Costa Mesa, CA 92626
(714) 557-8800
Fax (714) 557-5445

Interactive Update
Alexander & Associates
38 E. 29th Street, 10th Fl.
New York, NY 10016
(212) 684-2333

Mega Play
Sendai Publishing Group, Inc.
1920 Highland Ave., Suite 222
Lombard, IL 60148

Morph's Outpost
125 Lombardi Lane
Orinda, CA 94563
(510) 254-3145

Multimedia World
501 Second Street
San Francisco, CA 94107
(415) 281-8650
Fax (415) 281-3915

New Media
Hypermedia Communications, Inc.
901 Mariner's Island Blvd., Suite 365
San Mateo, CA 94404

Newtype Gaming
427 Merchant Street
San Francisco, CA 94111
(415) 788-4263

Play Meter Magazine
Skybird Publishing Company
6600 Fleur de Lis
New Orleans, LA 70124

Play Right
Infotainment World, Inc.
951 Mariner's Island Blvd., Suite 700
San Mateo, CA 94404
(800) 337-PLAY

Sega Force
Sega of America Inc.
130 Shoreline Drive
Redwood City, CA 94065
(415) 508-2800
Fax (415) 802-1448

SEGA Visions
Sega of America Inc.
130 Shoreline Drive
Redwood City, CA 94065
(415) 508-2800
Fax (415) 802-1448

Strategy Plus
P.O. Box 21
Hancock, VT 05748
(802) 860-6467
Fax (802) 860-6009

S.W.A.T. Pro
Infotainment World, Inc.
951 Mariner's Island Blvd., Suite 700
San Mateo, CA 94404
(800) 377-PLAY

Turbo Force
P.O. Box 7597
Red Oak, IA 51591-0597
(800) 444-2884

Video Games
L.F.P. Inc.
9171 Wilshire Blvd., Suite 300
Beverly Hills, CA 90210
(310) 858-7100

Wired
Wired USA Ltd.
544 Second Street
San Francisco, CA 94107-1427
(415) 904-0660

ORGANIZATIONS AND CONFERENCES

A number of organizations and professional associations offer conferences and expositions throughout the year. They also publish literature and provide many services for professionals in the field of interactive entertainment.

Amusement & Music Operators Association
401 N. Michigan Ave
Chicago, IL 60611
(312) 245-1021

Abbreviated: AMOA

Electronic and Entertainment Expo
Knowledge Industry Publications
701 Westchester Ave
White Plains, NY 10604
(800) 800-5474

Abbreviated: E3

Electronic Industries Association - Consumer Electronics Show
2001 Pennsylvania Ave, NW
Washington, DC 20006-1813
(202) 457-8700

Abbreviated: EIA - CES

IEEE Data Communications
10662 Los Vaqueros Circle
Los Alamitos, CA 90720
(714) 821-8380

IICS
11251 Morrison Street, Suite 205
North Hollywood, CA 91601
(310) 312-9060

Interactive Information Expo
Bruno Blenheim Inc.
Fort Lee Executive Park
One Executive Drive
Fort Lee, NJ 07024
(800) 829-3976

Abbreviated: I2

Sybold Seminars
P.O. Box 6710
Malibu, CA 90264-6710
(800) 433-5200

National Cable Show - Miami; May 1994

ONLINE SERVICES

The following online services can be accessed by any personal computer with a modem. All these services have online games.

America Online
8619 Westwood Center Drive
Vienna, VA 22182-2285
(703) 448-8700

CompuServe
5000 Arlington Centre Blvd.
P.O. Box 20212
Columbus, OH 43220
(800) 848-8199

Delphi
General Videotex Corporation
3 Blackstone Street
Cambridge, MA 02139
(800) 544-4005

GEnie
GE Company Information Services Division
401 N Washington St.
Rockville, MD 20850
(800) 638-9636

ImagiNation Network, The
41486 Old Barn Way
Oakhurst, CA 93644
(209) 642-0700
Fax (209) 683-3633

Multi-Players Game Network (MPG-Net)
P.O. Box 2310
Key West, FL 33045
(800) 245-0317
Fax (305) 292-7835

Prodigy Services Co.
445 Hamilton Ave.
White Plains, NY 10601
(800) 776-0845
Fax (914) 684-0278

INTERACTIVE ENTERTAINMENT PROVIDERS

The following companies provide Interactive Entertainment software and hardware.

Absolute Entertainment, Inc.
251 Rock Road, P.O. Box 116
Glen Rock, NJ 07452
(201) 818-4800
Fax (201) 818-3324

Access Software, Inc.
4910 W. Amelia Earhart Drive
Salt Lake City, UT 84116
(800) 800-4880
Fax (801) 359-2968

Acclaim Entertainment, Inc.
71 Audrey Ave.
Oyster Bay, NY 11771
(516) 624-8888
Fax (516) 624-2885

Accolade
5300 Stevens Creek Blvd.
San Jose, CA 95129
(408) 985-1700
Fax (408) 246-0885

Activision Studios
11440 San Vicente Boulevard
Los Angeles, CA 90049
(310) 207-4500
Fax (310) 820-6131

A.L.S. Industries, Inc.
P.O. Box 6513
1942 W. Artesia Blvd.
Torrance, CA 90504-0513
(310) 532-9262
Fax (310) 329-0982

American Laser Games
4801 Lincoln Road, NE
Albuquerque, NM 87109
(505) 880-1718
Fax (505) 880-1557

American Sammy Corp.
901 Cambridge Drive
Elk Grove, IL 60007
(708) 364-9787
Fax (708) 364-9831

American Softworks International Corp.
24 Richmond Hill Ave., 8th Fl.
Stamford, CT 06901
(203) 327-6545
Fax (203) 327-3676

American Technos, Inc.
19200 Stevens Creek Blvd., Suite 120
Cupertino, CA 95014
(408) 996-8736
Fax (408) 996-8736

Aris Multimedia Entertainment, Inc.
4444 Via Marina, Suite 811
Marina del Rey, CA 90292
(310) 821-0234

Arnowitz Studio
650 E. Blithedale Ave., #A
Mill Valley, CA 94941
(415) 383-2878

Asciiware
366A Lakeside Drive
Foster City, CA 94404
(415) 570-6200
Fax (415) 570-6433

Atari Corporation
1196 Borregas
Sunnyvale, CA 94088-1302
(408) 745-2000
Fax (408) 745-2088

Atari Games
675 Sycamore Drive
Milpitas, CA 95035
(408) 434-3748
Fax (408) 434-3776

Atlus Software
17145 Von Karman Ave., Suite 110
Irvine, CA 92714
(714) 263-0582
Fax (714) 757-1288

AT&T
5 Wood Hollow Road
Parsippany, NJ 07054
(201) 581-4800
Fax (201) 503-0865

Avalon Hill Game Company
4517 Harford Rd.
Baltimore, MD 21214
(800) 999-3222
Fax (410) 254-0991

Aztech Labs
46707 Fremont Blvd.
Fremont, CA 94538
(510) 623-8988
Fax (510) 623-8989

Baker & Taylor, Inc.
3850 Royal Ave.
Simi Valley, CA 93065
(800) 775-4100
Fax (805) 522-7300

Bethesda Softworks
1370 Picard Drive, Suite 120
Rockville, MD 20850
(301) 926-8300
Fax (301) 926-8010

Brøderbund Software, Inc.
17 Paul Drive
San Rafael, CA 94903-2101
(415) 492-3299
Fax (415) 492-3154

Bullet-Proof Software
8337 154th Ave. N.E.
Redmond, WA 98052
(206) 861-9200

Bureau of Electronic Publishing, Inc.
141 New Road
Parsippany, NJ 07054
(201) 808-2700
Fax (201) 808-2676

Capcom U.S.A.
3303 Scott Blvd.
Santa Clara, CA 95054
(408) 727-0400
Fax (408) 496-5720

Capitol Multimedia
2121 Wisconsin Ave., N.W.
Washington, DC 20007
(202) 625-0204
Fax (202) 625-0210

Capstone Software
7200 N.W. 19th St. #500
Miami, FL 33126
(305) 591-5900

CH Products
970 Park Center Drive
Vista, CA 92083
(619) 598-2518
Fax (619) 598-2524

Champion Glove
2200 East Ovid
DesMoines, IA 50313
(515) 265-2551
Fax (515) 265-7210

Chaos Technology
275 Community Drive
Lake Success, NY 11021
(516) 482-4000
Fax (516) 482-4057

Codemasters
Lower Farm House
Southam, Warwickshire
England
011-44-926-81-4132
Fax 011-44-926-81-7595

Commodore Business Machines, Inc.
1200 Wilson Drive
Brandywine Industrial Park
West Chester, PA 19380
(800) 66-AMIGA
Fax (215) 431-9465

Compact Publishing, Inc.
5141 MacArthur Blvd., N.W.
Washington, DC 20016
(206) 244-4770

Compton's New Media
2320 Camino Vida Roble
Carlsbad, CA 92009
(619) 929-2500
Fax (619) 929-2555

Compu-Teach
16451 Redmond Way, Suite 137-C
Redmond, WA 98502-4482
(206) 885-0517 x13
Fax (206) 883-9169

Core Design
Tradewinds House
69/71A Ashbourne Road
Derby DE3
011-44-332-297-797
Fax 011-44-332-381-511

Creative Labs, Inc.
1901 McCarthy Blvd.
Milpitas, CA 95035
(800) 998-5227
Fax (408) 428-6611

Crystal Dynamics Inc.
2460 Embarcadero Way
Palo Alto, CA 94303
(415) 858-4990
Fax (415) 858-3640

Culture Brain USA, Inc.
18133 N.E. 68th Street, Building D-130
Redmond, WA 98052
(206) 882-2339
Fax (206) 882-2320

Cyberdreams, Inc.
21243 Ventura Boulevard Suite 208
Woodland Hills, CA 91364
(818) 348-3711
Fax (818) 348-3772

Data East
1850 Little Orchard St.
San Jose, CA 95125
(408) 286-7080
Fax (408) 286-0842

Davidson & Associates, Inc.
19840 Pioneer Ave.
Torrance, CA 90503
(800) 545-7677
Fax (310) 793-0601

DC True
1840 Oak Ave.
Evanston, IL 60201-3686
(708) 866-1804
Fax (708) 866-1808

DigiTek Software
1916 Twisting Lane
Wesley Chapel, FL 33543
(800) 783-8023
Fax (813) 973-7888

Discovery Channel, The
7700 Wisconsin Ave.
Bethesda, MD 20814
(301) 986-0444
Fax (301) 986-9537

Domark Software Ltd.
1900 South Norfolk Street, Suite 202
San Mateo, CA 94403
(415) 513-8929
Fax (415) 571-0437

Dr. T's Music Software, Inc.
124 Crescent Rd.
Needham, MA 02194
(800) 989-6434
Fax (617) 455-1460

DTMC Inc.
270 Convention Way, Suite 202
Redwood City, CA 94063
(415) 367-9891
Fax (415) 368-4829

Dynamix, Inc.
1600 Mill Race Dr.
Eugene, OR 97404
(800) 326-6654
Fax (503) 344-1754

Dynasound Organizer, Inc.
1801 Old Hwy. 8, Suite 124
New Brighton, MN 55112
(612) 635-0828
Fax (612) 635-0927

Ebook Inc.
32970 Alvarado Niles Road, Suite 704
Union City, CA 94587
(510) 429-1331
Fax (510) 429-1394

Edmark
P.O. Box 3218
Redmond, WA 98073
(206) 556-8486
Fax (206) 556-8998

EduQuest/IBM
411 Northside Parkway
Atlanta, GA 30327
(404) 238-1233
Fax (404) 238-4301

Electro Brain Corporation
573 East 300 South
Salt Lake City, UT 84102
(801) 531-1867

Electronic Arts
1450 Fashion Island Blvd.
San Mateo, CA 94404
(800) 245-4525
Fax (415) 571-7995

Elpin Software
45 S. Park Victoria, Suite 401
Milpitas, CA 95035
(408) 956-0720
Fax (408) 956-0729

Enix America Corp.
2679 151st Place N.E.
Redmond, WA 98052
(206) 885-9611
Fax (206) 883-2197

Extreme Entertainment Group
BigNet USA
2755 Campus Drive, Suite 130
San Mateo, CA 94403
(415) 525-3000
Fax (415) 525-3010

Fujisankei Communications International - FCI
150 East 52nd Street, 34th Fl.
New York, NY 10022
(212) 753-8100
Fax (212) 688-0392

Future Trends
1508 Osprey Drive, Suite 103
DeSoto, TX 75115
(214) 224-3228
Fax (214) 224-3228

GameTek
2999 Northeast 191st St., Suite 800
North Miami Beach, FL 33180
(305) 935-3995
Fax (305) 932-8651

Gazelle Technologies / Educorp
7434 Trade Street
San Diego, CA 92121
(619) 636-9999

HeartBeat
700 Canal St.
Stamford, CT 06902
(203) 328-3003
Fax (203) 328-3004

Hi-Tech Expressions
584 Broadway
New York, NY 10012
(800) 447-6543
Fax (212) 941-1521

Hudson Soft USA, Inc.
400 Oyster Point Blvd. #515
South San Francisco, CA 94080-8540
(415) 871-8540

Humongous Entertainment, Inc.
12930 N. E. 178th St.
Woodinville, WA 98072
(206) 487-0505
Fax (206) 486-9494

Hyacinth
5508 Chimany Hollow
Norcross, GA 30093
(404) 416-6321

HyperGlot Software Co., Inc.
P.O. Box 10746, 5108-D Kingston Pike
Knoxville, TN 37919-0746
(800) 800-8270
Fax (615) 588-6569

IBM Multimedia Publishing Studio
1374 W. Peachtree St., Suite 200
Atlanta, GA 30309
(404) 877-1313

Icom Simulations, Inc. / Viacom New Media
648 S. Wheeling Road
Wheeling, IL 60090
(708) 520-4440
Fax (708) 459-7456

Imagineer
15317 N.E. 90th St.
Redmond, WA 98052
(206) 867-5790
Fax (206) 867-5792

Impressions Software
222 Third Street, Suite 0234
Cambridge, MA 02142
(617) 225-0500
Fax (617) 225-0993

Innovation Technologies
1491 Boston Post Road
Old Saybrook, CT 06475
(203) 395-3087
Fax (203) 388-0084

InterActive Publishing Corp.
300 Airport Exec. Park
Spring Valley, NY 10977
(914) 426-0400
Fax (914) 426-2606

Interplay Productions, Inc.
17922 Fitch Ave.
Irvine, CA 92714
(714) 553-6655
Fax (714) 252-2820

IREM America Corp.
8335 154th Ave, N.E.
Redmond, WA 98052
(206) 882-1093
Fax (206) 883-8038

Jaleco USA, Inc.
685 Chaddick Drive
Wheeling, IL 60090
(708) 215-1811
Fax (708) 215-2642

JVC Musical Industries, Inc.
3800 Barham Blvd., Suite 305
Los Angeles, CA 90068
(213) 878-0101
Fax (213) 878-0202

Kaneko USA, Inc.
1370 Busch Parkway
Buffalo Grove, IL 60089
(708) 808-1370
Fax (708) 808-1375

Kemco
Westpark -D, 8415 154th Ave, N.E.
Redmond, WA 98052
(206) 869-8000
Fax (206) 869-8080

Knowledge Adventure, Inc.
4502 Dyer Street
La Crescenta, CA 91214
(818) 542-4200
Fax (818) 542-4205

Koei Corp.
One Bay Plaza, 1350 Bayshore Hwy., Suite 540
Burlingame, CA 94010
(415) 348-0200
Fax (415) 348-8967

Konami, Inc.
900 Deerfield Pkwy,
Buffalo Grove, IL 60089
(708) 215-5100
Fax (708) 215-5122

Labtec Enterprises, Inc.
11010 N.E. 37th Circle, Unit #110
Vancouver, WA 98682
(206) 896-2000
Fax (206) 896-2020

Learning Company, The
6493 Kaiser Blvd.
Fremont, CA 94555
(510) 792-2101

Lewis Gloob Toys, Inc.
500 Forbes Blvd. South
San Francisco, CA 94080
(415) 952-1678
Fax (415) 952-7084

LucasArts Entertainment Company
Lucasfilm Games
P.O. Box 10307
San Rafael, CA 94912
(415) 721-3334
Fax (415) 721-3344

Macmillan New Media
124 Mt. Auburn St.
Cambridge, MA 02138
(800) 342-1338

Mallard Software, Inc.
3207 Justin Rd.
Flower Mound, TX 75028
(800) WEB-FEET
Fax (214) 539-5330

Maxis
2 Theatre Square, Suite 230
Orinda, CA 94563-3346
(510) 254-9700
Fax (510) 253-3736

MECC
6160 Summit Drive North
Minneapolis, MN 55430-4003
(612) 569-1692
Fax (612) 569-1551

Media Vision, Inc.
47300 Bayside Pkwy.
Fremont, CA 94538
(800) 348-7116
Fax (510) 770-8648

Megatech Software
1606 Lockness Place
Torrance, CA 90501
(310) 539-6452
Fax (310) 539-8450

Mentrix Software, Inc.
21213B Hawthorne Blvd. #5322
Torrance, CA 90509
(310) 517-9817
Fax (310) 517-9914

Merit Software
13635 Gamma Rd.
Dallas, TX 75244-4407
(800) 238-4277
Fax (214) 385-8205

MicroLeague Interactive Software
U.O.P. 201 Bellevue Bldg
Newark, DE 19702
(302) 368-9990
Fax (302) 368-8600

Microlytics, Inc.
Two Tobey Village Office Park
Pittsford, NY 14534
(800) 828-6293
Fax (716) 248-3868

MicroProse Software
180 Lakefront Drive
Hunt Valley, MD 21030
(401) 771-1151
Fax (301) 771-1174

Microsoft Corp.
One Microsoft Way
Redmond, WA 98052-6399
(800) 426-9400
Fax (206) 883-8101

MindCraft Software, Inc.
2291 205th St., Suite 201
Torrance, CA 90501
(800) 525-4933
Fax (310) 320-1522

Mindplay
3130 N. Dodge Blvd.
Tucson, AZ 85716
(800) 221-7911
Fax (602) 322-0363

Morgan Interactive, Inc.
160 Pine St., Suite 509
San Francisco, CA 94104
(415) 693-9596
Fax (415) 693-9597

Multicom Publishing
1100 Olive Way, Suite 1250
Seattle, WA 98101
(510) 777-1211
Fax (510) 777-1311

Namco Hometek, Inc.
150 Charcot Ave., Suite A
San Jose, CA 95131-1102
(408) 922-0712
Fax (408) 321-0618

National Geographic Society
1145 17th Street, N.W.
Washington, DC 20036
(202) 857-7675

New World Computing, Inc.
20301 Ventura Blvd., Suite 200
Woodland Hills, CA 91364
(818) 999-0606
Fax (818) 593-3455

Ninga Software Corp.
736 8th Ave., SW, Suite 330
Calgary, AL, CD T2P 1H4
(800) 265-5555
Fax (403) 265-5760

Nintendo of America, Inc.
4820 150th Ave, N.E.
Redmond, WA 98052
(206) 882-2040
Fax (206) 882-3585

NovaLogic, Inc.
19510 Ventura Blvd., Suite 200
Tarzana, CA 91356
(818) 774-0600
Fax (818) 774-0684

Ocean Isle Software, Inc.
1201 19th Place, 2nd Fl.
Vero Beach, FL 32960
(800) 677-6232
Fax (407) 770-4779

Ocean of America, Inc.
1855 O'Toole Ave.
La Miranda, CA 90638
(408) 954-0201
Fax (408) 954-0243

Origin Systems, Inc.
110 Wild Basin Road, Suite 230
Austin, TX 78746
(512) 328-5490

Panasonic Corp.
Matsushita Electric Corp. of America
One Panasonic Way
Secaucus, NJ 07094
(201) 348-7000
Fax (201) 348-7209

Paramount Interactive
700 Hansen Way
Palo Alto, CA 94304
(800) 821-1177
Fax (415) 813-8055

Park Place Systems
5421 Avenida Encinas
Carlsbad, CA 92008
(619) 929-2010 x211
Fax (619) 929-2035

Parker Brothers
50 Dunham Road
Beverly, MA 01915
(508) 921-3160
Fax (508) 921-3521

Philips Interactive Media
11111 Santa Monica Blvd.
Los Angeles, CA 90025
(310) 444-6600
Fax (310) 478-4810

Pioneer Electronics USA, Inc.
2265 East 220th St.
Long Beach, CA 90810
(213) PIONEER
Fax (213) 952-2260

Pixel Perfect, Inc.
10460 S. Tropical Trail
Merritt Island, FL 32952
(800) 788-2099
Fax (407) 777-0323

PlayMates Toys, Inc.
16200 Trojan Way
La Miranda, CA 90638
(714) 739-1929
Fax (714) 739-7164

Pop Rocket, Inc.
P.O. Box 170460
San Francisco, CA 94117
(415) 731-9112

Presto Studios, Inc.
P.O. Box 262535
San Diego, CA 92196-2535
(619) 689-4895

Pride Plastics, Inc.
6320 Caballero Blvd.
Buena Park, CA 90620
(800) 833-7308
Fax (714) 739-2203

Psygnosis, Ltd.
Sony Electronic Publishing Co.
675 Massachusetts Ave.
Cambridge, MA 02139
(800) 438-7794
Fax (617) 497-6759

QQP
495 Highway 202
Flemington, NJ 08822
(908) 788-2799
Fax (908) 788-7684

Quadra Interactive, Inc.
701 Palomar Airport Rd., Suite 300
Carlsbad, CA 92009
(619) 931-4755
Fax (619) 931-0660

RazorSoft, Inc.
7416 N. Broadway, Suite A
Oklahoma City, OK 73116
(405) 843-3505
Fax (405) 843-8409

Reactor, Inc.
445 W. Erie, Suite 5B
Chicago, IL 60610
(312) 573-0800
Fax (312) 573-0891

Readysoft, Inc.
30 Weirheirm Court, Unit 2
Richmond Hill, Canada l4B 1B9
(416) 731-3589
Fax (416) 764-8867

Renovation Products, Inc.
4655 Old Ironsides Drive, Suite 265
Santa Clara, CA 95054
(408) 982-2700
Fax (408) 982-2710

Revell-Monogram
8601 Waukegan Road
Morton Grove, IL 60063
(708) 966-3500
Fax (708) 967-5857

Saddleback Graphics
12812 Garden Grove Blvd.
Garden Grove, CA 92643
(714) 741-7093
Fax (714) 741-7095

Sanctuary Woods Multimedia Corp.
1006 Government St.
Victoria, BC, CD V8W 1X7
(800) 665-2544
Fax (604) 388-4852

Sega of America, Inc.
130 Shoreline Dr.
Redwood City, CA 94065
(415) 508-2800
Fax (415) 802-1448

Seika Corp.
20000 Mariner Ave., Suite 100
Torrance, CA 90503
(310) 373-0404
Fax (310) 375-6394

Seta USA, Inc.
105 East Reno Ave., Suite 22
Las Vegas, NV 89119
(702) 795-7996
Fax (702) 795-8096

Sierra On-line, Inc.
Coarsegold, CA 93614
(209) 683-4468
Fax (209) 683-3924

Silicon Graphics, Inc.
2011 N. Shoreline Blvd.
Mountain View, CA 94043-1389
(800) 800-7441
Fax (415) 961-0595

Sims Co., Ltd.
Miyamura Building 6-1
Shimoochai 1-Chome
Shinjuku-ku, Tokyo
Japan
03-5389-6921
Fax 03-5389-7031

Sir-Tech Software
P.O. Box 245
Charleston Mall
Ogdensburg, NY 13669
(315) 393-6451
Fax (315) 393-1525

Software Toolworks, The
60 Leveroni Court
Novato, CA 94949
(415) 883-3000
Fax (415) 883-0298

Sony Electronic Publishing Co.
1 Lower Ragsdale Dr., Suite 160
Monterey, CA 93940
(800) 654-8802
Fax (408) 372-9267

Spectrum HoloByte, Inc.
2490 Mariner Square Loop
Alameda, CA 94501
(510) 522-3584
Fax (510) 522-3587

Spinnaker Software Corp.
201 Broadway, 6th Fl.
Cambridge, MA 02139-1901
(800) 323-8088
Fax (617) 494-1219

Spirit of Discovery
5421 Avenida Encinas
Carlsbad, CA 92008
(619) 929-2010 x211
Fax (619) 929-2035

Sport Sciences, Inc.
2075 Case Parkway South
Twinsburg, OH 44087
(216) 963-0660
Fax (216) 963-0661

Square Soft, Inc.
Westpark G-1, 8351 154th Ave, N.E.
Redmond, WA 98052
(206) 861-0101
Fax (206) 861-0505

Strategic Simulations, Inc.
675 Almanor Ave., Suite 201
Sunnyvale, CA 94086-2901
(408) 737-6800
Fax (408) 737-6814

Sublogic
501 Kenyon Road
Champaign, IL 61820
(217) 359-8482
Fax (217) 352-1472

Sunsoft
11165 Knott Ave.
Cypress, CA 90630
(714) 891-4500
Fax (714) 892-0150

Takara USA Corp.
230 5th Ave., Suite 1201-6
New York, NY 10001
(212) 689-1212
Fax (212) 689-6889

Tatio America Corp.
390 Holbrook Drive
Wheeling, IL 60090
(708) 520-9280
Fax (708) 520-1309

Technological Computer Innovations
255 N. Cherrywood Dr.
Lafayette, CO 80026-2726
(303) 673-9046
Fax (303) 673-9085

Tecmagik, Inc.
3 Lagoon Drive, Suite 160
Redwood City, CA 94065
(415) 637-1350
Fax (415) 637-1995

Tecmo, Inc.
Sequoia Commerce Center
19260 S. Van Ness Ave.
Torrance, CA 90501
(310) 787-2900
Fax (310) 787-3131

Tengen, Inc.
675 Sycamore Drive
Milipitas, CA 95035
(408) 473-9400
Fax (408) 435-7470

Texas Caviar
3933 Steck Ave., Suite B-115
Austin, TX 78759-8608
(512) 346-7887
Fax (512) 346-1393

T H Q, Inc.
5016 North Parkway Calabasas, Suite 100
Calabasas, CA 91302
(818) 591-1310
Fax (818) 591-1615

3DO Company
600 Galveston Drive
Redwood City, CA 94063
(415) 261-3000
Fax (415) 261-3120

3E
7946 Grand Ave.
Bainbridge Island, WA 98110
(206) 842-0913
Fax (206) 842-4208

Three-Sixty Pacific, Inc.
2105 S. Bascom Ave., Suite 165
Campbell, CA 95008
(408) 879-9144
Fax (408) 879-9739

Thrustmaster Inc.
10150 S.W. Nimbus Ave.
Portland, OR 97223-4337
(503) 639-3200
Fax (503) 620-8094

Time Works
625 Academy Drive
Northbrook, IL 60062
(708) 559-1399
Fax (708) 559-1399

Titus Software Corp.
20432 Corisco St.
Chatsworth, CA 91311
(818) 709-3692
Fax (818) 709-6537

Toy Headquarters, Inc.
5016 No. Parkway, Suite 100
Calabasas, CA 91302
(818) 591-1310
Fax (818) 591-1615

Tradewest
2400 South Hwy 75
Corsicana, TX
(903) 874-2683
Fax (408) 872-8000

Trilobyte, Inc.
Box 1412, 110 S. 3rd St.
Jacksonville, OR 97530
(503) 899-1113
Fax (503) 899-7114

TriMark Interactive
2644 30th Street
Santa Monica, CA 90405-3009
(310) 314-2000
Fax (310) 392-8170

Turbo Technologies, Inc.
6701 Center Drive West, Suite 500
Los Angeles, CA 90045
(310) 641-4622
Fax (310) 641-4626

Twin Dolphin Games, Inc.
590 Taylor Way, Suite B
Belmont, CA 94002-4032
(415) 637-9300
Fax (415) 637-9310

Tyco Toys
6000 Midatlantic Drive
Mt Laurel, NJ 08054
(609) 840-1562
Fax (609) 722-0431

UBI Soft, Inc.
1505 Bridgeway, Suite 105
Sausalito, CA 94965
(415) 332-8749
Fax (415) 332-8757

US Gold
303 Sacamento Street, 4th Fl.
San Francisco, CA 94111
(415) 693-0297
Fax (415) 693-0698

Velocity Development Corp.
1644 Colonial Pkwy.
Inverness, IL 60067
(800) 453-6126
Fax (708) 991-4408

Viacom New Media
648 S. Wheeling Rd.
Wheeling, IL 60090
(800) 877-4266
Fax (708) 459-7456

Vic Tokai, Inc.
22904 Lockness Ave.
Torrance, CA 90501
(310) 326-8880
Fax (310) 326-8300

Virgin Games
18061 Fitch Avenue
Irvine, CA 92714
(714) 833-8710
Fax (714) 833-8717

Voyager Co., The
578 Broadway, Suite 406
New York, NY 10012
(800) 446-2001
Fax (212) 431-5799

Voyetra Technologies
5 O'Dell Plaza
Yonkers, NY 10701-1406
(800) 233-9377
Fax (914) 966-1102

Walt Disney Computer Software, Inc.
500 S. Buena Vista St.,
Burbank Centre, 20th Fl.
Burbank, CA 91521-6385
(800) 688-1520
Fax (818) 846-0454

Wayzata Technology
P.O. Box 807
Grand Rapids, MI 55744
(800) 377-7321

Working Designs
1701 Clear Creek Road
Redding, CA 96001
(916) 243-3417
Fax (916) 243-3157

INTERACTIVE TELEVISION RELATED COMPANIES

The following companies are currently working on ITV technology, services and programming.

Apple Computer, Inc.
20525 Mariani Ave.
Cupertino, CA 95014
(800) 776-2333
Fax (408) 996-0275

AT&T
295 N. Maple Ave.
Basking Ridge, NJ 07960
(800) 242-6005

Bell Atlantic Corp.
14 Washington Rd., Bldg. 2
Princeton Junction, NJ 08550
(609) 936-2900
Fax (609) 936-2859

E*ON Coporation
1941 Roland Clarke Place
Reston, VA 22091-1405
(703) 715-8600
Fax (703) 715-8853

GeoWorks, Inc.
2150 Shattuck Ave.
Berkeley, CA 94704
(800) 772-0001
Fax (510) 644-0928

GTE
2385 Camino Vida Roble
Carlsbad, CA 92009
(619) 431-8801

ICTV, Inc.
280 Martin Avenue
Santa Clara, CA 95050-4320
(408) 562-9200
Fax (408) 986-9566

Info Telecom
Rue De La Foret BP 9
Vendenheim 67550
France
88694533

Interactive Network
1991 Landings Drive
Mountain View, CA 94043
(415) 960-1000
Fax (415) 960-3331

Interactive Network Television
400 Tamal Plaza, Suite 403
Corta Madera, CA 94925
(415) 924-6688

Interactive Systems
15275 S.W. Koll Parkway, Suite 3C
Beaverton, OR 97006
(503) 627-0149
Fax (503) 627-0149

LodgeNet Entertainment
808 West Avenue North
Sioux Falls, SD 57104
(800) 257-2345
Fax (605) 332-4592

Mark Goodson Productions
5750 Wilshire Blvd., #475W
Los Angeles, CA 90036
(213) 965-6500

Microsoft Corp.
One Microsoft Way
Redmond, WA 98052-6399
(800) 426-9400
Fax (206) 883-8101

Microware Systems Corp.
1900 Northwest 114th St.
Des Moines, IA 50325-7077
(800) 475-9000
Fax (515) 224-1352

Novell, Inc.
122 East 1700 South
Provo, UT 84606-6194
(800) 453-1267
Fax (801) 429-5775

NTN Communications
2121 Palomar Airport Road, Suite 205
Carlsbad, CA 92009
(619) 438-7400

Paramount Communications, Inc.
Paramount Interactive
700 Hansen Way
Palo Alto, CA 94304
(800) 821-1177
Fax (415) 813-8055

Studio Interactive / The Game Channel
650 N. Bronson Street, #223
Hollywood, CA 90004
(213) 856-8048

TCI
5619 DTC Parkway
Englewood, CO 80111
(800) 800-2824

Viacom Corp.
648 S. Wheeling Rd.
Wheeling, IL 60090
(800) 877-4266
Fax (708) 459-7456

VideoWay
Le Groupe Videotron Ltee
2000 Berri St.
Montreal, Quebec, H2L 4V7
Canada
(514) 281-1232

Zing Systems
8480 East Orchid Road, Suite 6600
Englewood, CO 80111
(303) 488-2500

I

Index

Symbols

A

B

C

D

J-K

L

Q-R

T

U-V

W

X–Y–Z

CD

Using the Companion CD-ROM

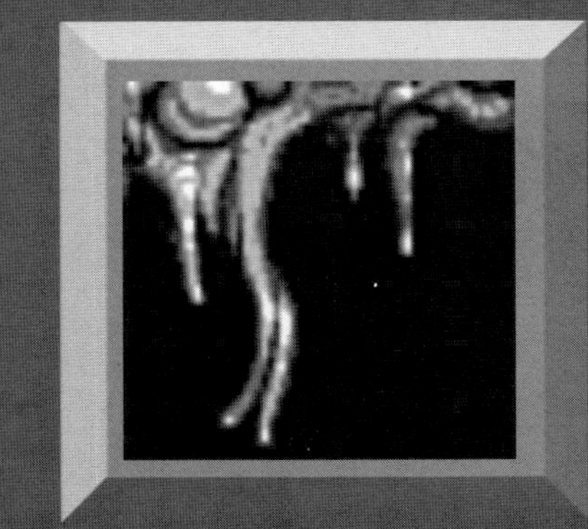

This CD-ROM contains more than 80 "test-drive" versions of interactive software for the PC and Macintosh.

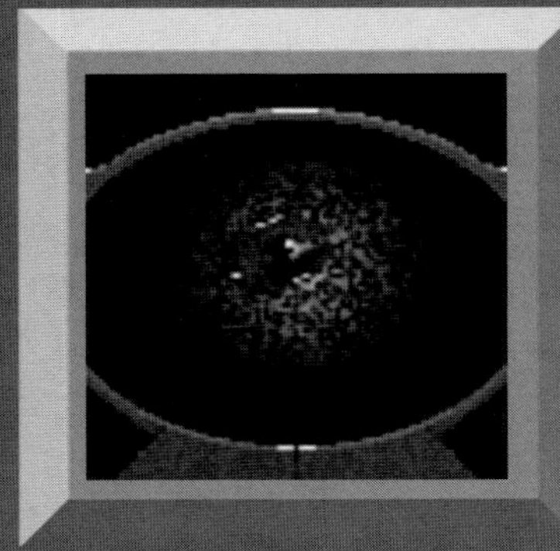

Using the Companion CD-ROM

The CD-ROM accompanying this book includes "test-drive" versions of more than 80 interactive software titles. You'll find DOS, Windows, and Macintosh software on the disc.

The PC DOS software features an easy-to-use graphical menu that allows you to navigate through the software on the CD-ROM. A Windows setup program will create a special Program Manager group with icons for all the Windows demos and text files that need to be read. Macintosh users will find each demo in its own folder.

Nearly every demo on this CD-ROM is playable, so each demo is assumed to be interactive and playable directly from the CD-ROM. If not, the entry for that demo tells you that it needs to be installed to your hard drive or is a show only. The DOS menu item, Windows icon, or Mac icon for each demo tells you whether the demo is playable and if it needs to be installed first.

SYSTEM REQUIREMENTS

Each of these trial versions has its own set of requirements, but you should make sure that your computer meets at least the minimum requirements listed below. Of course, there will be some demos that have even greater requirements than these.

Each demo usually includes a text file that describes the demo and any special requirements for running it. You can easily read these files to determine if there is something special you need to do before you run the software.

Whether you're running the DOS menu, using Windows Program Manager, or using a Macintosh, you can easily select items that allow you to read about the requirements for each demo.

Windows

To run the Windows software with the CD-ROM, you need:

- A computer with a 386 or better processor
- Windows 3.1
- 2 MB of RAM

To fully enjoy many of the demos, you'll need at least 4 MB of RAM, a Windows-compatible sound card, and speakers. Some of the demos require SVGA (256-color) graphics.

NOTE

Be sure to read the README.TXT file (PC users) or Read Me First! file (Mac users) before you start running any of the software. This file contains any late-breaking information about the software on the CD-ROM.

DOS

To run the DOS software on the CD-ROM, you need:

- A computer with a 12 MHz 286 or better processor
- DOS 5.0 or higher
- At least 1 MB of RAM
- VGA graphics

To fully enjoy many of the demos, you'll need at least 2 MB of RAM, a compatible sound card, and speakers. Some of the software requires a 386 or better processor.

Macintosh

To run the Macintosh software on the CD-ROM, you need:

- Macintosh LC, II-series or better computer
- System 6 or greater
- At least 2 MB of RAM

Before you run some of the demos, you must install special system extensions or control panels, such as QuickTime. These files are located in the folder for a demo.

Some of the demos require System 7 and 4 MB of RAM.

BEFORE YOU GET STARTED

To make it easy for you to navigate through this CD-ROM, we've created menus, icons, and folders that allow you to click with your mouse and run a software title.

DOS Menu Program

A graphical menu program allows you to easily run the DOS software titles on the CD-ROM. Follow these steps to start the menu program:

1. At the DOS prompt, switch to the drive holding the CD-ROM. For example, if your CD-ROM drive is D:, type **D:** and press the Enter key.
2. Type **MENU** and press the Enter Key. This will start the menu program.

On the first page of the menu system, you'll see buttons with the names of the software publishers that contributed demos for this project. Click on any of these buttons with your mouse, and a new screen appears with buttons for running software demos from this publisher. If software needs to be installed to your hard drive before it's run, the menu item will tell you.

If a demo has a text file that describes system requirements or gives instructions on how to use the software, it will be displayed below the button for running the demo. Be sure to read this information, as it may affect whether you can run the demo or not. You can navigate through the text by clicking on the scroll bar to the right of the text.

At the bottom of the menu screens are several buttons:

- Quit—exit the menu program. You can also exit by pressing the Escape key.
- Help—opens a file with information on how to use the menu program.
- Up and down arrows—moves up and down through the screens of the menu.

Special thanks go to NeoSoft Corporation, which publishes the NeoBook software that was used to create the DOS menu system. You'll find a trial version of the NeoBook software in the \DOSDEMOS\NEOBOOK directory. For information, you can contact NeoSoft at:

NeoSoft Corporation
354 NE Greenwood Avenue, Suite 108
Bend, OR 97701-4631
(503) 389-5489

Windows Setup

Before you run the Windows demos on the CD-ROM, you need to run a Windows setup program. This will create a Program Manager group named *Magic of Interactive Entertainment.* Follow these steps to run the setup program:

1. Start Windows if it isn't already running.
2. Click on the **F**ile menu in Program Manager.
3. Choose **R**un from the **F**ile menu.
4. In the Command Line: box, type **D:\SETUP** and click on OK. If your CD-ROM drive is not drive D, substitute the proper drive letter in this entry. For example, if your CD-ROM drive is F:, type **F:\SETUP**.
5. The setup program will start. Click on the **C**ontinue button.
6. The program will now create a Program Manager group named *Interactive Entertainment*. Click the **C**reate button to continue.
7. The setup program will inform you when the icons have been created. Then, click the OK button to exit.

This setup program doesn't copy any files to your hard drive—it simply creates icons for all the Windows demos on the CD-ROM. You can now double-click on an icon in the *Interactive Entertainment* group to run or install any of the Windows demos. Icons are also created for any text files that need to be read.

MACINTOSH NOTES

Each demo is stored in a separate folder, named for the software. Inside the folder, you'll find an icon for either running the demo or installing the demo to your hard drive. Before you run a demo, be sure to read the documentation or any ReadMe files that you see in the folder. They contain important information on how to run the software, plus any special system requirements.

SPECIAL BONUS SOFTWARE

Through a special arrangement with Virtual Reality Laboratories, this CD-ROM contains complete working versions of two award-winning products—Vistapro 1 for the PC and Distant Suns for PC and Macintosh. These are the complete versions, as sold in stores, not just demos.

Vistapro 1 and Distant Suns 1 are being provided to you through a special arrangement with Virtual Reality Laboratories, Inc. This software is not public domain, and you must abide by the terms of the company's license agreement:

> *The program Vistapro and the related user manual are copyrighted. You may not copy, modify, distribute, transfer, or transmit this program or the related manual except as is expressly provided in this agreement.*
>
> *You have the nonexclusive right to use this program on a single computer. You may make one backup copy of this program to protect against media damage. Call Virtual Reality Laboratories for use on local area networks—usually there is no charge.*
>
> *This program is sold as entertainment, without warranty as to its suitability to be used as any other purpose.*
>
> *This license agreement shall be governed by the laws of the United States of America and the State of California.*

Vistapro 1 (DOS)

Vistapro is a three-dimensional landscape simulation program. Using U.S. Geological Survey data, Vistapro can accurately re-create real world landscapes in vivid detail. You can modify and reshape the landscapes that are provided, or you can create your own from scratch! In addition, by simply clicking on several buttons, rivers and lakes can be created in a landscape where none existed previously.

The Vistapro software included with this book is the complete version of Vistapro 1.0. You can upgrade to the newest version for a special price—see the Vistapro registration card in the back of the book.

When you install the Vistapro software from the CD-ROM, the on-line user's manual will also be installed. It will be located in the \VISTAPRO\MANUAL directory of your hard drive, after Vistapro has been installed.

The manual is a series of text files, arranged by chapters and appendices. To view the manual, change to the \VISTAPRO\MANUAL directory, type MANUAL and press Enter. You will see a menu of choices, which represents a table of contents for the manual. When you select a choice, the text for that chapter will be displayed.

Be sure to check out the demo version of Vistapro 3, included on the CD-ROM. See the following "PC DOS Demos" section.

Distant Suns 1 (for Windows and Macintosh)

Distant Suns for Windows is a complete planetarium program, allowing you to explore the night sky in detail. You can click on objects in the sky to identify them and see detailed information about them. It displays up to 10,000 stars and 2,000 deep-space objects, such as galaxies, nebulas, and star clusters.

Windows Version

To install the Windows version to your hard drive, double-click on the *Install Distant Suns 1* icon in the *Interactive Entertainment* group that was created in Program Manager. This will start the installation program for the software—follow the on-screen instructions in the program to complete the installation.

This creates a new Program Manager group named *Distant Suns*. You can then double-click on the *Distant Suns* icon in this group to start the program.

Macintosh version

Distant Suns requires a minimum of two megabytes of memory (RAM), System 6.0.2 or greater, and at least 4 megabytes of free hard drive space. For optimum performance, a color system in 256 color mode and a math coprocessor are recommended.

To install the Macintosh version to your hard drive, drag the Distant Suns 1 (retail version) folder to your hard drive icon.

You will see two program files in this folder, ds.fpu and ds.sfp. The file ds.fpu is the program for computers with a math coprocessor; the file ds.sfp is the program which doesn't require a math coprocessor. If you're not sure whether you have a math coprocessor, try running the ds.fpu version. It should exit with an "error 90" if no coprocessor is available. Once you've determined which version of Distant Suns program to use on your machine, you can delete the other version of the program file.

PC DOS DEMOS

Start the DOS menu program to run these demos. You need to run the menu program and these demos from DOS; they will not run properly from a DOS session in Windows. The directory names in these lists are for your reference only. When you run the new program, it knows where to find each demo.

Activision

114400 San Vincente Blvd.
Suite 300
Los Angeles, CA 90049

Return to Zork

Directory: \DOSDEMOS\RTZ
(installs from \DOSDEMOS\ACTIVIS)

MechWarrior 2

Directory: \DOSDEMOS\MECH2

Richard Scarry's Busiest and Best Neighborhood

Directory: \DOSDEMOS\RSCARRY
(installs from \DOSDEMOS\ACTIVIS)

Cyberdreams

23586 Calabafas Rd.
Suite 102
Calabafas, CA 91302

CyberRace

Directory: \DOSDEMOS\CYBERACE

Electronic Arts

1450 Fashion Island Blvd.
San Mateo, CA 94404

EA Kids Theater

Directory: \DOSDEMOS\EAKIDS

Contains demos of:

Peter Pan's Story Painting

Eagle Eye Mysteries

Ping & Kooky's Cuckoo Zoo

Scooter's Magic Castle

Video Jam

GameTek

2999 Northeast 191st St.
Suite 800
North Miami Beach, FL 33180

Jeopardy

Directory: \DOSDEMOS\JEOPARDY

Tessarae

Directory: \DOSDEMOS\TESSARAE

Wilson ProStaff Golf

Directory: \DOSDEMOS\WILSON

Nomad

Directory: \DOSDEMOS\NOMAD

Humongous Entertainment

13110 NE 177th Place #180
Woodinville, WA 98072-9965

Putt-Putt Goes to the Moon

Directory: \DOSDEMOS\PUTTMOON

Putt-Putt Joins the Parade

Directory: \DOSDEMOS\PUTTPUTT

Fatty Bear's Birthday Surprise

Directory: \DOSDEMOS\FBEAR

Impressions Software

222 Third Street, Suite 0234
Cambridge, MA 02142

Detroit

Directory: \DOSDEMOS\DETROIT

My First World Atlas

Directory: \DOSDEMOS\ATLAS

Interplay Productions

17922 Fitch Ave.
Irvine, CA 92714

Alone in the Dark 1

Directory: \DOSDEMOS\ALONE1

Alone in the Dark 2

Directory: \DOSDEMOS\ALONE2

Star Trek: Judgement Rites

Directory: \DOSSHOWS\STARTREK

Rags to Riches

Directory: \DOSDEMOS\RAGSRICH

The Lost Vikings

Directory: \DOSDEMOS\VIKINGS

Mario Teaches Typing

Directory: \DOSDEMOS\MARIO

Battle Chess 4000

Directory: \DOSSHOWS\BCHESS

Another World

Directory: \DOSDEMOS\ANOTHER

Omar Sharif on Bridge

Directory: \DOSDEMOS\BRIDGE

Legend Entertainment

14200 Park Meadow Dr.
Chantilly, VA 22021

Gateway 2

Directory: \DOSDEMOS\GATEWAY2

MicroLeague Interactive Software

262 Chapman Rd.
University Office Plaza
Bellevue Bldg., Suite 201
Newark, DE 19702

Body Blows

Directory: \DOSDEMOS\BODYBLOW

Silverball

Directory: \DOSDEMOS\SILVBALL

Time Out Sports

Directory: \DOSDEMOS\TIMEOUT

MicroProse Software

180 Lakefront Dr.
PO Box 509
Hunt Valley, MD 21030

Taskforce 1942

Directory: \DOSDEMOS\TASK1942

DragonSphere

Directory: \DOSDEMOS\DRAGON

F-117a Stealth Fighter

Directory: \DOSDEMOS\F117A

NFL Coaches Club Football

Directory: \DOSDEMOS\FOOTBALL

Return of the Phantom

Directory: \DOSDEMOS\PHANTOM

David Leadbetter's Greens

Directory: \DOSDEMOS\GREENS

Master of Orion

Directory: \DOSDEMOS\ORION

Rex Nebular

Directory: \DOSDEMOS\REXNEB

Paramount Interactive

700 Hansen Way
Palo Alto, CA 94304

BusyTown

Directory: \DOSDEMOS\BUSYTOWN

Sierra On-Line

PO Box 485
Coarsegold, CA 93614

Gabriel Knight–The Sins of the Father

Directory: \DOSDEMOS\GKNIGHT

Freddy Pharkas-Frontier Pharmacist

Directory: \DOSDEMOS\FREDDY

Spectrum Holobyte

2490 Mariner Square Loop, Suite 100
Alameda, CA 94501

Chess Maniac Five Billion and One

Directory: \DOSDEMOS\CMANIAC

Falcon 3: Art of the Kill

Directory: \DOSDEMOS\FALCON3

Tornado

Directory: \DOSDEMOS\TORNADO

SSI (Strategic Simulations, Inc.)

675 Almanor Ave.
Suite 201
Sunnyvale, CA 94086

Ravenloft: Strahd's Possession

Directory: \DOSDEMOS\RAVEN

Dark Legions

Directory: \DOSDEMOS\DLEGIONS

Velocity Development

5 Embarcadero Center
Suite 3100
San Francisco, CA 94111

Spectre VR–DOS

Directory: \DOSDEMOS\SPECTRE

Virtual Reality Laboratories

2341 Ganador Court
San Luis Obispo, CA 93401

Vistapro 3.0

Directory: \DOSDEMOS\VISTA3

PC WINDOWS DEMOS

The setup program on the CD-ROM creates a Program Manager group named *Interactive Entertainment*, which contains icons for these demos. Double-click on a demo's icon to run the demo. If a program needs to be installed to your hard drive, the title of the icon will tell you.

EBook, Inc.

32970 Alvarado-Niles Rd., Suite 704
Union City, CA 94587

Aesop's Multimedia Fables

Directory: \WINDEMOS\AESOP

Aladdin and His Lamp

Directory: \WINDEMOS\ALADDIN

Mowgli

Directory: \WINDEMOS\MOWGLI

The White Horse Child

Directory: \WINDEMOS\WHCHILD

Don Quixote

Directory: \WINDEMOS\QUIXOTE

Renaissance Masters #1

Directory: \WINDEMOS\RENAISS1

Renaissance Masters #2

Directory: \WINDEMOS\RENAISS2

Impressionism and Its Sources

Directory: \WINDEMOS\IMPRESS

Multimedia Music: Mozart

Directory: \WINDEMOS\MOZART

Multimedia Music: Vivaldi

Directory: \WINDEMOS\VIVALDI

The Star Child

Directory: \WINDEMOS\SCHILD

A Christmas Carol

Directory: \WINDEMOS\CCAROL

Masque Publishing

P.O. Box 5223
Englewood, CO 80155

Solitaire Antics

Directory: \WINDEMOS\SOLANTIC

Masque Blackjack

Video Poker

Chess Net

Directory: \WINDEMOS\MASQUE

Morgan Interactive

160 Pine Street
San Francisco, CA 94111

The Ugly Duckling

Directory: \WINDEMOS\UGLYDUCK

Paramount Interactive

700 Hansen Way
Palo Alto, CA 94304

Rock, Rap 'n Roll

Directory: \WINDEMOS\ROCKRAP

Movie Select

Directory: \WINDEMOS\MOVIESEL

Lenny's Music Toons

Directory: \WINDEMOS\LENNY

Spectrum Holobyte

2490 Mariner Square Loop
Suite 100
Alameda, CA 94501

Iron Helix

Directory: \WINSHOW\HELIX

Velocity Development

5 Embarcadero Center
Suite 3100
San Francisco, CA 94111

Spectre VR–Windows

Directory: \WINDEMOS\SPECTRE

Remind Me

Directory: \WINDEMOS\REMINDME

Virtual Reality Laboratories

2341 Ganador Court
San Luis Obispo, CA 93401

Distant Suns 2.0

Directory: \WINDEMOS\DSUNS2

MACINTOSH DEMOS

Each of these Mac demos is located in a folder of the same name as the software. If a demo is not interactive, the title of the icon will indicate it.

Changeling Software

596 Elm Street
Windsor Locks, CT 06096

Pax Imperia

Cyberdreams

23586 Calabafas Rd.
Suite 102
Calabafas, CA 91302

Dark Seed

GameTek

2999 Northeast 191st St.
Suite 800
North Miami Beach, FL 33180

Mac Attack

Valkyrie

Wheel of Fortune

Jeopardy

Humongous Entertainment

13110 NE 177th Place #180
Woodinville, WA 98072-9965

Putt-Putt Goes to the Moon

Putt-Putt Joins the Parade

Fatty Bear's Birthday Surprise

Impressions Software

7 Melrose Dr.
Farmington, CT 06032

My First World Atlas

Interplay Productions

17922 Fitch Ave.
Irvine, CA 92714

Another World

MicroProse Software

180 Lakefront Dr.
PO Box 509
Hunt Valley, MD 21030

Civilization

Morgan Interactive

160 Pine Street
San Francisco, CA 94111

The Ugly Duckling

Paramount Interactive

700 Hansen Way
Palo Alto, CA 94304

BusyTown

Lunicus

Jump Raven

Rock, Rap 'N Roll

Movie Select

Pop Rocket

PO Box 170460
San Francisco, CA 94117

Total Distortion

Psygnosis

675 Massachusetts Ave.
Cambridge, MA 02139

Lemmings

Sanctuary Woods Multimedia Corp.

1875 South Grant Street, Suite 260
San Mateo, CA 94402

Sitting on the Farm

Spectrum Holobyte

2490 Mariner Square Loop, Suite 100
Alameda, CA 94501

Iron Helix

Falcon MC

Super Tetris

WordTris

Velocity Development

5 Embarcadero Center
Suite 3100
San Francisco, CA 94111

Spectre VR

PC SHAREWARE

In addition the to demos of software sold through retail outlets, we've included a selection of the best in PC shareware programs.

Shareware products are marketed by companies (often small ones) that cannot afford the time and frustration of packaging and distributing a software product through other means. This gives users the chance to try out different programs *before* paying for them. If you try a shareware program and continue to use it, you need to register the program with the author.

Many of the software titles in this section let you play through a complete single level of their games. When you register, many of these companies or authors will send you the complete game with many additional levels, plus a manual, hints or other valuable extras. See the documentation for a particular product to see what you get upon registering.

Epic Megagames

354 NE Greenwood Avenue
Suite 108
Bend, OR 97701-4631

Xargon

Directory: \DOSSHARE\XARGON

Zone 66

Directory: \DOSSHARE\ZONE66

Jill of the Jungle

Directory: \DOSSHARE\JILL

Electro Man

Directory: \DOSSHARE\ELECTRO

Heartlight

Directory: \DOSSHARE\HEART

Ken's Labyrinth

Directory: \DOSSHARE\KENSLAB

Epic Pinball

Directory: \DOSSHARE\EPICBALL

Adventure Math

Directory: \DOSSHARE\ADVMATH

Overkill

Directory: \DOSSHARE\OVERKILL

Kiloblaster

Directory: \DOSSHARE\KILO

Brix

Directory: \DOSSHARE\BRIX

Solar Winds

Directory: \DOSSHARE\SOLAR

Apogee Software Productions

3960 Broadway
Suite 235
Garland, TX 75043

Blake Stone: Aliens of Gold

Directory: \DOSSHARE\BLAKE

Halloween Harry

Directory: \DOSSHARE\HHARRY

Wolfenstein 3-D

Directory: \DOSSHARE\WOLF3D

Monster Bash

Directory: \DOSSHARE\MONSTER

Math Rescue

Directory: \DOSSHARE\MATHRESC

Word Rescue

Directory: \DOSSHARE\WORDRESC

Major Stryker

Directory: \DOSSHARE\MAJOR

Cosmo's Cosmic Adventure

Directory: \DOSSHARE\COSMO

Id Software

c/o StarPak
P.O. Box 1230
Greeley, CO 80632

Doom

Directory: \DOSSHARE\DOOM

ImagiSOFT, Inc.

Computer Games Division
P.O. Box 13208
Albuquerque, NM 87192

Movies to Go

Directory: \DOSSHARE\MOVIES

Redhook's Revenge

Directory: \DOSSHARE\REDHOOK

Chinese Checkers

Directory: \DOSSHARE\CCHECKER

Software Creations

26 Harris St.
Clinton, MA 01510

God of Thunder

Directory: \DOSSHARE\THUNDER

Hexxagon

Directory: \DOSSHARE\HEXXAGON

Argo Checkers

Directory: \DOSSHARE\CHECKERS

Night Raid

Directory: \DOSSHARE\NITERAID

Trivia Shell

Directory: \DOSSHARE\TRIVIA

(Each Trivia Shell program is stored in its own subdirectory.)

Picture Puzzle

Directory: \DOSSHARE\PUZZLE

John Dee Stanley

6959 California Ave SW
Seattle, WA 98136

Megatron VGA

Directory: \DOSSHARE\MEGATRON

Carr Software

P.O. Box 3919
Merced, CA 95344-1919

Capture the Flag

Directory: \DOSSHARE\CAPTURE

The Magic of Interactive Entertainment CD-ROM

The CD-ROM allows you to test drive more than 80 interactive software titles. Nearly every software demo is playable, letting you interact with the action, sights, and sounds.

Works with both PC and Macintosh systems!

System Requirements

Each software title has its own set of requirements, but you should make sure that your computer meets at least the minimum requirements listed below. Of course, there will be some demos that have greater requirements.

Windows

- A computer with a 386 or better processor
- Windows 3.1
- 2 MB of RAM
- Windows-compatible mouse
- VGA graphics

To fully enjoy some of the demos, you'll need at least 4 MB of RAM, a Windows-compatible sound card and speakers, and SVGA (256-color) graphics.

DOS

- A computer with a 12 MHz 286 or better processor
- DOS 5.0 or higher
- At least 1 MB of RAM
- VGA graphics

To fully enjoy many of the demos, you'll need at least 2 MB of RAM, a compatible sound card, and speakers. Some of the demos require a 386 or better processor.

Macintosh

- Macintosh LC, II-series or better computer
- 12 inch or larger color monitor
- System 6 or greater
- At least 2 MB of RAM

Before you run some of the software, you'll need to install special system extensions or control panels, which are included in the demo's folder. Some of the demos require System 7 and 4 MB of RAM.

Getting Started

The CD-ROM makes it easy to navigate through the wealth of software that's included. See "Using the Companion CD-ROM" for more information on the demos and how to explore them. You'll learn more about the graphical menu program for DOS demos, the special Program Manager group for Windows demos, and the arrangement of folders for Macintosh demos.